Goa

Paul Harding

LONELY PLANET PUBLICATIONS
Melbourne • Oakland • London • Paris

GOA

ELEVATION
- 600 m
- 300 m
- 150 m
- 50 m
- 0 m

KARNATAKA

MAHARASHTRA

To Savantvadi (32km)

To Mumbai (580km)

To Londa (111km), Dharwar (146km) & Belgaum (155km)

To Londa Junction & Castle Rock

ARAMBOL
Explore north Goa's most laid-back beaches and kick back in a cliff-side chalet

OLD GOA
Explore magnificent churches and cathedrals in the old Portuguese capital

PONDA
Marvel at Goa's unique Hindu temples and enjoy a buffet lunch at a spice plantation around Ponda

ANJUNA BEACH
Join the party scene and check out the famous flea market

FORT AGUADA
Climb the walls for superb views from this 17th-century fortress

PANAJI (PANJIM)
Explore Goa's most charming city with its fine church and fading Portuguese architecture

Hindu Temples

PERNEM

BICHOLIM

BARDEZ

SATARI

TISWADI

PONDA

MORMUGAO

Terekhol Fort
Querim
Arambol
Mandrem
Chopdem
Asvem
Morjim
Siolim
Chapora Fort
Vagator
Anjuna
Baga
Calangute
Candolim
Reis Magos Fort
Fort Aguada
Cabo Raj Niwas
Dona Paula
Mormugao
Pequeno Island

Pernem
Pernem Train Station

Chapora River
Terekhol River
Chapora River

Covale
Thivim (Mapusa Road) Train Station

Mapusa
Aldona
Corjuem Fort

Bicholim
Mayem Lake
Saptakoteshwara Temple

Sanquelim

Gontel
Anjunem
Valpoi

Onda

Cotorem
Nanus Fort

Molem National Park
Molem
Madei Protected Area

Ugao
Bondla Wildlife Sanctuary
Ugao Tisk
Darbandora

Bhagvan Mahavir Wildlife Sanctuary
Tambdi Surla Mahadeva Temple

Safa Shahouri Masjid
Mangaid Temple
Shantadurga Temple
Mahalsa Temple
Ramnath Temple

Ponda

Savoi Verem

Naroa
Chorao Island
Dr Salim Ali Bird Sanctuary
Divar Island
Karmali (Old Goa) Train Station
Old Goa
Carambolim
Britona
Panaji (Panjim)
Gaspar Dias
Goa Velha
Pilar
Agassaim
Cortalim
Verna

Vasco da Gama
Dabolim
Dabolim Airport

Mandovi River

17

4A

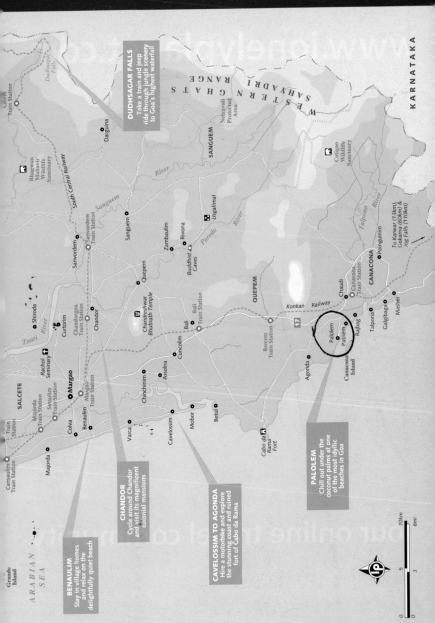

KARNATAKA

WESTERN GHATS
SAHYADRI RANGE

DUDHSAGAR FALLS
Take a train and jeep ride through jungle scenery to Goa's highest waterfall

Bhagwan Mahavir Wildlife Sanctuary

Lolem Train Station

Darguna

Dudhsagar Falls

South Central Railway

SANGUEM

Netravali Protected Area

Cotigao Wildlife Sanctuary

River

Sanguem River

Sanvordem Train Station

Sanvordem

Sanguem

Usgalimal

Pareda River

Shiroda

Curtorim

Chandorgoa Train Station

Chandor

Quepem

Zambaulim

Rivona

Buddhist Caves

QUEPEM

Chaudi

Talpona River

CANACONA

Poinguinim

To Karwar (13km);
Gokarna (60km) &
Jog Falls (110km)

Zuari River

Rachol Seminary

Margao

Magao Train Station

Chandreshwar Bhutnath Temple

Bali Train Station

Bali

Konkan Railway

Canacona Train Station

Rajbag

Talpona

Galgibaga

Mashel

SALCETE

Majorda Train Station

Benaulim Train Station

Colva

Benaulim

Chinchinim

Cuncolim

Assolna

17

Barcem Train Station

Palolem

Patnem

Majorda

Cansaulim Train Station

Varca

Cavelossim

Mobor

Betul

Agonda

Canacona Island

ARABIAN SEA

Grande Island

Cabo da Rama Fort

BENAULIM
Stay in village homes and relax on the delightfully quiet beach

CHANDOR
Cycle around Chandor and visit its magnificent colonial mansions

CAVELOSSIM TO AGONDA
Hire a motorbike and explore the stunning coast and ruined fort of Cabo da Rama

PALOLEM
Chill out under the coconut palms at one of the most idyllic beaches in Goa

0   5   10km
0   3   6mi

On the beach

Beach shacks offer an alternative Goan experience to hotel restaurants and established street cafés. They occupy an unrivalled breezy position with views of the sea and the distant horizon and their relaxed atmosphere make them ideal spots for sundowners. They often have an interesting selection of dishes, but there are a few points to note.

Most shacks have no power supply, so drinks, cooked food and fresh ingredients (including meat, fish and milk products) are kept chilled over ice. The few that have electricity generators usually only operate these for part of the day, with consequent risks to stored food. Often, the oil used for frying fish and meat is used repeatedly. To be on the safe side it is best to select from the day's fresh catch and order a grilled dish. Since there is no running water, all water for cooking and washing has to be carried in; glasses may be cleaned by dipping in a bucket. There are rarely any washing or toilet facilities.

Water

Drinking water used to be regarded as one of India's biggest hazards. It is still true that water from taps or wells should never be regarded as safe to drink. Public water supplies are nearly always polluted and unsafe. However bottled purified water is now widely available (not all bottled water is mineral water; some is simply purified water from an urban supply). Check the seal carefully (some are now double sealed) and avoid street hawkers; Crush the bottles when disposing of bottles. Water sterilization tablets can be bought from many chemists in Goa. This method reduces the amount of plastic bottles used throughout your trip and is a 'greener' option. Always carry plenty with you when travelling. **NB** It is important to use pure water for cleaning teeth.

Don't add ice cubes to any drink – the water used may be contaminated

Tea & coffee

Tea and coffee are safe and widely available. If you wish to order it black say 'no sugar', 'no milk' when ordering. At a roadside stall, however, *chai* or *chaa* is milky and sweet. *Nescafe*, *espresso* and *capuccino* coffee are sometimes on offer but may not turn out as you would expect in the West. UHT milk in litre packs is sold widely.

Soft drinks

There is a huge variety of bottled soft drinks, including well known international brands (eg *Coca-Cola*, *Pepsi*, *Fanta*), which are perfectly safe. Popular and safe Indian brands include *Limca* or *Teem* (lime and lemon), *Thums Up* (cola) and *Mirinda* (lemon), but some find them too sweet. Fruit juice, including mango, pineapple and apples is available in cartons; Prices of pre-packed drinks range from Rs 8-15.

Fruit juice

Fresh fruit juice (prepared hygienically) is a good option as is fresh lime-soda (plain, sweet or salty). Cool and refreshing fruit-flavoured milk-shakes and yoghurt-based *lassis* cost around Rs 35. Plain *lassi* is cheaper at about Rs 20.

Alcohol

A wide range of alcoholic drinks is available in Goa including some foreign brands in the major centres. Drinks in Goa remain relatively cheap compared with elsewhere in India. The increase in alcoholism (especially among Goan men) has led certain groups to call for prohibition.

The fermented juice of cashew apples, distilled for the local brew *kaju feni* (*fen*, froth), is strong and potent. Coconut or *palm feni* is made from the sap of the coconut palm. *Feni* is an acquired taste so it is often mixed with soda. It can also be taken "on the rocks" (poured on ice), as a cocktail mixed with fruit juice (bottle, about Rs 25) or pre-flavoured (eg with ginger). Don't drink this on an empty stomach. Sip slowly and avoid taking more than a couple of 'tots' when you are new to it.

Beer is usually available in three popular brands– *Kingfisher, Fosters, Kings, Pilsner*

Contents – Text

Contents – Maps

MAP INDEX

North Goa's Beaches p146

Terekhol River

Arambol (Harmal) p174

Vagator & Chapora p166

Anjuna p162

Bardez & Bicholim p177

Mapusa p159

Calangute & Baga p152

Candolim, Sinquerim & Fort Aguada p148

Panaji (Panjim) pp112-3

Old Goa p130

Vasco da Gama p188

Ponda & Around p139

Zuari River

Colva p192

Margao (Madgaon) p182

Benaulim p195

Central Goa p109

ARABIAN SEA

Palolem p201

South Goa p180

0   5   10km
0   3   6mi

The Authors

Paul Harding
After several years of journalism in Australia, Melbourne-born Paul set off around Europe and Asia with a backpack and a knack for losing things. He spent almost three years living in and around London, mostly subsisting but also writing and working as editor of a travel magazine.

In 1996 he returned to Australia and landed at Lonely Planet's Melbourne home for wayward travellers, where he worked as an editor until realising that the writers were having more fun. Paul's travels for Lonely Planet have taken him back to India (including Goa) several times, along the overland trail from Kathmandu to Istanbul and to points as diverse and far removed as Finland and New Zealand. He has contributed to many books, including *India*, *South India* and *Sacred India*.

Bryn Thomas
Born in Zimbabwe, Bryn contracted an incurable case of wanderlust during camping holidays by the Indian Ocean in Mozambique. Since then, his travel on five continents has included eight Himalayan treks, a 2500km Andean cycling trip and 45,000km of rail travel in India and Siberia.

Bryn has also co-authored the Lonely Planet guides to *Britain* and *India*.

FROM THE AUTHOR

Paul Harding Thanks, firstly, to Hilary Ericksen and Janine Eberle at Lonely Planet for offering me the job and for briefing and encouraging me along the way.

Many people in and out of Goa contributed to my research in many ways. In particular, thanks to journalist Frederick Noronha; to Ajit and Jack Sukhija – far more than mere hosts; to the lovely Walter and Marina Lobo in Calangute for entertainment, advice and hospitality; to Jaishima Dutta at the Government of India tourist office in Panaji – a true professional; to the knowledgeable Prajal Sakhardande; and to Aggie and his friends down in Palolem. Thanks also to the people at Goacom, an excellent Internet resource; the Goa Foundation; and all the travellers I met who provided information or inspiration. In Mumbai, thanks to Kamlesh Amin for his unfailing assistance.

At home, thanks to Jase and Rachel for keeping York St warm and occasionally emailing me, to Melina for being there, and to my family, who I never bother to thank but who always help keep me sane.

Finally thanks to Helen Christinis, Jolyon Philcox and Shahara Ahmed at LP for their hard work on this book.

This Book

Bryn Thomas, with assistance from Douglas Streatfeild-James, researched and wrote the 1st and 2nd editions of *Goa*. Paul Harding took up the reins to research and update this 3rd edition. Lucas Vidgen provided the information on Chennai for the Gateway Cities chapter, and Susan Derby researched the Excursions chapter.

FROM THE PUBLISHER

This 3rd edition of *Goa* was commissioned and developed by Janine Eberle. Jolyon Philcox coordinated the mapping and was assisted by Anneka Imkamp, Amanda Sierp and Chris Thomas. Helen Christinis coordinated the editing and was assisted by Daniel Caleo and Julia Taylor. Quentin Frayne updated the Language chapter.

The layout designer was Yvonne Bischofberger, with assistance from Sally Darmody. Sonya Brooke chose the colour images. Brendan Dempsey designed the cover. Eoin Dunlevy efficiently managed the project.

Thanks to Brigitte Ellemor and Shahara Ahmed for overseeing the editing and mapping processes.

Foreword

ABOUT LONELY PLANET GUIDEBOOKS

The story begins with a classic travel adventure: Tony and Maureen Wheeler's 1972 journey across Europe and Asia to Australia. There was no useful information about the overland trail then, so Tony and Maureen published the first Lonely Planet guidebook to meet a growing need.

From a kitchen table, Lonely Planet has grown to become the largest independent travel publisher in the world, with offices in Melbourne (Australia), Oakland (USA), London (UK) and Paris (France).

Today Lonely Planet guidebooks cover the globe. There is an ever-growing list of books and information in a variety of media. Some things haven't changed. The main aim is still to make it possible for adventurous travellers to get out there – to explore and better understand the world.

At Lonely Planet we believe travellers can make a positive contribution to the countries they visit – if they respect their host communities and spend their money wisely. Since 1986 a percentage of the income from each book has been donated to aid projects and human rights campaigns, and, more recently, to wildlife conservation.

> Although inclusion in a guidebook usually implies a recommendation we cannot list every good place. Exclusion does not necessarily imply criticism. In fact there are a number of reasons why we might exclude a place – sometimes it is simply inappropriate to encourage an influx of travellers.

UPDATES & READER FEEDBACK

Things change – prices go up, schedules change, good places go bad and bad places go bankrupt. Nothing stays the same. So, if you find things better or worse, recently opened or long-since closed, please tell us and help make the next edition even more accurate and useful.

Lonely Planet thoroughly updates each guidebook as often as possible – usually every two years, although for some destinations the gap can be longer. Between editions, up-to-date information is available in our free, monthly email bulletin *Comet* (w www.lonelyplanet.com/newsletters). You can also check out the *Thorn Tree* bulletin board and *Postcards* section of our website, which carry unverified, but fascinating, reports from travellers.

Tell us about it! We genuinely value your feedback. A well-travelled team at Lonely Planet reads and acknowledges every email and letter we receive and ensures that every morsel of information finds its way to the relevant authors, editors and cartographers.

Everyone who writes to us will find their name listed in the next edition of the appropriate guidebook. The very best contributions will be rewarded with a free guidebook.

We may edit, reproduce and incorporate your comments in Lonely Planet products such as guidebooks, websites and digital products, so let us know if you don't want your comments reproduced or your name acknowledged.

How to contact Lonely Planet:
Online: e talk2us@lonelyplanet.com.au, w www.lonelyplanet.com
Australia: Locked Bag 1, Footscray, Victoria 3011
UK: 72-82 Rosebery Ave, London, EC1R 4RW
USA: 150 Linden St, Oakland, CA 94607

Introduction

Goa is, and always has been, unlike any other part of India. Cocooned between the Arabian Sea and the Western Ghats (mountains), tiny Goa was fought over, ruled by the Portuguese for four centuries, and finally emerged as an independent, prosperous state.

After Independence, Goans discovered that their beautiful shores were still in high demand from interlopers – as a hippy paradise where travellers and 'freaks' would come to laze and party on the beaches. The heady flower-power days of the 1960s and '70s were the beginnings of modern-day tourism in Goa – and tourism is something that has been embraced here with abandon.

Today, in winter at least, Goa is one of the continent's biggest tourism draws – still popular with the trance-party ravers, but equally attractive to backpackers, package tourists on charter flights and Indian holiday-makers filing in from Mumbai and other places around the country.

Part of Goa's attraction is that it has a character quite distinct from the rest of India. The Christianisation of Goa by the Portuguese has left an indelible mark on the people and the landscape. Although possessing a minority of followers, Roman Catholicism remains a major religion, skirts outnumber saris, and the people display an

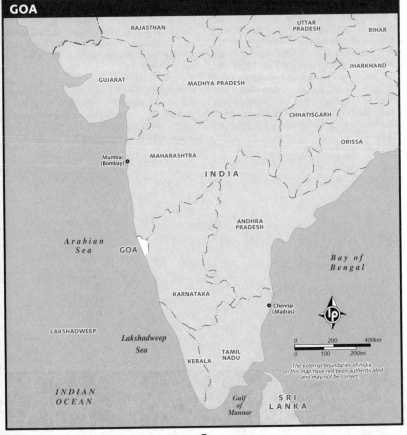

GOA

easy-going tropical indulgence, humour and civility. Goans love to celebrate their unique culture, and that can readily by seen and experienced in the many festivals, the music, the food and the customs.

For most visitors, this cultural aspect comes later – the first call is the beach. For 105km, beautiful beaches stretch almost uninterrupted along the coastline. In some places (unfortunately now in the minority) these gently shelving stretches of sand are almost untouched; traditional fishing boats line the sand; and behind the dunes, among coconut palms, lie sleepy villages. And while some locals despair at the ugly development on Calangute and Candolim beaches, even the busiest resorts show little of the high-rise development that has blighted some of the better known of the world's beach resorts. Within a few metres of the water's edge are palm-thatched 'beach shacks', restaurants where you can while away an afternoon with a drink, reading a book or watching the world go by. The beaches can at times be a carnival: cows stand around looking lost, fishermen mend nets, ear-cleaners and masseurs offer their services and Indian women take a tentative dip wearing a full sari. Hippies still wander the northern beaches and rave parties occasionally erupt on the sands at Anjuna and Vagator.

But Goa offers more than just sun, sand and hedonism, and its compact size makes it a pleasure to explore. Bird-watchers, naturalists, history buffs and curious travellers will find plenty of interest away from the beaches. Richly decorated, whitewashed churches are scattered throughout the countryside, while the magnificent churches and cathedrals at Old Goa (a World Heritage site) provide a fascinating insight into the state's colonial history. Standing almost side by side with the churches are Goa's distinctive Hindu temples. Explore the old Portuguese quarter and the riverfront of Panaji, India's most relaxed state capital; glide through the mangroves in a dugout canoe at the Dr Salim Ali Bird Sanctuary on Chorao Island; or get caught up in one of Goa's famous markets.

For many, the best way to see Goa is to hire a bicycle or motorbike. With the freedom of your own transport, you can discover empty beaches, crumbling old forts and narrow lanes that meander past paddy fields and spice plantations.

Most of all, visitors to Goa are likely to remember the peaceful, unhurried nature of the state, and the friendliness of its people. Siestas, the *susegad* (relaxed) attitude and smiles can sum up the Goan nature – and that makes it a great place for a holiday.

Facts about Goa

HISTORY
Prehistory
According to Hindu legend, Goa and the Konkan coastline were created by the god Parasurama, the sixth incarnation of Vishnu. After many years of fighting to avenge the murder of his father, Parasurama finally came to the Sahyadri mountains, or Western Ghats, that now form the border between Goa and Karnataka. In search of a completely pure piece of land on which to perform his sacrifices, Parasurama shot an arrow into the sea below the mountains and commanded the waves to retreat to the point where the arrow landed. The arrow fell, it is said, at the point where Benaulim village now stands, and the stretch of coastline that was revealed as the waves receded is the coastal plain of Goa. Parasurama performed his fire sacrifice in the north of the country (modern-day Pernem), and then peopled his new land with 96 Brahmin families.

Historians are at odds regarding the origins of the area's first seminomadic settlers. Some believe that the first Goans arrived as migrants from Africa, while others say that they were from eastern Asia, or perhaps were a northern tribe forced southwards by some instability in their homeland.

As the lifestyle of the early Goans became more settled, formal agriculture developed and villages sprang up. The people became almost self-sufficient in food production and they soon began to look outwards from the confines of their coastal territory, establishing links with the other peoples of southern India. The society would have been profoundly altered, in particular, by the arrival of Aryan migrants from the north in around 2400 BC, who brought with them the early strands of Hinduism. A second wave of Aryans came southwards in around 700 BC, which may have included important groups who came to precedence over the coming centuries – the Bhojas, Chediyas and Saraswat Brahmins.

Early History
It is known that during the Mauryan empire (321–184 BC), Goa became part of an administrative area known as Kuntala. During this period Buddhism arrived on India's west coast, brought by a monk named Punna who resided near modern-day Zambaulim in south Goa. With the rapid demise of the Mauryans after the death of emperor Ashoka in 232 BC, Goa came under the control of the Marathis, who ruled for about two centuries before being ousted in 50 BC by the temporarily powerful Anand-Chuttus.

Within a century Goa had changed hands again, this time becoming part of the powerful Satavahana empire, which controlled the whole of the west coast of India. During this period Goa emerged as an international trading centre, and evidence exists of regular trade with Africa, the Middle East and even with the Romans.

Further dynastic upheaval during the 2nd century AD saw Goa passing to the Bhojas, who ruled from the city of Chandrapur, near the present village of Chandor in south Goa, for nearly 300 years. Again, during the periods of peace, trade blossomed, but towards the end of the dynasty power began to be ceded to other smaller states that had come to prominence in the area, including the Konkan Mauryas and the Kadambas. At the end of the 6th century the powerful Chalukyas of Badami succeeded in bringing the whole area under their control. Despite the change of power, the Kadambas managed to retain their position, administering the area as a feudatory state to the new Chalukya rulers.

In the middle of the 8th century the Chalukyas were defeated by the Shilaharas, who held on to power for the next 200 years. There was considerable infighting throughout the reign, but the Shilaharas appear to have thrived until eventually challenged in AD 973 by their old enemies, the Chalukyas. The ensuing struggle between the two great adversaries gave the Kadambas (who had served both of them as local chieftains) a chance to claim the area as their own. After several attempts, the Kadamba leader Shastadeva captured the capital of Chandrapur in AD 979. The Chalukyas, although still the most powerful empire on the west coast, were content to let the Kadambas rule for them, and thus began one of the most glorious periods in the history of Goa.

The Kadambas

Finally, Goa had some stability, for although the Kadambas were feudatories to the Chalukyas, they succeeded in hanging on to power for 300 years. During this period Chandrapur grew into a large and beautiful city; it was used as the capital until around AD 1050, when a newer port on the Zuari River, known as Govepuri or Gopaka (now called Goa Velha) was adopted.

A unique mixture of cultural influences centred on Goa, with merchants coming from as far afield as Malabar, Bengal and Sumatra. In contrast with what was to come, this was a period of religious tolerance. Under the patronage of the Kadambas, Hinduism flourished and Goa became a pilgrimage destination with large temples and prestigious academic institutions.

The Muslims

The peace was shattered at the beginning of the 14th century by a series of Muslim invasions from the north. In 1312 Govepuri, and much else along with it, was destroyed; 15 years later the Muslims returned under Mohammed Tughlaq and the old capital of Chandrapur was levelled. Raids continued until finally, in 1352, Goa came under the permanent Muslim rule of the Bahmanis.

Although the Bahmanis held Goa for a quarter of a century, they were in constant conflict with the mighty Vijayanagar empire, which had its capital at Hampi and controlled much of southern India. The persecution of Hindus in Goa at this time forced many to flee south until, in 1378, the Vijayanagar army finally succeeded in wresting Goa from the Bahmanis.

A period of peace followed, accompanied by excellent trade. In particular, Goa was used to import Arab horses for the Vijayanagar cavalry, while spices flowed as export goods back to the Arab countries.

In the early 15th century the ousted Bahmanis made concerted attempts to win back their old territory. In all, four expeditions were mounted, the last of which, under Mahmud Gawan, struck in 1469. Despite a lightning attack from land and sea, it took three years to bring Goa back under control, and it became part of the Bahmani kingdom again in 1472. As if in revenge for the effort that had been expended, the Bahmanis wreaked havoc; Hindu temples and the capital Govepuri caught the brunt of it. With Govepuri in ruins and the waters near it badly silted up, the Bahmanis established a new capital, Gove, near Ela, on the Mandovi River.

There was little time for the Bahmanis to celebrate their success for within 20 years the kingdom had become riven by dispute and it split into four factions. One of these, the kingdom of Bijapur under its ruler Yussuf Adil Shah, inherited Gove. He was so impressed by the new city that he made it his second capital.

Arrival of the Portuguese

Almost before the city could adjust to its new-found prosperity, it was threatened again. In 1498 Vasco da Gama, a Portuguese sea captain, landed south of Goa at Calicut (present-day Kozhikode) on the Malabar Coast. The first European to reach India via the sea route around the Cape of Good Hope, he arrived 'seeking Christians and spices.' Although the kingdom of Prester John, the legendary Christian ruler, was nowhere to be found, there were spices in abundance.

For the Portuguese, who were approaching the height of their powers as a seafaring nation, the prospect of controlling the spice trade to Europe (which so far had been monopolised by Arab traders) was too good to miss. A subsequent expedition managed to establish a small fortress in Cochin (present-day Kochi). In 1503 a nobleman named Afonso de Albuquerque sailed from Portugal to reinforce this base, and returned home full of enthusiasm for the opportunities on offer.

In 1506 Albuquerque was dispatched again with orders to take over as the second Portuguese viceroy of what amounted to little more than two fortresses, one at Cochin and the other at Cannanore (present-day Kannur). The voyage was long and it wasn't until 1508 that Albuquerque arrived in India. It was evident that a more permanent base was required on the Indian coastline and that the Portuguese needed to consolidate their presence in the area. Rumours were rife that the Arab rulers of the coastal states were concerned about Portuguese sea power and were planning to attack the Portuguese fleet.

Wasting little time, Albuquerque sailed for Goa, and in March 1510 attacked and occupied the main island in the river – where Panaji (formerly Panjim) and Old Goa stand today. Although the element of surprise had been on his side, his success was short-lived, for Yussuf Adil Shah soon recovered and counterattacked, driving him out barely two months later.

With the monsoon setting in, there was little that Albuquerque could do except withdraw his ships out of range of the enemy guns and find as much cover from the elements as possible. He and his men rode out the monsoon in miserable conditions before retreating down the coast to recover.

Albuquerque attacked again, and on 25 November (St Catherine's Day) he retook Gove. As a punishment to those who assisted the sultan in his defence of the city, Albuquerque ordered that all Muslim occupants of the city should be put to death. He then set about fortifying the city and rebuilding the fort at Panaji.

Four months later, having put the new territory in order, Albuquerque departed on another voyage. During his absence there was a further attempt to recapture Goa, this time by Yussuf Adil Shah's son, Ismail Adil Shah. For several months the garrison managed to hold out until, reinforced by new arrivals from Portugal, they were able to establish a sound defence. In late 1512 Albuquerque returned victorious from having conquered Malacca and, organising the combined forces into two groups, attacked and defeated the Muslims.

After fortifying the colony, Albuquerque sailed west to consolidate his gains in the Gulf. He returned in 1513 in time to sign a treaty with the new ruler of Calicut and start on the serious work of laying out his new city.

Perhaps Albuquerque's greatest achievement during this period was the skilful political balancing act he performed. Both the Vijayanagar empire and the Bijapuris were potentially lethal threats, and Albuquerque played them off one against the other. The only bargaining tool he had was that both armies were keen to import horses (to use in attacks against each other) and he turned this to financial as well as political advantage by making them promise that they would only buy their horses from him, thus making a tidy profit on the existing trade through Goa's ports.

In 1515 he was on the move again, this time to the Gulf, but it was his final voyage: he returned fatally ill. He died aboard his ship in Goa harbour on 15 December 1515, having been brought up on deck to see Goa one last time.

Conquest & Expansion

Although the initial threat to the Portuguese had been beaten off, their position was anything but secure. The conquistadors still held only the islands in the river estuary, while their enemies held the far banks to both the north and south.

An uncommonly good piece of luck fell to the Portuguese in 1520 when, after a spate of successes against the Muslims, the Hindus offered their conquests to the Portuguese. They swiftly occupied the areas of Ponda, Salcete and Bardez and, although the Muslims took most of the territory back fairly quickly, some parts, notably Rachol Fort, remained in Portuguese hands.

At this point a little political cunning did the trick; the Portuguese brought in Mir Ali, a rival for the Muslim throne, and threatened to support his bid to overthrow the sultan. As a compromise, in 1543 the existing sultan ceded Bardez and Salcete permanently, on condition that Mir Ali was deported from the region. The areas that the Portuguese now held – Tiswadi, Bardez and Salcete – marked the extent of Portuguese territory in Goa for the next 250 years, and are now known as the Old Conquests, or Velhas Conquistas.

In 1565 the balance of power that had existed in the region collapsed when a coalition of Muslim rulers finally crushed the Vijayanagar army at the Battle of Talikota. The subsequent sack of the magnificent Vijayanagar capital at Hampi is reputed to have taken several months.

With the Muslim kingdoms in alliance and rid of their greatest enemy, it was inevitable that the Portuguese would come under threat. In 1570 the combined forces of Bijapur, Ahmednagar and Calicut besieged Goa with huge forces. Despite the overwhelming superiority in numbers, they failed to break the defence and after a 10-month siege they gave up and withdrew.

Christianisation of Goa

Although a handful of priests had arrived in Goa with Albuquerque's fleet, and the Franciscans had managed to send a few friars in 1517, missionary work was relatively low-key in Goa for almost 30 years. Initially the approach was enlightened, and the religious conversion that did take place was unforced.

In 1541, following the arrival of a handful of zealots, laws were passed that all Hindu temples should be destroyed, along with strict laws forbidding the observance of Hindu rituals, and other regulations stating that only those who were baptised could retain the rights to their land.

In 1560 the Inquisition unleashed a period of nearly 200 years of brutal suppression and religious terrorism. During this period many Hindus fled across the Mandovi River to escape persecution, smuggling their religious statuary to safety with them.

Although the Roman Catholic Church had much to answer for, there were also undoubtedly many good aspects to the work of the religious orders. By the middle of the 16th century the Franciscans, Dominicans, Augustinians and Jesuits, among others, were present in Goa. The missionaries established hospitals and schools and taught alternative methods of farming and forestry. They also masterminded much of the building work that was taking place; work on the Se Cathedral was commenced in 1560, and the Basilica of Bom Jesus was built between 1594 and 1605.

Portugal Fades & Marathas Attack

At the same time that the most magnificent buildings of Old Goa were being constructed, Portugal's fortunes were beginning to wane.

In 1580, bankrupted by a disastrous campaign in North Africa, Portugal was annexed by Spain, and it was not until 1640 that the Portuguese regained Independence. While this dealt an understandable blow to morale, finances and even manpower, a greater threat was the emergence of European rivals in the eastern oceans. In 1612 the Portuguese fleet was defeated off the coast of Surat in western Gujarat by the ships of the British East India Company, and the British suddenly became the power to be reckoned with in the Arabian Sea. The threat was eventually dealt with only by allowing the British to trade freely in all of Portugal's eastern ports, an agreement reached by the Convention of Goa in 1635.

By the early 1660s the Portuguese were also facing a threat from the east. Shivaji, the great leader of the Marathas, succeeded in taking the neighbouring territories of Bicholim and Pernem in 1664, before being forced to withdraw to deal with the Muslim leader Aurangzeb. His army was a constant worry around the Goan borders until his death in 1680.

In 1683 the Maratha army, now commanded by Shivaji's son, Sambhaji, got so close to Old Goa that defeat seemed inevitable. Ordering the coffin of St Francis Xavier to be opened, the viceroy laid the cane of office next to the saint's body and prayed for him to intercede. Miraculously, the Marathas withdrew at the last minute, again threatened by Mughal forces to their rear. The following year they took Chapora in Bardez taluka (district).

The Marathas returned again in 1737, taking the whole of Bardez except for the forts at Aguada and Reis Magos, and the whole of Salcete apart from Mormugao and Rachol. Finally a negotiated peace forced the Portuguese to hand over the territory of Bassein, near Mumbai (Bombay), in return for a Maratha withdrawal from Goa.

Expansion & Decline

The latter half of the 18th century saw both the expansion of the colony and the acceleration of its decline.

In 1764 the raja of Sonda, beset by his enemy Hyder Ali of Mysore, asked the Portuguese to occupy his lands in order to protect them for him. Although he intended the occupation to be temporary, the Portuguese obligingly moved into what today are Ponda, Sanguem, Quepem and Canacona, and the acquisition became permanent.

Between 1781 and 1788 the three northern talukas of Pernem, Bicholim and Satari were also added to the colony, bringing under Portuguese control the entire area that Goa occupies today.

At the same time, the character of the colony was changing hugely because of the repression of the religious orders (the Jesuits were banned in 1759) and the effective end of the Inquisition in 1774. Thus the new territorial acquisitions were spared the forced conversions and crusading Christianity that had been forced on the Old Conquests. By this stage too, Old Goa, once a city of more than 200,000 inhabitants, was practically abandoned due to recurring disease. The senate was formally moved to Panjim (present-day Panaji) in

1835, although it was another eight years before the city officially became the capital.

In 1787 there was a short-lived attempt at revolt from within Goa. The conspirators in the Pinto Revolt were mainly Goan churchmen, disaffected at the unequal status of Goans in the church hierarchy. The revolt was discovered while it was still in the planning stages, and several of the leaders were tortured and put to death, while others were imprisoned or shipped off to Portugal (see the boxed text 'The Pinto Revolt' in the North Goa chapter).

Right at the end of the century, Goa was temporarily occupied without a shot being fired. The British, engaged in a struggle against the southern monarch Tipu Sultan (who had formed an alliance with the French), marched into Goa in 1797. Although they departed a year later, they were back in 1802, this time guarding against a possible invasion attempt by the French. Despite repeated Portuguese protests, the British garrison remained in Goa until 1813. Although there was never any attempt to annex Goa, several years later (in 1839) the British government offered to buy Goa from the Portuguese for half a million pounds.

End of Empire

By this stage, retaining possession of Goa was, for the Portuguese, a matter of keeping face rather than of expediency.

While many uneducated Goans were willing to accept the status quo, among the educated classes there were already rumblings of a nascent Independence movement. The first manifestations of this were a series of uprisings by a clan called the Ranes, who came from Satari taluka in the northeast. For more than 50 years there was sporadic violence dealt with by Portuguese viceroys with a mixture of military suppression and concessions. Finally in 1912, after 14 rebellions, the movement was crushed by military force.

In 1910 when the Portuguese monarchy came to an end, it looked briefly as though the calls for self-determination were about to be answered. At the last moment, however, the proposed measures were withheld. The anger caused by this abrupt change in policy led to the emergence of a determined Goan Independence movement, with figures like Luís de Menezes Braganza championing the cause. By the 1940s the Goan leaders were taking their example from the Independence movement across the border in British India.

On 18 June 1946 a demonstration led to the public arrest of a prominent activist, Dr Ram Manohar Lohia, after he had been threatened at gunpoint not to address the crowd. The event provided the incentive needed to motivate the people, and large-scale demonstrations were held.

Many activists were arrested, and in all an estimated 1500 people were incarcerated. A militant wing of the Independence movement was formed, calling itself 'Azad Gomank Dal', who carried out a number of raids on police stations, public industries and stray security patrols.

The attacks led to an increased police and military presence and made for a defiant mood in Lisbon.

On 10 June 1947 the Portuguese Minister of Colonies, Captain Teofilo Duarte, warned that the 'Portuguese flag will not fall down in India without some thousands of Portuguese, white and coloured, shedding their blood in its defence.'

When overtures by the newly independent Indian government were made to the Portuguese in 1953, the lack of any formal response made it apparent that the Portuguese had no intention of withdrawing. Consequently, diplomatic relations between the two countries were broken off on 11 June 1953.

Within Goa the Independence movement continued in two distinct forms. A peaceful wing was directed under the auspices of the National Congress Goa, and on 15 August 1954 a huge satyagraha (nonviolent protest) commenced. Many were arrested, beaten and imprisoned.

Exactly a year later, as a mark of indignation at the treatment of the Goan satyagrahis, a second protest was organised, this time to be conducted by Indians from outside Goa.

On the morning of the rally more than 3000 protesters, including women and children, entered Goa at various points along the border with India. In response to this openly peaceful protest, Portuguese security forces charged the protesters with batons and opened fire. Some of the protesters were killed and hundreds more injured.

During this period India manoeuvred for international support, and tried to exert pressure on more established members of the United Nations (UN) to persuade the

Portuguese to leave peacefully. India's prime minister, Jawaharlal Nehru, in particular was opposed to taking Goa by force, as he believed that this would jeopardise the whole ethos of achieving political aims by peaceful means. He also recognised that it was possible that Goans might not vote for Independence if they were given a free choice.

In order to allay Goan fears, Nehru addressed the issue publicly:

Goa has a distinct personality, and we have recognised it. It will be a pity to destroy that individuality, and we have decided to maintain it. With the influx of time, a change may come. But it will be gradual and will be made by the Goans themselves. We have decided to preserve the separate identity of Goa in the Union of India and we hold to it firmly. No agitation against it will be to any purpose.

Although the pledge to respect Goa's integrity was upheld, Nehru could not resist the forces pushing for India to take Goa by force. During the night of 17 to 18 December 1961, Operation Vijay began with Indian troops crossing the border. Little resistance was met and by the evening of the 18th, troops were outside Panjim. There was a brief gunfight at Fort Aguada when a 'rescue operation' attempted to liberate a number of political prisoners, but to all intents the surrender itself was a mere formality.

At 8.30am on 19 December, troops of the Punjab Regiment occupied the Secretariat Building. The Portuguese left shortly afterwards, leaving most of their buildings intact, despite direct orders from Dr Antonio de Oliveira Salazar, the Portuguese dictator, that they should destroy everything before departing.

Post-Independence

After the liberation, the commander of the expeditionary force, Major General Candeth, was appointed the military governor of Goa. Under the provisions of the Constitution 12th Amendment Act of 1962, the former Portuguese colonies of Goa, Daman and Diu were integrated with the Indian Union, effective from the first day of the liberation.

Towards the end of 1962, the new political system started to take root through a number of elections. In September an informal consultative council was formed and in October the first panchayat (local government council) elections were held. In December there were elections for the state assembly and Goa's two parliamentary seats, and the first proper state government was operating in Goa by the end of December 1962.

The major question that was left unanswered was that of statehood. Neighbouring Maharashtra insisted that Goa should be added to its own territory and that Konkani, the language of the Goans, should not be recognised as an official language. The issue was finally settled on 16 January 1967 when, in an opinion poll, Goa, Daman and Diu opted to remain as a Union Territory, rather than being assimilated into their neighbouring states.

In May 1987 Goa split from Daman and Diu, and was officially recognised as the 25th state of the Indian Union. The struggle has been won too, to retain Konkani, which was recognised in 1992 as one of the official languages of India.

For most of the 1990s political instability, the bane of the country as a whole during this period, disrupted life in Goa. The practice of 'floor-crossing' (ministers switching parties) continues and in 1999 alone there were three changes of government coupled with a four-month period of President's Rule. Although the Congress Party had held sway for much of the 1990s, at the end of the decade it was the Hindu nationalist Bharatiya Janata Party (BJP) which came to power after Congress was riven with defections. Under the dominating leadership of Chief Minister Manohar Parrikar, the BJP ousted its own rebellious Congress Party allies to ride to power in its own right in October 2000. In mid-term elections in 2002 – hurriedly called because the government was reportedly close to collapse due to defections – the BJP failed to win an absolute majority, gaining 17 of the 40 seats. Cobbling together an alliance of the United Goans Democrat Party (UGDP), the Hindu Maharashtrawadi Gomantak Party (MGP) and an independent, Parrikar again won government.

Goa entered the new millennium with a burgeoning tourist industry and growing environmental problems, but the BJP has shown some commitment to Goa's heritage and conservation, and made moves to appeal to the Catholic minority as well as the Hindu 'vote bank'. Politics in Goa, however, continues to

The Changing Face of Goa

Goa has always had its fair share of visitors, some welcome, others not so. Early visitors were looking to conquer or colonise – beginning with a succession of Hindu dynasties, then Muslims from the north and east, and finally the seafaring Portuguese. Over four centuries the Portuguese radically changed the face of Goa, demolishing temples, building churches and converting people to Christianity.

But that's history. The latest challenge facing this tiny state comes from tourism – balancing economic advantages with environmental issues and the inexorably changing character of Goa. The first 'tourists' arrived on Goa's beaches not long after Independence in the early 1960s. Overlanding hippies found not only beautiful, untouched beaches (initially they settled on Calangute), but a relatively liberal, easy-going local attitude and enough ganja to keep them happy for the winter. Since there was little or no accommodation they threw up palm-leaf shelters on the beach or rented rooms in village homes for a pittance. Over the next 15 years a regular stream of 'freaks' turned up and gave Goa a rather unwanted reputation as a den of drugs, all-night partying and nudism that quickly upset local sensibilities. Hotels and beach shack restaurants began to sprout up in Calangute as locals who had previously made a living from fishing and farming realised they could cash in on the influx. Indian tourists also began flocking to Goa to get a look at the infamous debauched Westerners. Hippies became so synonymous with Goa that locals to this day still call all independent travellers 'hippies'.

Already the sleepy, rural nature of Goa was beginning to change. Lonely Planet's first guide to Goa in 1981 noted that Calangute was already becoming overdeveloped and that most travellers had moved up to Anjuna (where there were two hotels and the flea market was just getting into full swing) and Chapora. Colva beach, we said, was a palm-fringed 'paradise...without equal in India.' Few travellers had even heard of Arambol or Palolem – two beaches now favoured by many travellers. By the time the first direct charter flights from the UK arrived in 1985, Goa was firmly on the backpacker trail.

The arrival of charters brought a new type of tourist – short-stay, higher-spending package tourists – which sparked a building boom at the established beach resorts. Five-star luxury resorts, usually owned by outside interests, began popping up on some of Goa's deserted beach frontages at places like Cavelossim, Varca and Majorda. With swimming pools, golf courses and manicured lawns, they put on a strain on Goa's water resources, but give little back to the local economy. Goan journalist Frederick Noronha has tracked the changes first-hand and says many old-timers lament the change from 'a simple and green Goa' to one where pressure from tourism may be responsible for killing the golden goose that the tourists once came to see.

Environmental and cultural issues are at the forefront of politics these days – the Goa Foundation is particularly vocal in this area and the BJP government is taking steps to implement conservation and heritage preservation controls – but continued development and the ongoing scramble for the tourist dollar continue to change the face of Goa. Whether the tourist industry can be sustained in the current global climate is another question. There are simply too many hotels and restaurants in Calangute for all to remain viable in anything but the peak season and, with almost half the Goan population reliant on the tourist industry in some way, many worried locals are just waiting for the bubble to burst.

be fought on religious and caste lines, with ideology taking a back seat.

GEOGRAPHY & GEOLOGY

Goa occupies a narrow strip of the western Indian coastline, approximately 105km long and 65km wide, with a total area of 3701 sq km. It shares state borders to the north and northeast with Maharashtra, and to the south and southeast with Karnataka.

Administratively the state is divided up into two districts – north and south Goa –

with the major towns in each being Panaji (formerly Panjim, the state capital) and Margao (formerly Madgaon) respectively. Beyond this simple subdivision the state is further divided into 11 talukas: Pernem, Bicholim, Satari, Bardez, Tiswadi and Ponda lie in north Goa, while Mormugao, Salcete, Sanguem, Quepem and Canacona are in the south.

In terms of topography, Goa falls into three distinct areas: the Western Ghats, the midland region and the coastal region.

Western Ghats

In the east of the state lie the foothills and some of the peaks of the Western Ghats, the mountain range that runs along the west coast of India, separating the Deccan Plateau from the low-lying coastal areas. In Goa, the Western Ghats, made up locally of the Sahyadri Range, comprise about 600 sq km of the total area of the state. Some of the main peaks are Sonsagar (1166m), Catlanchimauli (1107m), Vaguerim (1067m) and Morlemchogor (1036m). All seven of Goa's main rivers (the longest of which, the Mandovi, is only 77km in length) have their sources in the Ghats.

Midland Region

Between the Ghats and the coast lies Goa's hinterland, a huge area mostly made up of laterite plateaus of between 30m and 100m in elevation. The laterite rock that comprises much of Goa is nearest to the surface on many of these plateaus, and since it is rich in both iron and manganese ores, the plateaus have become the scenes of large-scale open-cast mining.

Spice, fruit and areca nut plantations have become established in this region, particularly in the lower areas where soil is richer. Making efficient use of the water sources available, the terraced orchards support coconut palms and fruits such as jackfruit, pineapples and mangoes.

Coastal Region

Despite only making up a fraction of the total area of the state, the coastal region is undoubtedly the best known to most of Goa's visitors.

Lining the sides of many of Goa's tidal rivers are mangroves that thrive on the saline soil, and provide a unique habitat for birds and marine animals. The inland areas, known to the Goans as the *khazans*, are lands reclaimed by the building of 'bunds' or embankments. The skilful placement of sluices and floodgates allows the use of the land to be controlled. While the majority of the land is irrigated using fresh water, many of the drainage canals are allowed to fill at least partially with salt water, so that they can be used for fish farming. Other areas are allowed to flood with salt water, which is then left to evaporate for the collection of salt.

CLIMATE

The main feature of the Goan climate is the monsoon, which occurs between June and the end of September. Goa is in the path of the southwest monsoon and experiences a dry period lasting six to eight months of the year, followed by the annual rainfall over the remaining four months. During the two months preceding the onset of the monsoon, the humidity increases dramatically, and the normally clear skies become hazy and then cloudy. The period immediately prior to the rain is marked by high winds and lightning. During the monsoon season, 250cm to 300cm of rain is normal on the coast.

The pre-monsoon period is one of preparation for the Goans, who store enough firewood and food to last them through the rains. Although much agriculture takes place over the four-month monsoon period, fishing ceases almost completely because of the stormy conditions.

Once the monsoon has run its course the skies clear and the weather becomes pleasant. For four to five months from late October to February the climate is near perfect – cloudless blue skies, warm but not oppressively hot days, and calm seas. By mid-March the humidity starts to rise as the monsoon begins to approach again.

Surprisingly, the temperature throughout the year in Goa is fairly constant, varying from a maximum of 28°C or 29°C in July and August to a maximum of 33°C in May, and minimums for the same months of 24°C and 26.5°C.

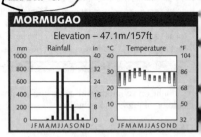

MORMUGAO
Elevation – 47.1m/157ft

ECOLOGY & ENVIRONMENT

The greatest environmental threat facing Goa today comes as a result of the state's headlong rush to keep up with the economic fortunes of the rest of India.

Goa's system of land management via *comunidades* – self-regulating communities under which land belonging to the estab-lished families in the village was leased to tenant farmers who then employed manual labourers to work it – ensured the best use of land, produce and labour for the good of the community as a whole. The panchayat sys-tem (which has now taken over many of the functions of the *communidades*) and Indian business-wallahs and land developers have been less respectful of the common good.

Deforestation

Over-cutting of the forested Western Ghats started at the beginning of the 20th century, and by the time the Portuguese departed, considerable damage had already been done. Shortly after Independence, licences were granted for further large-scale felling. In some cases the cleared land was replanted with imported crops such as eucalyptus and rubber plants. In many cases, however, the deforestation was permanent, with the land being used for roads, open-cast mining and other development.

The construction of reservoirs in the hills near the Maharashtra border has been par-ticularly damaging. Whole valleys are sub-merged under the new reservoirs, while neighbouring areas are deforested to rehouse the families made homeless.

Environmental groups estimate that more than 500 hectares of Goa's forests are dis-appearing every year, and that a mere 8% to 12% of the state is now under dense forest.

The damage caused by deforestation is far-reaching. The habitats of many of Goa's native animals are disappearing, as are the homelands of several of the minority peo-ples of the state. The Dhangars, Kunbis and Velips, all traditionally forest dwellers whose way of life revolves around agricul-ture and animal husbandry, have been forced into smaller and smaller pockets of land.

Mining

Nearly half of the iron ore exported annually from India comes from Goa. Goa's mines produce ore exclusively for export, and for eight months of the year both the Zuari and Mandovi Rivers are the scene of constant ac-tivity, as a stream of huge barges ferry the ore to the ships waiting in Mormugao Harbour.

Such large-scale extraction of ore has had a destructive effect on the environment of the Goan hinterland, and has also had some ad-

---

Fading Fisheries

Goa's once-abundant waters are facing a very real threat from overfishing. More than 40,000 Goans are dependent on fishing for their livelihood and although many *ram-ponkars* (traditional fishermen) also make some money by letting rooms or operating beach shacks, the continued vitality of the fishing industry is extremely important.

Locals wistfully reminisce of their childhood days when the *ramponkars* would give away 60cm-long kingfish because they had so many to spare. These days it's difficult to buy fish direct from the boats, and even the local markets offer slim pickings because much of the best fish is sold direct to upmarket hotels or shipped to interstate markets where the best prices can be found. Much of the best shellfish (prawns, crabs and lobsters) is ex-ported. Naturally this has driven up the price of seafood, not only for tourists, but for Goans who rely on their staple fish curry rice.

Overfishing has become a threat since modern motorised trawlers started to replace traditional fishing methods. The fact that the trawlers stay relatively close to the shore has adversely affected the catches of the *ram-ponkars*. The use of tighter nets, which do not allow juvenile fish to escape (these are either thrown away or used for fish fertilizer) has further dwindled fish stocks. Although the *ramponkars* have been agitating for some sort of restrictions on trawler fishing for a number of years, little has been done to avert what some ecologists believe will be a marine re-source disaster.

---

verse effects on the coastal region. Because no stipulation for environmental reconstruc-tion was made when the mining concessions were issued, many of the mines have simply been abandoned once the extraction was complete.

Out of the 80 million tonnes of rock and soil extracted annually, only 13 million tonnes are saleable ore and a huge amount of surplus is dumped on the spoil tips. Particu-larly during the monsoon, a huge quantity of soil is washed away and contributes to smothering both river and marine life. Other side effects of mining have been the destruc-tion of the local water table and the pollution of drinking water supplies.

Tourism

In 2001 1.38 million foreign and domestic tourists visited Goa (the domestic sector is by far the majority at 1.12 million) – slightly more than the entire population of Goa. While many Goans welcome tourism as a valuable source of income, there is legitimate concern about the sheer numbers involved.

The problem with the huge numbers is not only pollution and overcrowding; most Goans also realise that the charm of their coastline lies in its peaceful, unspoiled condition. The village of Calangute is now so overbuilt that sewage from the hotels is polluting well water.

The changing face of tourism is bringing new environmental problems, and mass tourism is actively being encouraged by the government. The hippies and backpackers are being replaced by a higher-spending, short-term package tourist. Five-star hotels with lush grounds and golf courses, and even the proliferation of mid-range hotels with swimming pools, puts increasing strain on water resources. Many Goans question whether water from reservoirs built in deforested areas should be used to maintain golf courses that will not even be used by the people of Goa.

Pressure groups point out that hotel developers have violated environmental protection laws. Originally the laws forbade the construction of any building within 500m of the high-water mark; this has now been reduced to 200m, and has still been completely ignored by some developers. Regulations that no boreholes should be dug within 500m of the high-water mark have been ignored by some of the larger hotels, who draw water for swimming pools. The disastrous result of this has been that the water table has lowered, local village wells in the area frequently run dry weeks before the monsoon, and there is a real danger that if saline intrusion occurs, the ground water supplies could be ruined permanently.

In the more remote beaches entrepreneurs have chosen to build bamboo and palm-thatch huts that are more environmentally sound than the concrete hotels of the developed resorts. When the high season is over, they are simply dismantled and put away.

Conservation

Three wildlife sanctuaries and one bird sanctuary have been set up since Independence and the state government appears willing at least to listen to the warnings of the environmental agencies. It was, however, only during the period of President's Rule in 1999 when the national government took control of the state, that the governor placed a section (419 sq km) of the Western Ghats region under the Wildlife Protection Act. This includes three of the wildlife sanctuaries. Two new reserves, Madei and Netravali, were notified as protected areas in 1999.

The Archaeological Survey of India took over responsibility for conservation of the state's monuments, including the buildings of Old Goa, in 1964 so there is some funding for essential maintenance and restoration work.

FLORA

The Western Ghats have the greatest diversity of plant life, including areas of jungle (which can be seen around Dudhsagar Falls and the Bhagwan Mahavir Wildlife Sanctuary). The vegetation here is, for the most part, tropical evergreen, although there are large areas of cane, bamboo and semi-evergreen trees.

On the lower slopes of the Ghats, thinner, dry soil supports lateritic semi-evergreen forest. In many places (for example, Cotigao Wildlife Sanctuary) the arid nature of the landscape leads to savannalike vegetation. In the less dry patches of the lower slopes, timbers such as teak are grown.

In the midland region the lateritic rock is extremely close to the surface and the soil is too thin in many places to support much more than coarse grass and scrub. Where possible, cashew trees, a significant cash crop which are able to withstand the hot dry conditions, have been laid out in large plantations.

In the folds between the hills, however, where there is shade and springs are to be found, the small valleys are often extremely fertile. Here, centuries-old methods are still followed in the cultivation of spices and fruits. Coconut palms are cultivated not only for the nuts and toddy (sap that is collected, fermented and distilled), but also to give shade to the less hardy trees.

Beneath the canopy of the coconut palms and mango trees, the tall, slender areca nut palms (which provide betel nuts for *paan* – a mixture chewed for its mildly intoxicating effect and as a digestive) are grown. These shelter an incredible variety of fruit trees and spice plants, ranging from pineapples to bananas, and pepper to cinnamon. Although many of these plants are indigenous to Goa, others were introduced by the Portuguese, including rubber trees, pineapples and chillies.

The coastal region has a similarly wide range of flora. The saline conditions support a substantial area of mangroves (estimated at a total area of 20 sq km).

Along the coast, coconut palms, perhaps the most useful of all trees grown in Goa, predominate. Another distinctive feature in the area is the large banyan trees that often provide a shady meeting spot in each village.

FAUNA
Despite Goa's small size, the state's unique topographical and environmental variation allows for an incredible variety of fauna, but some species now occur in only very small numbers. The forested areas of the Western Ghats have traditionally provided a habitat for some extremely rare animals. Goa is particularly notable for its spectacular birdlife

(see the boxed text 'Finding Those Feathered Friends' in the Central Goa chapter).

Mammals
Although Goa Tourism's brochures would have you believe differently, wild elephants are rarely found in the state's forests nowadays. Most members of the cat family are now extremely rare too, and sightings of tigers and leopards – known as panthers in India – are few and far between.

More common in this family is the jungle cat, which is about 60cm long excluding the tail. Notable for its long limbs and short tail, it is able to kill animals larger than itself. Also common are small Indian civets and common palm civets. Among the dog family, jackals, striped hyenas and wild dogs are occasionally sighted.

Goa has two common types of monkey that are frequently seen – bonnet macaques and common langurs. Much less commonly seen are slender loris, which are occasionally found in the dense forests of Molem and Canacona. There are also very occasional sightings of sloth bears, which can grow up to 1.5m long and generally feed on bees and termites.

Other more frequently seen inhabitants are common mongooses, which are found near settlements, and common otters and smooth Indian otters, both of which are seen near water. The Western Ghats are also home to Indian giant squirrels, which are found in the forests of Molem, Valpoi and Canacona. Other relatives in Goa are three-striped palm squirrels, five-striped palm squirrels and flying squirrels.

Among the animals to be found at ground level are common Indian porcupines and the wild boar, both of which are notorious for damaging crops. Particularly common are the large Indian bison or gaur. The animals you're most likely to see in Goa's wildlife sanctuaries are sambars and chitals, both species of deer. One of the rarer animals to inhabit Goa's forests today are nocturnal pangolins, otherwise known as scaly anteaters.

Common dolphins are found off the coastline and can often be seen on 'dolphin-spotting' boat tours.

Reptiles & Amphibians
The ubiquitous common house gecko is often seen in buildings at night feeding off insects

attracted to light. Snakes are common in Goa but the only place you're likely to see one is in a snake charmer's basket at a market.

Among the nonpoisonous variety are common blind snakes. Much higher in the Ghats, locally named *torava* snakes grow up to 50cm in length and are notable for their yellowish colouring and rough tails. Indian pythons are undoubtedly the largest of the snakes found in Goa; they have been known to grow up to 4.5m in length.

There are relatively few venomous snakes in Goa. The most distinctive are cobras, which are found near the coast and inland. There are three common varieties, as well as the much larger (and now rare) king cobras.

Care for Stray Dogs

You can't help noticing that Goa has a serious problem with stray dogs. Packs of them roam the streets, beg at the beach restaurants and will often keep you awake at night with their barking. Some are in very poor condition, ill fed and have parasites and skin conditions. Government policy in the past has been to shoot them, and it was not unusual to see contractors (paid on a per-dog basis) roaming the streets and beaches taking pot-shots at hapless pooches, until local and international petitioning to the courts put a stop to it (at the time of writing the matter was before the High Court).

In 1998 **International Animal Rescue** *(in the UK ☎ 01825-767688; **W** www.iar.org.uk)*, a UK-based charity, set up a shelter in Goa to care for sick dogs and cats and to implement a sterilisation programme. A team of vets now performs up to 85 sterilisations a week, mostly on dogs, and claims to have treated some 10,000 animals over four years. The dogs are also given a rabies vaccination and have their ear clipped to identify them.

Volunteers are sometimes needed to befriend timid dogs prior to sterilisation, and visitors are welcome (as are donations) to the centre near Mapusa: **International Animal Rescue** *(☎ 2268272)*, Animal Tracks, Murdungo Waddo, Assagao, Bardez.

If you see a sick or distressed animal, contact the centre; they will often come out and collect the dog, but during busy times, or if they're short-staffed, you may have to put it in a taxi and send it off to the centre, which many animal-lovers are happy to do.

The common varieties can grow to more than 1.5m in length, and the venom is likely to be lethal if not treated quickly with antivenin. Common Indian kraits are more poisonous still, needing only half the volume of poison injected by a cobra to kill a human adult.

Mention also needs to be given to the sea snakes known locally as *kusadas*. Although common along the coastline and extremely poisonous, they are very timid and their fangs are so far back that they rarely get enough grip to give a proper bite. Dead *kusadas* are occasionally seen on the beach where the *ramponkars* throw them. Since they are completely adapted for life in the water, they cannot move on land, and if stranded, will die.

Goa has a small population of other reptiles including two species of crocodile. Although rare, it is still possible to see these along the banks of a few inland waterways, and several companies advertise 'crocodile-spotting' trips by motorboat along likely stretches.

Freshwater turtles are found throughout the state and Goa is also a traditional breeding ground for marine turtles, which struggle ashore between October and December to lay their eggs in the sand. The survival of these amazing animals is growing increasingly doubtful, not only because more and more of Goa's beaches are being turned over to tourism, but also because the eggs are highly valued by the local *ramponkars*. (See the boxed text 'Turtle Beaches' in the North Goa chapter.)

Birdlife

Although Goa's flora and fauna may seem impressive on the page, you really have to know what you are looking for to appreciate the variety. Not so with the birdlife; keen bird-watchers will be in seventh heaven, and even those who have previously had little interest in birds will wonder at the richness.

A trip to the Dr Salim Ali Bird Sanctuary on Chorao Island is recommended. Other sites of interest are the wetlands at Carambolim (12km east of Panaji), at Shiroda (40km southeast of Panaji) and even the marshland south of the Baga River.

One of the best ways to see birds in Goa is to join an ecotour with **Southern Birdwing** *(☎ 2402957; **W** www.southernbirdwing.com)*; or contact locally based ornithologist and guide **Gordon Frost** *(☎ 2275301)*.

See the boxed text 'Finding Those Feathered Friends' in the Central Goa chapter for more information.

WILDLIFE SANCTUARIES

Goa has three wildlife sanctuaries: Bondla, Bhagwan Mahavir (which also contains Molem National Park) and Cotigao. The three were all established in the late 1960s, barely in time to save many species. There's also the tiny Dr Salim Ali Bird Sanctuary on Chorao Island. In 1999 two new wildlife reserves – Madei (208 sq km) in Satari taluka and Netravali (211 sq km) in Sanguem taluka – were notified as protected areas, but there is no infrastructure here for visitors. The creation of these protected areas links the sanctuaries running along the Western Ghats, providing a corridor for wildlife.

Advance bookings and requests for further information can be made via the Forest Department. Contact the **Assistant Conservator of Forests, Wildlife and Eco-Tourism** (☎ 2229701; *4th floor, Junta House, Panaji 403001*). The Forest Department has an informative website at ⓦ www.goaforest.com.

Bondla

Bondla Wildlife Sanctuary is the state's smallest, with an area of only 8 sq km, but is also the most accessible from Panaji or Margao. It has just one basic forest watchtower overlooking a small water hole. Regular sightings in the sanctuary include gaurs, barking deer and sambars. The park has a **Nature Interpretation Centre**, and a small **zoo**, and there is accommodation at the park entrance.

Bhagwan Mahavir & Molem

At 240 sq km, this is the largest of the wildlife sanctuaries in Goa. There are a couple of watchtowers from where it's possible to observe the wildlife in the morning or evening, and there's accommodation at Molem. As with the other parks, visitors will need to be patient to see much beyond a few deer. The countryside and the forest inside the park are wonderful and it's worth a visit for the scenery alone. Within the sanctuary is Goa's highest waterfall, Dudhsagar.

Cotigao

In the far south of the state, this 86-sq-km wildlife sanctuary offers regular sightings of sambars and gaurs from its two tree-top watchtowers. There are also very occasional sightings of large predators such as panthers, which have strayed into the park. There is a small **Nature Interpretation Centre** and limited accommodation, but it's best visited as a day trip from Palolem.

GOVERNMENT & POLITICS

India has a parliamentary system of government with two houses – a lower house known as the Lok Sabha (House of the People) and an upper house known as the Rajya Sabha (Council of States).

Goa has one representative in the Rajya Sabha and two in the Lok Sabha – one for south Goa and one for north Goa.

The two national houses and the various state houses elect the Indian president, who is a figurehead – the prime minister wields the real power. There is a strict division between the activities handled by the states and by the national government. The police force, education, agriculture and industry are reserved for the state governments. The central government has the controversial right to assume power in any state if the situation in that state is deemed to be unmanageable. Known as President's Rule, it has been enforced several times in other states, and most recently in Goa in 1999.

At the lowest level of local politics, Goa's 374 villages are split into 183 panchayats. Each panchayat has a number of wards (large villages will have several wards – Calangute has 11) each of which can elect one *panch* (member) to the panchayat. Elections take place by secret ballot every five years and the candidates are local residents who, if successful, carry out their duties in their spare time. The job is unpaid (although, as most Goans point out, there are plenty of ways in which being a *panch* can have financial compensations). Once the members have been elected, they then declare their party affiliations (if they have any) and the panchayat becomes affiliated to a political party.

Elections for the 40-member state government are staggered so as not to coincide with the panchayat elections. Typically, five or six panchayats are grouped together and the electoral district returns a Member of the Legislative Assembly (MLA).

The assembly elects a chief minister, deputy minister and other ministers. Although the chief minister is free in almost all matters of policy, he and the assembly are answerable to the state governor, who resides in the huge house on Cabo Raj Niwas in Panaji.

There are constant accusations of vote buying, many of which seem to be valid, but this is a widespread problem throughout India. There is a fine line, anyway, between the politicians who claim that if they are elected their constituents will get water connections, and those who agree to give preferential treatment in such cases to anyone who votes for them.

ECONOMY

Prior to Independence in 1961, Goa's economy was largely based on fishing, agriculture and the export of primary products such as timber and rubber. Because there was only a relatively small market for goods, industrialisation was minimal, and consisted only of small-scale fish and fruit canning plants and a few small factories. Because of the lack of employment opportunities, many young Goans were forced to travel – to Mumbai or even abroad – in order to earn a decent income. In 1961 the annual per capita income, assessed at current prices, has been estimated at Rs 434. Today, the per capita income is over Rs 26,000, the highest in India.

Industry

The bulk of this new-found wealth comes from industry. Although industrial growth was initially slow after Independence, expansion took off in the 1970s and the growth continues: today there are estimated to be 6500 small industries employing 40,000 people and more than 100 large factories employing another 40,000.

While ministers have been only too happy to attract large companies, local inhabitants have not always been so keen. An example of this was a project initiated by the multinational DuPont corporation to build a chemical plant in Goa. After mass demonstrations by local villagers, the plan was finally abandoned in 1995 and the plant relocated in Tamil Nadu. In 1999 local people tried to stop the opening of a copper processing factory Meta Strips in Sancoale. The matter was fought through the courts and while the plant remains open and operational, severe controls on hazardous waste, polluting emissions and water use were imposed.

More recently, Goa has pushed for a piece of India's technology pie, attempting to attract information technology (IT) and software companies and setting up software technology parks at Porvorim and Dona Paula.

Goans are also discovering that employment security is not always to be taken for granted. There is no restriction on the number of workers from outside the state who can come in search of employment. Labourers from Kerala, Karnataka and further afield are often so poor that they will accept any work available, at any price.

Agriculture

More than half of the state's population is involved in agriculture at various times of the year, although fewer Goans rely on it totally for their livelihood. This is generally because land holdings are small and irrigation facilities are limited. Despite great schemes to boost these facilities, many areas still run short of water.

Of Goa's area of 370,000 hectares, approximately 162,000 hectares are cropped. Main crops include rice, ragi, maize, pulses and oil seed. Cash crops such as sugar cane and rubber are also grown. Other main crops include cashew, coconut and various fruits and spices. The area under cultivation has increased substantially since 1961, as has production of almost all major crops. In particular, rice production has increased by well over 100% – a rise largely attributed to the introduction of high yield rice strains. Where irrigation allows, two rice crops are grown every year.

Mining

Mining started in Goa a century ago and today it is big business. Iron ore, manganese ore and bauxite are the main minerals extracted, but limestone, kaolin and a few other minerals are also mined in smaller quantities. The iron ore is of fairly low quality and is produced entirely for export, Japan being the main customer. As the open-cast mining has continued, further deposits have been discovered at lower levels, so that the original estimate of 411 million tonnes of reserves has increased considerably.

However, the mining companies are working against a law of diminishing returns because the lower deposits are not only of poorer quality but also harder to extract. Thus, while some estimates have it that the ore will last for about another 80 years, others claim that mining will cease being economically viable in 25 years.

One thing that is certain is that when mining does come to a halt, there will be considerable financial and social problems. It is estimated that 8000 people are directly employed by mining, and more than 20,000 others work in mining-related industries. The port of Mormugao, for example, owes 90% of its traffic to the export of ore.

Tourism

Tourism is a major source of income. In 1990 the state attracted 834,081 tourists; by 2001 the annual figure had risen to 1.38 million. An estimated 40% of Goans are involved directly or indirectly and there are grave concerns about the consequences should the current boom end.

There are already too many people who rely solely on tourism – in effect, supply of tourism-related services, including accommodation, exceeds demand in all but the busiest seasons. The effects of terrorism on the world travel industry have also hit Goa. In 2002 many hotels on the coastal belt were half empty for much of the season, and even the peak Christmas period was relatively quiet.

Arguments rage too about the direction the industry should be taking. The state government is discussing ways to encourage a higher spending category of tourists, as it feels, with some justification, that the huge numbers of package tourists actually spend little money while they are in Goa. Among the facilities proposed to encourage up-market tourists are more five-star resorts, golf courses and offshore casinos – the *Caravela*, a shipboard casino, began operating from Panaji in 2001.

The Goa Foundation and local tradespeople argue, however, that if higher spending tourists are encouraged, they will never stray out of the large hotel complexes, and all the income will go straight to the hotel chains. While package tourists and low-budget backpackers do not spend a lot of money, at least they spend it in the cafés, shops and markets run by local people.

Pressure groups have also pointed out that tourism was simply imposed on the people

Who's Coming to Goa?

Goa's economy and employment sector relies heavily on tourism, at least for part of the year. By far the biggest slice of the tourism market – and the fastest growing – is domestic tourism, which was boosted by the opening of the Konkan Railway. In 1990, 777,000 domestic tourists filed into Goa; in 2001 the figure was 1.12 million. By comparison 260,000 foreigners entered Goa in 2001, a considerable drop from the peak of 292,000 the previous year.

Official tourism statistics for 2001 show that the highest number of foreign visitors came from the UK (90,756 or 34.9%). Next came Germans (17,823), French (9095), Swiss (8708), Italians (8567), Swedes (8341), Finns (7898), Americans (5978), Portuguese (5461) and Canadians (4620). Australians come in at No 14 (3696) and Russians at No 19 (1892). Although it seems as though there are a lot of Israeli travellers in parts of Goa, their numbers don't make the top 20.

In the 2001/2002 season (October to May), there were 279 charter flights to Goa, carrying 76,410 tourists – a substantial drop from the peak of 419 flights in 2000/2001.

without them being consulted. The earnings from tourism may be considerable, but most of the money goes into a few pockets, many of those outside Goa. Tourism does provide jobs but these are often simply menial jobs, and the large hotel chains have used the Apprenticeship Act to enable them to get away with paying absurdly low wages. A waiter serves the tourist a lobster priced at Rs 900, which represents only a little less than what the same waiter earns in a month.

POPULATION & PEOPLE

Goa's population has grown hugely since Independence. In 1961 the population was 590,000, at the last national census (2001) it had burgeoned to around 1.34 million. The spiralling figures reflect more than anything else, the huge influx of Indians from elsewhere in the country.

The state's huge migrant population is predominantly made up of extremely poor workers who arrive in Goa during the dry season in search of employment, mostly as labourers. There is another influx of visitors from as far afield as Nepal and Kashmir

The Caste System in Goa

Although the origins of the Hindu caste system are hazy, it seems to have been developed by the Brahmins (priest class) in order to maintain their superiority over indigenous Dravidians. Eventually, the caste system became formalised into four distinct classes, each with its own rules of conduct and behaviour.

These four castes, in order of hierarchy, are said to have come from Brahma's mouth (Brahmins; priest caste), arms (Kshatriyas; warrior caste), thighs (Vaisyas; caste of tradespeople and farmers), and feet (Sudras; caste of farmers and peasants). Beneath the four main castes is a fifth group, the Untouchables, or Scheduled Castes, who literally have no caste. They perform the most menial and degrading jobs. Hindus cannot change their caste – they're born into it and stuck with it for the rest of their life.

The caste system does not play so large a part in Goa as elsewhere in India, but it is still recognised and is treated in a uniquely Goan way. Naturally, the Hindu population of Goa still observes the caste system, but surprisingly the Christian community too, retains a distinct awareness of it. This can be traced back to the incentives that were offered to high caste Goan families to convert to Catholicism – namely that they would be able to keep their caste privileges if they did so. Furthermore, when the religious orders were recruiting lay clergy from the local population, only Brahmins were considered to be suitable, as it was felt that only they would be able to command the respect of the rest of the people.

Today Goa's Catholics consider caste important mainly when it comes to marriage, where a suitable match includes finding a partner from the right sort of caste background.

who come to sell goods to tourists. Whole families of women and children from Karnataka, Kerala and even Rajasthan travel to Goa to peddle handicrafts and fruit on the beaches.

Goa has a unique mix of people. Just under 30% of the population are Christian, most of whom are based in the central talukas that made up the area of the Old Conquests – Tiswadi, Mormugao, Bardez and Salcete. Approximately 65% of Goans are Hindus who tend to predominate in the areas of the outlying talukas that formed the New Conquests (Novas Conquistas) – Pernem, Bicholim, Satari, Ponda, Sanguem, Quepem and Canacona. Another 5% of the state's population are Muslims and less than 1% belong to other religions. Of particular note are the members of three dwindling minorities – the Dhangars, Velips and Kunbis – who live in the forested areas of the east and southeast of Goa. Only 2% of Goa's population is made up of the Scheduled Castes (the official term for Dalits or Untouchables) and 0.03% belong to Scheduled Tribes.

EDUCATION

Goa enjoys a higher average level of education than the rest of India (76% literacy compared with a national average of 52%).

The region has a long history of higher learning. After the arrival of the Portuguese, educational duties fell to the Christian religious institutions, which played an important role in educating novices at the two major seminaries. At Rachol Seminary, which boasted the third printing press in the east, the first-ever grammar of Konkani was produced, and the Bible was first translated into Konkani. Priests also served as village teachers and taught music.

Today, the percentage of children attending school is higher in Goa than in most Indian states. Schooling is based on the English system and starts at age five with pre-primary education.

Generally, education to 10th standard is free, and there are nominal charges for education to 12th standard. Beyond 12th standard, the majority of degree courses are for three years. Goa has 21 universities for general studies.

Although students can attend any university, the chances for degree-level education have become considerably better since Goa University was established in June 1985. The Goa Medical College and the Dental College in Bambolim also foster the education of the state's future medics.

ARTS

As any visitor will perceive soon after arrival, Goans love music and dance, and have a rich artistic and cultural heritage.

Dance

Although a distinction must be made between Hindu and Christian traditions, it's fair to say Goa's most famous song and dance is the *mando*. Dubbed the 'love song of the people of Goa', the form blends the rhythms of Indian music with traces of Portuguese melody and is accompanied by Konkani words. It is accompanied by a *ghumot* (drum).

The dance is highly stylised: men and women face each other in two rows; the women hold fans while the men hold colourful handkerchiefs. Just as important as the dance itself are the words of the songs. The *mando* was performed at weddings and its lyrics speak of the love between the bride and groom, the union between them and the separation from their old families.

A product of upper-class Christian families, the main *mandos* were composed between 1880 and 1920 and originate from Salcete taluka – in particular the villages of Loutolim, Chandor and Curtorim. At weddings the *mando* is often followed by other traditional dances; the faster and more lively *dulpod*, and sometimes by a dance known as the *deaknni*, performed by female dancers.

Although visitors are unlikely to see other dances, except at a tourist department event, there are a number of traditional dances in Goa, the most famous of which are those of the farmers and the *ramponkars* to celebrate harvest and good catches respectively.

Music

Goa is particularly rich in folk music, although you are unlikely to hear much of it in the normal course of events because most shops, restaurants and taxis blare out modern Hindi, Latin or Western music.

Nonetheless, for aficionados, there's a strong tradition of local music, from the labouring songs of Goa's poorest indigenous people, the Kunbis, to the formalised songs of the Christian community for singing at weddings and festivals. The *mando* again takes pride of place in the Catholic tradition, but there are plenty of other *zoitis*, songs common to both the Hindu and Christian communities that are sung at various stages of the marriage ceremonies. In fact there are folk songs for almost all occasions – children's lullabies or *piannos*, songs for singing at planting and harvesting in the fields, *ramponkars'* songs, and even songs

traditionally sung by the saltpan workers and toddy tappers.

In the classical Hindustani tradition too, Goa is well represented. Kesarbai Kerkar, who was born in the village of Keri in Ponda taluka, is remembered as one of the greatest vocalists of the 20th century. Lata Mangeshkar, whose family comes from Goa, is India's most famous movie singer. She's reputed to have made the most recordings of any artist in the world.

Goa's most famous son in the entertainment business is Remo Fernandes, who is one of the best-known popular singers in India – his first album, *Goan Crazy*, is probably his best. Another album worth looking out for is *Forwards into the Past*, which has arrangements by Fernandes and vocals by Lucio Miranda.

For a real insight into traditional Goan music it might be worth getting any of the albums by Gavana, a cultural group dedicated to preserving and promoting Goan music and dance.

Live music is very much a part of the Goan culture and there are some excellent bands that do the rounds of the parties, especially at Christmas time. Many of them play cover versions of Western music, but there are some more authentic sounds too. Worth a visit if you're in Goa at the right time is the **Pop, Beat & Jazz Music Festival**, which is held every February at the Kala Academy in Panaji.

Goa Trance In the 1990s Goan DJs developed their own brand of techno, now known as Goa Trance or Psy-Trance, and this is what you'll hear played at the infamous raves. Difficult to describe but easily recognisable once you've heard it, Goa Trance is a hypnotic mix of a heavy electronic beat (up to 170 beats per minute), with lighter levels said to be derived from classical Indian music. Artists stress the spiritual side of the music, calling the style an 'interface between technology and spirituality.' Goa Trance is performed by DJs and artists around the world, especially in Europe, Scandinavia and Israel, but probably the most famous artist is still Goa Gil, the dreadlocked and bearded maestro who started the full moon parties in the early 1970s and developed the concept of Goa Trance. Gil first came to India from San Francisco in 1969, studying yoga in the Himalaya before settling in Goa. He has released 13 albums and tours the world performing at raves, although his appearances in Goa are relatively rare these days.

Other Goa Trance DJs include Pscychify, DJ Anti, Rajaram and Astral Projection. Mainstream house and techno DJ's performing in Goa include DJ Ryan Sparks and Ryan Beck.

Literature

Although it's difficult to get hold of English-language Goan literature (books go out of print very quickly), Konkani literature is thriving and there is also some interesting writing by Goans in English.

Ferry Crossings by Manohar Shetty (ed) is a fascinating showcase of Goan writing talent and also highlights the diversity of cultural influences that have shaped the state. The short stories, translated into English from the four main languages in use in Goa, deal with everyday subjects of Goan life.

Frank Simoes passed his early childhood in Goa, before travelling the world. His book *Glad Seasons in Goa* is a light-hearted account of his adventures as he rediscovers his Goan roots.

Sorrowing Lies My Land by Lambert Mascarenhas, first published in 1955, has since been reprinted. The subject is the struggle for Goan Independence and the book is held to be a classic of Goan literature.

The subjects and settings of the short stories of *In the Womb of Saudade* by Lambert Mascarenhas are drawn from Goan life.

Also see Books in the Facts for the Visitor chapter.

Architecture

Goan architecture, as everything else Goan, is fascinating for its combination of forms taken from different cultural traditions.

Temples Goa's temples are interesting because they combine aspects of Muslim and Christian architecture into basically Hindu layouts. The domed roofs are a Muslim trait, while the whitewashed octagonal towers and balustraded facades have been borrowed from Portuguese church architecture.

Of particular note are the *deepastambhas* (lamp towers) that are practically exclusive to Goan temples and are decorated with oil lamps at festival times. Early *deepastambhas* such as the one at the Saptakoteshwara Temple in Naroa, are distinctively eastern in shape and ornament, whereas later examples like the one at the Shantadurga Temple near Ponda, with its whitewashed pillars and baroque decoration, seem to have been lifted straight from the Catholic architecture of Old Goa.

Despite these unique aspects, Goa's temples share many common features with Hindu shrines throughout India, and the layout is pretty much standard to all. The pillared pavilion, which is large enough to accommodate worshippers and local gatherings, is known as the *mandapa*. Between the *mandapa* and the inner sanctum where the deity resides is the area known as the *antaralya*, and the sanctum itself is called the *garbhagriha*. On either side of the *antaralya* there are usually smaller shrines to the associated deities worshipped at the temple.

Outside the main building, the temple's courtyard is generally surrounded by *agarshalas* (accommodation blocks) for visiting pilgrims. Larger temples tend to have a storage area somewhere in these buildings where the ratha (ceremonial chariot) is stored. This huge ornamented cart (sometimes there are two or even three of them) is used to transport the representation of the deity around the village on feast days and is pulled by teams of worshippers.

All temples, and indeed all Hindu houses, have a *tulsi vrindavan* near the front of the building. The *vrindavan* itself is a large ornamental container – which holds the (usually very straggly) *tulsi* plant. According to Hindu mythology, the *tulsi* is actually one of Vishnu's lovers who Lakshmi, Vishnu's consort, turned into a shrub in a fit of jealousy.

Churches Goa's churches obviously owe the majority of their design features to the European traditions of their time, and in the case of some, they are openly copies of buildings in Rome or Lisbon (St Cajetan's in Old Goa is basically a replica of Rome's St Peter's). There are, however, some features that distinguish them from their European counterparts. In some cases these are practical modifications to suit the local climate. Large windows are set deep into the walls for example, to allow plenty of light to penetrate, but to keep out direct sunlight.

The churches were constructed from the local rock laterite, which is porous, so there was a need to whitewash it regularly. The lime compound with which this was done was made from oyster shells. This had the effect of proofing the walls against moisture, although the heavy monsoon rainfall meant that the work had to be repeated every three or four years. Since laterite was coarse and unsuited to fine carving, the more important churches, such as the Basilica of Bom Jesus in Old Goa, have facades of basalt that had to be specially imported, but which could be sculpted with ease.

Apart from these deliberate concessions, other features that make the churches unique are due to the work of the local Indian artisans who built them. The floral decoration inside the Church of St Francis of Assisi in Old Goa is very Indian, as is some of the flamboyant woodcarving to be found in churches throughout Goa.

All churches in Goa share several common features. The most striking of these is the reredos, or ornamented backdrop, to the altar. Since most of Goa's large churches were built in the 16th and 17th centuries, the reredos designs conform to the styles of the age – mainly massive, very ornate and heavily gilded. In front of the reredos is the main altar and then the chancel, which is sometimes decorated with carvings or paintings on the walls. Many of Goa's churches are constructed in a cruciform design with side altars in the transepts.

Houses Sadly the houses of the landed gentry are gradually disappearing, although there are still a few excellent examples to be seen and a couple that can be visited. In the grandest houses, the layout allows for a huge frontage, often with floor to ceiling glass patio doors and tiny wrought-iron balconies in front of each window.

In the smaller houses the emphasis is on a wide veranda that almost encircles the house and provides plenty of welcome shade. In almost all cases the central feature of the facade is the *balcao* (shady porch) that stands in front of the main entrance.

Within the houses, the layout is generally dominated by a *saquão* (central courtyard) where the family could carry out their affairs away from public scrutiny. Larger houses have a chapel or a family altar where daily prayers were said. Perhaps the most distinctive feature of the houses, however, is the windows. Until relatively recently translucent discs of oyster shell were used instead of glass. The 7cm to 10cm diameter discs are set in wooden frames and allow a gentle, cool light to filter into the rooms.

Houses of Goa, available from bookshops in Goa, is a lavish study of the architecture of 150 Goan houses. See the boxed text 'Chandor's Colonial Mansions' in the South Goa chapter for information on two houses that are open to the public.

Painting

Although there is no style that is particularly distinctive to Goa, there is a long tradition of painting, evidence of which can be seen in the murals in the Rachol Seminary, near the village of Raia. Today, Goa's budding artists are nurtured at the College of Art in Panaji, after which most opt to travel out of the state to study art at a higher level elsewhere.

In Goa, Odette Gonsalves is famous for her paintings of horses, and Dr Subodh Kerkar, who runs a small gallery in Calangute, depicts typically Goan scenes in a variety of styles and disciplines. The work of artist and illustrator Mario Miranda adorns everything from books to cassette covers, and cartoonist Alexys Fernandes is well known for his contributions to many of the newspapers and magazines in Goa and elsewhere.

For those interested in the art scene, there are several galleries that can be visited. Between Calangute and Candolim, the Kerkar Gallery mostly shows work by Dr Kerkar himself, although there's also a small section of Goan handicrafts. In Panaji, the Galleria Ralino on the east side of the Municipal Gardens is worth a browse, and the Gitanjali Gallery at the Panjim Pousada has changing exhibitions of Goan and Indian artists.

In January 2003 the inaugural Fountainhas Arts Festival was held in Panaji, where a number of houses were turned into art galleries exhibiting Indian and Goan art.

Theatre

Goa's very active theatre scene is dominated by the unique local street plays known as *tiatr* and *kell tiatr*. The *tiatrs*, almost all of which are in Konkani, are generally very humorous and provide a platform for satire on politics and current affairs. There are several well-known *tiatr* writers who regularly produce new plays. An annual **tiatr festival** is held at the Kala Academy in Panaji, and the productions frequently do the rounds of the villages and towns in the area.

SOCIETY & CONDUCT
Traditional Culture

Despite the fact that most Catholic families in Goa converted from Hinduism 400 or so years ago, there are remarkably strong links between the Christian and Hindu communities. The relationship extends way beyond mere tolerance and neighbourliness. Both communities recognise the religious festivals of the other, and in many cases they participate in the same festivals and share the same customs. Nonetheless there are inevitably differences, and so any survey of Goan society has to differentiate between the habits and conduct of each group.

It should also be noted that, partly because Goa receives more than one million visitors a year, many aspects of traditional Goan life are fast disappearing. While certain families or communities may observe a particular

Susegad

Susegad is a term that crops up frequently in connection with Goans. To a Goan *susegad* is an attitude along the lines of 'relax and enjoy life while you can,' It's a philosophy of not getting overwrought if the work takes a day longer than planned, of making an appointment for 10am knowing full well that the other party won't turn up until at least 10.30am, and of taking time to sit and gossip.

The original Portuguese word *socegado* (literally meaning 'quiet') may have been used more by the Catholic community than the Hindus, but Goans are alike in their understanding of *susegad*. On the 25th anniversary of Goan Independence, Prime Minister Rajiv Gandhi described how 'an inherent non-acquisitiveness and contentment with what one has, described by that uniquely Goan word *socegado*, has been an enduring strength of Goan character.'

It is *susegad* that makes a visit to Goa special; there are always people ready to smile and say hello, to let you onto a crowded bus or to sit and chat about any subject that comes to mind.

ritual, others will not, and indeed will be amazed that anyone still does so. The following commentary on traditional customs then must be read in the light of the fact that times are changing.

Birth Among Hindus it is still considered preferable to have a boy rather than a girl. This is less important in Catholic families, but there is nonetheless a tradition that the birth of a girl is greeted by letting off one packet of firecrackers, while the birth of a boy merits two packets! Although in Goa there is none of the ill-treatment of girls that occurs elsewhere in India, it was only relatively recently that determination of sex of the unborn child, with a possible view to terminating the pregnancy should it be female, was made illegal.

In Hindu communities it is considered the privilege of the young wife to go to her parents' house for the confinement. After the birth the mother and child are rubbed with turmeric and oil and the child is swathed in cloth bandages. The first ritual, albeit one that is now dying out, comes on the sixth day after the birth. Known as 'mother sixth' or *sathi*, a drum is beaten throughout the night and the family keeps a vigil in order to ward off evil spirits from the child.

For 10 days after the birth the mother is considered impure and is not touched by anyone except the midwife. On the 11th day the mother and child are bathed, and the house is symbolically purified. On the 12th or 13th day the *barse* (naming) takes place.

Christian communities celebrate the birth of the child and it is subsequently named at its baptism.

Marriage Among both the Christian and Hindu communities a similar process is undertaken to procure a suitable partner for a son or daughter. Unless the matter has already been decided between close friends, this will generally begin with discreet inquiries among the community. If this fails, advertisements may be placed in local newspapers, emphasising the professional qualifications of the individual and the calmness and maturity of their character.

Dowries are still required to be paid by the bride's family in both Christian and Hindu weddings. This can either facilitate a match or hinder it; intercaste marriages become much more acceptable if there's a good dowry, but a high-caste girl whose family has no money can find it very difficult to secure a partner from the same sort of background.

The wedding ceremony itself is a lengthy and noisy affair. Towards the end of the proceedings the bride and groom join hands in a ritual known as *kanyadana*, while water and silver coins are poured over their clasped hands. The final ritual of the marriage, known as *saptapadi*, takes place when the couple walks together seven times around the sacred fire, thus making the marriage irrevocable.

Christian weddings are similar to those in the West, although some rituals are borrowed from Hindu traditions, such as ritual bathing of the bride before the wedding. *Chuddo* (green bracelets traditionally worn by married women) are also worn by Christian brides, and tradition dictates that should her husband die before her, the widow should break the bangles on his coffin at the funeral.

A traditional wedding among the minority Gauda people is unusual for the theatricality of the customs leading up to the ceremony. The day before the wedding the groom is given a haircut and is bathed, and he then attempts to run away from his family and friends, refusing to marry the chosen bride. He is brought back to the house and the next day he goes to the house of the bride with his family, where the ceremony is to take place.

Death Funeral ceremonies in the Hindu community are similar throughout all the castes. Children below the age of eight are buried, while all others are cremated. In preparation for the cremation, the body is washed, laid on a bier and covered with a shroud. The chief mourner (usually the eldest son) also bathes, and then the body is carried by members of the family or friends to the funeral pyre. The son lights the pyre, and then walks three times around it with a pot of water, finally standing at the head of the pyre.

On the third day after the cremation, the son, accompanied by a few friends and family, collects the ashes, which are then consigned to water – possibly the sea or a stream. Those who can afford it will travel north to scatter the ashes on the sacred Ganges River.

On the 10th day after the cremation, all members of the house take a purificatory bath, and on the 11th day *panchagavya* (a liquid consisting of cow's milk, cow's urine

and other substances) is sprinkled over the house in a ritual purification.

In the Christian community deaths are followed by burial. Personal items are placed with the deceased in the grave, including, if they're suitable for the person who has died, cigarettes and a bottle of alcohol!

There are numerous superstitions in the Hindu and Christian communities about unrestful spirits – particularly of those who committed suicide or died before being given last rites. A number of measures are made at the funeral to discourage the spirit from returning. The clothing and funeral shroud are cut, and a needle and thread are placed in the coffin. The spirit of the deceased who wishes to come back must first repair its torn clothing, a task that takes until daylight, at which time departure from the grave is impossible.

Women in Society

Generally, the position of women in Goa is much better than that elsewhere in India. Not only do women in Goa have property rights that are not shared by women in other states, but Goan society has also been much more enlightened about the education of women.

Over the years a number of convents were established exclusively to educate girls, and modern Indian education now makes no discrimination between the sexes.

A result of Goa's progressive policies has been that women are well represented in the professions and in positions of influence. While men undoubtedly still dominate these areas, women fill large numbers of places as doctors, teachers and university lecturers, and 30% of panchayat seats are reserved for women. There are, however, aspects that still point to an inbuilt prejudice – a trend that the discrepancy between male and female literacy in the state confirms (89% for men, 76% for women).

There are two major women's groups in Goa that can be contacted for further information. The **All India Women's Conference** has a Goa branch, which has its headquarters at the Institute Menezes Braganza in Panaji. **Bailancho Saad** *(Women's Voice; 304 Prema Bldg, Rua de Ourem, Panaji 400001)* is a women's collective that addresses issues such dowry harassment, education, and community issues. Contact **Albertina Almeida** *(e alal@goatelecom.com)* for more information.

RELIGION

Census figures show the proportionate mix of Christians, Hindus and Muslims to be found in Goa, but they fail to express the unique religious blend that is found in the state. In the early years of Portuguese rule, many Goan Hindus converted to Christianity simply to be able to retain their property rights. In many cases half the family departed for Hindu-held areas, while the other half remained in Portuguese territory, converted to the new faith, and looked after the family land. Thus from the start, families contained members of different faiths.

In addition to the family links between the two religious communities, distinctions were further blurred by the ways in which the religious orders adapted their teaching to suit the local population. As early as 1616 the Bible was translated into Konkani in the form of a folk tale that the villagers would understand. In 1623 Pope Gregory gave permission for Brahmin families converting to Catholicism to retain their caste, and a number of local festivals and traditions continued to be observed.

Goan Christians and Hindus often observe the same festivals, or at least pay respects to those of the other faith. In Siolim, to the north of Chapora, for example, an annual wake is held in honour of the local deity. Every Christian and Hindu household in the community sends offerings to the shrine before a procession starts off around the village. During the course of the proceedings prayers containing attributes of both faiths are offered in Konkani for the unity of the whole village.

There are plenty of other examples. In Mapusa, for example, the Church of Our Lady of Miracles was built on the site of an old Hindu temple and the annual feast day, on the Monday of the third week after Easter, sees crowds of Hindus and Christians paying tribute together.

There are few Muslims in Goa today. The largest Muslim community is in Ponda, where the state's oldest mosque is located.

Hinduism

Despite the proliferation of churches in Goa, Hinduism has far more followers than Christianity. Hinduism is one of the oldest extant religions, with firm roots extending back to beyond 1000 BC.

Hinduism today has a number of hol books, the most important being the fou Vedas (Divine Knowledge), the foundatio of Hindu philosophy. The Upanishads, con tained within the Vedas, delve into th metaphysical nature of the universe an soul.

Also important is the Mahabharata (Grea War of the Bharatas), an epic poem contain ing more than 220,000 lines. It describes th battles between the Kauravas and Pandavas who were descendants of the Induvans (Lunar Race). In it is the story of Rama, an it is probable that the most famous Hind epic, the Ramayana, was based on this. Th Bhagavad Gita is a famous episode of th Mahabharata where Krishna relates hi philosophies to Arjuna.

Hindu Philosophy & Practice Basicall the religion postulates that we will all g through a series of rebirths or reincarna tions that will eventually lead to moksha the spiritual salvation that frees one fron the cycle of rebirths. With each rebirth yo can move closer to or further from eventua moksha; the deciding factor is your karm which is literally a law of cause and effec Bad actions during your life result in ba karma, which ends in a lower reincarnatio Conversely , if your deeds and actions hav been good, you will reincarnate on a highe level and be a step closer to eventual free dom from rebirth.

Dharma, or the natural law, defines th total social, ethical and spiritual harmony o life. There are three categories of dharma, th first being the eternal harmony that involve the whole universe. The second category i the dharma that controls castes and the rela tions between castes. The third dharma is th moral code that an individual should follow

The Hindu religion has three basic prac tices. They are *puja* (worship), the crematio of the dead and the rules and regulations o the caste system.

A guru is not so much a teacher as a spi itual guide, somebody who by example o simply by their presence indicates what pat you should follow. In a spiritual search on always needs a guru. A sadhu is an individ ual on a spiritual search. They're an easil recognised group, usually wandering aroun half-naked, smeared in dust with their hai and beards matted.

Hindu Pantheon Westerners may have trouble understanding Hinduism principally because of its vast pantheon of gods. In fact you can look upon all the different gods simply as pictorial representations of the many attributes of one god. The one omnipresent god usually has three physical representations. Brahma is the creator, Vishnu is the reserver and Shiva is the destroyer and reproducer. Each god has an associated animal known as the 'vehicle' on which he rides, as well as a consort with certain attributes and abilities.

Brahma, despite his supreme position, appears much less often than Vishnu or Shiva. Brahma has four arms and four heads, which symbolise his all-seeing presence.

Vishnu is usually shown in one of the physical forms in which he has visited earth. In all, Vishnu has paid nine visits and on his 10th he is expected as a Kalki, riding a horse. On earlier visits he appeared in animal form, as in his boar or man-lion (Narasimha) incarnations, but on visit seven he appeared as Rama, regarded as the personification of the ideal man and the hero of the Ramayana. Rama's consort is Sita. Rama also managed to provide a number of secondary gods, including his helpful ally Hanuman, the monkey god.

On visit eight Vishnu came as Krishna, who was brought up with peasants and thus became a great favourite of the working classes. Krishna is renowned for his exploits with the *gopis* (milkmaids) and his consorts are Radha, the head of the *gopis*, Rukmani and Satyabhama. Krishna is often blue in colour and plays a flute. Vishnu's last incarnation was on visit nine, as the Buddha. This was arguably a ploy to bring the Buddhist splinter group back into the Hindu fold.

When Vishnu appears as Vishnu, rather than as one of his incarnations, he sits on a couch made from the coils of a serpent and in his hands he holds two symbols, the conch shell and the discus. Vishnu's vehicle is the half-man half-eagle known as the Garuda. His consort is the beautiful Lakshmi who came from the sea and is the goddess of wealth and prosperity.

Shiva's creative role is symbolised by the frequently worshipped lingam (phallus). Shiva rides on the bull Nandi and his matted hair is said to have Ganga, the goddess of the Ganges River, in it. Shiva's consort is Parvati, the beautiful. Parvati has, however, a dark side when she appears as Durga, the terrible. In this role she holds weapons in her 10 hands and rides a tiger. As Kali, the fiercest of the gods, she demands sacrifices and wears a garland of skulls.

Shiva and Parvati have two children. Ganesh is the elephant-headed god of good fortune and is probably the most popular of all the gods. Ganesh obtained his elephant head due to his father's notorious temper. Coming back from a long trip, Shiva discovered Parvati in her chambers with a young man. Not pausing to think that their son might have grown up during his absence, Shiva lopped his head off. He was then forced by Parvati to bring his son back to life but could only do so by giving him the head of the first living thing he saw – an elephant. Ganesh's vehicle is a rat. Shiva and Parvati's other son is Kartikiya, the god of war.

A variety of lesser gods and goddesses also make up the Hindu pantheon. Most of India's temples are dedicated to one or other of the gods, but curiously there are very few temples dedicated to Brahma. Most Hindus profess to be either Vaishnavaites (followers of Vishnu) or Shaivites (followers of Shiva).

The cow is the holy animal of Hinduism – it represents fertility and nurturing, benign aspects of the mother goddess, and is a symbol of Mother India.

Facts for the Visitor

HIGHLIGHTS
Beaches

Goa's prime attraction and biggest draw is, without doubt, its string of wonderful beaches. They run in an almost unbroken stretch from the northern border with Maharashtra all the way to Karnataka in the south. See the boxed text 'The Beach Files' later in this chapter to help you decide which beach you want to be at.

Churches

No visit to Goa would be complete without seeing Old Goa. You may not be an architecture buff, or even have a fondness for history, but a visit to this former Portuguese capital really does bring Goa's glorious past to life. Although impressive today, it's still hard to imagine that at one time this place was renowned as the greatest city in the east, and that it was a centre of trade and learning. The highlights here are the Basilica of Bom Jesus and the Se Cathedral, but there are several other well-preserved churches.

Goa has plenty of smaller, whitewashed churches, which are often the focus of village life. If you're fortunate enough to catch one during its annual feast celebrations you'll be in for a treat. Three parish churches that stand out are the small and historic chapel at Reis Magos, the parish church of Nossa Senhora de Penha de Franca at Britona, and St Anthony's Church in Siolim.

Forts

Goa's coastline has a long history of fortification and defence. The main fort is Fort Aguada, which still stands sentinel above the northern entrance to the Mandovi River.

A fantastic place to get away from it all is Terekhol Fort in the far north of the state. The small hotel that now operates in the fort is superb, and you couldn't get a more peaceful setting. On the southern coast the fort of Cabo da Rama has a stunning setting and makes a good day trip from Palolem or Colva. Inland is the tiny Corjuem Fort, which has the atmosphere of an isolated outpost.

Temples

The majority of the best-known Hindu temples in Goa are based in Ponda taluka (dis-

---

Seven Things You Should Do...

- Cycle out to the churches of the former capital of Old Goa
- Tour and lunch at a spice plantation in Ponda taluka
- Browse, haggle and get lost in Anjuna's Flea Market
- Take to the water – cruise on the Mandovi, go dolphin-spotting on the open sea, or bird-watching on the Sal River or in a dugout canoe at the Dr Salim Ali Bird Sanctuary
- Sip feni on the balcony of Panaji's Hotel Venite
- Take an early-morning yoga class at any beach resort
- Sleep in a bamboo hut on Palolem beach

---

trict), and are easily visited from Panaji (Panjim) or Margao (Madgaon). Possibly the two most interesting temples, however, are further afield. In the far east of Goa is the oldest surviving temple in the state, the Mahadeva Temple at Tambdi Surla. It dates from the Kadamba dynasty, and is reached by driving through some of the most attractive and unspoiled countryside in Goa. Much nearer to the coast is the Chandreshwar Bhutnath Temple, impressively set on the top of Chandranath Hill in south Goa.

Wildlife Sanctuaries

For its size, Goa boasts a relatively large area devoted to national parks and sanctuaries, but as far as wildlife goes, it's the birds that are the biggest draw. The Dr Salim Ali Bird Sanctuary on Chorao Island, near Panaji, is a fascinating place to visit, even for those who are not dedicated bird-watchers.

For ardent naturalists, the state's three wildlife sanctuaries provide opportunities to explore some unspoiled countryside. If you're prepared to spend several hours (or days) in the forest watchtowers you can expect to glimpse animals such as sambars, gaurs, macaque monkeys and even mongooses. Bhagwan Mahavir Wildlife Sanctuary is the largest of the three wildlife reserves and also contains the Dudhsagar Falls, the

BRYN THOMAS

Daytime ravers, Anjuna

BRYN THOMAS

Palolem beach

Bungalows, Arambol

LINDY HICKMAN

PAUL BIGLAND

Beach cricket, Arambol

ALAIN EVRARD

Paragliding over Vagator beach

Paddling in the sea, Little Vagator Beach

Selling fruit, Little Vagator Beach

Bicycles at sunset, Colva beach

second-highest waterfall in India, and a popular destination for a day excursion from the coast. Bondla Wildlife Sanctuary is the smallest and most accessible of Goa's sanctuaries, easily visited from Panaji or Margao.

Highways & Byways

Even away from the coast, the forest and Western Ghats, one of the most memorable things about Goa is its scenery. Detouring off the main highway by car or motorcycle is a pleasure in itself. Along the way you'll pass rural villages, colonial-era houses, verdant paddy fields, spice and cashew plantations and gleaming whitewashed churches.

Taking the coastal roads either north or south from Panaji, you'll stumble upon almost-empty beaches, spectacular headlands and forts, and broad rivers where you may have to wait with the locals while a ferry comes to haul you across. Or head inland to explore Old Goa, and the islands of Divar and Chorao, which have a way of life that seems to have stopped shortly after Independence.

Another good area to explore is along the eastern border of Salcete taluka, where the small villages (such as Chandor) still hold some of the best examples of Goan architecture to be found anywhere in the state.

Markets & Festivals

No visit to Goa is complete without visiting one of its markets. The most famous is the Anjuna Flea Market, held every Wednesday (from mid- to late-October until the start of the monsoon) at the southern end of Anjuna beach. From humble hippy beginnings, it has developed into a juggernaut of up to 2000 stalls attracting traders and tourists from all over India. Even if you're not in the market for a Kashmiri blanket or an elephant carving, it's a weird and wonderful experience and not to be missed. The Friday Mapusa Market has a lot more local colour, bringing traders from all over the state to hawk their wares; this a place to pick up some bargains.

With its unique Christian and Hindu mix, Goa is renowned for its annual festivals, from statewide religious celebrations such as Carnival, to local village fairs and tourist-oriented events. Getting caught up in one of the traditional Goan celebrations may well be a highlight of your visit. See Public Holidays & Special Events later in this chapter for more information and dates.

SUGGESTED ITINERARIES

Because of its small size and ease of travel, planning an itinerary for Goa may not be necessary – simply base yourself at a beach or town and make excursions and day trips from there. But if your time is short, you might want to prioritise and plan you trip to fit in as much as possible. Consider these options.

Beach Hopping

If you're travelling independently (without pre-booked accommodation), it's worth staying at a few different beaches to take in the varying atmosphere – see the boxed text 'The Beach Files' later for more information. A sample itinerary from Panaji might be to head up to Calangute or Baga for a couple of days – there's plenty of accommodation in a variety of budgets, great restaurants, good shopping and some manic nightlife. If the Goan party scene is for you, a couple of days based in Anjuna or Vagator during the high season should be on the cards. Backpackers and budget travellers will enjoy a couple of days in Arambol with its laid-back scene and occasional parties. In south Goa, Benaulim is an easy place to spend a few days, but the pick of the beaches is Palolem. From here you can easily check out Agonda and Patnem beaches for something a little quieter.

One Week

If your time in Goa is short but you still want to see a bit of the state away from the beach, you'll need to plan your time. Spend a day in Panaji exploring the Latin Quarter and taking an evening cruise on the Mandovi. The following morning head out to the churches of Old Goa, and perhaps spend the afternoon at one or two of the Hindu temples near Ponda and lunch at a spice plantation. Hiring a motorcycle or chartering a taxi will speed things up. For day three, move up to the beach, basing yourself anywhere between Candolim and Chapora. Take in a sunset at Fort Aguada, catch the Anjuna Market on Wednesday or one of the Saturday night markets at Baga or Arpora. Hire a motorcycle and take the coast road via Morjim and Mandrem to Arambol. Stay overnight then continue up to Terekhol Fort before returning to Panaji.

Two Weeks

With two weeks you can cover the above itinerary and add in a boat tour (dolphin- or

The Beach Files

Goa's biggest attraction for Western (and increasingly Indian) visitors is its beaches. The beaches themselves, the associated villages and resorts that have grown up around them, and the people that are drawn to them, are all quite different in character. Some have changed beyond recognition in the past 10 years, others are just being discovered, and a few pockets remain unspoilt. Here's a brief snapshot of Goa's beaches from north to south.

Querim This virtually deserted stretch of sand, just south of the Terekhol River, has a handful of beach shacks serving food at its northern end but no accommodation to speak of. You can walk here from Arambol.

Arambol The most northern of Goa's developed beaches, Arambol (formerly Harmal) has an attractive rocky headland and chilled-out, but increasingly busy, scene with music bars and some good restaurants; it attracts backpackers and some of the old Anjuna crowd looking for a quieter time. There's a small freshwater lake and opportunities for paragliding.

Mandrem The next beach south is clean with a small knot of bamboo huts between the road and the beach and some good mid-range accommodation among the coconut groves near the Mandrem Creek. This is a quiet beach with no 'nightlife' as such and the only restaurants are attached to accommodation places.

Asvem South of the Mandrem River, Asvem is a very peaceful beach popular with travellers drifting up to escape the 'scene' further south. There's a growing number of bamboo and palm-thatch huts, but essentially it's a quiet place – bring a book and chill out.

Morjim This is another long stretch of sand, almost deserted in places and backed by palms, casuarinas and a typical coastal village. The southern end, near the mouth of the Chapora River, has a few beach shacks popular with day-trippers, but no accommodation near the beach; the northern end has a handful of accommodation places, cafés and beach shacks, but again this is a place to relax and do nothing. Rare olive ridley turtles nest at the southern end of the beach (see the boxed text 'Turtle Beaches' in the North Goa chapter).

Chapora There is no beach here but the village is one of the favourite haunts of long-term visitors – backpackers, hippies, ravers and Goa regulars. Chapora village has a ruined Portuguese fort and a colourful harbour. Accommodation is mainly in homes for rent.

Vagator There are three relatively small, attractive beaches here backed by rocky cliffs that attract lots of day-trippers. Mostly budget accommodation is scattered around the village. Vagator is Goa's main party centre with a couple of sites for rave parties and late-night party places such as Primrose Cafe. The crowd here is a mix of budget travellers, European and Israeli ravers and a few mid-range tourists.

Anjuna Famous for its Wednesday flea market, Anjuna has long been a hippy hang-out, but now attracts a range of mostly younger or alternative travellers, including the party crowd. Accommodation is scattered over a wide area, mostly back from the beach. The beach itself is lovely at the southern end – not too crowded but with a few laid-back beach shacks.

Baga This is the northern end of the main package-tourist strip, running from the mouth of the Baga River straight into Calangute. The beach is good but crowded, with plenty of beach shacks and mid-range hotels. It attracts a slighter younger crowd than Calangute – a mix of backpackers and charter tourists.

Calangute Package tourism central. Goa's original holiday beach is now a mass of concrete mid-range hotels, shops, bars, some quality restaurants, touts and all the tourist trappings that go with it. Good if you want to be in the thick of the 'holiday action', bad if you want to avoid the crowds in the high season. The beach is long and crowded with sun beds, umbrellas and beach shacks.

Candolim & Sinquerim A bit more upmarket than Calangute, these beaches attract a slightly older crowd. The beaches are equally appealing and less crowded than Calangute. Mostly mid-range and top-end charter tourists come here, but there are a few cheap places to stay and some good restaurants. Sinquerim is the beach below Fort Aguada, dominated by the five-star Taj resort.

The Beach Files

Miramar & Dona Paula Panaji's town beach, Miramar is not much for swimming or sunbathing, but it's a popular spot to watch the sunset from. There is limited accommodation here and further south at Dona Paula, the small peninsula at the mouth of the Zuari River. It's handy for Panaji, but not suitable if you want to be close to a decent ocean beach.

Bogmalo A small, exclusive beach south of Vasco da Gama, Bogmalo is set up for charter tourists. You can enjoy water sports here and there is a dive centre.

Majorda & Velsao On this 6km stretch of relatively deserted beach between the Mormugao headland and Colva, there are a few beach shacks, a handful of upmarket resorts and typical coastal villages back from the beach, but not much excitement for the independent traveller.

Colva The beach here is similar to Calangute, but it's much quieter and still has a noticeable fishing industry. In Colva village there's a mix of package tourists, Indian tourists and backpackers, but no party scene – generally the crowd is older than at the northern beaches.

Benaulim The beach is similar to Colva but quieter again – beautiful sand, a string of beach shacks and some deserted spaces. There's some budget accommodation on the beach, and cheap guesthouses and family homes in the village. It's a popular place to rent long term, but there's little in the way of nightlife or even restaurants.

Varca & Cavelossim This 10km strip of relatively undeveloped, pristine beach is punctuated by some of Goa's finest resorts. Apart from a few mid-range places in Cavelossim, it's pretty much left to upmarket tourists content to move between the pool and their little piece of beach.

Agonda North of Palolem, Agonda is a largely undeveloped beach with a few sets of bamboo huts and budget accommodation places. The southern end of the beach is quite exposed but it's a lovely place. There's nothing to do here but chill out. The village is so far unfettered by the tourism rush occurring elsewhere in south Goa.

Palolem This is Goa's 'paradise lost' according to some. Palolem is still the most idyllic and picture-perfect beach in the state, but fast filling up with travellers and the businesses set up to service them. Accommodation is mostly in the string of bamboo huts fronting the beach and there are plenty of beach shacks playing music into the night. It's easy to meet people here which makes it popular with both short-term tourists and travellers stopping off on the trip around India.

Patnem A short distance south of Palolem, Patnem is much quieter, with just a few beach shacks and bamboo huts, and some decent surf.

Rajbag Between Patnem and the Talpona River, Rajbag is an exposed beach now dominated by the five-star Goa Intercontinental Resort.

Bringing in the catch of the day, Colva beach

crocodile-spotting) or a trip out to Bondla Wildlife Sanctuary and Dudhsagar Falls.

During the second week, head down to south Goa for a change of pace. An excellent day trip from Margao (or Colva) is to explore Salcete taluka, visiting Chandor, Rachol and Loutolim. Colva and Benaulim are fine beaches close to Margao, but if you really want to explore, hire a motorcycle and ride down the coast via Cavelossim and Betul to the fort at Cabo da Rama, then on to Palolem – a great beach to spend a couple of days at. From here you can easily visit Agonda or Patnem beaches, or Cotigao Wildlife Sanctuary.

One Month

With a month you can do all of the above plus more, checking out the various beaches and basing yourself at the one that suits you best. You'll also have time to check out some attractions outside Goa – see the Excursions chapter for suggestions on trips to Karnataka.

PLANNING
When to Go

The best time to visit Goa is during the cooler months from November to March. If you arrive in October, right at the start of the tourist season, you'll find the beaches pleasantly empty, but may also find that some of the facilities (such as beach shacks) haven't yet bothered to open.

At the end of the high season, April and May can be very humid, and suffer from the same problems as the beginning of the season: most beach shacks pack up after Easter and swimming becomes less pleasant as the sea gets rougher.

The monsoon, which visits Goa between June and the end of September, is felt by many Goans to be when the state is at its best. Parties and celebrations are held to welcome the rain, and the countryside turns lush and green almost overnight. In terms of tourism, however, this period is virtually dead. Some guesthouses simply close up while all energies are devoted to farming. Swimming in the sea is out of the question.

Without doubt the peak time for visitors to Goa is over Christmas and New Year, and some people have been coming back annually for a decade or more. The massive influx of visitors at Christmas allows hotels and guesthouses to charge exorbitant prices

and many are booked solid, but it's a great time to be in Goa. The weather is perfect, the place is buzzing, and in typical Goan fashion there are parties most nights.

Maps

Good road maps of Goa are virtually impossible to get hold of, which is annoying as this is one of the few states in India where visitors can easily hire a motorcycle and head off exploring by themselves. There are adequate maps available, but none accurate enough to guide you around the back roads without having to stop and ask for directions. The best is *Goa and its Beaches*, published by Roger Lascelles in the UK and available through Stamfords. Other road maps are produced by the Discover India series (Rs 65) and you can get free state maps from the Goa Tourism Development Corporation (GTDC).

If you have access to the Internet, check out the website W www.johnthemap.co.uk. It has full-colour maps of Goa's beaches, as well as maps of the main towns and talukas, all of which can be downloaded and printed.

Fin Doll publishes a small booklet *Goa Maps with Yellow Pages* which includes pretty good maps of the main tourist areas. The booklet costs Rs 60 and is available at hotels, bars and bookshops in Goa, or on the Internet at W www.goacom.com.

What to Bring

It's unnecessary to fill your backpack or suitcase full of clothes and gear. The climate is warm even in winter, and everything you might need is available cheaply in Goa.

Light clothing is all you'll need, along with one warm top just in case there's a chill late at night, but you can leave the quilted jackets and hiking boots behind. Although shorts are accepted as a Western eccentricity, they should at least be of a decent length. Bring some dress clothes – wearing shorts or a T-shirt in a formal situation is definitely impolite.

Soap, toothpaste and other toiletries are readily available from supermarkets and pharmacies. Tampons are available in most major places but pads are more widely available.

For budget travellers, a sturdy padlock is a virtual necessity. Most cheap hotels, beach huts and even a few mid-range places

Close Shave

Men can leave the safety razor at home – one of the pleasures of travel in India is popping into a barber shop every few days for a full-service shave. For around Rs 20, or US$0.50 (at beach resorts some barbers jack up the price for tourists), you get lathered up, shaved with a blade razor, then the process is repeated for a closer shave. Then there's the hot, damp towel, a cooling stick of balm and sometimes talcum powder or aftershave.

Before you know it you're also in for a vigorous scalp massage and neck-cracking experience: this is a common scam to extract an inflated amount from a tourist – if you want a shave, agree on a price first. For hygiene, choose a barber shop that looks clean and ensure that a fresh blade is used.

have doors locked by a flimsy latch and padlock. A knife (preferably Swiss army) has a whole range of uses, such as peeling fruit and opening cans and bottles. Insect repellent is worth bringing, though you can buy Indian-brand repellents in Goa. Electric mosquito zappers are available from local shops and if you buy one in India it will have the right plug fitting.

Power cuts in Goa are frequent ('load shedding' as it is euphemistically known) and there's little street lighting at night so bring a torch (flashlight).

RESPONSIBLE TOURISM

Common sense and courtesy go a long way when you are travelling. Think about the impact you may be having on the environment and the people who inhabit it. One very simple way of minimising your impact is to reduce the amount of plastic you use. Recycle plastic bags; try to recycle plastic drinking bottles, or purify your water.

As exotic and tempting as they may be, avoid buying products such as sea shells, coral or ivory.

For information on environmental organisations see the boxed text 'Conservation Contacts' in the Facts about Goa chapter.

Child Prostitution

Since Anglo-Indian Freddy Peat was convicted in 1996 of horrific sex crimes against children in Goa, there has been increasing acceptance that child prostitution is a problem that needs to be tackled. There is now greater vigilance by both police and locals, and the legal procedure is in place to deal with paedophiles. Offenders face life imprisonment in an Indian jail if they are convicted.

If you know, witness or suspect anyone engaged in these activities you should report them to police in Goa. **Stop Paedophilia** (☎ 2420141) in Panaji is an organisation that promotes awareness of the issue and encourages people to report any suspicious activity, such as an adult taking unrelated children to hotels.

Cleaning Up

When visiting Goa spare a thought for one of the toughest environmental problems facing the state at the moment – the battle against litter and, in particular, plastic nonbiodegradable rubbish. Quite simply, the state's infrastructure does not have the means to cope with the volume of rubbish created by more than one million tourists who visit annually. The problem has been exacerbated over the past few years by the widespread use of plastic mineral-water bottles and plastic bags given by shops (previously goods were wrapped in newspaper or left unpackaged). Although beach cleanups are frequently organised, the rubbish is often simply dumped elsewhere.

Steps to manage the problem have met with little success, even though the government has recognised the impact of tourism and has declared certain beaches and historic areas such as Calangute beach and Old Goa 'plastic free zones', where the sale and use of plastic bottles is prohibited. Even if the litter could be collected properly there is presently no recycling facility for plastics in Goa. The only real solution is to cut down on the amount of plastic used. There are simple steps that everyone can take to help: don't drop litter, and refuse plastic bags from shops.

You can also refill mineral water bottles where possible. A few restaurants now have efficient water filters and offer to fill up water bottles from their supply. Contact the **Goa Foundation** (☎ 2256479) in Mapusa for information on current schemes to reduce waste.

TOURIST OFFICES
Local Tourist Offices
Within Goa there are representatives of the national (Government of India) tourist office, and the state tourist organisation, the Goa Tourism Development Corporation (GTDC). The Government of India tourist office is next to the Municipal Gardens in Panaji, and there are GTDC tourist information counters in Panaji, Margao, Mapusa, Vasco da Gama and at Dabolim Airport.

Tourist Offices Abroad
The Government of India Department of Tourism maintains a string of tourist offices in other countries where you can get brochures, leaflets and some information about India.

Australia
(☎ 02-9264 4855, fax 9264 4860, e info@ india.com.au) Level 2, Piccadilly, 210 Pitt St, Sydney NSW 2000
Canada
(☎ 416-962 3787, fax 962 6279, e india@ istar.ca) 60 Bloor St West, Suite No 1003, Toronto, Ontario M4W 3B8
France
(☎ 01 45 23 30 45, fax 45 23 33 45, e info -fr@india-tourism.com) 1-13 Bis Blv Hausmann, 75008 Paris
Germany
(☎ 069-242 9490, fax 242 94977, e info@ india-tourism.com) Baseler Strasse 48, 60329 Frankfurt-am-Main
Israel
(☎ 03-510 1431, fax 510 1434, e info-il@ india-tourism.com) 4 Kaufman St, Tel Aviv
Italy
(☎ 02-805 3506, fax 7202 1681, e info .it@india-tourism.com) Via Albricci 9, 20122 Milan
Japan
(☎ 03-5715062, fax 5715235, w www.indo tour.or.jp) Pearl Bldg, 7-9-18 Ginza Chou-Ku, Tokyo 104
Netherlands
(☎ 020-620 8991, fax 638 3059, e info.nl@ india-tourism.com) Rokin 9-15, 1012 KK Amsterdam
Sweden
(☎ 08-215081, fax 210186, e info.se@ india-tourism.com) Sveavagen 9-11, S-III 57, Stockholm 11157
UK
(☎ 020-7437 3677, fax 7494 1048, e info@ indiatouristoffice.org) 7 Cork St, London W1X 2LN

USA
New York: (☎ 212-586 4901, fax 582 3274, e ny@itonyc.com) 1270 Avenue of the Americas, Suite 1808, New York, NY 10020
Los Angeles: (☎ 213-380 8855, fax 380 6111, e goitola@aol.com) 3550 Wilshire Blvd, Suite 204, Los Angeles CA 90010

VISAS & DOCUMENTS
Visas
Just about everyone needs a visa for India and it must be obtained before you enter the country.

Six-month multiple-entry visas (valid from the date of issue) are issued to most nationalities regardless of whether you intend staying that long or are re-entering the country. Visa applications can be made at your nearest embassy or consulate in person or by post. You need to provide a completed visa application form, passport photographs, visa fee and, in some cases, an itinerary and proof of onward travel (such as a flight ticket out of India). Check with your embassy for specific requirements. Many embassies have a website where you can download and print a visa application form and get all the information you need (see Embassies & Consulates later in this chapter). Visa fees vary from country to country: the cost is A$88 for Australians, UK£30 for Britons, €50 (or equivalent) for Dutch and most European passport holders and US$60 for US passport holders.

Visa Extensions Officially, visa extensions are only obtainable in Delhi and, even then, only in extenuating circumstances. If your visa is about to run out and you're desperate, check first with the **Foreigners' Registration Office** (☎ 2225360; open 9.30am-1pm Mon Fri) inside the **police headquarters**, but they may direct you to the Home Department at the Secretariat Building. In Panaji, visa extensions are not granted as a matter of course in Panaji. If you're unsuccessful here, Mumbai and Bangalore are the nearest alternatives.

You can only get another six-month visa by leaving the country and coming back in on a new visa.

Tax Clearance Certificates
If you stay in India for more than 120 days you officially need a 'tax clearance certificate' to leave the country, but we've never yet heard from anyone who has actually been

asked for this document on departure. In Panaji, go to the foreign section of the **Income Tax Office** *(Shanta Bldg, Emidio Gracia Rd)*, bringing your passport and a handful of bank exchange or ATM receipts (to show you really have been changing foreign currency into rupees officially).

Travel Insurance

A travel insurance policy to cover theft, loss and medical problems is definitely a wise idea. There is a wide variety of policies and your travel agent will have recommendations. Some policies specifically exclude 'dangerous activities', which can mean motorcycling and even trekking. This is especially relevant in Goa, where most people hire a scooter or motorcycle at some time. Other increasingly popular activities in Goa are scuba diving and water sports such as water-skiing and paragliding, all of which may require special stipulations when you take out your travel insurance.

Driving Licence & Permits

If you are considering hiring a car or motorcycle in Goa (as many do), get an international driving permit. While not essential in Goa, the permit will certainly keep you out of trouble if you're stopped by police. Contact the automobile association in your own country to get one – obviously you need a valid driving licence to be eligible for it.

Copies

All important documents, eg, passport data and visa pages, credit cards, travel insurance policy, air/bus/train tickets, driving licence) should be photocopied before you leave home. Leave one copy with someone at home and keep another with you, separate from the originals. It's also a good idea to store details of your vital travel documents in Lonely Planet's free online **Travel Vault** (W *www.ekno.lonelyplanet.com)* in case you lose the photocopies.

EMBASSIES & CONSULATES
Indian Embassies & Consulates

India's embassies, consulates and high commissions abroad include:

Australia
High Commission: (☎ 02-6273 3999, fax 6273 3328, W www.indianconsulate.org) 3/5 Moonah Place, Yarralumla, ACT 2600

Consulate General: (☎ 02-9223 9500, fax 9223 9246) Level 27, 25 Bligh St, Sydney, NSW 2000
Honorary Consulate: (☎ 03-9384 0141, fax 9384 1609) 7 Munro St, Coburg, Melbourne, VIC 3058

Belgium & Luxembourg
Embassy: (☎ 02-6409140, fax 6489638, W www.indembassy.be) 217 Chaussee de Vleurgat, 1050 Brussels; also Honorary Consulates in Antwerp and Luxembourg

Canada
High Commission: (☎ 613-744 3751, fax 744 0913, W www.hciottawa.ca) 10 Springfield Rd, Ottawa, Ontario K1M 1C9
Consulate General: (☎ 416-960 0751, fax 960 9812) 1835 Yonge St, Toronto, Ontario M4S 1X8
Consulate General: (☎ 604-662 8811, fax 682 2471, W www.cgivancouver.com) 325 How St, 2F, Vancouver, BC V6C 1Z7

Denmark
Embassy: (☎ 045-3918 2888, fax 3927 0218, W www.indian-embassy.dk) Vangehusvej 15, 2100 Copenhagen

France
Embassy: (☎ 01 40 50 71 71, fax 01 40 50 09 96, W www.amb-inde.fr) 15 rue Alfred Dehodencq, 75016 Paris

Germany
Embassy: (☎ 030-2579 5611, fax 2579 5620, W www.indianembassy.de) Tiergartenstrasse 17, Berlin 10185
Consulate: (☎ 089-210 2390) Widenmayer Strasse 15, Munich D-80538; (☎ 069-1530050, W www.cgifrankfurt.de) Friedrich Ebert Anlarge 26, Frankfurt 60325

Ireland
Embassy: (☎ 01-497 0483, fax 497 8074) 6 Leeson Park, Dublin 6

Israel
Embassy: (☎ 03-510 1431, fax 510 1434) 4 Kaufman St, Sharbat House, Tel Aviv 68012

Italy
Embassy: (☎ 06-488 4642, fax 481 9539) Via XX Settembre 5, 00187 Rome

Japan
Embassy: (☎ 03-3262 2391, fax 3234 4866, W www.embassy-avenue.jp) 2-2-11 Kudan Minami, Chiyoda-ku, Tokyo 102

Nepal
Embassy: (☎ 01-413174, fax 413132, W www.south-asia.com/Embassy-India/) Kapurdhara Marg, Kathmandu 410900

Netherlands
Embassy: (☎ 070-346 9771, fax 361 7072, W www.indianembassy.nl) Buitenrustweg 2, 2517 KD, Den Hague

New Zealand
High Commission: (☎ 04-473 6390, fax 499 0665) 180 Molesworth St, Wellington
Sweden
Embassy: (☎ 08-10 70 08, fax 24 85 05, Ⓦ www.indianembassy.se) Adolf Fredriks kyrkogata 12, Stockholm 11183
UK
High Commission: (☎ 020-7836 8484, fax 7836 4331, Ⓦ www.hcilondon.net) India House, Aldwych, London WC2B 4NA
USA
Embassy: (☎ 202-939 7000, fax 265 4351, Ⓦ www.indianembassy.org) 2107 Massachusetts Ave NW, Washington, DC 20008
Consulate General: (☎ 212-774 0600, fax 861 3788, Ⓦ www.indiacgny.org) 3 East 64th St, Manhattan, New York, NY 10021-7097
Consulate General: (☎ 415-668 0662, fax 668 9764, Ⓦ www.indianconsulate-sf.org) 540 Arguello Blvd, San Francisco, CA 94118
Consulate General: (☎ 312-595 0405, fax 595 0416, Ⓦ www.chicago.indianconsulate.com) NBC Tower, 455 North Cityfront Plaza Drive, Suite 850, Chicago, IL 60611

Embassies & Consulates in India

Most foreign diplomatic missions are in Delhi, but there are also quite a few consulates in the other major cities of Mumbai (Bombay), Kolkata (Calcutta) and Chennai (Madras). Austria, Germany, Italy, Mexico, Portugal and the UK have honorary consuls in Goa. We've listed each country's embassy that is closest to Goa:

Australia
Consulate General: (☎ 022-22181071) 16th floor, Maker Tower, E Block, Cuffe Parade, Colaba, Mumbai
Austria
Honorary Consul: (☎ 0832-2232011, fax 2232013) 2nd floor, Kamat Centre, Dayanand Bandodkar Marg, Panaji
Canada
Consulate: (☎ 022-22876027) 41/42 Maker Chambers VI, Nariman Point, Mumbai
Denmark
Embassy: (☎ 011-23010900, fax 3792019; ⓔ denmark@vsnl.com) 11 Aurangzeb Rd, Delhi
Finland
Embassy: (☎ 011-26111473, fax 6885380) E-3 Nyaya Marg, Chanakyapuri, Delhi
France
Embassy: (☎ 022-24950918) 2nd floor, Datta Prasad Bldg, 10 NG Cross Rd, Cumballa Hill, Mumbai

Germany
Honorary Consul: (☎ 0832-2223261), c/o Cosme Matias Menezes Group, Rua de Ourem, Panaji
Honorary Consul: (☎ 022-22832422) 10th floor, Hoechst House, Vinayak K Shah Rd, Nariman Point, Mumbai
Ireland
Embassy: (☎ 022-22024607) 2nd floor, Royal Bombay Yacht Club, Shivaji Marg, Colaba, Mumbai
Israel
Embassy: (☎ 022-22819993) 16th floor, Earnest House, Nariman Point, Mumbai
Italy
Honorary Consul: (☎ 0832-2230697, fax 2229907) Sesa Ghor, Pato, Panaji
Embassy: (☎ 011-26114355) 50E Chandragupta Marg, Chanakyapuri, Delhi
Japan
Embassy: (☎ 022-24933843) 1 ML Dahanukar Rd, Mumbai
Mexico
Honorary Consul: (☎ 0832-2226281, fax 2225098) 1st floor, Dempo House, Dayanand Bandodkar Marg, Panaji
Netherlands
Embassy: (☎ 022-22016750) 1st floor, Forbes Bldg, Charanjit Rai Marg, Mumbai
New Zealand
High Commission: (☎ 011-26883170) 50N Nyaya Marg, Chanakyapuri, Delhi
Portugal
Honorary Consul: (☎ 0832-2229266) LIC Bldg, Pato, Panaji
South Africa
Embassy: (☎ 011-26149411) B18 Vasant Marg, Vasant Vihar, Delhi
Spain
Embassy: (☎ 011-23792085, fax 3793375) 12 Prithviraj Rd, Delhi
Sweden
Embassy: (☎ 011-26875760, fax 6885401) Nyaya Marg, Chanakyapuri, Delhi
Switzerland
Consulate General: (☎ 022-22884563) 102 Makers Chambers IV, Nariman Point, Mumbai
UK
Deputy High Commissioner: (☎ 0832-2228571, fax 2232828) 3rd floor, Manguirish Bldg, 18th June Rd, Panaji
Embassy: (☎ 022-22830517) 2nd floor, Maker Chambers IV, J Bajaj Marg, Nariman Point, Mumbai
USA
Embassy: (☎ 022-23633611) Lincoln House, 78 Bhulabai Desai Rd, Cumballa Hill, Mumbai

Your Own Embassy

It's important to realise what your own embassy – the embassy of the country of which you are a citizen – can and can't do to help you if you get into trouble. Generally speaking, it won't be much help in emergencies if the trouble you're in is remotely your own fault. Remember that you are bound by the laws of the country you are in. Your embassy will not be sympathetic if you end up in jail after committing a crime locally, even if such actions are legal in your own country. See Embassies & Consulates in India for contact details.

CUSTOMS

The usual duty-free regulations apply for India; that is, 1L of spirits and 200 cigarettes.

You're allowed to bring in all sorts of Western technological wonders, but expensive items, such as video cameras, are likely to be entered on a 'Tourist Baggage Re-Export' form to ensure you take them out when you leave. It's not necessary to declare still cameras. See the Indian customs website (w www.customs.gov.in) for more information.

MONEY
Currency

The rupee (Rs) is divided into 100 paise (p). There are coins of 5, 10, 20, 25 and 50 paise, Rs 1, 2 and 5, and notes of Rs 10, 20, 50, 100 and 500.

You are officially not allowed to bring Indian currency into the country or take it out. You are allowed to bring in unlimited amounts of foreign currency or travellers cheques, but you are supposed to declare anything over US$1000 on arrival.

One of the most annoying things about India is that no-one ever seems to have *any* change, and you'll find on numerous occasions you'll be left waiting for five minutes while a shopkeeper hawks your Rs 100 note around other shops to secure change. ATMs routinely dispense only Rs 500 notes which are a nightmare to change!

Exchange Rates

The subwwway section of Lonely Planet's website (w www.lonelyplanet.com/subwwway/) provides links to currency converters for up-to-the-minute exchange rates. At the time of going to press, the exchange rates were:

country	unit		rupees
Australia	A$1	=	Rs 31
Canada	C$1	=	Rs 34
Euro zone	€1	=	Rs 56
Japan	¥100	=	Rs 40
New Zealand	NZ$1	=	Rs 27
UK	UK£1	=	Rs 78
USA	US$1	=	Rs 47

Exchanging Money

Cash It pays to have some US dollars, pounds sterling or euros in cash for times when you can't change travellers cheques or use a credit card. You won't have any problem changing money in the tourist areas. The best rates are usually at the State Bank of India and Thomas Cook. Next best are the private moneychangers. Hotels offer the least attractive rates.

Travellers Cheques All major brands are accepted in India, with American Express (AmEx) and Thomas Cook being the most widely traded. Pounds sterling, euros and US dollars are the safest bet. Charges for changing travellers cheques vary from place to place and bank to bank, but hot competition among private moneychangers means you can usually change cheques commission-free.

All travellers cheques are replaceable, but this does you little good if you have to go home and apply for them at your bank. You should keep an emergency stash of cash in a totally separate place from your cheques, along with a record of the cheque serial numbers, proof of purchase slips and your passport number.

AmEx and Thomas Cook travellers cheques are the easiest to have replaced in Goa, provided you have the right documentation. If your travellers cheques are lost or stolen, contact the following offices in Panaji immediately:

American Express Menezes Air Travel (☎ 2432960), Ourem Rd
Thomas Cook (☎ 2221312), 8 Alcon Chambers, Dayanand Bandodkar

ATMs Several banks have introduced 24-hour ATMs into Goa and there are more opening each year. These take international cards using the Cirrus, Maestro, Master-Card and Visa networks. The main banks with ATMs are ICICI, Centurion, HDFC and UTI. In most cases the ATMs are not actually attached to a bank branch but are installed in shopping areas purely as cash-dispensing machines. They are usually in an air-conditioned cubicle (which you may need your card to access) and are guarded by 24-hour armed security. You can currently find ATMs in Panaji, Margao, Mapusa, Calangute, Candolim, Vasco da Gama, Ponda and Colva.

Credit Cards These are accepted in most major tourist centres, but don't expect to be able to use a card in budget hotels and restaurants. Upmarket hotels accept them, as do most travel agencies and practically all department stores. MasterCard and Visa are the most widely accepted cards. Cash advances on credit cards can be made at branches of Thomas Cook and Bank of Baroda, as well as at most moneychangers (which are often travel agencies) at the beach resorts.

International Transfers International money transfers can be arranged through Thomas Cook's Moneygram service or Western Union, both of which have branches in Panaji and some other towns in Goa. Charges for this service are high – if you have a credit card it's cheaper to get someone to deposit money in your home account and draw a cash advance.

Airport Scams

If you change rupees back into non-Indian currencies at the airport make double sure you're getting the correct rate and have been given the correct amount of money. Because you're not supposed to take Indian currency out of the country, some bureaux de change charge ridiculous (unadvertised) commission fees.

If you arrive on a charter flight you may be besieged by children and assorted beggars asking for just 'one pound coin', the sort of loose change that you can't exchange in India. When you depart you'll probably see the same kids trying to sell the coins back to departing tourists. A pound is worth almost Rs 80 – a tidy profit for doing nothing!

Moneychangers Private moneychangers are everywhere in towns and beach resorts. They keep longer hours than banks, and are quick and efficient. Many travel agencies double as exchange offices and give cash advances on credit cards. Shop around and check rates at the banks first.

Encashment Certificates All money is supposed to be changed at official banks or moneychangers, and you are supposed to be given an encashment certificate for each transaction. Banks will usually give you one, and they can be useful if you want to re-exchange excess rupees for hard currency, buy a tourist-quota train ticket, or if you need to show a tax clearance certificate. ATM receipts serve the same purpose.

Costs

India as a whole is a very cheap country to visit. However, costs in Goa often depend on whether or not you're being charged as a rich foreign tourist. Some things seem ridiculously cheap: a haircut for US$1, a veg thali (traditional all-you-can-eat meal) for 50c; a one-hour bus ride for 30c and a packet of Indian cigarettes for 50c. But souvenirs, many hotels, petrol (gas) and imported goods will seem relatively expensive in comparison.

By staying in rock-bottom budget hotels or guesthouses, eating fish curry rice at local restaurants and not moving around or partying too much, it's possible to get by in Goa on Rs 250 (US$6) a day. Also, outside the November–March high season, accommodation costs are substantially reduced – see Accommodation later in this chapter for more details. At the other end of the scale, staying at a five-star resort and living it up can easily cost US$250 a day or more.

Most visitors will opt for a middle ground. On a budget, but allowing for clean, secure accommodation, meals in cheap restaurants or beach shacks, the occasional taxi or motorcycle hire and a bit of nightlife, expect to pay US$15 to US$25 a day. A mid-range budget – staying in a decent hotel with a pool, eating in touristy restaurants and testing out the seafood, taking taxis everywhere and buying souvenirs – set aside perhaps US$50 a day. If you're on a package deal with accommodation included, you should find US$25 to US$30 is ample.

Sample costs in Goa include:

Item	Price Rs
Small beer	30
Newspaper	2
Camera film	100
Budget meal	30
Restaurant meal	60
Cigarettes (10)	20

Tipping & Bargaining

Although tipping is not necessary, particularly if you're hanging out on one of the more remote beaches, most people do tip both the staff in their hotel and in restaurants. A waiter in a restaurant, or a room boy at a hotel, get paid about Rs 1000 to 2000 a month (US$25 to US$50), so they rely on the tips they pick up in the tourist season.

There's no need to go overboard; Rs 10 to 20 is about right for members of the hotel staff who help you out, and the normal 10% figure is quite adequate in restaurants. Some hotels and restaurants prefer that you contribute to a general tips box so that money can be distributed evenly among staff. It's not necessary to tip taxi drivers for short trips, but

Baksheesh

In many Asian countries tipping is virtually unknown, but India is an exception – although tipping has a rather different role in India than in the West. The term 'baksheesh', which encompasses tipping and a lot more besides, aptly describes the concept in India. You 'tip' not so much for good service, but to get things done.

Judicious baksheesh will open closed doors, find missing letters and perform other small miracles. Tipping is not necessary for taxis nor for cheaper restaurants, but if you're going to be using something repeatedly, an initial tip will ensure the standards are kept up – for example, this may explain why the service is slower every time you eat in your hotel restaurant. Keep things in perspective, though. Demands for baksheesh can quickly become never-ending. Ask yourself if it's really necessary or desirable before shelling out.

Many Westerners find this aspect of Indian travel the most trying – the constant demands for baksheesh and the expectations that because you're a foreigner, you'll tip. However, from an Indian perspective, baksheesh is an integral part of the system – it wasn't invented simply to extract money from tourists. Take some time to observe how Indians (even those who are obviously not excessively wealthy) deal with baksheesh situations; they always give something, and it's expected and accepted by both sides.

Although you may not consider yourself well off, think of how an Indian who earns Rs 800 a month sees you. Foreigners who spend their whole time trying to fight the system, instead of rolling with it philosophically, inevitably find themselves constantly involved in vitriolic and unpleasant arguments with people over what is, in the end, a pittance. No-one would be naive enough to suggest that all demands for baksheesh are justified, or that the amount demanded is always reasonable, but if you can accept the fact that this is how things work here, and tip fairly, chances are you'll find that things are a whole lot easier.

Although most people think of baksheesh in terms of tipping, it also refers to giving alms to beggars. Wherever you turn in India you'll be confronted by beggars – many of them (often handicapped or hideously disfigured) genuinely in dire need, others, such as kids hassling for a rupee or a pen, obviously not.

All sorts of stories about beggars do the rounds of the travellers' hang-outs, many of them with little basis in fact. Stories such as rupee millionaire beggars, people (usually kids) being deliberately mutilated by their parents so they can beg, and a beggars' Mafia are all common.

It's a matter of personal choice how you approach the issue of beggars and baksheesh. Some people feel it is best to give nothing to any beggar as it 'only encourages them' and to contribute by helping out at a charity such as Mother Teresa's Missionaries of Charity; others give away loose change when they have it; unfortunately, others insulate themselves entirely and give nothing in any way. It's up to you.

Whether or not you decide to give to beggars on the street, the 'one pen, one pen' brigades of children should be firmly discouraged.

it's normal to tip the driver if you've hired a car for a day of sightseeing.

While there are fixed-price stores in the larger towns, in bazaars and at markets specifically geared to tourists, you are generally expected to bargain. The trick with bargaining is that you should have some idea of what you should be paying for any given article. You can find out by checking prices at fixed-price stores, asking other travellers what they have paid, and shopping around before settling on a vendor. If all else fails, a general rule of thumb is to offer half the original asking price and work up from there.

At the Anjuna Flea Market, in particular, traders start very high with their prices, so bargain hard and be prepared to walk away – the same item will be in another stall nearby anyway. See the boxed text 'The Art of Haggling' later in this chapter.

POST & COMMUNICATIONS

The Indian postal and poste restante services are generally good. Letters almost always reach you and letters you send almost invariably reach their destination, although they take up to three weeks.

Postal Rates

It costs Rs 8 to send a small postcard or aerogramme anywhere in the world from India, and Rs 15 for a large postcard or a standard letter (up to 20g).

Sending Mail

Sending parcels from Goa, or anywhere in India, requires a little more than fronting up at the post office with your package. First, take the parcel to a tailor (there's usually one very close to the post office) and ask to get it stitched up in cheap linen or calico. At the post office you'll get the necessary customs declaration forms which will be attached to the parcel. To avoid excise duty at the delivery end, it's best to specify that the contents are a 'gift' with a value less than Rs 1000.

Express Mail Service (EMS) Speedpost is available at major post offices (such as Panaji and Margao) and, although more expensive than ordinary post, this is a much faster and more reliable way of sending parcels overseas. A parcel to Europe costs Rs 675 for the first 250g and Rs 50 for each additional 250g; to North America it costs Rs 425 plus Rs 100 per additional 250g and to Australasia it's Rs 425 plus Rs 75 per additional 250g.

If you are sending books or printed matter (maximum 5kg), these can go by book post, which is considerably cheaper than parcel post, but the package must be able to be opened for inspection.

Sending parcels in the other direction (to India) is an extremely hit-and-miss affair. Don't count on anything bigger than a letter getting to you. And don't count on a letter getting to you if there's anything of value inside it.

Receiving Mail

Have letters addressed to you with your surname in capitals and underlined, followed by poste restante, GPO and the city or town in question. Many 'lost' letters are simply misfiled under given (Christian) names, so always check under both your given and last names. Letters sent via poste restante are generally held for one month only, after which, if unclaimed, they might be returned to the sender or just left in a box under the counter until they disintegrate.

Telephone

The area code for all places within the state of Goa is ☎ 0832, which you only need to dial when calling from outside the state or from a mobile phone.

All over Goa, even in the smallest places, you'll find private STD/ISD call booths that have direct local, interstate and international dialling. Usually found in shops or other businesses, they are easy to spot because of the large STD/ISD/PCO signs advertising the service. Travel agencies and Internet places generally offer a telephone service. A digital meter lets you keep an eye on the call cost, and gives you a print out at the end. You then just pay the shop owner. Some booths offer a call back service for a small per minute charge, but there's no such thing as a free reverse-charge call.

Direct international calls from these phones cost Rs 25 to 40 per minute, depending on the country you are calling. At the time of writing, not many Internet cafés were offering Internet phone calls (which can cost as little as Rs 5 a minute to Europe or North America) but this situation is likely to change, so it's worth asking.

To make an international call, you will need to dial the following: 00 (international access code from India) + country code (of the country you are calling) + area code + local number.

To make a call to Goa, dial the following: international access code of the country you are in + 91 (international country code for India) + 832 (Goa's area code omitting the initial 0) + local number.

Mobile Phones These have been embraced with a passion in India, and if you intend to spend some time in Goa it may be worth getting hooked up to the local network. Call costs – even international calls – are relatively cheap in India and having a mobile phone means you can easily be contacted at any time, and make calls if you need to.

You can bring your own handset and instantly get connected to a prepaid account on one of the local networks. The main companies offering prepaid mobile phone accounts in Goa are **Airtel** (W www.airtel world.com), **Idea** (formerly AT&T) and **BPL** (W www.bplmobile.com). They all offer similar rates but Airtel is generally considered the best. Note that your phone will only work in Goa and parts of Maharashtra, although most operators have a 'roaming' facility that allows you to receive calls and send SMS messages outside Goa. A SIM card costs around Rs 325 plus you pay for an initial amount of call time. You can buy SIM cards practically anywhere, such as PCO/STD/ISD booths and Internet cafés, and the vendor will usually help you set it up. Top-up cards come in various denominations, but you'll always pay an additional 'line rental' charge each time you buy one.

The more credit you have on your phone, the cheaper the call rate. Average call rates within India are around Rs 1 per minute and you can call internationally for less than Rs 30 per minute. SMS messaging is even cheaper. Note that calls to your mobile phone are also charged to your account – shop around to find the deal that best suits you.

Cell Tone, in Panaji, is a reliable place to get hooked up to the local mobile phone network.

Fax

Faxes can also be sent from many telephone offices but are not cheap at around Rs 70 per page for international faxes and Rs 10 for faxes sent within India. You can receive faxes for around Rs 10 per page.

Email & Internet Access

Internet and email services in Goa are plentiful, reliable and relatively cheap. In all major towns, beach resorts from Arambol to Palolem, and even some small villages, you'll easily find somewhere to check email. The most common places offering Internet access are travel agencies and STD/ISD phone offices, but you'll also find a few dedicated Internet cafés. Many hotels and guesthouses also offer Internet access for guests. Average charges are around Rs 40 per hour, usually with a minimum of 15 minutes (Rs 10 to 15), but there are places in Margao, Vasco and Mapusa charging as little as Rs 20 per hour.

DIGITAL RESOURCES

There's no better place to start your Web explorations than with **Lonely Planet** (W www .lonelyplanet.com). Here you'll find succinct summaries on travelling to most places on earth, postcards from other travellers, and the Thorn Tree bulletin board, where you can ask questions before you go or dispense advice when you get back.

India in general, and Goa in particular, is very Web savvy and you'll find countless excellent websites devoted to Goan travel, activities, culture, history, news and the trance party scene. Goa-specific websites worth checking out include:

Goacom (W www.goacom.com) This is one of the best websites for information on Goa for both tourists and residents; it features a monthly webzine.

Goa Gil (W www.goagil.com) This is the site of acclaimed Goa Trance DJ, Goa Gil; it includes tour dates.

Goa Tourism (W www.goatourism.org, www .goa-tourism.com) The state tourism body, the GDTC, has two sites.

Goa Unleashed (W www.goaunleashed.com) This is a great site for tourist information, activities and Goan lifestyle tips.

Goa World (W www.goa-world.com) This site has information on everything from history and culture to recipes and Konkani; it also has links to some 300 Goa-related sites.

Goenkar (W www.goenkar.com) A community site with members' pages and cultural news.

BOOKS

Goa is a great place for reading – apart from anything else there's plenty of scope for leisure time, and there are lots of bookshops where you can purchase reading matter. India is one of the world's largest publishers of books in English, and Indian publishers also do cheap reprints of Western bestsellers at prices far below Western levels.

Lonely Planet

It's pleasing to be able to say that for more information on India and its neighbours, and for travel beyond India, most of the best guides come from Lonely Planet! Lonely Planet's award-winning *India* is now in its 10th edition. One of Lonely Planet's most successful and popular titles, this is the most comprehensive guide to the country you'll find.

Lonely Planet's handy pocket-sized city guide to *Delhi* has more information on the capital. There's also a *South India* guide and the *Hindi & Urdu phrasebook*.

Hello Goodnight: A Life of Goa by David Tomory and published by Lonely Planet's travel literature series explores what Goa has meant to travellers over time.

Guidebooks

Window on Goa by Maurice Hall is a labour of love that took nearly 10 years to research and write. Breaking the subject down into comprehensive sections, the author writes authoritatively about the churches, forts and villages, and much else besides. The book manages to be incredibly comprehensive while avoiding being purely academic.

Goa: A Traveller's Historical and Architectural Guide by Anthony Hutt is hard to get hold of but well worth the effort if you can find a copy. It contains excellent photographs and a comprehensive historical commentary.

Although in scope it's less comprehensive than *Window on Goa*, JM Richards' *Goa* is acknowledged to be an excellent overview. The sections on Old Goa include a wonderful tour of the city. The sections on Goan history are similarly engaging.

There are many books on wildlife, but bird-watchers might want to get hold of *Pocket Guide to the Birds of the Indian Subcontinent* by Christopher Helm.

A Guide to the Flora and Fauna of Goa by P Killips is a slim volume that doesn't aim to cover everything you might see in Goa, but it has excellent colour illustrations of the main animals and plants.

Travel

Chasing the Monsoon by Alexander Frater is an Englishman's account of a journey north from Kovalam in Kerala all the way to one of the wettest places on earth (Cherrapunji in Meghalaya), following the onset of the monsoon as it moves north across the country. It's a fascinating insight into the significance of the monsoon, and its effect on people.

Goa and the Blue Mountains or Six Months of Sick Leave by Richard Burton is the earliest travelogue that is readily obtainable. Originally published in 1851, this account by Lt Richard Burton of his journey through Goa and thence southwards to Ootacamund makes great reading. The book is interesting for the historical perspective but is also highly enjoyable because of Burton's irreverent sense of humour. Reprinted in 1991 it's available at the Other India Bookstore in Mapusa.

Ecology & Environment

Undoubtedly the best single publication about the Goan environment, *Fish Curry and Rice* is a comprehensive survey of the state of the environment today, and the threats that face it. The book is published by the Goa Foundation, a nongovernment organisation (NGO) dedicated to heightening public awareness of environmental matters. It costs a hefty Rs 750.

The Transforming of Goa is a collection of essays, edited by Norman Dantas, dealing with topics such as Goan identity, politics, language and religion. Although the scope is much wider than merely environmental matters, the environment features prominently.

Religion

If you want a better understanding of India's religions there are plenty of books available in India. Pauline Book & Media Centre in Panaji also stocks many titles on Christianity and St Francis Xavier.

A Handbook of Living Religions, edited by John R Hinnewls, provides a succinct and readable summary of all the religions you will find in India, including Christianity and Judaism.

Hinduism by KM Sen is brief and to the point.

A Classical Dictionary of Hindu Mythology & Religion by John Dowson is an Indian paperback reprint of an old English hardback. As the name suggests, it is in dictionary form and is one of the best sources for unravelling who's who in Hinduism.

Guru – the Search for Enlightenment by John Mitchiner is an excellent, detailed and dispassionate introduction to 16 of India's best-known gurus and religious teachers.

General

Anjuna: Profile of a Village in Goa by Teresa Albuquerque is a fascinating, in-depth look at the history of one Goan village through the years. Dr Albuquerque has both the academic background and the family connections in the community to be able to sketch an unrivalled portrait of the life of the village. History, architecture, folklore and traditions are all covered.

The Boarding Party by James Leasor tells the true story of the wartime drama that took place in Mormugao Harbour. Although Portugal and Goa were technically neutral, a British raid by members of the Calcutta Light Horse successfully destroyed a number of German ships that were using the harbour as a base. The book was made into a film called *The Sea Wolves* starring Gregory Peck and Roger Moore.

Goa Remembered – Vignettes of Fading Traditions by Angelo Pereira is one of several books that make an effort to record what life in Goa was like in the first half of the 20th century.

Legends of Goa by Mario Cabral E Sa and illustrated by one of Goa's best-known artists, Mario de Miranda, is a reworking of some of the best folktales of Goa. It lends extra colour to the state's traditions and history, and is an interesting read.

Goa Freaks: My Hippie Years in India by Cleo Odzer is a mind-blowing account of the author's time living in Anjuna during the crazy 1970s and of her drug-running scams during the monsoon that financed her 'freak' lifestyle.

Of Umbrellas, Goddesses & Dreams by Robert S Newman is a series of essays on Goan culture and the changes of the past two decades by an American writer and regular visitor to Goa.

Dust: and Other Short Stories from Goa is a collection of short stories by Goan writer and conservationist Heta Pandit. The character-driven stories bring to life aspects of everyday life in Goa.

NEWSPAPERS & MAGAZINES

English-language dailies for India as a whole include the *Times of India*, the *Hindustan Times*, the *Indian Express* and the *Statesman*. Indian weekly news magazines include *India Today*, the *Week*, *Sunday* and the *Illustrated Weekly of India*. They're widely available.

Goa has three English-language dailies of its own: the *Herald*; the *Navhind Times*; and the *Gomantak Times*. All three are pretty similar, typically consisting of two or three pages of local news, about the same of national and international news, and an all-important sports section with the usual emphasis on cricket. Goa also has its own monthly magazine *Goa Today*, which is well written and focuses on a particular issue of local interest every month.

Time and *Newsweek* are available in the bookshops of larger hotels and at some of the more established newsstands in Panaji, although compared with Indian newspapers they're ridiculously expensive.

RADIO & TV

Satellite TV runs 24 hours and offers up to 30 channels including BBC, CNN, Discovery, Star TV, Star Sports and Asianet. Many mid-range and all top-end hotels have satellite TV. Various local channels broadcast in the vernacular. The national broadcaster is Doordashan; it has the news in English every evening (check the local newspapers for broadcast times).

Radio programmes can be heard on All India Radio (AIR), which provide interviews, music and news features. The only FM station is AIR 105.4FM, which broadcasts a mix of Western, Konkani, Hindi and Marathi music. Some programmes are in English. Details on programmes and frequencies are provided in the major English-language dailies. You can also tune in to stations such as BBC World.

PHOTOGRAPHY & VIDEO
Film & Equipment
Colour print film processing facilities are readily available throughout Goa – around Rs 180 for same-day processing. Film is relatively cheap (Rs 100 for a roll of 36 exposures) and the quality is usually (but not always) good, so if you want to be sure that it is, it's best to bring film with you.

If you're taking slides bring the film with you. Colour slide film is available at a few shops in Panaji, Margao and Calangute, but usually only Kodak Ektachrome 100ISO. Colour slides have to be sent out of the state for processing (usually to Mumbai) – take your film home with you. Kodachrome and other 'process paid' film will have to be sent overseas.

It's possible to obtain video cartridges in Goa but try to take all you need with you.

Restrictions & Photographing People
Be careful what you photograph. India is touchy about places of military importance – this can include train stations, bridges, airports and military installations. Some temples prohibit photography in the forechamber and inner sanctum. If in doubt, ask.

Goans are generally easy-going about photography – children especially love to the photographed – but always ask before photographing people at close range. A zoom is a less intrusive means of taking portraits – even when you've obtained permission to take a portrait, shoving a lens in your subject's face can be disconcerting. A reasonable distance between you and your subject will help to reduce your subject's discomfort, and will result in more natural shots.

TIME
India is 5½ hours ahead of GMT/UTC, 4½ hours behind Australia (EST) and 10½ hours ahead of America (EST). It is officially known as IST – Indian Standard Time, although many Indians prefer to think it stands for Indian Stretchable Time! When it's noon in London, it's 5.30pm in Goa.

ELECTRICITY
The electric current is 230V to 240V AC, 50 cycles. Even in Panaji the electricity is unpredictable, and away from the city whole villages can be cut off for half an hour or more, although usually the power cuts only last for a minute or two. This can be a problem if you're in an Internet café and half way through a long email (save your work!) though many businesses have a back-up generator for precisely that reason. If you are bringing any sensitive electrical equipment, eg, a laptop computer, a voltage regulator is useful to protect it against the power fluctuations. Bulky, primitive regulators can be bought in electrical shops in Goa for around Rs 1000, but it's much more convenient to buy a compact one at home and bring it with you.

Sockets are of a three round-pin variety, similar (but not identical) to European sockets. There are two sizes of socket, one large, one small (the latter is more common). European round-pin plugs will go into the smaller sockets, but as the pins on Indian plugs are somewhat thicker, the fit is loose and connection is not good. Universal adaptors are widely available at electrical shops in Goa.

WEIGHTS & MEASURES
Although India is officially metricated, imperial weights and measures are still used in some areas of commerce. When referring to numbers (amounts) you will often hear people referring to lakhs (one lakh = 100,000) and crores (one crore = 10 million) of rupees, cars, apples or whatever. A metric conversion chart is included on the inside back cover of this book.

LAUNDRY
Most hotels offer laundry service. Top-end and mid-range hotels will charge a relatively high rate for the service but it's still cheap by Western standards and is almost always charged per item of clothing. Even budget guesthouses or bamboo beach accommodation will arrange for your laundry to be done for Rs 5 to 10 per piece and it invariably comes back immaculately washed, ironed and folded.

TOILETS
In most hotels and guesthouses geared mainly for foreign tourists, sit-down flush toilets and toilet paper are invariably supplied. Off the beaten track, at train stations (and other public places) and in places that don't specifically cater for foreigners, there are squat toilets only. In such circumstances it's

customary to use your left hand and water, not paper. A strategically placed tap (and usually a water container) is available in squat toilets. If you can't get used to the Indian method, bring your own paper (none is supplied, but is widely available to buy). But remember that stuffing paper (and tampons) down the toilet is simply going to clog an already overloaded sewerage system even further. Sometimes a plastic bin is provided for the disposal of paper and tampons.

By far Goa's most environmentally friendly toilets – but rarely seen, let alone used by most tourists – are the 'pig loos' (see the boxed text 'Ecofriendly Pigs' under Benaulim in the South Goa chapter).

HEALTH

Travel health depends on your predeparture preparations, your daily health care while travelling and how you handle any medical problem that does develop. While the potential dangers can seem quite frightening, in reality few travellers to Goa will experience anything more than upset stomachs.

There are reasonably well-stocked pharmacies in all the towns in Goa selling drugs manufactured under licence to Western companies. You can buy more medications over the counter in an Indian pharmacy than you'd be able to in the West.

If you need a doctor the more upmarket hotels will usually have a reliable one on call.

Hospitals

Although there are reasonable facilities available in Panaji, Margao and Vasco da Gama, Goa does not have the quality of medical care available in the West. The best facilities in Goa are at the **Goa Medical College Hospital** (☎ 2225727) at Bambolim, 9km south of Panaji on the National Highway (NH) 17. In the event of a serious accident this is the best place to go; it has a brain scanner and most other facilities.

There are also many qualified doctors with their own private clinics who can provide excellent service. It's probably best to ask at your hotel for the nearest recommended doctor. If you are unlucky enough to be injured in an accident, the best bone specialist in Goa is **Dr Bhale** (☎ 2217053) who runs an X-ray clinic at Porvorim, 4km north of Panaji on the NH17.

Emergency Numbers

Throughout Goa there are 24-hour numbers you can call in an emergency. For police call ☎ 100, for fire call ☎ 101 and for an ambulance or accident call ☎ 102.

The ambulance service in Goa is unreliable, with only a handful of vehicles operated by **Goa Accident & Trauma Emergency** *(GATE;* ☎ *102).* Unless a local knows how to get hold of an ambulance, the quickest way to get to hospital is by taxi or private car.

Predeparture Planning

Immunisations Vaccinations are recommended but not required for India. It pays to make sure your standard immunisations are up to date and Hepatitis A is worth considering.

Plan ahead for getting your vaccinations: some of them require more than one injection, while some vaccinations should not be given together. It is recommended you seek medical advice at least six weeks before travel.

Record all vaccinations on an International Health Certificate, available from your doctor or government health department, and carry it with you. A yellow fever vaccine is the only vaccine that is a legal requirement for entry into India, usually only enforced when coming from an infected area.

Discuss your requirements with your doctor, but vaccinations you should consider for a trip to Goa include the following.

Diphtheria & Tetanus Both these diseases occur worldwide and can be fatal. Everyone should have these vaccinations, which are usually combined. After an initial course of three injections, boosters are necessary every 10 years.

Hepatitis A This is the most common travel-acquired illness after diarrhoea. Hepatitis A vaccine (eg, Havrix 1440 or VAQTA) provides long-term immunity (possibly more than 10 years) after an initial injection and a booster at six to 12 months.

Hepatitis B Travellers who should consider a hepatitis B vaccination include those visiting countries (including India) where there are high levels of hepatitis B infection, where blood transfusions may not be adequately screened or where sexual contact or needle sharing is a possibility. It involves three injections, the quickest course being over three weeks with a booster at

12 months. A combined hepatitis A and hepatitis B vaccination, Twinrix, is also available. Three injections over a six-month period are required.

Malaria On the increase in Goa and in some parts of the state, malaria is now endemic. Antimalarial drugs do not prevent you from being infected, but kill the malaria parasites during a stage in their development and significantly reduce the risk of becoming very ill or dying. Seek expert advice on medication, as there are many factors to consider including the side effects of medication, your medical history and whether you are a child or adult or pregnant.

Meningococcal Meningitis Vaccination is recommended for travellers to certain parts of India, including Goa, and Nepal. A single injection will give good protection for three years. Protection may be less effective in children under two years.

Polio Everyone should keep up to date with this vaccination, which is normally given in childhood. A booster every 10 years maintains immunity.

Rabies Vaccination should be considered by those who will spend a month or longer in India, especially if they are cycling, handling animals, caving, travelling to remote areas, and for children (who may not report a bite). Stray dogs in Goa present a risk of rabies. Pretravel rabies vaccination involves having three injections over 21 to 28 days. If someone who has been vaccinated is bitten or scratched by an infected animal they will require two booster injections of vaccine; those not vaccinated require more.

Typhoid This is an important vaccination to have where hygiene is a problem. It's available either as an injection or as oral capsules.

Travel Health Guides Lonely Planet's *Healthy Travel Asia & India* is a handy pocket size and packed with useful information including pretrip planning, emergency first aid, immunisation and disease information and advice on what to do if you get sick on the road.

There are also several excellent travel health sites on the Internet. From the Lonely Planet home page there are links (**W** www .lonelyplanet.com/subwwway/) to the World Health Organization and the US Centers for Disease Control & Prevention.

Basic Rules

Food & Water An old colonial adage says: 'If you can cook it, boil it or peel it you can eat it…otherwise forget it.' Vegetables and fruit should be washed with purified water or peeled where possible. Beware of ice cream that is sold in the street or anywhere it might have been melted and refrozen.

If a place looks clean and well run and the vendor also looks clean and healthy, then the food is probably safe. In general places that are packed with travellers or locals will be fine, while empty restaurants are questionable. The food in busy restaurants is cooked and eaten quite quickly with little time standing around and is probably not reheated. Seafood is fresh and generally safe in Goa, even in beach shacks.

The number one rule in India is *be careful of the water*, including ice. Forget about drinking untreated tap water. If you don't know for certain that the water is safe assume the worst. Reputable brands of bottled water (often called mineral water in Goa) or soft drinks are generally fine, although various surveys over the years have established that the purification processes used by bottled water manufacturers leave a lot to be desired. Only use water from containers with a serrated seal – not tops or corks. Take care with fruit juice, particularly if water may have been added. Milk should be treated with suspicion as it is often unpasteurised, though boiled milk is fine if it is kept hygienically, as is milk powder.

Water Purification The simplest and most effective way of purifying water is to boil it thoroughly.

Consider purchasing a water filter for an extended trip. Apart from being economical and safe, it's environmentally friendly as it means you won't be contributing to the problem of plastic bottles. It's very important when buying a filter to read the specifications so that you know exactly what it removes from the water and what it doesn't. Simple filtering will not remove all dangerous organisms, so if you cannot boil water it should be treated chemically. Chlorine tablets such as Puritabs, Steritabs or other brands, will kill many pathogens, but not some parasites such as those that cause giardiasis and amoebic cysts. Iodine is more effective in purifying water and is available in tablet form (such as Potable Aqua). Follow the directions carefully and remember that too much iodine can be harmful.

Environmental Hazards

Heat Exhaustion Dehydration and salt deficiency can cause heat exhaustion. Take time to acclimatise to high temperatures, drink sufficient liquids and do not do anything too physically demanding.

Salt deficiency is characterised by fatigue, lethargy, headaches, giddiness and muscle cramps; salt tablets may help, but adding extra salt to your food is better.

Prickly Heat This is an itchy rash caused by excessive perspiration trapped under the skin. It usually strikes people who have just arrived in a hot climate. Keeping cool, bathing often, drying the skin or resorting to air-conditioning may help.

Sunburn In Goa you can get sunburnt surprisingly quickly, even through cloud. Use a sunscreen, hat, and barrier cream for your nose and lips. Calamine lotion or a sting-relief spray are good for mild sunburn. Protect your eyes with good-quality sunglasses, particularly if you will be near water or sand.

Infectious Diseases

Diarrhoea Simple things like a change of water, food or climate can all cause a mild bout of diarrhoea, but a few rushed toilet trips with no other symptoms is not indicative of a major problem.

Dehydration is the main danger with any diarrhoea, particularly in children or the elderly, as dehydration can occur quite quickly. Under all circumstances fluid replacement (at least equal to the volume being lost) is the most important thing to remember. Weak black tea with a little sugar, soda water, or soft drinks allowed to go flat and diluted 50% with clean water, are all good. With severe diarrhoea a rehydrating solution is preferable to replace minerals and salts lost. Commercially available oral rehydration salts (ORS) are very useful; add them to boiled or bottled water. In an emergency you can make up a solution of six teaspoons of sugar and a half teaspoon of salt to a litre of boiled or bottled water. Urine is the best guide to the adequacy of replacement – if you have small amounts of concentrated urine, you need to drink more. Keep drinking small amounts often.

Gut-paralysing drugs such as loperamide or diphenoxylate can be used to bring relief from the symptoms, although they do not actually cure the problem. Only use these drugs if you do not have access to toilets,

eg, if you must travel. These drugs should not be used if the person has a high fever or is severely dehydrated, and are not recommended in children under 12 years.

In certain situations antibiotics may be required: diarrhoea with blood or mucus (dysentery), any diarrhoea with fever, profuse watery diarrhoea, persistent diarrhoea not improving after 48 hours and severe diarrhoea. These suggest a more serious cause of diarrhoea and gut-paralysing drugs should be avoided. Seek medical help.

Fungal Infections These occur more commonly in hot weather, and are usually found on the scalp, between the toes (athlete's foot) or fingers, in the groin and on the body (ringworm). You get ringworm (which is a fungal infection, not a worm) from infected animals or other people. Moisture encourages these infections.

To prevent fungal infections wear loose, comfortable clothes, avoid artificial fibres, wash frequently and dry yourself carefully. If you do get an infection, wash the infected area at least daily with a disinfectant or medicated soap and water, and rinse and dry well. Apply an antifungal cream or powder such as tolnaftate. Try to expose the infected area to air or sunlight as much as possible and wash all towels and underwear in hot water, change them often and let them dry in the sun.

Hepatitis This is a general term for inflammation of the liver. It is a common disease in India, and worldwide. There are several different viruses that cause hepatitis, and they differ in the way that they are transmitted. The symptoms are similar in all forms of the illness, and include fever, chills, headache, fatigue, feelings of weakness and aches and pains, followed by loss of appetite, nausea, vomiting, abdominal pain, dark urine, light-coloured faeces, jaundiced (yellow) skin and yellowing of the whites of the eyes. People who have had hepatitis should avoid alcohol for some time after the illness, as the liver needs time to recover.

Hepatitis A is transmitted by contaminated food and drinking water. You should seek medical advice, but there is not much you can do apart from resting, drinking lots of fluids, eating lightly and avoiding fatty foods. Hepatitis E is transmitted in the same way as hepatitis A.

There are almost 300 million chronic carriers of **hepatitis B** in the world. It is spread through contact with infected blood, blood products or body fluids, such as through sexual contact, unsterilised needles and blood transfusions, or contact with blood via small breaks in the skin. Other high-risk situations include having a shave, being tattooed or having your body pierced with contaminated equipment. The symptoms of hepatitis B may be more severe than type A, and the disease can lead to long-term problems such as chronic liver damage, liver cancer or a long-term carrier state. Hepatitis C and D are spread in the same way as hepatitis B and can also lead to long-term complications.

HIV & AIDS Infection with the human immunodeficiency virus (HIV) may lead to AIDS, which is a fatal disease. Any exposure to blood, blood products or body fluids may put the individual at risk. The disease is often transmitted through sexual contact or dirty needles – vaccinations, acupuncture, tattooing and body piercing can be potentially as dangerous as intravenous drug use. HIV/AIDS can also be spread through infected blood transfusions.

If you do need an injection, ask to see the syringe unwrapped in front of you, or take a needle and syringe pack with you.

Fear of infection with HIV should never preclude treatment for serious medical conditions.

Intestinal Worms These parasites are most common in rural, tropical areas. The different worms have different ways of infecting people. Some may be ingested with food such as undercooked meat (eg, tapeworms) and some enter through your skin (eg, hookworms). Infestations may not show up for some time, and although they are generally not serious, if left untreated some can cause severe health problems later. Consider having a stool test when you return home and then determine the appropriate treatment.

Meningococcal Meningitis This serious disease can be fatal. There are recurring epidemics in northern India and Nepal.

A fever, severe headache, sensitivity to light and neck stiffness that prevents forward bending of the head are the first symptoms. There may also be purple patches on the skin. Death can occur within a few hours, so urgent medical treatment is required.

Treatment is large doses of penicillin given intravenously, or chloramphenicol injections.

Typhoid This is a dangerous gut infection caused by contaminated water and food. Medical help must be sought.

In its early stages sufferers may feel they have a bad cold or flu on the way, as early symptoms are a headache, body aches and a fever that rises a little each day until it is around 40°C (104°F) or more. The victim's pulse is often slow relative to the degree of fever present – unlike a normal fever where the pulse increases. There may also be vomiting, abdominal pain, diarrhoea or constipation.

In the second week the high fever and slow pulse continue and a few pink spots may appear on the body; trembling, delirium, weakness, weight loss and dehydration may occur. Complications such as pneumonia, perforated bowel or meningitis may occur.

Malaria This serious and potentially fatal disease is spread by mosquito bites. If you are travelling in endemic areas such as Goa, it is extremely important to avoid mosquito bites and to take tablets to prevent this disease. Symptoms range from fever, chills and sweating, headache, diarrhoea and abdominal pains, to a vague feeling of ill-health. Seek medical help immediately if malaria is suspected. Without treatment it can rapidly become more serious and can be fatal.

If medical care is not available, malaria tablets can be used for treatment. You need to use a malaria tablet that is different from the one you were taking when you contracted malaria. The standard treatment dose of mefloquine is two 250mg tablets and a further two, six hours later. For Fansidar, it's a single dose of three tablets. If you were previously taking mefloquine and cannot obtain Fansidar, then other alternatives are Malarone (atovaquone-proguanil; four tablets once daily for three days) or quinine sulphate (600mg every six hours). There is a greater risk of side effects with these dosages than in normal use if used with mefloquine, so medical advice is preferable. Ways to prevent mosquito bites include:

• Wear light-coloured clothing
• Wear long trousers and long-sleeved shirts
• Use mosquito repellents containing the compound DEET on exposed areas (prolonged overuse of DEET may be harmful, especially to children, but its use is considered preferable to being bitten by disease-transmitting mosquitoes)
• Use a mosquito net impregnated with mosquito repellent (permethrin) – it may be worth taking your own
• Impregnating clothes with permethrin effectively deters mosquitoes and other insects

Dengue Fever This viral disease is transmitted by mosquitoes and occurs mainly in tropical and subtropical areas of the world, including India. Generally, the risk to travellers is small except during epidemics, which are usually seasonal (during and just after the rainy season).

The *Aedes aegypti* mosquito that transmits the dengue virus is most active during the day, unlike the malaria mosquito, and is found mainly in urban areas, in and around human dwellings.

Signs and symptoms of dengue fever include a sudden onset of high fever, headache, joint and muscle pains (hence its old name, 'breakbone fever') and nausea and vomiting. A rash of small red spots appears three to four days after the onset of fever. Dengue is commonly mistaken for other infectious diseases, including influenza.

You should seek medical attention if you think you may be infected, although there is no specific treatment. Infection can be diagnosed by a blood test.

Japanese B Encephalitis This viral infection of the brain is transmitted by mosquitoes. Most cases occur in rural areas as the virus exists in pigs and wading birds; there have been cases in Goa in the monsoon season. Symptoms include fever, headache and alteration in consciousness. Hospitalisation is needed for correct diagnosis and treatment. There is a high mortality rate; of those who survive many are intellectually disabled.

Cuts, Bites & Stings
See Less Common Diseases later in this chapter for details of rabies, which is transmitted through animal bites.

Bedbugs & Lice Bedbugs live in various places, but particularly in dirty mattresses and bedding, evidenced by spots of blood on bedclothes or on the wall. Bedbugs leave itchy bites in neat rows. Calamine lotion or a sting-relief spray may help.

All lice cause itching and discomfort. They make themselves at home in your hair (head lice), your clothing (body lice) or in your pubic hair (crabs). You catch lice through direct contact with infected people or by sharing combs, clothing and the like. Powder or shampoo treatment will kill the lice and infected clothing should then be washed in very hot, soapy water and left in the sun to dry.

Bites & Stings Bee and wasp stings are usually painful rather than dangerous. However, in people who are allergic to them, severe breathing difficulties may occur and require urgent medical care. Calamine lotion or a sting-relief spray will ease the discomfort, and ice packs will reduce the pain and swelling. There are some spiders with dangerous bites but antivenins are usually available. Scorpion stings are notoriously painful and can actually be fatal. Scorpions often shelter in shoes or clothing.

There are various fish and other sea creatures in the sea around Goa that can sting or bite dangerously or that are dangerous to eat. Again, local advice is the best suggestion (also see the boxed text 'Taking the Perilous Plunge').

Cuts & Scratches Wash well and treat any cut with an antiseptic such as povidone-iodine. Where possible avoid bandages and Band-Aids, which can keep wounds wet. Coral cuts are notoriously slow to heal and if they are not adequately cleaned, small pieces of coral can become embedded in the wound.

Jellyfish See the boxed text 'Taking the Perilous Plunge' for information about jellyfish stings.

Leeches & Ticks Leeches may be present in damp rainforests (for example, around Jog Falls during the wet season); they attach themselves to your skin to suck your blood. Trekkers often get them on their legs or in their boots. Salt or a lighted cigarette end will make them fall off. Do not pull them off, as the bite is then more likely to become infected. Clean and apply pressure if the point of attachment is bleeding. An insect repellent may keep them away.

You should always check all over your body if you have been walking through a potentially tick-infested area as ticks can cause skin infections and other more serious diseases. If a tick is found attached, press down around the tick's head with tweezers, grab the head and gently pull upwards. Avoid pulling the rear of the body as this

Taking the Perilous Plunge

Hundreds of thousands of visitors come to Goa each year to swim and paddle in the clear, warm waters of the Arabian Sea. There's not much surf and, outside of the monsoon season, these are some of the safest waters in the world. But the sea off Goa's coastline can be deceptive and there are a few dangers it pays to be aware of.

Swimming

Every year there are drowning deaths along the coastline. Undertows and currents can be strong even close to the beach, especially early and late in the season. Don't swim just after you have eaten, and definitely do not go in the water if you have been drinking alcohol. Remain within your depth, and remember that the underwater slope is not always even – the beach may suddenly drop in places leaving you in deep water. Despite the romantic temptation, it's not wise to take a midnight dip, especially if you've been out partying.

In the monsoon, when even the fishermen don't bother going out, swimming in the sea is out of the question. You should also be careful in October and November, as the sand bars near the beaches are still in a state of transition. This is because during the monsoon large volumes of sand get swept inshore, and when the normal sea conditions return they are gradually eroded by the currents. At the beginning of this process, in the weeks following the monsoon, there are only a few channels through the sandbanks, and very strong rips are generated as the water courses through these points.

Jellyfish

The waters off Goa contain significant numbers of jellyfish. Although they generally stay out in deeper water, it's not unheard of for jellyfish to drift into shallower water, particularly during the early and late months of the season (ie, October to November and March to April). A jellyfish sting won't kill you, but it will cause considerable pain. First aid for a jellyfish sting is to calm the victim and wash off the tendrils with sea water. An acid solution should then be used to soak the stings – if you're near a beach shack ask them for vinegar or lime juice. Having done this, the sting then needs to be subjected to heat treatment, as the protein toxins of the venom break down in temperatures of between 43°C and 45°C. Divers often carry heat packs for just this contingency, but for swimmers again the answer lies in the beach shacks. Get someone to fill a basin with hot water, and immerse the affected area, gradually adding more hot water, getting the temperature as high as possible. *Do not* treat the sting with an ice pack, as this will make the symptoms worse.

Other Sea Creatures

Although you may see the occasional dead **sea snake** (called *kusada* in Goa) on the sand, you are extremely unlikely (or unlucky enough) ever to spot a live one, and even less likely to be bitten by one. They're extremely timid and will try to avoid swimmers at all costs.

Scorpion fish (sometimes also known as stonefish) and **lionfish** both inhabit areas of the Goan coastline, although you're unlikely to find them on the sandy bottom of the main swimming beaches. They tend to hang out where there's a bit of shelter (rocks and stones, for example) and are found in shallow waters around one or two of the small islands off the coast of Goa. Both types of fish have poisonous dorsal fins and, if stepped on by an unwary bather, the venom injected into the person's foot can be very painful. As with a jellyfish sting, heat treatment breaks down the protein toxins, and medical treatment should be sought as soon as possible.

may squeeze the tick's gut contents through the attached mouth parts into the skin, increasing the risk of infection and disease. Smearing chemicals on the tick will not make it let go and is not recommended.

Snakes To minimise your chances of being bitten, always wear boots, socks and long trousers when walking through undergrowth where snakes may be present. Don't put your hands into holes and crevices, and be careful when collecting firewood.

Snake bites do not cause instantaneous death and antivenins are usually available. Immediately wrap the bitten limb tightly, as you would for a sprained ankle, and then attach a splint to immobilise it. Keep the victim still and seek medical help, if possible with the dead snake for identification. Don't attempt to catch the snake if there is a possibility of being bitten again. Tourniquets and sucking out the poison are now comprehensively discredited.

Less Common Diseases
The following diseases pose a small risk to travellers, and so are only mentioned in passing. Seek medical advice if you think you may have any of these diseases.

Cholera This is the worst of the watery diarrhoeas and medical help should be sought. Outbreaks of cholera are generally widely reported, so you can avoid such problem areas. Fluid replacement is the most vital treatment – the risk of dehydration is severe as you may lose up to 20L a day. If there is a delay in getting to hospital then begin taking tetracycline. The adult dose is 250mg four times daily. It is not recommended for children under nine years, nor for pregnant women.

Filariasis This is a mosquito-transmitted parasitic infection found in India and other parts of Asia. Possible symptoms include fever, pain and swelling of the lymph glands; inflammation of lymph drainage areas; swelling of a limb or the scrotum; skin rashes and blindness.

Lyme Disease This is a tick-transmitted infection that may be acquired in India. The illness usually begins with a spreading rash at the site of the tick bite and is accompanied by fever, headache, extreme fatigue, aching joints and muscle and mild neck stiffness.

Rabies This fatal viral infection is found in many countries, including India. Many animals can be infected (eg, dogs, cats, bats and monkeys) and it is their saliva that is infectious. Any bite, scratch or even lick from an animal should be cleaned immediately and thoroughly. Scrub with soap and running water, and then apply alcohol or iodine solution. Medical help should be sought promptly to receive a course of injections to prevent the onset of symptoms and death.

Tetanus This disease is caused by a germ that lives in soil and the faeces of horses and other animals. It enters the body via breaks in the skin. The first symptom may be discomfort in swallowing, or stiffening of the jaw and neck; this is followed by painful convulsions of the jaw and whole body. The disease can be fatal. It can be prevented by vaccination.

Tuberculosis (TB) This is a bacterial infection usually transmitted from person to person by coughing, but which may be transmitted through consumption of unpasteurised milk. Milk that has been boiled is safe to drink, and the souring of milk to make yogurt or cheese also kills the bacilli. Travellers are generally not at great risk as close household contact with the infected person is usually required before the disease is passed on.

Typhus This disease is spread by ticks, mites or lice. It begins with fever, chills, headache and muscle pains followed a few days later by a body rash. There is often a large painful sore at the site of the bite and nearby lymph nodes are swollen and painful. Typhus can be treated under medical supervision. Seek local advice on areas where ticks pose a danger and always check your skin carefully for them after walking in a danger area such as a tropical forest.

SOCIAL GRACES
Goans are hospitable and friendly people and it befits visitors, in return, not to take advantage of the welcome they receive. Sadly, a number of tourists (domestic as well as foreign) see Goa's relatively liberal attitudes

as an excuse to pay scant attention to the feelings of the local community. In order to avoid causing offence there are a number of things that you should and shouldn't do.

Dress

Many Western tourists seem to give little or no consideration to the fact that in India it is polite to dress slightly more formally than it is back at home. While there is no need to go overboard, you will see few, if any, of even the poorest Goans walking around town without wearing a shirt. Shorts and T-shirts are fine, but off the beach you should cover up – particularly when visiting churches and temples and in social situations. Likewise for both men and women, clothing should not be too revealing. Wearing very short shorts, swimming trunks or a

Cover Up

Nudism (which for Indians includes going topless) is illegal now in Goa, although many foreigners continue to do it. Signs on some beaches warn of this and police occasionally patrol beaches (mainly to discourage illegal vendors), but there is generally a reluctance to enforce the law.

Though many Goans living along the beach belt have become resigned to it, many people are offended by displays of nudity and some blame incidents of assault and harassment of foreign women on such behaviour. They won't say anything because, like everyone else, they are aware that their livelihoods depend on keeping tourists happy. Since in Goa there is no longer such a thing as a totally deserted beach, wandering a few hundred metres from the nearest café won't amount to modesty if women wish to go topless.

Much more worrying for tourists and locals alike, Goa is rapidly becoming famous throughout India for the fact that women tourists are seen to be 'on show'. This has spawned a new and unwanted form of tourism, as Indian men from other states use Goa as a bolt hole for a weekend's boozing and ogling. Free from family and community constraints, they can spend two or three days drinking (alcohol is much cheaper in Goa than elsewhere in India) and staring at sunbathers. If you wish to avoid this kind of unwanted attention, cover up while at the beach.

bikini top for a trip into town are all frowned upon. Once again, no-one is going to stop you and object, but you'll help prevent the general image of foreigners from taking yet another dive.

It is customary to take off your shoes before entering a Hindu temple. In most cases it is also polite to remove your shoes at the door to a person's house. There is no hard and fast rule, but if there's a pile of shoes by the front door, or if your host or hostess slips off their sandals before entering the house, do likewise.

Photography

Goans are generally quite mellow about having their photograph taken, regarding it as the price one has to pay for encouraging the tourist industry. Do ask, however, before you poke your camera into someone's face – particularly before you take pictures of women or older people. If they do object, respect their wishes.

An easy way to make friends is to take their address and offer to send a copy of the photo when you get home (as long as you do it, of course). It can also be very tempting to take photos of some of the colourful scenes at the Anjuna Flea Market, but some of the Western travellers object quite strongly to being photographed. Again, it is only polite to ask and, if there are any objections, to respect the wishes of the subject.

Do not take photos inside temples, and ask before you use a camera and flash in a church.

Religious Etiquette

It's important to behave respectfully when visiting any religious site and particularly when attending a service. Don't talk loudly or smoke, and dress conservatively (no shorts or singlet tops). Never touch a carving or statue of a deity.

Food Etiquette

You should use your right hand for all social interactions, whether passing money, food or any other item. Eat with your right hand only. If you are invited to dine with a family, always take off your shoes and wash your hands before taking your meal. The hearth is the sacred centre of the home, so never approach it unless you have been invited to do so.

WOMEN TRAVELLERS

Foreign women travelling in India have always been viewed by Indian men as free and easy, based largely on what they believe to be true from watching cheap Western soaps. Women have been hassled, groped, stared at and spied on in hotel rooms.

Recently the situation has become more difficult for women travellers, mainly because the 'sexual revolution' that swept the West 35 years ago has now hit India. The message getting through to the middle-class Indian male is that sex before and outside of marriage is less of a taboo than in the past, and so foreign women are seen as even more free and easy than before.

Goa is one of the places where this problem is at its worst, as it has gained a reputation for being a place where Western women frequently go naked on the beach. Thus for some Indian men, the idea of a perfect weekend away with their (male) friends is a trip to Goa, where booze is cheap and there are plenty of women to ogle. Generally it doesn't get beyond being extremely annoying – groups of men wander down the beach and either try to chat up women who are alone, or just stand and stare.

Goa's reputation as a relatively safe, easy-going destination took a battering in recent years; the rape of two Swedish women in Anjuna in early 1997 (the offenders were sentenced to seven years in prison), the gang rape of a British woman in January 2000 in Calangute, and the rape of another British tourist in Betalbatim in 2000 all received media attention. At Christmas several of the beach shacks that host parties actually put up signs requesting that women be accompanied if they're leaving the shack – even to answer the call of nature in the nearby sand dunes. The simple fact is that it is not safe to wander about alone after dark in Goa.

Close attention to standards of dress may go some way to minimising problems. Topless bathing is illegal, and bikinis and short skirts worn away from the beach will create unwanted attention.

Other harassment likely to be encountered includes obscene comments, inappropriate or unwanted touching, and jeering, particularly by groups of youths. Try to stay calm in all circumstances so that you are more able to deal with the problem at hand appropriately.

GAY & LESBIAN TRAVELLERS

While overt displays of affection between members of the opposite sex, such as cuddling and hand-holding, are frowned upon in India, it is not unusual to see Indian men holding hands with each other or engaged in other close affectionate behaviour. This does not necessarily suggest that they are gay.

The gay movement in India is confined almost exclusively to larger cities and Mumbai is really the only place where there's a gay 'scene'. Since marriage is seen as very important, to be gay has a particular stigma – most gays stay in the closet or risk being disowned by their families. Homosexual relations for men are illegal in India. There is no legislation forbidding lesbian relations.

However, Goa, with it's liberal reputation, draws a lot of gay men and there's a discreet scene happening in Calangute.

As with relations between heterosexual Western couples travelling in India, gay and lesbian travellers should exercise discretion and refrain from displaying overt affection towards each other in public.

Bombay Dost is a gay and lesbian magazine. Its website (W www.bombay-dost.com) has articles, information and back issues. The magazine is published in Mumbai.

DISABLED TRAVELLERS

There are few provisions for disabled travellers in Goa and thus, for the mobility-impaired traveller, there will be a number of challenges. Few older buildings have wheelchair access; toilets have certainly not been designed to accommodate wheelchairs; footpaths, where they exist (only in larger towns), are generally riddled with potholes and crevices, littered with obstacles and packed with throngs of people, severely restricting movement.

Nevertheless, increasing numbers of disabled travellers are visiting Goa, and the difficulties are far from insurmountable. If your mobility is restricted you will need a strong and able-bodied companion to accompany you, and it would be well worth considering hiring a private vehicle with a driver.

An organisation that may be able to offer information on travel practicalities within India for disabled travellers is the **Royal Association for Disability and Rehabilitation** (Radar; ☎ 020-72503222, fax 72500212;

W *www.radar.org.uk; 12 City Forum, 250 City Rd, London EC1V 8AF, UK).*

TRAVEL WITH CHILDREN

Goa is probably the most family-friendly state in India. Apart from the beach – which is enough to keep most kids happy for weeks – there are boating facilities, a science park in Panaji, and hotels that are used to accommodating children.

Children can enhance your encounters with local people, as they often possess little of the self-consciousness and sense of the cultural differences that can inhibit interaction between adults. For more information, get hold of a copy of Lonely Planet's *Travel with Children* by Cathy Lanigan.

DANGERS & ANNOYANCES

Goa is essentially a safe destination for travellers, but this is India and the tourist industry carries with it a few inherent dangers that you should be aware of. Touts, pressure sales tactics and minor scams are annoying, but more worrying is theft, harassment of women and the occasional muggings that occur.

Personal Security

In recent years there have been a number of robberies (some of them violent) on tourists in Goa. Much more disturbing have been recent attacks on women (see Women Travellers earlier in this chapter). Goans are understandably concerned by these incidents and blame them on criminals from neighbouring states. Some measures have been introduced, such as limited street lighting and security patrols on some beaches, but it's probably still not a good idea for women to go to beach shacks alone at night.

It pays for everyone, not just women, to be wary. The busy resorts are safe enough when there are people around, but late at night anyone can be vulnerable. Quiet resorts with poor street lighting, such as Benaulim, have proven to be risky for travellers wandering alone at night. If you are staying in a reasonable hotel or family house where there is a safe or similar facility, leave your passport and travellers cheques there rather than carrying them around. For more information see the boxed text 'Tips for Safe Travel'.

People visiting in the low season should avoid staying in isolated accommodation near the beach.

Theft

Never leave valuables (eg, passport, tickets, health certificates, money and travellers cheques) in your room; they should be with you or secured in a hotel safe. Use a money belt that goes under your clothing. Never walk around with valuables casually slung over your shoulder, and take extra care on crowded public transport.

One scam involves groups of teenage pickpockets posing as students with sponsorship forms. One of them engages victims in conversation while the others pick their pockets. The unfortunate part is that there are also a lot of genuine students who may stop you with a questionnaire or something similar.

From time to time there are also drugging episodes. As tempting as it may be when you befriend someone, don't accept drinks or food from strangers unless you can be absolutely certain it's safe.

Tips for Safe Travel

While the majority of travellers in Goa will have no serious or life-threatening problems, tourists have occasionally been the target of theft or assault. There are some common-sense steps you can take to minimise the risk:

- In your hotel room, never open the door to someone you don't know. Don't sleep with your windows or doors unlocked.
- Any time you go out at night, do so in the company of a friend or a group of people, rather than alone.
- Avoid poorly lit or quiet streets or lanes. Always walk with confidence and purpose. Have something handy that can be used as a weapon in an emergency, and be determined to use it to defend yourself.
- Use noise to attract attention if you are threatened – yell as loudly as you can or carry a loud whistle. Locals will usually come to your aid.
- If you are being sexually harassed or assaulted on public transport, embarrass the person by complaining in a loud voice and report them to the conductor or driver.
- Women should avoid returning male stares; just ignore them. Dark or reflective glasses can help.

Reporting Thefts to the Police

Despite the fact that Goans condemn the police almost as roundly as they do their politicians, one thing that they will all tell you is that individual policemen are very poorly paid. Little wonder then, they say, that the police try to get a little baksheesh (tip, bribe or donation) when they can. Little wonder too, that they are reluctant to do any more work than they absolutely have to.

If you have something stolen in Goa, assuming that you want to claim the money from your insurance company when you get home, you have to report it to the police. According to the accounts of several travellers your initial contact is likely to be frustrating.

Foreigners are often discouraged from making a report. First the policemen might claim that you staged the theft yourself to claim the insurance money. Then, weakening the case slightly, that it was your own fault for not taking adequate security precautions. Alternatively, some people are told that if they file a report of theft and the criminal is caught, they will have to wait in the country for up to six months until the case comes to trial. 'Much better,' the policeman argues, 'to forget the matter.' Finally, if all of the earlier attempts to persuade you to go away have been unsuccessful, it may be suggested that you record the matter as articles that have been 'lost' rather than stolen.

The only answer is to be patient, friendly and persistent. There is no way that reporting a theft is going to mean that you have to stay in Goa. If you keep explaining that you need a copy of the report for your insurance claim, the police will give way and do the paperwork.

Having said this, in recent years Goan police have come under pressure to be more sympathetic towards tourists, and some police are genuinely helpful. If you have trouble receiving help from the police, try contacting a tourist office – Goa Tourism or the Government of India tourist office in Panaji.

Beware also of your fellow travellers. Some make their money go further by helping themselves to other people's.

Remember that backpacks are very easy to rifle through – don't leave valuables in them. Remember also that something may be of little or no value to a thief, but to lose it would be a real heartbreak to you – like film or journals. Finally, a good travel insurance policy helps give you peace of mind as well as some compensation.

If you do have something stolen, you'll need to report it to the police (see the boxed text 'Reporting Thefts to the Police'). You'll also need a statement proving you have done so if you want to claim on insurance.

LEGAL MATTERS

If you find yourself in a sticky legal predicament, contact your embassy (see Embassies & Consulates in India earlier in this chapter). Carry your passport with you or keep it in a hotel safe.

Drugs

For a long time Goa was a place where you could indulge in all sorts of illicit drugs with relative ease – they were cheap, of high quality, readily available and the risks were minimal. Ecstasy and LSD (acid) are still the drug of choice for many ravers, and hashish (charas) is widely available – often brought down from Manali and the Kullu Valley in Himachal Pradesh and peddled around the beach resorts.

These days, however, a few things have changed and the state and federal governments and the Goan police have been taking a tough antidrugs line. A special court, the Narcotic Drugs and Psychotropic Substances Court has been established in Goa with its own judge, just to try drugs offences, and an Anti-Narcotics Cell, a division of the police force, conducts frequent raids and searches.

If you're unfortunate enough to fall foul of the law, it seems the prevailing attitude is 'if in doubt, convict' on the basis that the accused can always appeal to a higher court if they wish to do so. The standard sentence for possession of even a small amount of drugs (for instance, 10g of hashish) is 10 years 'rigorous imprisonment' (plus a fine of Rs 100,000), and the police are increasingly targeting likely beaches and events. Aguada Jail now houses a number of prisoners, including Westerners, who are serving drug-related sentences. Would-be users should not be lulled into a false sense of security in Goa, and should think extremely carefully about the risks before partaking.

Warning – Police Harassment

One evening in March 1998, a couple of travellers who had rented a house for the winter in Vagator answered the door to find five officers from the Goa police on their doorstep. The officers, from the Anti-Narcotics Cell (ANC), forced their way into the house following what they said was a tip-off that a stash of marijuana was hidden there. Notwithstanding the fact that one of the travellers was an asthmatic nonsmoker, an officer appeared from *outside* the house holding up a bag containing 165g of hash. 'Irrefutable evidence,' declared the police.

The travellers were given the option of making an immediate payment of US$3000 or facing charges. Not giving way to police extortion cost them 18 months in Aguada Jail and they were released only in October 1999 after an appeal hearing threw out the police case. There have been numerous other cases of police planting drugs on hapless foreigners and then demanding money. The Vagator area is especially notorious for 'raids'.

Why does it happen? It's undeniable that there is a drugs problem in Goa and that there are dealers and users who are breaking the law. The drugs laws in India are now some of the toughest in the world and possession of even a relatively small amount of hash can lead to 10 years in jail. The police, however, are poorly paid and the opportunities for raking in the rupees through extortion are so extensive that it is said that some officers actually bribe their way into their jobs for as much as US$5000. The real money, of course, comes from pay-offs from the drug barons to the police. Westerners are small fry, but occasionally useful to show the world that Goa is doing something to clean up the drugs problem.

Probably the best way to deal with police extortion should it happen to you is to try persuasion, but if that fails to work, attempt to bargain down the 'fine' and then pay up. While doing this, make a mental note of every distinguishing feature of the policeman to whom you are paying it. Immediately after the incident, write a letter describing exactly what happened, with as much detail as possible. Copies of the letter should go to the Government of India tourist office in Panaji (not the Goan Tourist Department), any one (or all) of the three daily English-language newspapers in Goa, and the Government of India tourist office in your own country (see Tourist Offices Abroad earlier in this chapter).

Smoking & Spitting

On 1 January 2000 a new law came into force in Goa banning smoking, spitting and the chewing of tobacco in all public places. It's a welcome move, but clearly virtually impossible to enforce, except in government buildings and places such as train stations. Transgressors face a Rs 1000 fine. Smoking is banned in many enclosed restaurants, especially if there is air-con, while other restaurants have nonsmoking areas.

BUSINESS HOURS

Just about the only important rule about business hours in Goa is that many Goan shops and offices knock off for lunch and a siesta from about 12.30pm to 3pm. Apart from this, government offices are open 10am to 5pm, Monday to Saturday, and are closed every second Saturday. Sunday is a day of rest, when the business districts of towns like Panaji and Margao are like ghost towns.

Banks are generally open 10am to 2pm Monday to Friday (weekdays), and 10am to noon Saturday. To compete with money-changers, which keep normal (and sometimes extended) business hours, some now have extended hours and even open on Sunday. In resort areas, tourist-oriented businesses such as travel agencies, Internet cafés and merchandise or souvenir shops stay open well into the evening and on Sundays.

PUBLIC HOLIDAYS & SPECIAL EVENTS

Goa could easily be called India's festival state. Goans love to celebrate, and due to its unusual religious mix, Goa has a huge number of holidays and festivals. At times it can seem as though there are as many public holidays as working days, and so frequently banks, post offices and transport services seem to be closed! Along with the nationwide Hindu festivals, Goans celebrate myriad Christian festivals – not only Christmas, Easter and Lent, but many feast days specific to certain villages or parishes, and truly Goan events such as the Feast of St Francis Xavier at Old Goa in early December. On top of this, more recent food, arts and cultural festivals have been developed during the winter season to capitalise on Goa's tourist numbers. Whereas most Christian festivals occur on set dates, Hindu religious festivals follow the lunar calendar and therefore change from year to year.

In the following list, national, state, and some of the more notable local holidays are given, but there are also many other local and village events.

January

Feast of the Three Kings On 6 January the villages of Reis Magos, Cansaulim and Chandor celebrate this unusual festival with local boys re-enacting the arrival of the three kings with gifts for Christ. There's lots of pageantry and a church service, which is followed by food and entertainment.

Republic Day 26 January marks the anniversary of India's establishment as a republic in 1950; despite the fact that Goa was not involved it is celebrated here too (Goans don't miss a chance to rejoice!).

February–March

Feast of Our Lady of Candelaria This feast is held on 2 February at the parish church in Pomburpao.

Pop, Beat & Jazz Music Festival This festival is held over two days in February at the Kala Academy in Panaji.

Fountainhas Arts Festival Homes in the Fountainhas district are turned into galleries for this exhibition of Goan and Indian art.

Shigmotsav or **Shigmo** Goa's version of Holi, this Hindu festival is held to mark the end of winter. It normally takes place on the full moon day of the month of Phalguna, and is widely celebrated by gangs of youths throwing coloured water and powder at one another. Tourists frequently become a target – sometimes it's in good humour, but just as often overexcited locals try to cover foreigners with the powders. This is not a day to go out dressed in your best clothes. Those touring Goa under their own steam may also find the road blocked, even a day or two before the feast, by gangs of local youths, who exact a donation for letting any hapless travellers past their stretch of tarmac. Shigmo parades are often held in Panaji, Margao, Mapusa and Vasco da Gama, with processions of colourful floats.

Carnival The original reason for the Carnival was to celebrate the arrival of spring, and it was observed within the Catholic community as three days of partying before Lent began (February–March). The Carnival is now really just one big party and one of Goa's maddest events. In Panaji the festivities centre around a procession of colourful floats, which takes place on Sabado Gordo (Fat Saturday). The event is opened by the arrival of King Momo, who makes a traditional decree ordering his subjects to forget their worries and have a good time.

March–April

Ramanavami The birth of Rama, an incarnation of Vishnu, is celebrated at the temple at Partagal in Canacona.

Procession of All Saints Held at Goa Velha on the fifth Monday in Lent, this is the only such procession of its sort outside Rome. Thirty statues of the saints are brought out from storage and paraded around the neighbouring villages. The main road through Goa Velha (the NH17) generally becomes blocked with the traffic, as people from all over Goa are drawn to the fair that takes place at this time.

Good Friday & Easter The Easter celebrations are marked by huge church services throughout Goa; the big congregations often overflow onto the street, or the services are held outside to accommodate everyone. Christians mark the event with large family gatherings.

Feast of Jesus of Nazareth This is held at Sindao, on the first Sunday after Easter.

Feast of Our Lady of Miracles Held in Mapusa, 16 days after Easter, this particular festival is famous for its common celebration by large numbers of Hindus and Christians.

Beach Bonanza On successive Sundays from mid-April onwards, this tourist-oriented festival of music, dancing and food stalls was originally held on the beach at Colva, but has been moved back to the football ground in the village.

Youth Fete This is pretty much the same as the Beach Bonanza, but takes place on Calangute beach.

May–June

Igitun Chalne Occurring in May, this is one of the most distinctive festivals in Goa, and is specific to the temple in Sirigao, in Bicholim taluka near Corjuem Fort. *Igitun chalne* literally means fire walking, and the high point of the festival, which occurs at night, comes when devotees of the goddess Lairaya walk across a pit of burning coals to prove their devotion.

Feast of St Anthony This is held on 13 June. It seems natural that the feast of St Anthony, Portugal's national saint, should be celebrated in Goa, although the festival has taken on a particular local significance. It is said that if the monsoon has not arrived by the time of the feast day, a statue of the saint should be lowered into the family well, to hasten the arrival of the rain.

Feast of St John the Baptist (Sao Joao) This feast is held on 24 June. Whereas St Anthony's feast day marks the onset of the rains, the Feast of St

John is a thanksgiving for the arrival of the monsoon. The most obvious manifestation of the rains is the fact that the wells start to fill up again, and to mark the event the young men of the community jump into the water. Since each well owner, by tradition, has to supply feni to the swimmers, the feast day is marked by increasingly high spirits.

Feast of St Peter & St Paul Held on 29 June this is another celebration of the monsoon, this time by the fishing community, particularly in Bardez taluka. The fishermen tie their boats together to form rafts, which serve as makeshift stages. After a church service in the morning, and a large feast, the festival of *sangodd* is held; *tiatrs* (local Konkani dramas), folk dances and music are performed before an audience that watches from the banks of the river.

August–September

Independence Day This holiday on 15 August celebrates the anniversary of India's Independence from the UK in 1947. The prime minister delivers an address from the ramparts of Delhi's Red Fort.

Feast of St Lawrence This feast day celebrates the end of the monsoon and the reopening of the Mandovi to river traffic.

Gokul Ashtami In some Krishna temples during the celebration of Krishna's birthday, the deity is symbolically placed in a cradle.

Bonderam Celebrated on Divar Island on the fourth Saturday of August, the festival features processions and mock battles that commemorate the disputes that took place over property on the island.

Navidades Held on 24 August, the offering of the first sheaves of rice is made to the head of state.

Ganesh Chaturthi This important Hindu festival is celebrated throughout the state, and commemorates the birth of Ganesh. The festival can last for 2½ days. Clay models of Ganesh are taken in procession around the areas of the temples, before being immersed in water. A period of fasting is observed.

September–October

Fama de Menino Jesus The feast is held at Colva on the second Monday of October and celebrates the 'miraculous' favours granted by the 'Menino Jesus', which resides within the Church of Our Lady of Mercy in Colva.

October–November

Diwali This Hindu festival, also known as the Festival of Lights, is second in importance only to Ganesh Chaturthi and marks the victory of good over evil. Symbolically, lamps are lit morning and evening within the homes of the worshippers.

Govardhana Puja This Hindu festival is dedicated to that holiest of animals, the cow.

November–December

Marathi Drama Festival This takes place at Kala Academy in Panaji from November to December.

Food & Cultural Festival This five-day festival is held on Miramar beach in November or December to highlight Goan cuisine and entertainment.

Konkani Drama Festival This is held at Kala Academy in November to December.

Feast of Our Lady of the Rosary This feast is held on the third Wednesday of November at Navelim, about 5km south of Margao.

Tiatr Festival This festival is held at the Kala Academy in November.

Goa Heritage Festival A two-day event of Goan food, folk music and dancing is held in Panaji's Campal Heritage Precinct in late November.

Feast of St Francis Xavier Celebrated in Old Goa on 3 December with processions and services.

Feast of Our Lady of Immaculate Conception Held on or around 8 December in Panaji and Margao, the feast is accompanied by a large fair.

Christmas Day Christmas, December 25, is celebrated as a holiday throughout Goa and India. Goa's Catholics flock to midnight mass services, traditionally called Missa de Galo or Cock Crow because they used to go on well into the early hours of the morning. Christmas day is marked with large family gatherings and feasting.

Christmas in Goa

Christmas is not only the most festive time to be in Goa, but also the busiest tourist season. Celebrations begin around mid-December with carol singing, concerts, street decorations and nativity scenes set up in villages. Groups of carol singers, often accompanied by Santa in the traditional red-and-white costume, roam around raising funds, which may be used for a party but are often contributed to the needy in the community. Stars made of paper stretched over a wooden frame are hung outside homes, and in villages families compete to make the best cribs or stars.

On Christmas Eve, Christian families gather for a late dinner before midnight mass at the parish church. Another service is held on Christmas Day but, for the most part, this is a family day, when presents are exchanged.

In the lead up to the New Year, local children make an effigy of an old man and flag down passing traffic and pedestrians to contribute to their fund – which some see as a form of extortion! The effigy is torched on a bonfire at the stroke of midnight, symbolising the end of the old year.

ACTIVITIES

Goa has long been seen as a place where tourists come to laze on the beaches but, in recent years, tour operators, locals and the tourists themselves have realised that a good book and a beach bar are not enough. As a result, the number of activities on offer has steadily increased.

Motorcycling & Cycling

Most tourists hire a moped or motorcycle at some time during their stay in Goa, but often they rarely venture further than the next beach or the nearest town. There are some worthwhile day rides:

From Benaulim or Cavelossim, ride down the coast road via Betul, Cabo da Rama and Agonda to Palolem
From Calangute, Anjuna or Vagator, head up the coast via Morjim and Mandrem to Arambol
From Arambol the ride up to Terekhol Fort is quite stunning
From Panaji, ride out to Old Goa and across to Divar Island, or continue to Ponda to explore the Hindu temples and spice plantations
From Margao, explore Salcete taluka around Chandor and Loutolim

The shorter rides (such as Panaji to Old Goa or Palolem to Rajbag) can also be done by bicycle. See the Getting Around chapter for details of hiring motorcycles and bicycles.

Diving

Although Goa is not internationally renowned as a diving destination, its waters are regarded as the third top spot for diving in India, after the Andaman and Lakshadweep islands. You can also make dive excursions to sites south of Goa off the Karnataka coast.

There are two dive schools, both of which offer courses and boat dives, and cater for a range of skills from novice to fully qualified. The shallow waters off the coast are ideal for less-experienced divers; typical dives are at depths of 10m to 12m with abundant marine life to be seen. The only problem is that visibility can be unpredictable; on some days it's 30m, while on other days it's closer to 2m. The dive season is November to April.

Marine life you are likely to encounter include tropical fish such an angelfish, parrotfish, wrasses and lionfish, sharks (reef tip

and shovel-nosed among others), stingrays, gropers, snapper, damselfish, barracuda, sea cucumbers and turtles. A highlight of diving in Goa are the wreck dives – there are literally hundreds of wrecks along Goa's coastline, including Portuguese and Spanish galleons and more recent wrecks of merchant and naval ships.

Popular dive sites include Grande Island and St George's Island. South of Goa, off the Karnataka coast, are Devbagh Island (near Karwar) and Pigeon Island, which are also popular.

The following dive schools are both Professional Association of Dive Instructors (PADI) affiliated:

Barracuda Diving (☎ 2437001, fax 2437020, W www.barracudadiving.com) This is a very professional operator based at the Goa Marriott Resort in Miramar. Most open-water dives are around Grande Island and Devbagh Island. Courses include a noncertificate introductory course (two mornings; Rs 3500); and a PADI introductory course (two mornings; Rs 8000) which both involve pool training and two shallow dives. A four-day PADI open-water course is Rs 15,000, a two-day advanced open-water course is Rs 10,000, and a 14-day dive master course is Rs 25,000. For qualified divers, two boat dives (depart 8.30am) cost Rs 2250, including equipment and guide supervision.
Goa Diving (☎ 2555036, W www.goadiving.com, House No 145P, Chapel Bhat, Chicalim 403711) Goa diving is based at Joets Guest House on Bogmalo beach and offers a full range of courses from an introductory dive for novices (Rs 2200) to the PADI open-water course (Rs 15,000), two-to five-day advanced courses (Rs 12,000 to 17,000) and seven-day dive master courses (costing Rs 20,000). Guided dives cost Rs 1430 (one tank) and Rs 2200 (two tanks), including equipment. Goa Diving uses St George's Island off Bogmalo beach and Pigeon Island, 85km south off the coast from Murudeshwar.

Water Sports

Water sports are now a regular feature of Goa's main tourist beaches and usually operate from November to March. There are three operators on Calangute and Baga beaches, and another two on Sinquerim beach. Bogmalo and Colva beaches also have water sports.

Activities on offer include parasailing, jet-skiing, water-skiing, windsurfing, wakeboarding and tube- or banana-boat rides.

Costs vary only slightly – obviously the five-star resort operators are more expensive. Parasailing costs around Rs 800 for one person, jet-ski hire costs around Rs 600 for a short spin.

Rafting & Kayaking

Although not in Goa itself, Dandeli Wildlife Sanctuary is only a couple of hours drive across the border in Karnataka, and here you can try white-water rafting, kayaking and caving. Kali O2 (☎ 08284-33360; W www .kailo2.com) is an adventure company offering rafting and kayaking on the Kali River, as well as mountain-biking, canyoning and canoeing. Accommodation is available at Dandeli and bookings can be made at Day Tripper Tours & Travel in Goa (see Organised Tours in the Getting Around chapter).

Paragliding

Fancy some high-flying excitement? The main paragliding operator is based at Arambol where you can launch off the northern headland or do a certified course – see Things to See & Do under Arambol in the North Goa chapter for details. You can also paraglide at Anjuna on market day.

Yoga, Meditation & Massage

Indian spirituality or plain yoga for better health is easy to find in Goa, though most of the traditions practiced are borrowed from other parts of India and brought here for the tourist demand.

On practically any beach resort you'll see flyers advertising yoga and meditation classes, Ayurvedic treatment, astrology and holistic healing. Some places to try yoga include Purple Valley Yoga Centre in Anjuna; Himalayan Iyengar Yoga Centre near Arambol; Zambala in Vagator; Pedro's in Benaulim; and Bhakti Kutir in Palolem.

For Ayurvedic treatment and massage, check out the Massage Academy in Baga; the Natural Healing Centre in Calangute; Pousada Tauma in Calangute; or the Ayurvedic Heritage Club Village on Arossim beach near Majorda. Ayurveda is an ancient holistic and natural healing system from Kerala. It uses oil massage and a range of herbal medicines, oils and powders to treat a variety of ailments or to simply 're-juvenate body and mind.'

VOLUNTEER WORK

Numerous charities and international aid and development agencies have branches in India, where there are a few work opportunities for foreigners. Though it may be possible to find temporary volunteer work when you are in India, you'll probably be of more use to the charity concerned if you write in advance and, if they need you, stay long enough to be of help. A week on a hospital ward may go a little way towards salving your own conscience, but you may actually not do much more than get in the way of the people who work there long term. Many volunteer organisations arrange long-term (one to two year) placements for volunteers in India. The best opportunity for volunteer work in Goa is with a locally based organisation such as El Shaddai. The following organisations may be able to help or offer advice and further contacts:

Co-ordinating Committee for International Voluntary Service (☎ 01 45 68 49 36. W www.unesco.org/ccivs) Unesco House, 1 rue Miollis, 75732 Paris Cedex 15, France

El Shaddai (☎ 2264798, W www.elshaddaigoa.com) St Anthony Apartments, C Block Mapusa Clinic Rd, Mapusa (for more information see the boxed text 'El Shaddai – Homes for Kids' in the North Goa chapter)

International Animal Rescue (☎ 2268272) This organisation sometimes needs volunteers to help with its dog-sterilisation programme by befriending animals (see the boxed text 'Care for Stray Dogs' in the Facts about Goa chapter)

Voluntary Service Overseas (VSO; ☎ 020-8780 7200, W www.vso.org.uk) 317 Putney Bridge Rd, Putney, London SW15 2PN, UK

Working Abroad (☎ 01273-711406, W www.workingabroad.com) 59 Lansdowne Place, Hove BN3 1FL, East Sussex, UK

ACCOMMODATION

From bamboo huts beneath shady beach palms to spectacular five-star resorts with lobbies the size of an airport departure lounge and lush nine-hole golf courses, Goa has accommodation in every price range and to suit every taste. This tiny state has probably the best range of places to stay in India.

You can rent a room in a village home for US$2 a night; stay on the beach surrounded by bamboo and palm-thatch for US$3; go for the comfort of a clean, mid-range hotel with air-con and TV for US$25; or enjoy

Basilica of Bom Jesus, Old Goa

Se Cathedral, Old Goa

Church of St Francis of Assisi, Old Goa

Sunset over paddy fields

Women carrying water jugs, Pernem

Shantadurga Temple, Ponda

uxurious resort hotel from US$75 to US$300.

If you arrive early in the season you'll find plenty of rooms available in all budgets, giving you room to bargain or shop around if the price isn't right. On the other hand, if you turn up at one of the more popular beaches in the high season you will come across some very average places that are vastly overpriced.

Most places to stay (apart from some bamboo huts and private homes) reviewed in this book have private bathrooms.

Seasons

Accommodation is all about supply and demand in Goa and the hottest demand is over the Christmas period from around 22 December to 5 January. At this time many hotels – particularly mid-range and top-end places at the popular beach resorts like Calangute and Colva – will jack their walkin rates up by two or three times. Many hotels are booked out with charter groups anyway. You may even find that if you book into a place before this peak season, but stay through the Christmas period, the price will suddenly shoot up during your stay as hoteliers try to capitalise on this busy period. If you're coming to Goa at this time, book ahead but shop around – not all hotel owners are greedy.

Generally the hotel prices in Goa are based on high, middle and low seasons. The high season covers the period from mid-December to late January (with the exception of the peak Christmas period), the middle (shoulder) seasons are from October to mid-December and February to June, and the low season runs from July to September. Unless otherwise stated, prices quoted in this book are high-season rates (not peak season). If you're in Goa during the rest of the year, count on discounts of about 25% in the middle season and up to 60% in the low season.

Costs & Taxes

There's a luxury tax of 8% on rooms over Rs 500 and 12% for those over Rs 800. For most of the budget places, the prices quoted will include this tax, but in mid-range and

The Bamboo Revolution

Six or seven years ago there wasn't a bamboo hut to be found on Goa's coastline. Tourism was booming and beach resorts like Calangute and Colva were rapidly developing into concrete jungles at odds with the laid-back tropical state.

In 1996 a British traveller to Goa, a carpenter, built himself a hut from bamboo, so he could hang out on deserted Asvem beach in north Goa. Travellers had been throwing up palm-leaf shelters for years, but the hut he built was one of the first of its kind used by a tourist in Goa. The idea caught on with local entrepreneurs looking to offer accommodation on some of the less-developed beaches – Palolem, Agonda, Morjim, Asvem and Mandrem. The concept was perfect; the huts were cheap and easy to construct, required no permanent building site and were popular with backpackers and travellers looking for cheap, environmentally friendly accommodation close to the beach. At the end of the season they could simply be dismantled and put away. Local panchayats (councils), tourism authorities and even conservation groups such as the Goa Foundation were happy to see this type of 'temporary' development.

So what happened? In the past three years or so, the beaches mentioned above have turned into mini bamboo and thatch villages, with more businesspeople eager to jump on this lucrative bandwagon. In Palolem there are so many huts that they're rarely full and travellers can sleep in one for Rs 100 or Rs 200 a night, even in peak season.

In an effort to attract travellers, the huts are becoming more sophisticated, from the original palm thatch four-walls-and-a-roof, to solid floors, fans and lights and even en suite bathrooms. Treehouses (huts built on stilts with raised verandas) are a popular variation. If you want to see the latest in imaginative bamboo hut design, check out the themed huts belonging to Bridge & Tunnel in Palolem.

One effect of this building boom is a potential bamboo shortage in Goa. One Palolem owner did complain to us that he was having trouble getting materials. 'I can't get a supplier,' he mused, 'they're all going up to Arambol!'

top-end hotels you can expect tax to be added to the bill. Some hotels add a further 10% 'service tax'.

Accommodation costs vary dramatically, depending on the location and the season. For simple cottage or hut accommodation on Palolem or Arambol beach you'll pay around Rs 200 to 300 per night in high season. For a simple but decent guesthouse in Vagator or Benaulim, expect to pay Rs 200 to 400 per double with private bathroom and cold water. A typical mid-range hotel with fan, TV, hot water and maybe a swimming pool in Calangute or Colva will cost Rs 600 to 1000 a double. Top-end hotels in Varca or Candolim can cost anything from Rs 1200 to 8000 per night.

In this book accommodation is categorised as budget (Rs 100 to 500), mid-range (Rs 500 to 1000) and top end (Rs 1000 to 10,000), although the lines are sometimes blurred depending on the location.

Checkout Times

Checkout times vary considerably in Goa. They can be as early as 8am – especially in Panaji where hotels want rooms vacated for early bus and train arrivals – or as late as noon. Unlike elsewhere in India, few hotels or guesthouses have 24-hour checkout policies. Make sure you know the checkout time and try not to sleep in on the day you're due to leave – some hotels demand an extra 50% of the daily rate for oversleeping, which is easy to do if you've just rolled in at 5am from a rave party!

Most places will store your luggage and some may give you some checkout grace time if you let them know in advance.

Touts

Throughout India, including Goa, visitors arriving by bus or train are likely to be met by taxi drivers and autorickshaw-wallahs (autorickshaw drivers) offering to take them to a nice hotel. The technique is simple – they take you not to the place you want to go to but to the place that pays the best commission. Some very good cheap hotels simply refuse to pay the touts and you'll then hear lots of stories about the hotel you want being 'full', 'closed for repairs', 'no good any more' or even 'flooded'. It's almost always a lie.

Touts do have a use, though – if you arrive during the high season, finding a place to stay can be difficult. Hop in a rickshaw tell the driver what price you will pay for a hotel, and off you go.

FOOD
Goan Specialities

The Goan identity is rooted, among other things, in a deep enjoyment of food and drink. Thus, when a Goan writer becomes nostalgic, he or she usually ends up reminiscing about the taste of their grandmother's *sorpotel*, the texture of a perfect *bebinca*, or the aroma of a large glass of feni.

The basic components of Goan cooking are, not surprisingly, local products. The claim that every part of the coconut is used for something is not an idle one. Coconut oil, milk and grated coconut flesh flavour many dishes, while toddy (the sap from the coconut palm), is also used to make vinegar and to act as a yeast substitute. Another important product of the palm is jaggery, a dark-coloured sweetener that is widely used in preparing Goan sweetmeats.

Goan cooking generally involves liberal amounts of spices, giving dishes a strong taste and distinctive aroma. The most commonly used include cumin, coriander, chillies, garlic and turmeric. Another local ingredient used to flavour fish curries is *kokum* (a dried fruit that is used as a spice). Particular combinations of spices have led to a number of styles of cooking, which have subtly differing flavours – masala, vindaloo and the seafood dish *balchão* being some of the most famous.

For the main content of the meal, seafood of all varieties is eaten, and pork and chicken are the most commonly used meats. The Portuguese influence in Goan cooking cannot be ignored. Seafood dishes such as *recheiado* and *caldeirada*, and *cabidela* (a rich pork dish) reflect the legacy of the state's colonial heritage.

Goan cuisine does not naturally cater for the vegetarian, and as a compromise cooking styles such as *xacuti* and *caldinho* (dishes cooked in spices and coconut milk) are sometimes used in the preparation of vegetables. Two vegetable dishes, however, are *mergolho*, which is made from pumpkin and papaya, and breadfruit curry.

Seafood Goa is famous for its seafood, the classic staple dish being fish curry rice. This dish of fish in a spicy sauce served over rice can be found in cheap restaurants for as little as Rs 20 – but up to Rs 120 in fancier places.

With the variety and range on offer, combined with the skills of the local cooks, there is a mouthwatering choice. Kingfish is probably the most common item on the menu, but there are many others including pomfret, shark, tuna and mackerel. Among the excellent shellfish available are crabs, tiger prawns and lobster. Other seafood includes squid and mussels.

For the sake of tourist tastebuds, many beach shacks and restaurants present seafood lightly spiced, or without spices at all. In this case the food is generally either fried, grilled or cooked in a garlic sauce. Traditional Goan cooking methods, however, generally involve seasoning the seafood in some way.

Among the most famous Goan dishes is *ambot tik*, a slightly sour curry dish that can be prepared with either fish or meat, but more usually fish. *Caldeirada* is a mildly flavoured offering in which fish or prawns are cooked into a kind of stew with vegetables, and often flavoured with wine. *Recheiado* is a delicious preparation in which a whole fish, usually a mackerel or pomfret, is slit down the centre and stuffed with a spicy red sauce, after which it is cooked normally. *Balchão* is a method of cooking either fish or prawns in a dark red and tangy tomato sauce. Because of the preservative qualities of the sauce, *balchão* can be cooked in advance and reheated up to four days after preparation. *Rissois* are snacks or starters that are made with prawns fried in pastry shells.

Meats *Sorpotel* is one of Goa's most famous meat dishes, and is prepared from pork, pork liver, heart and kidneys. These are diced and cooked in a thick and very spicy sauce flavoured with feni to give it an added kick. *Xacuti* is a traditional way of preparing meat, usually chicken, by cooking it in coconut milk, and adding grated coconut and a variety of spices. The result is a mild curry, but with a distinctive and delicious flavour.

Chouricos are spicy pork sausages, which owe more than a passing debt to Portuguese culinary traditions. Goan sausages are prepared using well-salted and well-spiced cubes of pork. Once they have been made, the strings of sausages are dried in the sun and then hung above the fire where they are gradually smoked. Traditionally they are eaten during the monsoon, when fish is scarce. In preparation, they are soaked in water and then usually fried and served with a hot sauce and rice.

Cafrial is a method of preparation, usually used with chicken, in which the meat is marinated in a sauce of chillies, garlic and ginger and then dry-fried. The result is a rather dry, but spicy dish.

Breads Bakers regularly do the rounds of each village in Goa, pushing bicycles laden with fresh bread and either ringing a bell or hooting a horn on the handlebars to let the villagers know they've arrived. There are several types of local bread. *Uned* are small, round, crusty rolls, usually served fresh from the bakery, and an ideal alternative to rice when eating a dish such as *sorpotel*. Particularly famous and unique to Goa are *sanna* (steamed rolls made with rice flour, ground coconut and coconut toddy), which are ideal to eat with any of the spicy Goan dishes.

Sweets The most famous of Goa's sweetmeats is *bebinca*, a wonderful concoction made from layer upon layer of coconut pancakes. Cooking the perfect *bebinca* is an art form, for not only does the cook have to get exactly the right mixture of egg yolk, flour, coconut milk and sugar, but the cooking has to be timed just right to ensure that all layers are cooked equally. It'll put inches on your waistline if you develop a taste for it, but it's not to be missed.

Dodol is another famous Goan sweet, traditionally eaten at Christmas, and made with rice flour, coconut milk, jaggery and cashew nuts. It is usually cooled in a flat pan and served in slices, and is very sweet. *Doce*, made with chickpeas and coconut, is another favourite.

Indian Cuisine

Most of the many different cuisines from around India are also available in Goa. In a country of India's size it's only natural that there are considerable variations in styles from around the country, partly because of climatic conditions and partly because of historical influences. In the north much more meat is eaten and the cooking is often 'Mughal style' (often spelt 'Mughlai'), which bears a closer relationship to food of the Middle East and central Asia. The emphasis is more on spices and less on chilli. In the north, grains and breads are eaten far more than rice. In the south more rice is eaten, there is more vegetarian food, and the curries tend to be hotter. Another feature of southern vegetarian food is that it's always eaten with fingers (of the right hand only).

In the most basic Indian restaurants and eating places, known as *dhabas* or *bhojanayalas*, the cooking is usually done right out the front so you can see exactly what is going on. In these basic places a meal of dhal (a stew of lentils), vegetables, rice and chapatis – called a thali after the metal plate it is served on – makes a filling lunch for around Rs 20.

Curries & Spices Believe it or not, there is no such thing as 'curry' in India. It's an English invention, an all-purpose term to cover the whole range of Indian food spicing.

Although all Indian food is certainly not curry, this is the basis of Indian cuisine. Curry doesn't have to be hot enough to blow your head off, although it can if it's made that way. Curry most definitely is not something found in a packet of curry powder. Indian cooks have about 25 spices on their regular list and it is from these that they produce the curry flavour. Normally the spices are freshly ground in a mortar and pestle known as a *silvatta*. Spices are usually blended in certain combinations to produce masalas (mixes). Garam masala (hot mix), for example, is a combination of cloves, cinnamon, cardamom, coriander, cumin and peppercorns.

Popular spices include saffron, an expensive flavouring produced from the stamens of certain crocus flowers. This is used to give rice that yellow colouring and delicate fragrance. Turmeric also has a yellow-colouring property, acts as a preservative and has a distinctive smell and taste. Chillies are ground, dried or added whole to supply the heat. Ginger is supposed to be good for the digestion, while many masalas contain coriander because it is said to cool the body. Strong and sweet cardamom are used in many desserts and in rich meat dishes.

Breads & Grains Rice, a staple in South India, is supplemented by a whole range of breads known as rotis or chapatis. Indian breads are varied but always delicious. Simplest is the chapati, which is simply a mixture of flour and water cooked on a hotplate known as a *tawa*. Direct heat causes them to rise, but how well that works depends on the gluten content of the wheat. A *paratha* is also cooked on the hotplate but ghee is used and the bread is rolled in a different way. Deep-fried bread that puffs up is known as a *puri* in the north and a *luchi* in the east. Bake the bread in a tandoori oven and you have naan.

Originating from the south are *dosas*. These are basically paper-thin pancakes made from lentil and rice flour. Curried vegetables wrapped inside a *dosa* makes it a *masala dosa* – a terrific snack meal. An *idli* is a kind of South Indian rice dumpling, often served with *dahi idli* (spicy curd sauce) or with spiced lentils and chutney. They're a popular breakfast dish in the south. Pappadams are crispy deep-fried lentil-flour wafers often served with thalis or other meals. An *uttapam* is like a *dosa*.

Basic Dishes Curries can be vegetable, meat (usually chicken or lamb) or fish, but they are always fried in ghee (clarified butter) or vegetable oil. There are a number of dishes that aren't really curries but are close enough to them for Western tastes. Vindaloos have a vinegar marinade and tend to be hotter than most curries. Korma, both meat and vegetable, are rich, substantial dishes prepared by braising. *Navratan korma* is a very tasty dish using nuts, while a *malai kofta* is a rich, cream-based dish. *Dopiaza* literally means 'two onions' and is a type of korma that uses onions at two stages in its preparation.

Probably the most basic of Indian dishes is dhal. Dhal is almost always there, whether as an accompaniment to a curry or as a very basic meal in itself with chapatis or rice. The common green lentils are called *moong*; dhal is also made with *rajmaa* (kidney beans).

Other basic dishes include *mattar panir* (peas and cheese in gravy), *saag gosh* (spinach and meat), *aalu dum* (potato curry), *palak panir* (spinach and cheese) and *aalu chhole* (diced potatoes and spicy-sour chickpeas). Some other vegetables include *paat gobi* (cabbage), *phuul gobi* (cauliflower), *baingan* (eggplant or brinjal) and *mattar* (peas).

Chewing the Paan – an Oral Experience

Although the Goans are not nearly such prolific *paan* chewers as their countryfolk elsewhere in India, they don't lack the resources. The main constituent of *paan* – the betel nut, which comes from the areca palm – is widely cultivated in Goa. The nut is mildly intoxicating and addictive, but is quite inedible by itself, and so is combined with other ingredients. *Paan* – the name given to the collection of spices and condiments wrapped in a leaf and chewed with betel nut – is usually taken at the end of an Indian meal, when it is chewed as a mild digestive.

Paan sellers have a whole collection of little trays, boxes and containers in which they mix either *saadha* (plain) or *mitha* (sweet) *paans*. The ingredients may include, apart from the betel nut, lime paste (the ash not the fruit), the powder known as *catachu*, various spices and even a dash of opium in a pricey *paan*. The whole concoction is folded up in a piece of edible leaf, which you pop in your mouth and chew. If that sounds easy, wait till you try it – inserting the average *paan* feels like stuffing a football into your gob. *Paan* can be made without the betel (which is hell for your teeth), in which case it's fine to swallow the fermenting liquid that floods your mouth, but usually the remains are spat out, adding another red blotch to the pavement – note that spitting in public places is officially illegal in Goa.

Over a long period of time, indulgence in *paan* will turn your teeth red-black and even addict you to the betel nut. Hundreds of thousands of people in Asia are addicted to betel nut in the same way that people are addicted to nicotine. More worryingly, a direct link between the consumption of *paan* and the incidence of oral cancer has been discovered. However, trying *paan* occasionally is not known to cause any harm.

Tandoori & Rice Dishes Tandoori is a northern speciality and refers to the clay oven in which the food is cooked, after first being marinated in a complex mix of herbs and yogurt. The result is not as hot as curry dishes, but has a wonderful spicy flavour that suits most Western palates. Tandoori chicken is a favourite, served as a full or half bird.

Biryani is another Mughal dish. The meat is mixed with a deliciously flavoured, orange-coloured rice that is sometimes spiced with nuts or dried fruit.

A *pulao* is flavoured rice often with pulses and with or without meat. You will also find it in other Asian countries further west. Those who have the idea that Indian food is always curry and always fiery hot will be surprised by tandoori and biryani dishes.

Side Dishes Indian food generally has a number of side dishes to go with the main meal. Probably the most popular is *dahi* – curd or yogurt. It has the useful ability of instantly cooling a fiery curry – either blend it into the curry or, if it's too late, you can administer it straight to your mouth. Curd is often used in the cooking or as a dessert and appears in the popular drink lassi.

Sabzi is curried vegetables, and *baingan bharta* is a pureed eggplant dish. *Mulligatawny* is a souplike dish, which is really just a milder, more liquid curry. It was adopted into the English menu by the Raj. Chutney is pickled fruit or vegetables and is the standard relish for a curry.

Chinese Food

For some reason almost every restaurant in Goa, be it in the largest hotel or the humblest beach shack, feels that it's necessary to have Chinese food on the menu. While in general the food is quite good, and can make a very tasty alternative to Goan or Indian dishes, you are extremely unlikely to find much genuine Chinese cuisine in Goa – if anything it's a bland fusion of all Southeast Asian cuisine (rice, noodles, Cantonese, Thai etc) with an Indian touch.

Western Food

Western tastes are well served too, and most restaurants in tourist areas will offer at least a few dishes that make a brave stab at being Western in flavour. While in many cases beach shacks will restrict themselves to some simple pasta or toasted sandwiches, the larger hotels that cater to British tourists will go all out with roast beef and other tastes of home. There are several restaurants in the northern beach resorts (Calangute, Baga, Candolim, Anjuna and Vagator) that specialise in Italian, French or

Mediterranean cuisine. Some do an excellent job, even using imported ingredients and chefs with experience in Europe, and this is usually reflected in the price.

In general the most common 'Western' items on the menu in the cheaper restaurants are the sort of snacks that have become the staple diet of travellers the world over: breakfast fare such as banana pancakes, porridge, omelettes and, of course, chips. There are a number of places that cater to the sweet-toothed visitor, and bakeries in almost all the major centres produce mouthwatering pastries and cakes; even fresh croissants are not hard to come by.

Fruit

Bananas, pineapples, mangoes, jackfruit, watermelons and papaya are all grown locally, and the Goan varieties are renowned for being small but particularly sweet. Goa has even been in the forefront of perfecting some strains of fruit; know-how when it comes to grafting plants has led to varieties of mango that even today bear the names of their creators – you'll find Fernandina, Costa and Afonso.

Watermelons, which are often sold by the slice on roadside stalls, are a fine thirst quencher when you're unsure about the water and fed up with soft drinks. Try to get the first slice before the flies discover it.

DRINKS
Nonalcoholic Drinks

Water Basically, you should not drink water unless you know that it has been boiled, filtered or sterilised. Water is generally safer to drink in the dry season than in the monsoon when it can really be dangerous. See Basic Rules under Health earlier in this chapter for more information.

Tea & Coffee Indians, for all the tea they grow, make some of the most hideously oversweetened, murkily milky excuses for tea that you'll ever taste. But Indian chai, which is stewed with the milk and sugar already added, is an acquired taste and even purists may come to like it eventually. A glass of chai from a street vendor costs less than Rs 5, and standing around drinking it with locals is a typically Indian social experience.

Coffee is available everywhere, although true coffee lovers are likely to be disappointed. The most widely produced brew is 'milk coffee' – which is simply Nescafé made with boiled milk. Tourist hotels and restaurants have adapted to Western tastes though, and most give you a pot of black coffee and a separate jug of milk. A number of restaurants and upmarket snack bars in Goa also offer freshly ground coffee - including cappuccino and espresso – and Calangute now has two specialist coffee shops serving exotic blends from Colombia, Kenya and Morocco.

Juices & Other Drinks Freshly squeezed and sold at stalls all over Goa, fruit juice is a refreshing, healthy and safe drink. Sugar cane juice is also available from street vendors and is one of the most thirst-quenching drinks around, especially if it's chilled (which means the vendor will have crushed the juice over ice). Vendors are easy to find as their stalls are usually decked with constantly jangling bells attached to the flywheel of the crushing machine. Although it's extremely sweet, sugar cane juice is great for an instant energy boost!

Green coconuts are even better and there are coconut stalls on just about every beach as well as in the towns. When you've drunk the milk the stallholder will split the coconut open and cut you a slice from the outer shell with which to scoop out the flesh.

Soft drinks are cheap (around Rs 12 a bottle) and ready available in Goa. Coca-Cola got the boot from India a couple of decades back for not cooperating with the government, but that company and Pepsi are back with a vengeance, sold alongside local Indian brands such as Thums Up, Limca and Teem.

Finally there's lassi, that oh so cool, refreshing and delicious iced-curd (yogurt) drink. Lassis are either mixed with sugar, salt or fruit.

Alcoholic Drinks

Because of lower taxes, Goa is one of the cheapest states in India for alcohol. This makes it a popular destination for Indians from neighbouring states, who often make a weekend of it, crossing the state border by car and having two days of bingeing before returning home on Sunday evening.

Still, alcohol is relatively expensive compared with food and other costs in Goa. A small bottled beer in a beach shack, restaurant or bar costs Rs 20 to 30 (depending on how trendy the place is). A shot of Indian-made spirits is about Rs 40 to 60 (mixers cost extra) and a shot of feni is Rs 20.

The Goan climate makes cold lager a natural choice, although many bar owners are yet to fully appreciate the value of ice-cold beer. There are several brands of very drinkable Indian beer available in Goa. The most famous is Kingfisher ('most thrilling chilled'), which many locals consider to be the best, but which beer connoisseurs agree has far too many added preservatives, giving you a whopping headache. King's lager (small bottles) is excellent, while Ice, San Miguel and Foster's are all available. Again, preservatives are added to combat the effects of climate on 'quality'.

Beer and other Indian interpretations of Western alcoholic drinks are known as IMFL (Indian Made Foreign Liquor). They include imitations of Scotch and brandy under a plethora of different brand names. The taste varies from hospital disinfectant to passable imitation Scotch.

Indian wines vary from sweet to sherry-like. Reds and whites are available, but quality varies from year to year and the red is usually very sweet – almost a port. Cheaper brands like Vin Ballet verge on the undrinkable; Grovers and Chantilly are much better. Imported wines from France, Chile and even Australia are available at a few restaurants, especially Italian and French restaurants in resorts like Calangute. It's naturally very expensive – usually around Rs 1000 a bottle.

Feni – Goa's Fire Water

It's clear as water, it tastes like aromatic gasoline and it really packs a punch – Goa's most famous spirit is the double-distilled and fearfully potent feni, a drink that deserves respect.

There are two types of feni, both of which are made from local ingredients. Coconut or palm feni is made from the sap drawn from the severed shoots on a coconut tree. In Goa this is known as toddy, and the men who collect it are toddy tappers. Toddy tappers at work are a common sight; crouched in the canopy of the palm tree they collect the terracotta pot that has filled with creamy white sap, then trim the shoots to facilitate further collection, tie a new pot over the top, and descend to move on to the next tree. Toddy can be collected year-round, so palm feni is in plentiful supply at all times.

Caju (cashew) feni can only be made during the cashew season in late March and early April. Cashews are an important crop in Goa and pretty much wherever you travel in early spring you can see them. The cashew apple, when ripe, turns a yellow-orange colour and the nut ripens below it. When the fruit is harvested the nuts are separated from the 'apples' and are laid out to dry in the sun. The apples are placed in a pit and trampled by foot to collect the juice. Both palm toddy and caju juice can be drunk fresh immediately after collection – but the important process of turning the juice into alcohol is yet to occur. Left for just a few hours they soon start to ferment.

Having been left to ferment for a day or so, the toddy or caju is distilled for the first time. In typical local stills, the juice is placed in a large terracotta pot over a wood fire; the vapour exits through a tube that typically passes through an oil drum filled with water, below which the distillate is collected. This result of this first process is called uraq, a medium-strength spirit (10% to 15% proof), some of which is kept (you can buy uraq in the shops). The majority is distilled again to make feni. By the time it comes out of the second distillation, Goa's national drink has an alcoholic strength of around 30% to 35% proof.

Although the feni is ready for drinking as soon as it has been collected, traditionally it is sealed in huge terracotta jars and may be left to mature for up to several years.

Many Goans enjoy drinking straight feni, but the uninitiated will probably find the alcoholic strength a bit unpleasant. The best idea is to mix it with a soft drink such as Limca or cola – or close your eyes and shoot it. Goans are keen to offer advice to foreigners; don't drink it on an empty stomach, don't mix it with other spirits, and certainly don't swim after a couple of fenis. And take it easy; you don't realise how strong it is until you stand up.

You can buy a shot of feni in any bar or restaurant, and you can buy colourful, decorative bottles, which make a good gift, from wine stores from Rs 100 to 400, depending on the quality.

Finally, there's Goa's own fire-water, the sledgehammer feni and its cousin *uraq*, made from distilled fruit of the cashew tree; see the boxed text 'Feni – Goa's Fire Water' earlier.

ENTERTAINMENT
Cinemas
The Indian film industry is the largest in the world in terms of volume – between 800 and 1000 films are registered for classification with the censorship board each year! The vast majority of what's produced are the average Bollywood 'masala' movies – cheap melodramas based on three vital ingredients: romance, violence and music. Most are dreadful but provide an element of escapism for the audience. It's worth seeing at least one Indian movie while you're here – if only for the experience. The best cinemas are in Panaji – some even show Western action films. Ask locals for recommendations.

Discos & Nightclubs
Goa has a more liberal attitude to nightlife than most places in India, but nightclubs are pretty much for tourists – both wealthy Indians and foreigners. For some time the only nightclub in Goa was in Calangute, and it's in this area where you'll still find the majority of Goa's Western-style nightlife – although it's gradually extending to Candolim and Arpora. At Calangute, roughly where it creeps into Baga beach, Tito's is Goa's longest-running and most famous bar and nightclub. There are many other bars in the area, but none come close to Tito's. In south Calangute, Club Antoos is a late-night haunt, and there are a couple of chic, new 'Mumbai-style' music bars with discos in Candolim. Further inland, at Saligao, Club Westend is a party place with raves a couple of nights a week.

In a spectacular hilltop location in Arpora, Club Cubana is something different again – a late night bar and club (with swimming pool) where you pay an entry fee and all drinks are free. In Anjuna, Paradiso is undoubtedly Goa's most awesome club – a huge terraced place with several levels overlooking the beach. It attracts top Goan and international DJs.

In south Goa, nightclubs are mostly limited to the five-star resort hotels, which all have their own discos, bars and sometimes gaming rooms. As you'd expect, these are mainly frequented by hotel guests – well-heeled Indian and foreign tourists – but they're open to any reasonably dressed patron. The Leela Palace and Holiday Inn Resort in Mobor, and the Goa Renaissance Resort and Club Mahindra in Varca are worth checking out, if you're staying in the vicinity.

Single guys should be aware that Indian nightclubs don't allow single men (often called 'stags') onto the dance floor or disco area – it's couples or ladies only. The reason is simple: to avoid lecherous groups of men coming in and giving women unwanted attention – and the trouble that that brings. Well-dressed, sober Western men may be able to get around this, but don't count on it.

Panaji also has a couple of nightclubs in the Campal district that are popular with local students.

Music & Dance
Some of the larger hotels and more upmarket restaurants lay on live music, which is usually Western and often good. Goan artistes give surprisingly authentic renditions of Western pop songs and are much in demand as entertainers in other parts of India.

A good place to see local live acts is at the Saturday night markets in Baga and Arpora. Ingo's Saturday Nite Bazaar, between Baga and Anjuna, features everything from rock fusion bands to jazz and Goan folk music.

The best place to catch a performance of Indian classical music and dance is at the Kerkar Art Complex in Calangute every Tuesday evening, or at the Kala Academy in Panaji. The Pop, Beat & Jazz Music Festival, held at the Kala Academy in February, is the best opportunity to see performances of all types of music.

Rave Parties
As much as the average Goan would hate to admit it, one thing that has made this tiny state famous is the all-night, full-moon rave parties that took root here in the hippy days almost 30 years ago. The parties, mostly staged around Anjuna and Vagator, evolved and developed into mainstream events attracting hardcore European and Israeli ravers gyrating to the distinctive Goa Trance. Over the Christmas–New Year period organisers manage to get around the laws banning loud music after 10pm, but at other times the plugs regularly get pulled on parties – much

to the relief of the locals. See the North Goa chapter for a rundown on what's happening.

SPECTATOR SPORTS

While everyone knows how passionate Indians are about cricket, it comes as a surprise to learn that Goa's top sport is football (soccer), another legacy of the Portuguese. Every village has at least one football team, sometimes a team for each ward of the village, and league games are fiercely contested. The result of this keen following at village level has been the creation of several teams that regularly perform well at national level, and even a number of Goan players in the national football squad. The main Goan teams are Salgaonkar, Dempo, Sesa Goa and Churchill Brothers, and major matches are played at the Nehru Stadium, Fatorda, which is near the Margao bus station. The season runs from October to April and tickets to the matches generally cost less than Rs 20.

The Goans are also keen cricketers and games take place everywhere at local levels. Goa's English-language daily papers publish reports on matches and upcoming fixtures.

Dhirio, the Goan equivalent of bullfighting, was finally banned in early 1997.

SHOPPING

Although Goa is not renowned for its handicrafts, there is a huge market in every tourist centre with traders from elsewhere in India who come to sell to foreigners.

While, sadly, this means that you are unlikely to take home much that is genuinely Goan (apart from the odd decorative bottle of feni), it also means that Goa has become a very varied place to shop for souvenirs. Where else can you find jewellery and carpets from Kashmir, fabrics from states as far apart as Rajasthan and Kerala, carvings from Karnataka or paintings from Nepal?

Be careful when buying items that include delivery to your home country. You may well be assured that the price includes home delivery and all customs and handling charges. Often this may not be the case, and you may find that you have to collect the item yourself from your country's main port or airport, and pay customs and handling charges.

Where to Shop

The obvious place to start shopping for handicrafts and souvenirs are the markets.

The state's biggest market – and very much a tourist magnet – is the Anjuna Flea Market held every Wednesday in season. There are two smaller Saturday night markets at Baga and Arpora. For local markets, check out Mapusa's Friday market, where you can buy everything from produce and furniture to clothing and crafts at reasonable prices. Panaji and Margao both have busy municipal markets which are interesting to browse around, but you won't find much worth buying.

In Panaji, the main shopping street is 18th June Rd, a long thoroughfare lined with craft and clothing shops, emporiums and shops selling cashews and spices. MG Rd has a collection of modern Western department stores, including Nike, Benetton and Levi's. Perhaps the greatest concentration of department stores, boutiques, jewellery and craft shops is in Calangute, on the road that

The Art of Haggling

The friendly art of haggling is an absolute must in most parts of Goa, unless you don't mind paying above the market value. Traders in towns and markets are accustomed to tourists who have lots of money and little time to spend it. This means that when you ask a shopkeeper 'How much?', the reply will probably be 'very good price,' but more often than not that price is daylight robbery.

In government emporiums, department stores and some larger shops, the prices are usually fixed (often quite high). But in most other shops catering to tourists, and in all markets, bargaining is the name of the game.

If you have absolutely no idea what something should really cost, start by slashing the price by at least half. The vendor will probably look aghast and tell you that this is impossible, as it's the very price they had to pay for the item themselves. This is the usual story. This is when the battle for a bargain begins and it's up to you and the salesperson to negotiate a price. You'll find that many shopkeepers lower their so called 'final price' if you proceed to head out of the shop and tell them that you'll 'think about it.'

Don't lose your sense of humour and fairness while haggling – it's not a battle to squeeze every last rupee out of a poor trader, and not all vendors are out to rip you off.

leads down to the main beach, and on the Calangute–Candolim road. Prices are high here but so is the quality of the merchandise.

The Calangute–Baga road is lined with many small shops selling handicrafts, souvenirs, music and clothing.

What to Buy

Carpets It may not surprise you that India produces and exports more handcrafted carpets than Iran, but it probably is more of a surprise that some of them are of virtually equal quality. India's best carpets come from Kashmir, and these can be found in traders' shops in Goa.

Carpets are either made of pure wool, wool with a small percentage of silk to give a sheen (known as silk touch) or pure silk. The latter are more for decoration than hard wear. Expect to pay from Rs 7000 for a good quality 1.2m by 1.8m carpet, but don't be surprised if the price is more than twice as high.

Papier-Mache This is probably the most characteristic Kashmiri craft. The basic papier-mache article is made in a mould, then painted and polished in successive layers until the final intricate design is produced. Prices depend upon the complexity and quality of the painted design and the amount of gold leaf used. Items include bowls, cups, containers, jewellery boxes, letter holders, tables, lamps, coasters, trays and so on. A cheap bowl might cost only Rs 25, a large, well-made item might approach Rs 1000.

The Commission Racket

Although Goa is nowhere near to being as bad for this kind of thing as, say, Agra, just about all taxi drivers are still able to collect a commission for taking their passengers to the right shops. Whatever you might be told, if you are taken by a rickshaw or taxi driver to a place, be it a hotel, craft shop, market or even restaurant, the price you pay will be inflated. This can be by as much as 50%, so try to visit these places on your own.

While it is certainly a minority of traders who are actually involved in dishonest schemes, virtually all are involved in the commission racket. You need to shop with care, so take your time, be firm and bargain hard. Good luck!

Jewellery For Western tastes the heavy folk-art jewellery of Rajasthan has particular appeal. Tibetan jewellery is even chunkier and more folklike than the Rajasthani variety. If you're looking for fine jewellery, as opposed to folk jewellery, you may well find, as most of those who are *au fait* with *haute couture* do, that much of what is produced in India is way over the top.

Leatherwork Indian leatherwork is not made from cowhide but from buffalo, camel, goat or some other hide. *Chappals,* the basic sandals found all over India, are the most popular buy.

Textiles This is still India's major industry and 40% of the total production is at the village level, where it is known as *khadi* (homespun cloth). Bedspreads, tablecloths, cushion covers or material for clothes are popular khadi purchases. There is an amazing variety of cloth styles, types and techniques around the country. In Gujarat and Rajasthan heavy material is embroidered with tiny mirrors and beads to produce everything from dresses to stuffed toys to wall hangings. Tie-dye work is also popular in Rajasthan and Kerala. In Kashmir embroidered materials are made into shirts and dresses. Batik is a fairly recent introduction from Indonesia but already widespread; *kalamkari* cloth from Andhra Pradesh and Gujarat is an associated but far older craft.

Silks & Saris Silk is cheap and the quality is often excellent. If you are buying a silk sari, it helps to know a bit about the silk and the sari. Saris are 5.5m long, unless they have fabric for a choli attached, in which case they are 6m. Sari silk is graded and sold by weight – in grams per metre.

Bronze Figures & Woodcarving Delightful small images of gods are made by the age-old lost-wax process. A wax figure is made, a mould is formed around it, then the wax is melted and poured out. Molten metal is poured in and once it's solidified the mould is broken open. Figures of Ganesh, and of Shiva in his incarnation as dancing Nataraja, are among the most popular.

In the south, images of the gods are also carved out of sandalwood. Rosewood is used to carve animals – elephants in particular.

Carved wooden furniture and other house-hold items, either in natural finish or lac-quered, are also made in various locations.

Antiques Articles more than 100 years old are not allowed to be exported from India without an export clearance certificate. If you have doubts about any item and think it could be defined as an antique, you can check with the **Archaeological Survey of India** (☎ 2286133), which is at the museum in Old Goa.

Musical Instruments Indian musical in-struments are an interesting buy in India and you'll see new and second-hand guitars, sitars and tablas at the Anjuna Flea Market. There are also instrument shops in Panaji and Margao. Easier to carry and even easier to play are CDs and tapes. You can find Bolly-wood soundtracks, Goan Trance and main-stream Western music at shops and stalls all over Goa for between Rs 100 and 600.

Clothing Western-brand clothing stores are all the rage in Panaji and Calangute these days. Big names like Benetton, Levi's, Nike, Reebok and Lacoste now have much of their produce made in India, and these shops, which cater almost exclusively to tourists, sell their brand-name gear at prices lower than you'd find at home. Don't ex-pect the type of cheap rubbish you might pick up in Bangkok – Levi jeans go for around Rs 2000, Lacoste polo shirts retail at Rs 1000 and Nike trainers from Rs 2000.

Getting There & Away

Goa's Dabolim Airport is owned and controlled by the Indian navy so there are currently no scheduled international flights direct to Goa – only domestic flights, a handful of Air India flights from the Middle East and charter flights. Since charter companies occasionally have spare seats to sell, it's worth contacting them even if you don't want a package trip. Most charter flights into Goa run from the UK and Germany, plus a few from the Netherlands, Russia and Finland. Direct charter flights from Israel are also being considered. A new international airport is being planned at Mopa in the north of the state, near the border with Maharashtra, but it will be several years before this comes to fruition.

For most independent travellers, getting to Goa involves a two-part journey that begins with a flight to Mumbai (Bombay) followed by another flight, or rail or bus trip, for the 600km south to Goa. If you're coming from Southeast Asia, Australia or New Zealand, it would be worth checking fares to Chennai (Madras), 1000km from Goa.

The first section of this chapter deals with travel from international destinations to India, the second section covers getting to Goa from elsewhere in India. See the Gateway Cities chapter for more detailed information on Mumbai and Chennai.

India

This section gives details of how to get to and from India from other countries.

AIR
Buying Tickets
The flight into India will represent a considerable slice of your budget, but you can reduce the cost by finding discounted fares. Stiff competition has resulted in widespread discounting, and websites specialising in cheap tickets have created an even more cut-throat market. Shop around at reputable travel agencies, 'bucket shops' (agencies specialising in discounted fares) and on the Internet – and start early as seats are usually sold in blocks with the cheapest economy fares on any flight going first.

> ## Warning
>
> The information in this chapter is particularly vulnerable to change: prices for international travel are volatile, routes are introduced and cancelled, schedules change, special deals come and go, and rules and visa requirements are amended. Airlines and governments seem to take a perverse pleasure in making price structures and regulations as complicated as possible. You should check directly with the airline or a travel agency to make sure you understand how a fare (and ticket you may buy) works. In addition, the travel industry is highly competitive and there are many lurks and perks.
>
> The upshot of this is that you should get opinions, quotes and advice from as many airlines and travel agencies as possible before you part with your hard-earned cash. The details given in this chapter should be regarded as pointers and are not a substitute for your own careful, up-to-date research.

It's also worth doing some research on the Internet when looking for your ticket. Many airlines, full-service and no-frills, offer some excellent fares to Web surfers. They may sell seats by auction or simply cut prices to reflect the reduced cost of electronic selling. Many travel agencies around the world have websites, which can make the Internet a quick and easy way to compare prices. Online ticket sales work well if you are doing a simple one-way or return trip on specified dates. However, online super-fast fare generators are certainly no substitute for a travel agent who knows all about special deals, has strategies for avoiding layovers and can offer advice on everything from which airline has the best vegetarian food, to the best travel insurance.

Departure Tax
Departure tax to most countries is Rs 500, but this is almost always included in the cost of your ticket and is not payable at the airport – check with your travel agent.

The UK
The majority of visitors from the UK arrive in Goa on a charter flight – with flight and

accommodation included as a package. See Charter Flights for information.

Various excursion fares are available from London to Mumbai, but you get better prices through London's many cheap ticket specialists. Check the travel page ads in the *Times*, the Sunday papers, *Time Out*, or free travel magazines like *TNT*. A good website to check fares is W www.cheapestflights .co.uk. Reliable London agencies include **Trailfinders** (☎ 020-7938 3939; W *www.trail finders.co.uk; 194 Kensington High St, W8*), **STA Travel** (☎ 0870 160 0599; W *www.sta travel.co.uk; 86 Old Brompton Rd, SW7*), **Flight Centre** (☎ 0870 890 8099; W *www .flightcentre.com*) and **Flightbookers** (☎ *0870 010 7000; W www.ebookers.com*).

London to Mumbai return fares start from around UK£350 in the low season, or UK£550 in the high season; cheaper short-term fares are also available. The cheapest fares are usually with Middle Eastern or Eastern European airlines, with at least one stopover.

Charter Flights You can fly direct to Goa from the UK (usually from Gatwick and Manchester), either on a seat-only charter flight or on a package trip that includes flight and accommodation. Package trips can work out to be great value, but if you want some flexibility and the option to move to a different beach or hotel, a flight-only option is worth considering. Either way, you must return home on a charter flight, not a scheduled flight. Charter flights are not available to Indian nationals and usually depart between Friday and Sunday.

For a direct seat-only flight to Goa, try the **Charter Flight Centre** (☎ *020-7854 8432; W www.charterflights.co.uk*), which sells limited seats online, as well as holiday packages. If you're flexible about dates and are travelling outside the peak season, you can get flights as cheap as UK£99 one way, but most start at UK£299.

Another good agency to check with is **Flightsearchers** (☎ 0800 093 5434; W *www .flightsearchers.co.uk*), which has a database of flights from agencies throughout the UK. Again, with a bit of flexibility you can get some amazing bargains, and they offer last-minute deals.

If you want to visit Goa on a package trip that includes flights and accommodation,

most travel agencies stock the brochures of the main operators, or you can search for deals on the Internet. Packages start at around UK£350 for two weeks, depending on the type of accommodation and location. Over Christmas there's little available for less than UK£900.

Try the following agencies:

Cosmos (☎ 0870 443 1821, W www.cosmos-holidays.co.uk)
Hayes & Jarvis (☎ 0870 898 9890, W www.hayes-jarvis.com)
The Imaginative Traveller (☎ 0800 316 2717, W www.imaginative-traveller.com)
JMC (☎ 0870 758 0203, W www.jmc.com)
Lazydays in Goa (☎ 01202-771 170, W www.lazydays.co.uk)
Manos (☎ 0870 238 7744, W www.manos.co.uk)
Somak Holidays (☎ 020-8423 3000, W www.somak.co.uk)
Sovereign (☎ 0870 366 1634, W www.sovereign.com)
Thomson Holidays/Faraway Shores (☎ 0870 165 0079, W www.thomson-holidays.com)

Continental Europe

Fares from continental Europe are generally more expensive than from London, although there are cheap flights available to Mumbai out of Frankfurt, Amsterdam and Paris, and there are a few charter-flight options direct to Goa. Again, the cheapest fares tend to be with Middle Eastern airlines such as Gulf Air and Emirates, but KLM, Lufthansa and Alitalia have some good deals. Expect to pay from €600 return to Mumbai in the low season, and €1000 return in the high season.

Germany There are charter flights direct from Germany to Goa and there are reasonably cheap Lufthansa flights out of Frankfurt. For scheduled flights to Mumbai, recommended agencies include **STA Travel** (☎ 01805 456 422; W *www.statravel.de*), **Just Travel** (☎ 089-747 3330; W *www.justtravel .de*), **Lastminute** (☎ 01805 284 366; W *www .lastminute.de*) and **Expedia** (☎ *01802 397 3342; W www.expedia.de*). Charter flights are available through **TUI** (☎ *01803-9998 8433; W www.tui.de*). Holiday packages cost from €850 to €1200.

The Netherlands Amsterdam is a good place to buy a cheap ticket. **NBBS Reizen** (☎ *0900 102 0300; W www.nbbs.nl; Rokin 66*) in Amsterdam is the official student travel agency. Other recommended agencies in Holland include **Kilroy Travels** (☎ 020-524 5100; W www.kilroytravels.com) and **Airfair** (☎ 020-620 5121; W www.airfair.nl).

France Recommended agencies in France include **OTU Voyages** (☎ 0820 817 817; W www.otu.fr), **Voyageurs du Monde** (☎ 01 42 86 16 00; W www.vdm.com), **Nouvelles Frontiéres** (☎ 0825 000 747; W www.nou velles-frontieres.fr), **Anyway** (☎ 0892 893 892; W www.anyway.fr) and **Lastminute** (☎ 0892 705 000; W www.lastminute.fr).

Italy & Spain Recommended agencies in Italy include **CTS Viaggi** (☎ 06-462 0431), which specialises in student and youth travel, **Passagi** (☎ 06-474 0923) and **Viaggi Wasteels** (☎ 06-446 6679).

In Spain, recommended agencies include **Barcelo Viajes** (☎ 902 116 226; W www .barceloviajes.com) and **Nouvelles Frontiéres** (☎ 91 547 42 00; W www.nouvelles.frontieres .com).

Scandinavia There are a handful of direct charter flights operating from Finland. The best agency to book through is **Aurinko-matkat Suntours** (☎ 09-1233 233; W www .aurinkomatkat.fi).

In Sweden, **Fritidsresor** (W www.fritidsre sor.se) handles charter flights from Stockholm's Arlanda Airport from around Skr6500.

For scheduled flights to Mumbai, a recommended agency operating throughout Scandinavia is **Kilroy Travels** (W www.kilroy travels.com).

The USA & Canada
Discount travel agencies in the USA are known as consolidators – San Francisco is the ticket consolidator capital of America, although some good deals can be found in Los Angeles, New York and other big cities. The *New York Times*, the *LA Times*, the *Chicago Tribune* and the *San Francisco Examiner* all produce weekly travel sections in which you'll find any number of travel agencies' advertisements.

STA Travel (☎ 800 781 4040; W www.sta travel.com) has offices throughout the USA. **Council Travel** (☎ 800 226 8624; W www .ciee.org) is America's largest student travel

organisation. Some recommended websites for online bookings include:

- W www.atevo.com
- W www.cheaptickets.com
- W www.expedia.com
- W www.lowestfare.com
- W www.orbitz.com

The cheapest return air fares from the US west coast to Mumbai are from around US$1100 to US$1400, and to Chennai from around US$1400 to US$1600. From the US east coast, the most convenient, and shortest, route to India is via Europe – flying to London and getting a cheap fare from there is an option. Return tickets from New York cost around US$1200 to Mumbai.

In Canada, **Travel Cuts** (☎ 800 667 2887; W www.travelcuts.com) is Canada's national student travel agency. For online bookings try W www.expedia.ca and W www.travel ocity.ca. Most flights to India are via Europe but a number of reasonably priced fares are also available from Vancouver via one of the major Asian cities. Low-season return fares from Vancouver to Mumbai start at around C$2250 flying via Hong Kong or Singapore, or C$3000 via Europe. Return fares from Montreal or Toronto are slightly more expensive. Fares to Mumbai in the low season cost from C$2500 to C$3000 with British Airways, via London, or with Lufthansa Airlines, via Frankfurt.

Australia & New Zealand
Most flights to India from Australia and New Zealand go via Southeast Asia, although there are a few via Korea and Japan. The cheapest airlines on this route are usually Malaysian Airlines, Thai Airways, Emirates and Singapore Airlines. Qantas also flies on this route in partnership with other airlines. Standard return fares from the east coast of Australia (Sydney or Melbourne) to Mumbai range from A$1300 to A$2200, depending on the season and availability. Fares are slightly cheaper to Chennai.

It's a similar situation from New Zealand. Return fares from Auckland or Wellington to Mumbai start at around NZ$1850.

Two of the best agencies for cheap fares in Australia are **Flight Centre** (☎ 133 133; W www.flightcentre.com.au) and **STA Travel** (☎ 1300 360 960; W www.statravel.com.au), which both have offices throughout the country. The best website for flights is ⓦ www.travel.com.au.

In New Zealand, again check out **Flight Centre** (☎ 0800 243 544; ⓦ www.flightcentre .co.nz) or **STA Travel** (☎ 0800 874 773; ⓦ www.statravel.co.nz), or the travel website ⓦ www.travel.co.nz.

Southeast Asia

Hong Kong This city has a reputation for being the discount ticket capital of the region, although its bucket shops are no cheaper than Bangkok or Singapore. One-way tickets to Mumbai or Chennai can be picked up from US$560 with Emirates or SriLankan Airlines. A useful agency is **Last Minute** (☎ 0852-2301 3188; ⓦ www.last minute.com.hk) or **STA Travel** (☎ 0852-2736 1618; ⓦ www.statravel.com.hk).

Singapore & Malaysia From Singapore you can pick up one-way tickets to Mumbai or Chennai for about US$450 with Singapore Airlines.

From Kuala Lumpur, Indian Airlines has flights to Chennai from US$550 or to Mumbai from US$650. **STA Travel** has offices in Singapore (☎ 6737 7188; ⓦ www.statravel .com.sg; 33a Cuppage Rd) and Kuala Lumpur (☎ 03-2148 9800; ⓦ www.statravel.com.my; 5th floor Magnum Plaza, 128 Jalan Pudu).

Thailand Bangkok is a popular departure point from Southeast Asia into India and the cheapest place to pick up flights. You can fly to Mumbai or Chennai for as little as US$300 with Thai Airways or Indian Airlines. In Bangkok, **STA Travel** (☎ 02-236 0262; ⓦ www.statravel.co.th; 33/70 Surawong Rd) is a reliable place to start.

Nepal

Royal Nepal Airlines Corporation (RNAC) and Indian Airlines share routes between India and Kathmandu. Flights from Kathmandu are around US$260/520 one way/ return to Mumbai. Both airlines give a 25% discount to travellers under 30 years of age on flights between Kathmandu and India.

Sri Lanka

There are flights to and from Colombo and Mumbai, Chennai or Thiruvananthapuram (Trivandrum). Flights are most frequent on the Chennai–Colombo route (US$140/280

one way/return). Indian Airlines flights to Trivandrum are around US$80/150.

Africa

Due to the large Indian population living in Southern and East Africa there are plenty of flights from here to Mumbai. Typical one way/return fares from Nairobi to Mumbai are about US$350/600 return with Ethiopian Airlines, Kenya Airways or Air India. Try **Flight Centres** (☎ 02-210024; Biashara St) in Nairobi.

Rennies Travel (ⓦ www.renniestravel.com) and **STA Travel** (ⓦ www.statravel.co.za) have offices throughout southern Africa. A one-way/return flight from Cape Town or Johannesburg costs around US$600/750.

Goa

This section gives details of how to get to Goa from other parts of India.

AIR

India's main domestic airlines, **Indian Airlines** (ⓦ www.indian-airlines.nic.in), **Jet Airways** (ⓦ www.jetairways.com) and **Air Sahara** (ⓦ www.airsahara.net) have regular domestic services between Goa and Mumbai, Delhi, Chennai, Kochi (Cochin), Kozhikode (Calicut), Pune and Bangalore. Most airlines have reasonable onward connections to other cities in India from Mumbai or Delhi (see the 'Goa Air Services' table later in this chapter).

Computerised booking systems mean getting flight information and making reservations is relatively simple, but flights into and out of Goa are heavily booked between December and February, so plan as far in advance as possible.

Infants up to two years old travel at 10% of the adult fare, but only one infant per adult can travel at this fare. Children aged two to 12 years old travel at 50% of the adult fare. There is no student reduction for overseas visitors, but there is a youth fare for people aged 12 to 29 years, offering a 25% reduction.

Some useful airlines addresses are:

Chennai

Air Sahara (☎ 044-7110202) Lokesh Towers, 18 Kodambakkam High Rd

Indian Airlines (☎ 044-28553039) 19 Rukmani Lakshmi Pathy Rd, Egmore

Goa Air Services

The following table shows direct flights between Goa and other Indian cities.

flight	flight No	day	departs	arrives	cost (US$)*
Mumbai–Goa					
Indian Airlines	IC663	daily	5.50am	6.45am	95
Indian Airlines	IC163	daily	12.40pm	1.40pm	95
Indian Airlines	IC865	daily	2.40pm	3.40pm	95
Indian Airlines	IC597	Mon, Wed, Fri	1.15pm	2.15pm	95
Air India	AI146/744	Mon, Thur	12.25pm	1.30pm	95
Jet Airways	9W 471	daily	12.30pm	1.30pm	103
Jet Airways	9W 473	daily	2.15pm	3.15pm	103
Jet Airways	9W 475	daily	noon	1pm	103
Jet Airways	9W 479	Mon-Sat	6.30am	7.30am	103
Air Sahara	S2 219	daily	12.10pm	1.10pm	95
Goa–Mumbai					
Indian Airlines	IC866	daily	7.25am	8.20am	95
Indian Airlines	IC164	daily	2.25pm	3.25pm	95
Indian Airlines	IC664	daily	4.20pm	5.20pm	95
Indian Airlines	IC598	Tues, Thur, Sat	7.10pm	10.10pm	95
Air India	AI6729/837	Mon, Thur	2.30pm	3.30pm	95
Jet Airways	9W 472	daily	2.10pm	3.10pm	103
Jet Airways	9W 474	daily	4.15pm	5.15pm	103
Jet Airways	9W 476	daily	1.45pm	2.45pm	103
Jet Airways	9W 480	Mon, Wed–Sat	8.05am	9.05pm	103
Air Sahara	S2 220	daily	1.40pm	2.20pm	95
Delhi–Goa					
Indian Airlines	IC865	daily	noon	3.40pm	245
Air Sahara	S2 117	daily	noon	2.25pm	245
Goa–Delhi					
Indian Airlines	IC866	daily	7.25am	10.55am	245
Air Sahara	S2 118	daily	1.40pm	5.15pm	245

Jet Airways (☎ 044-28414141) 43 Montieth Rd, Egmore.

Mumbai

Air Sahara (☎ 022-22836000, 24-hour toll-free ☎ 1600-115466, e bomcity@airsahara.net) 7 Tulsiani Chambers, Free Press Journal Marg, Nariman Point

Indian Airlines (☎ 022-22023031, 24-hour reservations ☎ 141) Air India Bldg, Nariman Point

Jet Airways (☎ 022-22855788) Amarchand Mansion, Madame Cama Rd

For addresses of airlines in Goa, see Getting There & Away under Panaji in the Central Goa chapter.

BUS

India has a comprehensive and extensive public bus system, but most of the state-run vehicles are tired, decrepit and overcrowded. From neighbouring states you'll find frequent bus services into Goa – it's just a matter of turning up at the bus station and checking timetables or jumping on the next available bus. There are also plenty of private bus companies running into Goa from Mumbai, Pune, Bangalore, Mangalore and other interstate cities. The private buses are marginally more expensive, but are also faster and more comfortable, with reclining seats and the option of air-con or even 'sleeper' class.

Goa Air Services

flight	flight No	day	departs	arrives	cost (US$)*
Pune–Goa					
Indian Airlines	IC917	daily	1.15pm	2.05pm	90
Goa–Pune	No direct flight				
Chennai–Goa					
Indian Airlines	IC575	Mon, Fri	12.55pm	1.55pm	150
Jet Airways	9W 3525	daily	11.30am	2.30pm	180
Goa–Chennai					
Indian Airlines	IC576	Tues, Sat	8.20am	11.35am	150
Bangalore–Goa					
Indian Airlines	IC917	daily	11.15am	12.05pm	115
Jet Airways	9W 3525	daily	1.40pm	3.15pm	115
Goa–Bangalore					
Indian Airlines	IC917	daily	2.25pm	3.40pm	115
Jet Airways	9W 3516	daily	3.40pm	5.10pm	115
Cochin–Goa					
Indian Airlines	IC575	Mon, Fri	2.45pm	3.55pm	135
Goa–Cochin					
Indian Airlines	IC576	Tues, Sat	8.20am	9.30am	135
Kozhikode–Goa					
Indian Airlines	IC598	Tues, Thur, Sat	7.20am	8.25am	115
Goa–Kozhikode					
Indian Airlines	IC597	Mon, Wed, Fri	1.05pm	4.10pm	115

* Tourist or nonresident economy-class fares; business-class fares are about 50% more

Mumbai

Getting to Goa by bus from Mumbai is not the most comfortable or quickest means – riding the rails on the Konkan Railway is far preferable – but it's not too bad, and very economical. The sleeper buses, with bunk beds, are popular. They're not as comfortable as a sleeper on a train and erratic driving means you might wake to find yourself flying out of your bed, but for a long overnight trip it beats sitting up all the way.

Private long-distance buses leave several times daily for Goa from Dr Anadrao Nair Rd, near Mumbai Central train station. Fares for nonair-con deluxe buses to Panaji are Rs 250 (14 to 18 hours depending on city traffic). Sleeper buses cost Rs 350 to 450. Fares are as much as 50% higher during the peak Christmas–New Year period. To check on departure times and current prices, try **National Travels** (☎ 022-230 15652; Dr Anadrao Nair Rd).

If you're staying in South Mumbai, a more convenient departure point for private buses to Goa is from MG Rd, just south of the Metro cinema (near Fashion St). It's best to purchase tickets directly from bus agents with pavement stalls clustered in either of these areas or contact **Ganesh Travels** (☎ 022-22674589; 35 Mint Rd, Fort).

Karnataka & Chennai

There are regular bus services into Goa from the neighbouring state of Karnataka, especially from Bangalore (Rs 360, 14 hours), Mysore (Rs 225, 17 hours), Hampi (Rs 350, 10 hours) and Mangalore (Rs 180, 11 hours). Private buses also have regular services on these routes – see Panaji and Margao later in this book for more information on interstate buses from Goa.

Taking the bus to or from Chennai is not really a viable option. There's one private bus a week from Goa to Chennai (Rs 700, 22 hours). The easiest option is to take the train or bus from Chennai to Bangalore and then a bus from here. Private bus companies in Chennai, with offices opposite Egmore station, run superdeluxe video buses daily to Bangalore (Rs 146, eight hours).

TRAIN

Two railway systems cross the state. The South Central Railway has its terminus in Mormugao (past Vasco da Gama) and runs due east, through Margao (Madgaon) and into Karnataka. The Konkan Railway, opened in 1998, runs from Mumbai to Mangalore through Goa, with some trains continuing south to Ernakulam and Trivandrum. The main stations in Goa include Pernem, for Arambol (Harmal); Thivim (Mapusa Road) station, for Anjuna, Baga and Calangute; Karmali (Old Goa) station, for Old Goa and Panaji; Margao, for Colva and Benaulim; and Canacona, for Palolem.

If coming from Mumbai or Mangalore you can book your ticket to these intermediate stations, but even if you book through to Margao you can get off at any station en route.

If you intend to do any serious train travel outside Goa, get hold of *Trains at a Glance* (Rs 25) from a bookstall in any major train station. It's a comprehensive book in English of timetables listing every major train service in India. As well as enabling you to find the right train for your journey, it gives the distance of the trip (enabling you to calculate the fare for the class you wish to travel) and the train number, which is useful for filling out reservation forms. You can also look up timetables, fares and make reservations on the Indian Railways website at ⓦ www.indian railways .com.

Most stations have a left-luggage facility. Backpacks can be left for Rs 2 to 5 per day.

Train Types & Classes

There are seven classes on mail and express trains, but not all trains have all classes. The most basic is 2nd-class seating, which has hard seats and is a free-for-all where five or six people will cram onto a bench seat made for three. Then comes 2nd-class sleeper (or sleeper class) which has open carriages where the seats are padded and fold down at night to form three tiers of beds. Air-con sleepers are more comfortable and secure as each carriage has compartments and you get bedding (sheets, blanket, pillow) on some classes. The most common are three-tier (six beds in a compartment) and two-tier (four beds). Two-tier air-con is about twice the price of three-tier air-con and 1st class (two beds) is about double that again. Sleeping berths are only available between 9pm and 6am.

Finally there's chair car, which comprises individual reclining seats on certain air-con trains (such as the *Shatabdi Express*), and 1st class, which is a more comfortable version of chair car.

Reservations

Reservation charges are from Rs 15 to 35 depending on the class. The easiest way to reserve a ticket is to stay well away from the station and do it over the Internet. **Indian Railways** (ⓦ *www.indianrailways.com*) has online reservations where you can check seat availability on the train you want, book a ticket, pay for it by credit card and either have it delivered or arrange to pick it up from a station collection centre. You first need to register on the site, then fill out an online form similar to the normal reservation forms.

At most major city stations there's a separate section or counter(s) in the booking hall that deals with the tourist quota. Only foreigners and nonresident Indians are allowed to use this facility. Here you can make your reservations in relative comfort away from the crowds, but you must pay in foreign currency (cash or travellers cheques in US dollars or pounds sterling only) or with rupees backed up by exchange certificates or ATM receipts. Only a limited number of seats are allocated to the tourist quota, so if you can't get on there it's also worth trying for a normal reservation. When booking any ticket at a train station you must fill out a reservation form *before* queuing up.

If the train you want is fully booked, it's often possible to get a Reservation Against Cancellation (RAC) ticket. This entitles you to board the train and have seating accommodation. Once the train is moving, the Travelling Ticket Examiner (TTE) will find a berth for you. This is different from a wait-listed ticket, as the latter does not give you the right to actually board the train.

Costs

Fares are calculated by distance and are fixed regardless of what train you are on and where you are travelling. The only exceptions are the high-speed *Shatabdi Express* and *Rajdhani Express* which have their own set of fares for each route. For other mail and express trains the timetables indicate the distance in kilometres between the stations and from this it is simple to calculate the cost between any two stations using the fare table published in *Trains at a Glance*. Sample fares for a journey of 100km in the various classes are:

2nd-class seat	Rs 35
2nd-class sleeper	Rs 56
chair car	Rs 122
three-tier air-con	Rs 158
two-tier air-con	Rs 322
1st-class air-con	Rs 542

Refunds Booked tickets are refundable but cancellation fees apply. If you present the ticket more than one day in advance, a fee of Rs 10 to 50 applies, depending on the class. Up to four hours before departure you lose 25% of the ticket value; within four hours before and up to three to 12 hours after departure (depending on the distance of the ticketed journey) you lose 50%.

From Mumbai

Mumbai is 588km by rail from Goa (Margao) – a journey of about 12 hours. From Mumbai's Chhatrapati Shivaji Terminus (CST; formerly Victoria Terminus) there's currently one fast day train and one overnight service between Mumbai and Goa. Note that on train timetables Margao is *always* referred to as Madgaon. The 0103 *Mandavi Express* departs daily at 7.05am, reaching Margao at 6.25pm the same day. The 0111 *Konkankanya Express* leaves daily at 10.50pm, arriving in Margao at 10.45am

the following morning. Fares to Margao on either train are Rs 130 for a 2nd-class seat, Rs 208 for a 2nd-class sleeper, Rs 584 for three-tier air-con; Rs 934 for two-tier air-con; and Rs 1815 for a 1st-class sleeper. Going to Mumbai, these trains depart from Margao at 10.30am and 6pm respectively.

The **reservation centre** *(open 8am-8pm Mon-Sat, 8am-2pm Sun)* is at the back of CST station where the taxis gather. Tourist-quota tickets are available at Counter 52 on the 1st floor *(open 8am to 3pm Mon-Sat, 8am-2pm Sun)* but can only be bought 24 hours before the date of travel. You can buy tickets (but not tourist-quota tickets) with a Visa or MasterCard at the credit card counters (10 and 11) up to 60 days in advance.

Another three day trains depart from Lokmanya Tilak station, 16km south of Mumbai CST. The best option – and, at the time of research, the fastest train to Goa – is the 2051 *Jan Shatabdi Express* which departs Mumbai at 5.35am and gets in to Margao at 1.30pm (Rs 272/800 in 2nd class/air-con chair car). The 6345 *Netravati Express* departs at 11.45am and arrives at 10.30pm, and the 2619 *Matsyagandha Express* departs at 2.20pm, arriving at 12.20am.

A planned 'bullet train' – expected to be the fastest train in India – should be operating on the Konkan Railway between Mumbai (Roha) and Goa by the time you read this. The *Swarna Shatabdi Express (Golden Century)* will travel at 150km/h and will cover the journey in about four hours.

From Chennai & Bangalore

A direct Chennai–Vasco da Gama train, the *Chennai–Vasco Express*, started in June 2003. Initially it will run only once a week, departing from Chennai on Sunday at 12.45pm and from Vasco da Gama on Saturday at 2.40pm. The trip goes via Margao in Goa and Hubli and Hospet in Karnataka (941km, Rs 288/810 in sleeper/three-tier air-con, 21 hours).

Other ways to reach Goa by train would be to take the 2007 *Shatabdi Express* leaving at 6am from Central Station (Rs 530/1075 in air-con chair class/1st class) for the 361km journey to Bangalore (five hours). There are another six daily services from Chennai to Bangalore which take six to seven hours but are cheaper, including the 2639 *Brindavan Express* departing at

7.15am (Rs 89/311 in 2nd class/chair car). From Bangalore to Goa you can take the afternoon *Intercity Express* to Hubli (7½ hours) and change there for Margao, or take the *Chennamma Express* to Londa and change here.

An alternative from Chennai is to catch the 7pm *Chennai–Mangalore Mail* to Mangalore (18 hours), then the 2.50pm *Matsyaghanda Express* (16 hours) to Margao.

In Chennai you can make train reservations on the 1st floor of the **Train Reservation Complex** *(open 8am-2pm & 2.15pm-8pm Mon-Sat, 8am-2pm Sun)*, which is next to Central Station.

Mangalore & the South

Getting from Mangalore or further south (from Kerala) to Goa is easy as the line runs up the coast. From Trivandrum in Kerala to Margao catch the 6346 *Netravati Express* departing at 1.30pm (Rs 290/816 in sleeper/three-tier air-con, 19 hours) or the 2431 *Rajdhani Express* at 7.15pm (Rs 940/1320, 11 hours). Both trains stop at Kankanadi, 5km from Mangalore.

There are seven daily trains from Kankanadi to Madgaon (Rs 127/356, six hours, 312km).

CAR & MOTORCYCLE

Renting a self-drive car in any of the main cities in India and driving to Goa is possible but not recommended. India holds the unenviable record of having the most dangerous roads in the world. **Hertz** (W *www.hertz.com)* has offices in Mumbai *(☎ 022-26910908)*, Chennai *(☎ 044-7126908)* and several other Indian cities. Rental is from around Rs 1000 per day, drivers must be 25 years old or over, and a deposit of Rs 5000 is required.

Sai Service (W *www.saiservice.com)* is a reliable company which rents out self-drive cars and chauffeur-driven cars. It has offices in Mumbai *(☎ 022-26396274)* and Panaji in Goa *(☎ 2417063, Dabolim Airport ☎ 257 4817)*, but the self-drive option is only available in Goa. A self-drive nonair-con Maruti car costs from Rs 900 for 24 hours with 150km per day, or Rs 6300 a week with unlimited mileage.

If you want to travel into Goa by car it's easy to hire a car and driver. Car-hire companies offer chauffeur-driven services, or you can simply make your way to the nearest taxi rank and start bargaining. The 600km trip from Mumbai to Goa takes about 14 hours; many drivers will happily do this in one stretch, although you can easily break it over two days, perhaps stopping overnight on the beach at Ganpatipule. You'll have to pay for the taxi's return trip, so the cost will be at least Rs 7000 – almost twice the cost of a one-way flight from Mumbai to Goa. Shop around for the taxi that offers you the lowest rate per kilometre. As a guide, Sai Service charges Rs 8 per kilometre plus Rs 150 chauffeur allowance, but the Maruti vehicles they use are considerably more comfortable than your average Mumbai Premier taxi!

Getting Around

BUS

The Kadamba Transport Corporation (KTC) is the state government bus service. It's over-worked and underfunded, with most of the buses in a poor state of repair, but it manages to provide cheap, regular services to most parts of the state. There are also a number of private operators that run parallel services.

With only short distances to cover and the relaxed approach of the local people, bus travel in Goa is a cheap and enjoyable way to get around. Unless you're in a hurry or have a lot of luggage, the bus costs a fraction of a taxi fare, and you will probably meet a few friendly people along the way. If you're travelling between major centres, eg, Panaji (Panjim) to Margao (Madgaon) or Panaji to Mapusa, take an express service. For a few extra rupees you are guaranteed a seat and you won't stop at every other house en route.

For travel between the northern beaches and southern beaches you'll generally have to change buses at one or more of the major centres – for instance, if you're going from Anjuna to Palolem, you'll have to catch a bus to Mapusa or Panaji, another to Margao and a third to Palolem.

At the bus stands in Panaji, Margao, Mapusa and Vasco da Gama, all destinations are written in English, so there's little problem in finding the bus you need. In addition, at all bus stands around the state the conductors stand beside their vehicles shouting out the destination and encouraging passengers to get on.

TRAIN

Goa has two railways. The South Central Railway has its terminus in Mormugao (past Vasco da Gama) and runs due east, through Margao and into Karnataka. This line is often used by tourists who want to day-trip to the Dudhsagar Falls in the east of the state, as well as by travellers heading towards Hampi in Karnataka (the nearest station is at Hospet).

The Konkan Railway runs from Mumbai (Bombay) to Mangalore (in Karnataka) through Goa. It's unlikely that you'll use the train much for travel within Goa but it may be useful if you're planning to travel from one end of the state to the other, ie, Arambol

(Harmal) to Palolem, which would otherwise require at least three changes by bus. In the north the stations of Pernem and Thivim (Mapusa Road) are not particularly convenient for the beaches, but in the south, Canacona station is only 3km from Palolem beach.

Konkan Railway stations in Goa, from north to south, are: Pernem (for Arambol), Thivim (for Mapusa), Karmali (for Old Goa and Panaji), Verna, Margao (for Colva and Benaulim), Bali, Barcem and Canacona (for Palolem).

CAR & MOTORCYCLE

Getting around Goa by motorcycle is almost *de rigueur*, especially around the northern beaches where packs of travellers are looking for some action. You only need to look at the sea of motorcycles parked behind the Wednesday Anjuna Flea Market, or standing along the lane outside Vagator's Primrose Cafe or Nine Bar, to realise that it borders on a cliche. If you plan to spend most of your time lying on the beach you may have little use for a motorcycle, but if you want to move around a bit, follow the parties, check out the scenes and restaurants at different beaches or head inland for the day, you'll soon find it's a hassle without your own transport. The freedom that a motorcycle affords is hard to beat. See the boxed text 'Hiring a Motor-cycle' later in this chapter for details.

Few visitors to Goa bother to a rent self-drive car. Given the crazy driving conditions, and the fact that you're likely to spend a large amount of time on the beach anyway, it's easier to hire a car and driver when required. What's more, hiring a car with a driver for a day is actually cheaper than hiring a self-drive vehicle.

Road Conditions & Safety

Because of the extreme congestion in towns and the narrow, bumpy roads in the country, driving is often a slow, stop-start process. The only genuine highways are the NH17 running north–south and passing through Margao, Panaji and Mapusa; and the NH4A which heads east from Panaji into Karnataka, bypassing close to Ponda.

The country roads away from these high-ways are much more pleasant for motoring,

The Helmet Issue

Life-saving accessories are clearly not a high priority among Goa's motorcycle riders. Helmets are officially compulsory but the law is – or at least has been – universally ignored in Goa and few riders bother to wear one. In 2003 the government renewed its push to legislate for the wearing of helmets for riders and pillion passengers, and for police to enforce the law with fines.

But motorcycle pilots and members of the Motorcycle Action Group (MAG) have strongly opposed this law, arguing that helmets should remain optional. Riders are concerned at the inconvenience of having to carry a helmet everywhere, plus a spare helmet for a passenger. One reported complaint was that a helmet would mess up the hair of women riders or passengers! If the law is enforced, motorcycle pilots should carry a spare helmet, and you'll need to ask for a helmet if renting a bike.

as there's very little heavy traffic (mostly motorcycles, cyclists, a few buses and tourist vehicles) and the countryside is scenic. Most main roads are in reasonable condition but are generally not well signposted – it's very easy to get lost if you don't continue to ask directions.

Of course, road safety is an important issue when you're out on a motorcycle. India has the worst record for road accidents in the world, and almost one person a day dies in a road accident in Goa alone. Inexperienced, helmetless foreigners on motorcycles are extremely vulnerable. Each season more than a few tourists travel home in a box via the state mortuary in Panaji.

Road Rules & Permits

Road rules in India are applied mainly in theory. Driving is on the left, vehicles give way to the right at uncontrolled intersections, and road signs are universal pictorial signs. At busy intersections in towns, traffic police are often on hand to reduce the chaos. Otherwise, make good use of your horn.

Never forget that the highway code in India can be reduced to one essential truth – 'Might is Right.' On a motorcycle you're pretty low in the rights hierarchy. Goan dri-vers often try unexpected moves, and Goan pigs have an unnerving habit of dashing onto the road without warning. Avoid riding at night – road surfaces in some places are very bad and many roads are unlit.

An international driving permit is technically not mandatory, but it's wise to bring one. The first thing a policeman will want to see if he stops you is your licence, and an international permit is incontrovertible. Permits are available from your home automobile association.

Fuel

Petrol is expensive compared to the cost of living in India – around Rs 29 per litre at the pump (diesel is much cheaper, costing around Rs 10 per litre). But distances are short and the small bikes in particular are very economical, so you won't spend a lot of money on fuel. There are petrol stations in all the main towns such as Panaji, Margao, Mapusa, Ponda and Vasco da Gama, including a 24-hour service station in Margao and another on the highway near Cuncolim. In villages, roadside shops often sell petrol (in varying states of dilution) in plastic mineral water bottles for around Rs 35 a litre – just ask around if you're running low.

While it's usually possible to find someone selling petrol, if you're heading for a day ride into the interior or even along the coast, make sure you have adequate fuel to begin with. Since many rental motorcycles (especially the Honda Kinetics) have broken gauges, you can't always rely on the needle to tell you when they're almost empty.

A Honda Kinetic holds 7L of fuel, and should go 40km on 1L. A 100cc Yamaha takes 10L to 11L and also does 40km per litre. Enfields hold about 18L; new models will do about 35km per litre, while older ones do considerably less.

Renting a Car

Finding a car and driver for hire is certainly not going to be a problem in the main towns or beach resorts – touts and drivers will invariably approach you. If you'd prefer to rent through a business, head to any travel agency. The typical cost for a day of sightseeing in a chauffeur-driven car, depending on the distance, is Rs 600 to 800. An air-con vehicle will cost more.

ROAD DISTANCE CHART (km)

	Bicholim	Calangute	Hampi	Mapusa	Margao	Molem	Old Goa	Palolem	Panaji	Pernem	Ponda	Vasco da Gama
Bicholim	---											
Calangute	35	---										
Hampi	390	396	---									
Mapusa	25	10	392	---								
Margao	53	50	370	46	---							
Molem	70	76	320	72	50	---						
Old Goa	23	26	370	22	37	50	---					
Palolem	93	90	403	86	40	83	75	---				
Panaji	19	16	380	12	34	60	10	74	---			
Pernem	43	28	410	18	64	90	40	104	30	---		
Ponda	38	43	350	39	25	30	19	53	29	47	---	
Vasco da Gama	49	46	390	42	30	70	35	70	30	60	34	---

If you do decide to choose the self-drive option, the main rental company is **Sai Service** (☎ 2417063; Dabolim Airport ☎ 257 4817; W www.saiservice.com), which has an office at Alto Porvorim. A nonair-con Maruti car costs from Rs 900 for 24 hours with 150km per day, or Rs 6300 per week with unlimited mileage. Sai Service also rents the same car with a driver for an eight-hour day for around Rs 700.

Almost any local taxi will quite happily set off on a long-distance trip and, after a little friendly bargaining, the costs are quite reasonable. Inquiring at a taxi rank is the easiest way to find a car, although the state-run Goa Tourism Development Corporation (GTDC or Goa Tourism) and several private agencies can also provide cars with drivers (the starting rate is Rs 8 per kilometre). Alternatively, you can ask your hotel to book a car for you.

Buying & Selling a Motorcycle

Buying (and later selling) a motorcycle during a stay in Goa is not really practical, economical or necessary – unless you are planning to do some extensive further motorcycle touring around India. Even if you're going to be in Goa for, say, three months, you can hire a scooter for as little as Rs 80 a day and a bigger bike for Rs 150 a day (these rates are based on a long hire period starting early in the tourist season when there are plenty of idle bikes around) and you can take it back to the hirer if something goes wrong.

If you do plan to buy a bike, there are plenty of second-hand machines around – check advertisements in the daily papers or simply ask around at mechanic shops or with people who rent out bikes. You can pick up a decent scooter for Rs 20,000 and an Enfield for Rs 40,000.

Organised Motorcycle Tours

Peter & Friends Classic Bike Adventure (☎ 2254467; W www.classic-bike-india.de; Casa Tres Amigos, Socol Vado No 425, Assagao) is an established German company that organises bike tours on Enfields with full insurance and support. Tours last two to three weeks and cover the Himalaya (near Manali); Nepal; or South India and Goa.

There are also day excursions around Goa and trips of several days to Hampi in Karnataka. The two-week Tropical South India Tour costs €1090 (around Rs 56,600), including accommodation and meals. The company has its own accommodation called Classic Bike Adventure Country Club, at its headquarters in Goa.

For dates, prices and more information on the tours, check the website (in English and German).

Hiring a Motorcycle

Hiring a motorcycle in Goa is easier than you might think – the hirers will probably find you! A private bike owner is technically not allowed to rent out a machine, and consequently you may be told that if the police stop you, you should say that the bike belongs to your friend and that you have borrowed it. This law is universally ignored in Goa and the police won't bother with the origins of the bike provided it has the correct registration papers and you have a valid licence. However, if you leave the state you may need to produce the original documents to the vehicle you are driving or riding. If you want to go further afield than Goa, therefore, you need a licensed rental agency to stay within the law.

Which Bike?

At the bottom end of the scale are the most popular rental bikes – gearless scooters like the 100cc Honda Kinetics or Bajaj scooters. They have absolutely *no* pose value, but are extremely practical and easy to ride which makes them the obvious choice if you don't have a lot of motorcycle-riding experience. You only need a car driving licence to ride these bikes.

Next up the scale are the 100/135cc bikes – Yamaha is the most common. Again fuel economy is good, they go faster than a Kinetic, and they tend to be a bit more comfortable over a long distance. Although they're easy to ride, you'll need to have had some experience on a motorcycle.

Finally, at the top of the pile are the real bikes – classic Enfield Bullets. Made in India since the 1950s, this old British-designed machine oozes street cred, and the thumping sound of the engine reverberates around the hills of Anjuna and Vagator in the high season. They are far less fuel friendly, require more maintenance than the others and take a little getting used to. Most of the Enfields available for hire are 350cc, but there are also some 500cc models around.

Costs & Where to Hire

Like everything in Goa, rental costs depend on the season as well as supply and demand. Outside the high season (December–February), when there's a glut of bikes around, you can hire a Honda Kinetic for Rs 100 a day for rental of a week or more. Yamahas cost around Rs 200 and Enfields cost Rs 300. Bargain with the bike owners – most are desperate to unload their machines for the season and secure an income.

In the high season – especially mid-December to mid-January – you'll pay top rupee, especially for short-term hire. Expect to pay Rs 300 a day for a scooter, Rs 400 for a 100cc bike and up to Rs 600 for an Enfield. The age and condition of the bike will also be a factor in the cost. Make absolutely sure

BICYCLE

Whether riding around the beach resorts, exploring the back lanes of Goa's coastal villages, or embarking on a more ambitious multiday ride into the interior, Goa is small enough to make getting around by bike a viable and enjoyable option.

Goa offers plenty of variety for a bicycle tourist, with relatively smooth-surfaced highways, rocky dirt tracks, coastal routes through coconut palms and winding country roads through spice plantations, rural villages and ancient temples.

Mountain bikes are especially suited to riding in India, but if you want a quality machine for serious bike touring, it's worth bringing your own. The downside is that your bike is likely to be a real curiosity and

subject to much pushing, pulling, probing and possibly theft. Bring spare tyres, tubes, patch kits, chassis, cables, freewheels, a pump with the necessary connection and spokes, tools and a repair manual.

Hiring a Bicycle

Hiring a bicycle is not difficult in Goa, but hiring a *good* bicycle is not so easy. India is a country of bicycles, but in Goa anyone with a moderate income owns a motorcycle of some sort and everyone else rides the typical Indian-made single-gear rattler. Every beach in Goa has a multitude of people who are prepared to rent out bicycles – just ask around and someone will rent you *their* bicycle. Panaji and Margao have bicycle-hire shops and at Calangute, Colva and Palolem

Hiring a Motorcycle

that you agree with the owner about the price; one ploy to extract extra cash from the unwitting tourist is to claim that the hire rate includes days only – since the bike was kept overnight that will be 'extra'.

There are no 'rental shops' in Goa as such. You simply rent the bike off the street at beach resorts, through your hotel, or through a tout who will no doubt approach you within minutes of your arrival. In Panaji, head to the cluster of bikes opposite the post office. In Calangute, ask around at the market area or near the steps to the beach. In Margao, try anywhere around the Municipal Gardens where taxis hang out. In Colva, Arambol or Palolem, head down to the main entrance to the beach and ask there.

Many travel agencies and tourist-oriented businesses also advertise motorcycles for rent. Ask if the bike owner or renter has a phone contact (they often have a mobile phone) so that you can call them if something goes wrong with the bike. You'll probably be asked to pay cash upfront, but get a written receipt and don't leave your passport or licence as security.

Peter & Friends Classic Bike Adventures (☎ 2254467; W www.classic-bike-india.de) rents well-maintained Royal Enfield 500cc Bullets with insurance for Rs 7900 a week in the peak season.

What to Look For
It makes sense to check the bike over before you hire it and make a note of any damage or broken part so that you're not blamed for it later. Make sure that the brakes work and that all the other parts, such as lights and horn, are fine too. Mirrors are very useful, but many older rental bikes are missing them. Also take a look at the condition of the tyres.

Getting Stopped by the Police
The travellers' grapevine is littered with tales of tourists being stopped by the police; 'no licence', 'no helmet' or 'dangerous driving' can all be reason enough for the police to demand on-the-spot payment of a 'fine' – baksheesh by any other name. The simplest answer is to keep away from areas where you are likely to bump into the police – avoid the national highways and the Zuari and Mandovi Bridges where there are often police checkpoints. Many people get away without any hassle, however, so there's no point in worrying too much about it. In recent years Goan police have been pulled into line and extortion of foreigners is on the decline. During our research trip the only run-in we had with police was when two young cops flagged us down at 3am on the back road between Baga and Anjuna – they merely wanted a lift to Anjuna police station! Make sure that you have correct documentation, such as an international driving permit.

---

you can rent India's answer to the mountain bike – a sturdy framed Raleigh or similar model which may or may not have gears. Away from the main tourist areas, however, you won't find any bicycle-hire places since bike rental is not in high demand.

Expect to pay around Rs 5 an hour or Rs 40 per day (less for rentals of a week or more). If you just want to hire a bike for a day in the high season you may have to pay up to Rs 80.

Purchase
For a long stay of three months or more in Goa, it's worth considering buying a bicycle locally. Finding an Indian bicycle is no problem: every town will have at least a couple of shops selling various brands of basic Indian bikes including Hero, Atlas, BSA and Raleigh, almost all painted jet black. You should be able to pick up a second-hand bike for Rs 1000 to 1500.

HITCHING
Hitching is never entirely safe in any country in the world, and we don't recommend it. Travellers who decide to hitch should understand that they are taking a small but potentially serious risk.

Besides the possible dangers, hitching isn't a particularly realistic option in Goa. Regional traffic on Goa's main roads comprises a large percentage of either motorcycles or tourist vehicles (hire cars, taxis etc) which are unlikely to pick you up. Locals occasionally try to flag down passing motorcycles for a short ride, so there's no reason why you can't, but don't count on it. The main highway running north–south through Goa carries a fair bit of traffic, including trucks, so it's possible to try hitching a lift there.

It's not a good idea for a woman on her own to hitch. India, unlike the West, provides little sympathy to rape – although Goa is particularly progressive in this regard. A woman in the cabin of a truck on a lonely road has, needless to say, only her own strength and resources to call upon should she be threatened.

BOAT

One of the joys of travelling around Goa is joining locals on flat-bottomed passenger/vehicle ferries that cross the state's many rivers. These ferries have been carrying people from mainland to islands and from village to town for decades, but some services have been put out of business by massive bridge-building projects (the most recent being the Siolim–Chopdem bridge) and more bridges are planned for the future. In some cases the ferry is merely a shortcut rather than an essential service – a road will usually get you to your intended destination eventually.

Most of the remaining ferries operate a half-hourly service from early morning until late evening. Foot passengers ride for free, motorcycles cost Rs 4. The main ferries of interest to travellers are: Panaji–Betim for the back road to Candolim and Calangute; Querim–Terekhol for Terekhol Fort; Old Goa–Divar Island; Ribandar–Chorao Island for Dr Salim Ali Bird Sanctuary and Chorao Island; and Cavelossim–Assolna, for the coastal ride from Benaulim to Palolem.

LOCAL TRANSPORT
Taxi

Although taxis are supposed to charge metered rates, the simple fact is that no taxi or autorickshaw in Goa uses its meter and many 'taxis' are simply vans or cars that don't have a meter anyway. Always agree on the fare beforehand, otherwise you can expect enormous arguments and hassles when you get to your destination. And agree on the fare clearly – if there is more than one of you make sure it covers all of you (ie, the fare is for the taxi, not per person).

The 'official' fare as printed on the taxi windscreen is Rs 8 per kilometre. Fares at the prepaid taxi stand at the airport are Rs 12 per kilometre, but for most trips you should be able to negotiate slightly cheaper rates than this. If a driver insists on an extortionate rate simply walk away – if he really wants the job the price will drop. If you can't agree on a reasonable fare, find another driver.

If you have luggage make sure there are no extra charges, or you may be asked for more at the end of the trip.

Autorickshaw

An autorickshaw is a yellow-and-black three-wheeled contraption powered by a noisy two-stroke motorcycle engine. It has a canopy, a driver up front and seats for two (or sometimes more) passengers behind. This typically Indian mode of transport is cheaper than a taxi and generally a better option for short trips – count on Rs 20 to 30 for a trip across Panaji. Even for a trip such as Anjuna Flea Market to Panaji (costing around Rs 70) it's a viable ride. Because of their size and manoeuvrability, they're quicker than a taxi for trips around town but their drivers are certifiably nuttier – hair-raising near misses are guaranteed and minor collisions are not infrequent!

Motorcycle Taxi

Goa is the only state in India where motorcycles are a licensed form of taxi. You can tell the motorcycle taxis (or pilots as they are sometimes called) by the yellow front mudguard and they gather, along with taxis and autorickshaws, at strategic points in towns and at beach resorts. If you're solo they're a fast, efficient and cheap method of getting around. The minimum charge is around Rs 10; a 10-minute journey will be about Rs 40. The great advantage, apart from price, is that motorcycle taxis can get straight through crowded traffic and, of course, it's a fun way to travel. The downside is that there's an increased element of danger – motorcycle pilots may be experienced riders but that doesn't stop them coming off or colliding with other vehicles and you've got little or no protection in the event of a crash.

ORGANISED TOURS

Tours of Goa are offered by private companies as well as by the GTDC. Book GTDC tours at the head office in Panaji (☎ 2224132, fax 2423926; W www.goa-tourism.com; Trionora Apartments, Dr Alvares Costa Rd), or at any of the GTDC hotels in Panaji, Margao, Calangute, Colva, Mapusa, Vasco da Gama, Mayem, Old Goa and Ponda.

GTDC's one-day tours are quite comprehensive, but they pack too much in, which means you spend a lot of time staring out of a bus window and end up seeing very little of the sights. They're really only good value if you're in a very big hurry, or if you're travelling solo and can't share the cost of a taxi with a group.

The **North Goa Tour** (with/without aircon Rs 150/120; 9.30am-6pm) starts in Panaji and visits Mapusa, Shri Pandurang Temple, Mayem Lake (lunch stop), Vagator, Anjuna, Calangute and Fort Aguada. There are two variations of this tour with one departing from Margao or Colva, the other from Calangute or Mapusa. The **South Goa Tour** (with/without air-con Rs 150/120; 9.30am-6pm) from Panaji takes in Miramar, Dona Paula, Old Goa, Shantadurga Temple, Manguesh Temple, Mormugao, Colva (lunch stop), Margao and Ancestral Goa at Loutolim. A similar tour departs from Mapusa or Calangute (8.30am to 8pm) and ends with an optional river cruise on the Mandovi. A slight variation is the **Traditional Tour** (Rs 120; 9.30am-8pm), which covers similar ground but starts in Colva or Margao with a lunch stop at Old Goa, and ends with an optional river cruise.

Other GTDC tours include the **Dudhsagar Special** (with/without air-con Rs 600/500; 9am-6pm), visiting Old Goa, Ponda, Dudhsagar Falls, lunch at Molem, and Tambdi Surla Mahadeva Temple; **Goa By Night** (Rs 140; 6.30pm-9.30pm), which includes a river cruise and an evening tour of Panaji's sights; **Pernem Tour** (Rs 120; 9.30am-6pm), which covers temples in the northern talukas, Arambol, Asvem and Morjim beaches; and the **South End Tour** (Rs 130; 9.30am-6pm) from Margao, visiting Chandor, Damodar Temple, Selaulim Dam and Palolem. There are also three- to five-night package tours which include accommodation (and meals if requested) from Rs 1250 to 3500 per person.

One of the best of the private tour operators is **Day Tripper Tours & Travel** (☎ 227-6726; W www.daytrippergoa.com) based in Calangute. It has a range of day and overnight tours within Goa, as well as interstate trips to Hampi, Ashy National Park in Karnataka, Mumbai, and even to the Taj Mahal. Short trips include dolphin-spotting cruises (Rs 330), full-day backwater cruises (Rs 1000), historical tours of Old Goa and the Hindu temples (Rs 730), Dudhsagar Falls (Rs 1020), and a day trip to Palolem (Rs 365). There's also a half-day guided bird-watching trip (Rs 875) and an overnight trip to Palolem (Rs 1460).

Southern Birdwing (☎ 2402957; W www.southernbirdwing.com) in Nerul runs wildlife and ecotours including crocodile-spotting on the Cumbrous Canal and bird-watching trips to Bondla and the Carambolim wetlands.

Ola Jeep Tours (☎ 2271249) has recommended trips in a 10-seater jeep to Dudhsagar Falls (Rs 950) and Ponda's temples and spice plantations (Rs 800).

Gateway Cities

On any scheduled flight to Goa, you'll first fly into a major international airport then either take a domestic connecting flight to Goa, or make your own way there. Mumbai (Bombay) is the closest and most logical entry point, but Chennai (Madras) is also an option. If you have the time, a few days spent exploring either of these fast-paced Indian metropolises – and experiencing a sharp contrast with Goa – should definitely be on your agenda.

Mumbai (Bombay)

☎ 022 • pop 16.4 million

Mumbai is the usual Indian gateway city for Goa. It's about 600km south to Goa, and road and rail transport is excellent – see the Getting There & Away chapter for details.

It may come as a surprise to find that Mumbai is an easy city to enjoy, and the longer you spend here, the better it gets. This is India's modern finance centre, the economic powerhouse of the nation, heart of the Hindi film industry, one of India's biggest software producers and the industrial hub of everything from textiles to petrochemicals. But it's also a magnet for the rural poor and it's these new migrants who continually reshape the city in their own image, making sure Mumbai keeps one foot in its hinterland and the other in the global marketplace.

Mumbai can be an exciting place, with vital street life, India's best nightlife, more bazaars than you could ever explore and the capacity to draw you in like no other Indian metropolis.

Orientation & Information

Mumbai is an island connected by bridges to the mainland. The principal part of the city is concentrated at the southern claw-shaped end of the island known as South Mumbai. The southernmost peninsula is Colaba, traditionally the travellers' nerve centre, and directly north of Colaba is the busy commercial area known as the Fort, where the old British fort once stood.

Tourist Offices The busy, but rather efficient, **Government of India tourist office**

(☎ 22207433; 123 Maharshi Karve Rd; oper 8.30am-6pm Mon-Fri, 8.30am-2pm Sat) is opposite Churchgate train station. It also has a **24-hour booth** (☎ 28325331) at the international airport (Arrival Hall 2A) and a **counter** (☎ 26156920) at the domestic airport.

Money The best place to exchange cash and travellers cheques is **American Express** (AmEx; ☎ 22048291; Shivaji Marg; oper 9.30am-6.30pm Mon-Fri, 9.30am-2.30pm Sat, in Colaba. **Thomas Cook** (☎ 22048556; 324 Dr D Naoroji Rd, Fort; open 9.30am-6pm Mon-Fri, 9.30am-5pm Sat) also provides swift foreign exchange.

There are **ATMs** on Colaba Causeway (Centurion and ICICI banks); Citibank has ATMs at its branches at 293 Dr D Naoroji Rd, Fort, and at Nariman Point in the Air India Building. HSBC has a handy ATM a Chhatrapati Shivaji Terminus (CST; formerly Victoria Terminus), just outside the reservation hall.

Post & Communications The main post office (☎ 22621671; open 9am-8pm Mon-Sat, 10am-5pm Sun) is an imposing building behind CST train station.

There are many Internet cafés in South Mumbai. Try **New Nikhil Communication** (Rs 30/hr; 45 Mint Rd) near CST station **Satyam i-way** (Rs 40/hr; Colaba Causeway, and **Cyber Zone** (Rs 30/hr; Arthur Bunder Rd) both in Colaba.

Colaba & Mumbai Harbour

The **Gateway of India** is an exaggerated colonial marker conceived of after the visit of King George V in 1911. The yellow basalt arch of triumph, derived from the Muslim styles of 16th-century Gujarat, faces out to Mumbai Harbour at the tip of Apollo Bunder in Colaba. Officially opened in 1924, it was redundant just 24 years later when the las British regiment ceremoniously departed India through its archway.

Anchored in Bombay harbour, the massive **Museum Ship Vikrant** (Rs 85; ferries 11am-4.30pm Tues-Sun) is a former aircraft carrier now serving as a fascinating museum. The ship was built by the British in 1945 and bought by the Indian Navy in 1957. The

Vikrant served in the India–Pakistan War of 1971, and in the liberation of Goa from the Portuguese. Admission includes the ferry ride out to the ship, departing in front of the Gateway of India every half hour.

Elephanta Island

The rock-cut temples on **Elephanta Island** *(citizen/foreigner Rs 10/US$5; caves open 9am-5.30pm Tues-Sun)* are Mumbai's premier tourist attraction. Little is known about their origins, but they are thought to have been created between AD 450 and 750, when the island was known as Gharapuri (Place of Caves). The Portuguese renamed it Elephanta because of a large stone elephant near the shore. This statue collapsed in 1814 and the British reassembled the remaining pieces at Victoria Gardens, where it stands today. There is one main cave with a number of large sculptured panels, all relating to Shiva. The most famous of the panels is the Trimurti, or Triple-Headed Shiva, where the god is depicted as destroyer, preserver and creator. The central bust of Shiva, its eyes closed in eternal contemplation, may be the most serene sight you witness in India.

Take advantage of the English-language guide service (free with deluxe boat tickets),

24 Hours in Mumbai

Although a sprawling metropolis, Mumbai's best sights and sounds can easily be experienced in a short stay – make sure you get an early start!

Morning

Head first to **Colaba**, the travellers' nerve centre, where you'll find the Gateway of India facing out into Mumbai Harbour. A short boat trip on the harbour is a good way to gain some perspective on the city, and you can visit the *Vikrant*, an aircraft carrier now preserved as a floating **museum**.

The best way to see the rest of Mumbai's finest sights is to take a **taxi tour** or hire a car and driver from the booths at Apollo Bunder (Rs 600 to 800 for a half day). They'll take you along **Marine Drive** past **Chowpatty Beach** to **Malabar Hill** and the **Hanging Gardens**, to Gandhi's former residence at **Mani Bhavan**, to **Haji Ali's Mosque**, and the **Mahalaxmi Dhobi Ghat**. Otherwise, just wander the streets by yourself, watch a game of cricket on the maidans and enjoy the Victorian **architecture** of the University, High Court and Victoria Terminus (now called Chhatrapati Shivaji Terminus).

Lunch

Mumbai is also a great place to eat. For lunch, there are travellers' restaurants on **Colaba Causeway**, trendy cafés on **Veer Nariman Rd** or, for a Mumbai treat, try one of the Mangalorean seafood restaurants such as **Mahesh Lunch Home**.

Afternoon

If galleries and museums are your thing, Mumbai's best are conveniently clumped together in an area known as Kala Ghoda, right next to Colaba. The **Chhatrapati Shivaji Maharaj Vastu Sangrahalaya** (formerly Prince of Wales Museum), **Jehangir Gallery** and **National Gallery of Modern Art** can all be visited in a couple of hours. If you'd rather **shop**, there are plenty of government emporiums and souvenir shops in Colaba and the Fort Area. For a real Mumbai experience, though, head up to the thriving street **markets** north of the train station (see Shopping later in this chapter).

Dinner

Bade Miya is a great street barbecue in Colaba, or splurge at the cosmopolitan **Indigo** or **Tendulkar's**.

Night

As dusk falls, head up to Chowpatty Beach, which takes on a mini carnival atmosphere. Try some **bhelpuri**, have your fortune read or put your scalp in the hands of a head masseur. Mumbai is one of the few cities in India where you can really party late. Start with a drink at **Leopold's** in Colaba then, depending on your budget and taste, you can salsa at **Copa Cobana** or mix it with Mumbai's beautiful people at **Insomnia** or **Athena**.

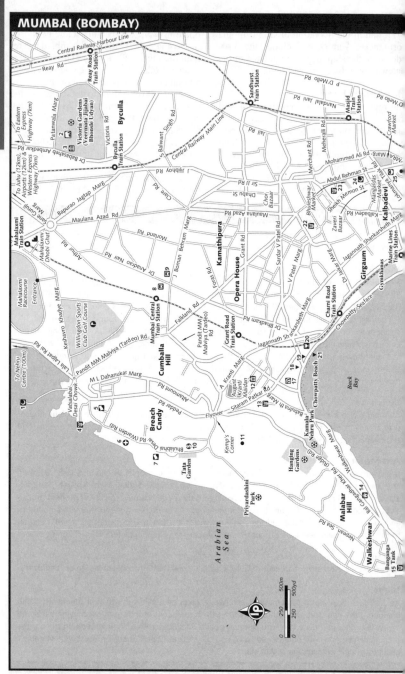

MUMBAI (BOMBAY)

MUMBAI (BOMBAY)

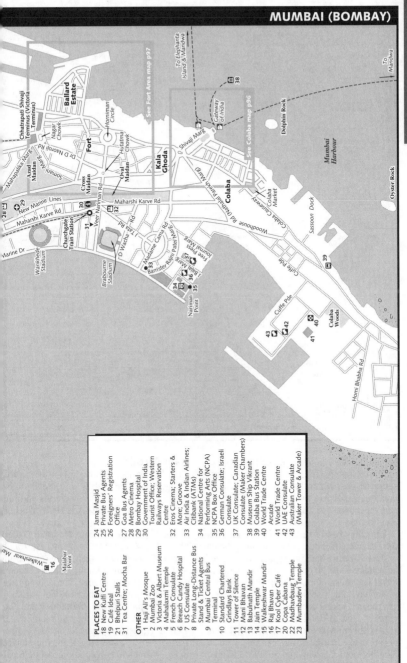

PLACES TO EAT
18 New Kulfi Centre
19 Café Ideal
21 Bhelpuri Stalls
31 Tea Centre; Mocha Bar

OTHER
1 Haji Ali's Mosque
2 Mumbai Zoo
3 Victoria & Albert Museum
4 Mahalaxmi Temple
5 French Consulate
6 Breach Candy Hospital
7 US Consulate
8 Private Long-Distance Bus Stand & Ticket Agents
9 Mumbai Central Bus Terminal
10 Standard Chartered Grindlays Bank
11 Tower of Silence
12 Mani Bhavan
13 Babulnath Mandir
14 Jain Temple
15 Walkeshwar Mandir
16 Raj Bhavan
17 Kool Cyber Café
20 Copa Cabana
22 Madhavbaug Temple
23 Mumbadevi Temple
24 Jama Masjid
25 Private Bus Agents
26 Foreigners' Registration Office
27 Goa Bus Agents
28 Metro Cinema
29 Bombay Hospital
30 Government of India Tourist Office; Western Railways Reservation Centre
32 Eros Cinema; Starters & More; Groove
33 Air India & Indian Airlines; Citibank (ATMs)
34 National Centre for Performing Arts (NCPA)
35 NCPA Box Office
36 German Consulate; Israeli Consulate
37 UK Consulate; Canadian Consulate (Maker Chambers)
38 Museum Ship Vikrant
39 Colaba Bus Station
40 World Trade Centre Arcade
41 World Trade Centre
42 UAE Consulate
43 Australian Consulate (Maker Tower & Arcade)

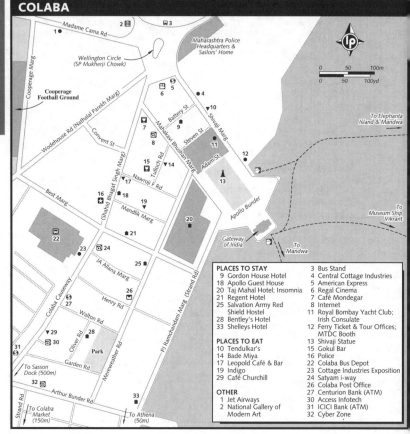

COLABA

PLACES TO STAY
9 Gordon House Hotel
18 Apollo Guest House
20 Taj Mahal Hotel; Insomnia
21 Regent Hotel
25 Salvation Army Red
    Shield Hostel
28 Bentley's Hotel
33 Shelleys Hotel

PLACES TO EAT
10 Tendulkar's
14 Bade Miya
17 Leopold Café & Bar
19 Indigo
29 Café Churchill

OTHER
1 Jet Airways
2 National Gallery of
  Modern Art

3 Bus Stand
4 Central Cottage Industries
5 American Express
6 Regal Cinema
7 Café Mondegar
8 Internet
11 Royal Bombay Yacht Club;
   Irish Consulate
12 Ferry Ticket & Tour Offices;
   MTDC Booth
13 Shivaji Statue
15 Gokul Bar
16 Police
22 Colaba Bus Depot
23 Cottage Industries Exposition
24 Satyam i-way
26 Colaba Post Office
27 Centurion Bank (ATM)
30 Access Infotech
31 ICICI Bank (ATM)
32 Cyber Zone

beginning every hour on the half-hour from the ticket booth. There's also a small **museum** on site, which has some informative pictorial panels on the origin of the caves and the history of Maharashtrian rock-cut architecture.

Launches head to Elephanta Island from the Gateway of India. Small economy boats cost Rs 70 return and more spacious 'deluxe' launches cost Rs 90 return. With an economy ticket you must return on an economy boat – if you have a deluxe ticket you can return on any boat. Tickets are sold by touts at the gateway and at booths lining the southern end of Shivaji Marg at Apollo Bunder. Boats depart every half-hour from around 9am to 3pm between Tuesday and Sunday and take just over an hour.

Kala Ghoda

Kala Ghoda is the name given to the area wedged between Colaba and the Fort that contains Mumbai's main galleries and museums. The **Kala Ghoda Arts Festival** is held here over two weeks in February.

The bright and spacious **National Gallery of Modern Art** (☎ 22852457; MG Rd; admission Rs 5; open 11am-6pm Tues-Sun), in the Sir Cowasji Jehangir Public Hall, is a modern space showcasing a range of changing exhibitions by Indian and international artists.

Chhatrapati Shivaji Maharaj Vastu Sangrahalaya (Prince of Wales Museum; ☎ 2284519; citizen/foreigner Rs 10/300; open 10.15am-6pm Tues-Sun) is a fine museum set in an ornamental garden and boasting a galleried central hall topped by a huge dome

Colourful street scenes, Panaji

Portuguese building, MG Rd, Panaji

Hotel Venite, Panaji

Portuguese architecture, Fontainhas, Panaji

Church of Our Lady of the Immaculate Conception, Panaji

Inside are paintings, sculptures and a natural history section.

The **Jehangir Art Gallery** (☎ 22048212; 161B MG Rd; admission free; open 11am-7pm daily), once the city's principal exhibition space, now hosts interesting weekly shows by Indian artists.

Other Attractions

Chowpatty Beach The little curve of beach called Chowpatty is still a favourite evening spot for courting couples, families, political rallies and anyone out to enjoy what passes for fresh air. Eating *bhelpuri* (thin, crisp fried rounds of dough mixed with puffed rice, fried lentil, lemon juice, chopped onion, herbs and chutney) at the collection of stalls on the edge of the beach

at night is an essential part of the Mumbai experience, as is getting a vigorous head rub from a *malish-wallah* (head masseur). Forget about visiting during the day for a sunbathe or a dip, as the water is filthy.

Malabar Hill On the northern promontory of Back Bay is the exclusive residential area of Malabar Hill. The formal **Hanging Gardens** (Pherozeshah Mehta Gardens) on top of the hill are a pleasant place for a stroll (popular with Mumbai's courting couples), while the smaller **Kamala Nehru Park** opposite has views of Chowpatty Beach, Marine Drive and the city.

Mani Bhavan The building where Mahatma Gandhi stayed during his visits to

FORT AREA

Azad Maidan

To Crawford Market (500m)

Chhatrapati Shivaji Terminus
(Victoria Terminus)

Nagar Chowk

St Georges Rd

P D'Mello Rd

Fashion Street

Ballard Estate

Alexandra Dock

Maruti Cross La

Cochin St

Shoorji Vallabhdas Marg

Rustom Sidhwa Marg

Ghoga St

Fort

The Mint

Flora Fountain

Veer Nariman Rd

Horniman Circle

Hutatma Chowk

High Court

Homi Modi St

Mumbai Harbour

University Rd

Bombay University

A'S D'Mello Rd

Dr VB Gandhi Marg

Naval Dock Yard

Secretariat

Art Plaza

Elphinstone College

Kala Ghoda

PLACES TO STAY & EAT	
6	Hotel City Palace
8	Residency Hotel
13	Mahesh Lunch Home
14	Mocambo Café & Bar;

OTHER	
1	Bus Stand
2	Central Railways Reservation Centre; (ATM)
3	Main Post Office
4	Main Post Office Parcel Counter
5	New Nikhil Communication
7	Sterling Cinema
9	Citibank (ATMs)
10	Reserve Bank of India
11	Bombay Store
12	UTI Bank (ATM)

15	Thomas Cook
16	Standard Chartered Grindlays Bank
17	Bookstalls
18	HSBC Bank (ATMs)
19	Sri Lankan Consulate
20	St Thomas' Cathedral
21	Town Hall; Asiatic Society of Bombay Library; State Central Library
22	Bombay Stock Exchange
23	Standard Chartered Grindlays Bank (ATMs)
24	Rajabai Clock Tower
25	Jehangir Art Gallery
26	Chhatrapati Shivaji Maharaj Vastu Sangrahalaya (Prince of Wales Museum)

Bombay from 1917 to 1934 is now a small, but engrossing, **museum** (☎ 23805864; 19 Laburnum Rd; admission free; open 9.30am-6pm daily) that shouldn't be missed. Many important events in India's struggle for Independence emanated from here. Gandhi's simple room remains untouched and there's a wonderful photographic record of his life.

Haji Ali's Mosque At the end of a long causeway snaking into the Arabian Sea is a whitewashed mosque containing the tomb of the Muslim saint Haji Ali. He is believed to have been a wealthy local businessman who renounced the material world and meditated on a nearby headland after a pilgrimage to Mecca. The mosque becomes an island at high tide, but is accessible at other times via the concrete causeway.

Mahalaxmi Dhobi Ghat At Mumbai's municipal laundry or dhobi ghat at Mahalaxmi, some 5000 men use rows of open-air troughs to beat the dirt out of the thousands of kilograms of soiled clothes brought from all over the city each day. The best view, and photo opportunity, is from the bridge across the railway tracks near Mahalaxmi train station, which can be reached from Churchgate station.

Organised Tours

The Maharashtra Tourism Development Corporation (MTDC) operates uninspiring city tours at 2pm daily (Rs 70), and one-hour, open-deck bus tours of the city's illuminated heritage buildings at 7pm and 8.30pm on weekend evenings (Rs 70), departing from the Gateway of India. All can be booked at the **MTDC booth** at Apollo Bunder near the Gateway of India.

Bombay By Night (☎ 22626066; US$25) is an eventful evening tour of the city, taking in the city sights. For an extra charge the tour can be done in an Ambassador stretch limousine! (Organise this by prior booking.)

Cruises on Mumbai Harbour are a good way to escape the city and offer the chance to see the Gateway of India as it was intended. Short ferry rides (one hour) cost Rs 30 and leave very frequently from the harbour.

Places to Stay

Mumbai is India's most expensive city for accommodation and pressure for a room can be intense during the Christmas season and Diwali. A budget place here is anything under Rs 1000 for a double, but you can get a reasonable room for half that.

Places to Stay – Budget

Most of the cheap hotels are in Colaba.

Salvation Army Red Shield Hostel (☎ 22 841824; 30 Mereweather Rd; dorm beds Rs 135, with full board Rs 205, doubles/triples with private bathroom & full board Rs 570/855) is a little institutional but, if you take the dorm option, easily the cheapest place to stay in Mumbai.

The central **Apollo Guest House** (☎ 220 45540; e hotel apollogh@hotmail.com; 43/ 45 Mathuradas Estate Bldg, 1st floor, Colaba Causeway; singles/doubles with shared bathroom Rs 360/460, doubles with private bathroom Rs 750, with air-con Rs 850) has clean but cramped rooms. The prices quoted include tax.

Hotel City Palace (☎ 22615515, fax 22676897; 121 City Terrace, W Hirachand Marg; economy singles/doubles with air-con Rs 475/650, larger rooms Rs 850/1050), in the Fort area, is a bit claustrophobic but spotlessly clean and surprisingly quiet given the location. It's directly opposite CST train station.

Places to Stay – Mid-Range

In Colaba, **Shelleys Hotel** (☎ 22840229, fax 22840385; e shelleyshotel@vsnl.com; 30 PJ Ramchandani Marg; doubles from Rs 1622) overlooks the waters of Mumbai Harbour. It's a lovely hotel with a slight hint of the Raj about it. Book ahead.

Bentley's Hotel (☎ 22841474, fax 22871846; e bentleyshotel@hotmail.com; 17 Oliver Rd; doubles Rs 670-1320) has loads of character. Rooms have cable TV and the price includes breakfast. The more expensive rooms are huge and spotless with colonial furniture and balconies. Rooms 31 and 21 are among the best. Reservations are recommended – the hotel takes email bookings and accepts major credit cards. The price includes tax.

Regent Hotel (☎ 22871854, fax 22020363; e hotelregent@vsnl.com; 8 Best Marg; singles/ doubles with breakfast Rs 2120/2332) is quite a stylish hotel that has plenty of marble surfaces and comfortable rooms with fridge, TV and air-con. The rooms have either a sitting room or enclosed balcony. The price includes tax.

Residency Hotel (☎ 22625525, fax 22619164; e residencyhotel@vsnl.com; 26 Rustom Sidhwa Marg; singles/doubles Rs 1380/1485) is one of the few comfortable options in the heart of the Fort. It has a marble lobby and spotless air-con rooms with private bathroom. The price includes tax.

Places to Stay – Top End

Next to the Gateway of India, the **Taj Mahal Hotel** (☎ 56653366, fax 56650323; w www.taj hotels.com; Apollo Bunder; tower wing from US$230/255; heritage wing singles/doubles from US$270/295, with harbour view US$330/ 345) is one of the finest hotels in India. Rooms in the superb heritage wing are plush, with some facing in to the pool and the more expensive rooms facing Mumbai Harbour. A 16% tax is payable.

Gordon House Hotel (☎ 22871122, fax 22872026; w www.ghhotel.com; 5 Battery St; singles/doubles Rs 4500/5000, suites from Rs 10,000) is a chalk-white, European-style boutique hotel with stylish rooms decorated in Mediterranean, country-style American and Scandinavian themes (anything but Indian!). There is also tax payable.

Places to Eat

Colaba A Mumbai institution dating back to 1871, **Leopold Café & Bar** (☎ 22020131; cnr Colaba Causeway & Nawroji F Rd; mains Rs 60-180) is the most popular travellers' hang-out in the city. There's an extensive Chinese, continental and Indian menu, an excellent juice bar (juices Rs 40 to 85), and consistently good, but overpriced, food.

Café Churchill (☎ 22844689; 103B Colaba Causeway) is a tiny, smoke-free place with booth seating so it can be hard to get a seat. The specialities are tasty sandwiches (Rs 40 to 70), reasonable pasta meals and some interesting desserts such as honey walnut tart (Rs 50).

Bade Miya (☎ 22841649; Tulloch Rd) is an evening barbecue street stall with a city-wide reputation. The constant spittle of meat and wafting smoke leads you to excellent kababs, tikkas and rotis, served to customers milling on the street or seated at tables on the roadside.

Indigo (☎ 56368999; 4 Mandlik Rd; mains Rs 285-385; open 12.30pm-3pm & 7.30pm-

midnight) is one of the trendiest places in Colaba. It's a stylish, modern restaurant and bar with casual furniture and a rooftop garden dining area.

Tendulkar's (☎ 22829934; 1st floor, Narang House Shivaji Marg, Apollo Bunder; mains Rs 275-475) is the ultramodern new restaurant owned by Indian cricket superstar Sachin Tendulkar. The food is a mix of Indian, European and Mediterranean, the decor an icy mix of neon, glass and booth seating. A beer at the bar (for mere people-watching) starts at Rs 100.

Fort Area With an open street frontage, **Mocambo Café & Bar** (☎ 22870458; 23A Sir P Mehta Rd; mains Rs 25-50) lets you absorb the atmosphere of the Fort. It's a convenient spot for breakfast, sandwiches and cold beer, and the menu includes Parsi, Mughlai and Chinese dishes.

Mahesh Lunch Home (☎ 22870938; 8B Cawasji Patel St; mains Rs 85-200) is the place to try Mangalorean seafood. Renowned for its ladyfish, pomfret, lobster and crabs, the rawas tikka (marinated white salmon) and pomfret tandoor are superb.

Churchgate & Chowpatty Beach A great place to hang out for the afternoon is **Mocha Bar** (☎ 22236070; 82 Veer Nariman Rd; tapas Rs 75-160), a mellow Arabian-style coffee house with low cushioned seating, hookah pipes, exotic coffee varieties and world music.

The **Tea Centre** (☎ 22819142; 78 Veer Nariman Rd; mains Rs 60-130, set lunch Rs 185) is a serene colonial-meets-contemporary place where you can pop in for a pot of tea (Rs 40 to 105) or a light meal.

Café Ideal (☎ 23630943; Fulchand Niwas, Chowpatty Seaface; mains Rs 35-80) is a bustling café, of the type made popular by Iranian Parsis early in the 20th century. It has a booming CD jukebox, a Chinese, Indian and continental menu, and views out to Back Bay.

New Kulfi Centre (cnr Chowpatty Seaface & Sardar V Patel Rd) has been making some of the city's most delicious kulfi (Rs 14 to 30) since 1965. It's weighed into 100g slabs, cut into cubes, and served on plates to customers gathered on the pavement.

The **stalls** at Bhel Plaza on Chowpatty Beach open up in the evening and are the most atmospheric spots to snack on *bhelpuri* (Rs 10), *panipuri* (deep-fried roti filled with dhal) and ice cream.

Entertainment

Mumbai has a more liberal attitude to drinking and nightlife than most Indian cities, and there are plenty of happening places in Colaba.

Café Mondegar *(☎ 22020591; Metro House, 5A Colaba Causeway; mains Rs 40-80; open 8am-midnight daily)* is a busy café-bar with a CD jukebox, draught beer (Rs 60) and a steady flow of travellers.

Gokul Bar *(☎ 22848428; Tulloch Rd, Colaba; open from 11am daily)* is a classic, 100% male, Indian drinking den. It can get pretty lively and the beer is cheap (starting at Rs 45).

Copa Cabana *(☎ 33680274; Darya Vihar, 39 Chowpatty Seaface; admission free; open 7pm-12.30am daily)* is a small, buzzing, Latin-flavoured club/bar with decent music, fine margaritas (Rs 200) and no elbow room. Draught beer costs Rs 60.

Two of Mumbai's most exclusive and fashionable nightclubs are located in Colaba. **Insomnia** *(☎ 22023366; open 8pm-3am daily)* at the Taj Mahal Hotel is the place to rub shoulders with Bollywood starlets and young professionals. Entry is Rs 600 per couple, or Rs 1000 on Friday and Saturday nights. **Athena** *(☎ 22028699; 41/44 Minoo Desai Marg)*, south of Arthur Bunder Rd, also attracts the cream of Mumbai's bright and brash young things. Admission is Rs 1000 per couple on weekends; midweek nights are sometimes free.

The **National Centre for Performing Arts** *(☎ 22833737; W www.tata.com/ncpa)*, at Nariman Point, hosts Indian theatre, dances and classical music in three theatre venues.

Shopping

You can buy just about anything in the dense bazaars north of the Fort. The main areas are **Crawford Market** (fruit and vegetables), **Mangaldas Market** (silk and cloth), **Zaveri Bazaar** (jewellery), **Bhuleshwar Market** (fruit and vegetables) and **Chor Bazaar** (Mumbai's 'thieves' market', for antiques and furniture).

Colourful Crawford Market (officially called Mahatma Phule Market) is the last outpost of British Bombay before the tumult of the central bazaars begins. The meat market is strictly for the brave, being one of the few places you can expect to be accosted and asked to buy a bloody goat's head.

Government emporiums such as **Central Cottage Industries** *(Colaba Causeway)* and the independent **Bombay Store** *(Sir P Mehta Rd, Fort)* are good places to browse for fixed-price handicrafts.

Getting There & Away

For information on getting to/from Goa from Mumbai, see the Getting There & Away chapter.

Getting Around

To/From the Airport There's a prepaid taxi booth at the international airport with set fares to various places. To Colaba, the Fort and Marine Drive the fare is Rs 325 during the day (Rs 405 for air-con) and takes about one to 1½ hours. Don't try to catch an autorickshaw from the airport to the city; they're prohibited from entering downtown Mumbai.

There's no prepaid taxi counter at the domestic airport, but the taxi queue is controlled by the police. The fare to the city centre is around Rs 300, plus extra for baggage.

An alternative from the domestic terminal is to catch an autorickshaw to Vile Parle train station (Rs 15), and a suburban train between Vile Parle and Churchgate or CST (Rs 7, 45 minutes). Don't attempt this during rush hour.

Bus & Train The red single and double-decker buses are one of the best ways to travel short distances in the city, except during rush hours (Rs 3 for a stage). Just jumping on a double-decker bus (eg, No 103) is a good, cheap way to have a look around South Mumbai.

Mumbai has an efficient, but overcrowded, suburban train network. There are three main lines; the most useful service operates from Churchgate heading north to stations such as Charni Rd (for Chowpatty Beach), Mumbai Central, Mahalaxmi (dhobi ghats), Vile Parle (domestic airport), Andheri (international airport) and Borivali (Sanjay Gandhi National Park).

Taxi & Autorickshaw Every second car on the streets of Mumbai seems to be a black-and-yellow Premier taxi and South Mumbai taxi drivers almost always use the vehicle's meter without prompting and give the correct change to passengers; the auto-rickshaws are confined to the suburbs north of Mahim Creek.

Taxi meters are out of date, so the fare is calculated using a conversion chart, which all drivers carry.

Chennai (Madras)

☎ 044 • pop 6.4 million

Capital of Tamil Nadu, Chennai is India's fourth-largest city and a fast-growing, heavily polluted metropolis. It's also a deeply conservative city with many reminders of the colonial past and a tradition of attracting and nurturing the region's finest thinkers, artists and craftspeople.

Chennai is a possible entry to India if you're flying in from Southeast Asia. While it's not an easy trip from here to Goa by bus, a new direct train from Chennai to Vasco da Gama, the *Chennai–Vasco Express*, has made getting to Goa much easier – see the Getting There & Away chapter for details.

Information

There are **Tamil Nadu Tourism Development Corporation** booths at Central and Egmore train stations.

The **Government of India Tourist Office** (☎ 28461459, fax 28460193; 154 Anna Salai; open 9.15am-5.45pm Mon-Fri, 9am-1pm Sat & public holidays) is also a useful first stop for information.

You can change cash and travellers cheques at **AmEx** (☎ 28523638; G17 Spencer Plaza, Anna Salai) or **Thomas Cook** branches (☎ 25342374; 20 Rajaji Salai, George Town • ☎ 28553276; 45 Montieth Rd, Egmore).

Banks with ATMS include **HSBC** (Rajaji Salai), **ICICI** (MG Rd) and **HDFC Bank** (Monteith Rd).

The **main post office** (Rajaji Salai; open 8am-8.30pm Mon-Sat, 10am-5pm Sun) is in George Town. There are plenty of places to check email. **Dishnet** (2nd floor, Apex Plaza, MG Rd, Nungambakkam; open 6am-midnight daily; Rs 15/30min) has 40 terminals and is quick and efficient. The **Internet Zone** (1 Kennett Lane, Egmore; open 9am-11pm daily; Rs 25/hr) has fast access and air-con.

Things to See & Do

The red Indo-Saracenic **High Court Building** at Parry's Corner is the main landmark in George Town. Built in 1892, it's said to be the largest judicial building in the world after the Courts of London.

Built around 1653 by the British East India Company, **Fort St George** has undergone many alterations. It presently houses the Secretariat and Legislative Assembly. The **Fort Museum** (citizen/foreigner Rs 5/100; open 10am-5pm Sat-Thur) has a fascinating collection of memorabilia from the British and French East India Companies, as well as the Raj and Muslim administrations.

The **Government Museum** (Pantheon Rd; citizen/foreigner Rs 5/250; open 9.30am-5pm Sat-Thur, closed public holidays) has a fine archaeological section representing all the major South Indian periods including Chola, Vijayanagar, Hoysala and Chalukya. The same ticket gets you into the **National Art Gallery**, which has a interesting array of Mughal, Rajasthani and Deccan artworks from the 10th to the 18th centuries.

Vivekananda Museum (admission Rs 2; South Beach Rd open 10am-12.30pm & 3pm-7pm Thur-Sat & Mon-Tues, 3pm-7pm Sun) is in a building formerly known as the Ice House, once used to store massive ice blocks transported by ship from North America. It later became the venue from which Vivekananda preached his ascetic philosophy, and now houses a collection of photographs and memorabilia from the swami's life.

Chennai's film industry now rivals Mumbai's Bollywood for output. the **AVM Studios** (☎ 24843183; 38 Arcot Rd, Vadapalani; admission free; open 8am-8pm daily) is the only one routinely open to the public – they just give you a pass to wander around the sets.

Places to Stay

Egmore, on and around Kennet Lane, is good for budget accommodation. The top hotels are mainly along and around Anna Salai.

Places to Stay – Budget

The **Hotel Regent** (☎ 28191347; 11 Kennet Lane; singles/doubles Rs 200/300) has quiet rooms with bucket hot water set around a central courtyard.

Tourist Home (☎ 28250079; 21 Gandhi Irwin Rd; singles/doubles Rs 300/360) has

CHENNAI (MADRAS)

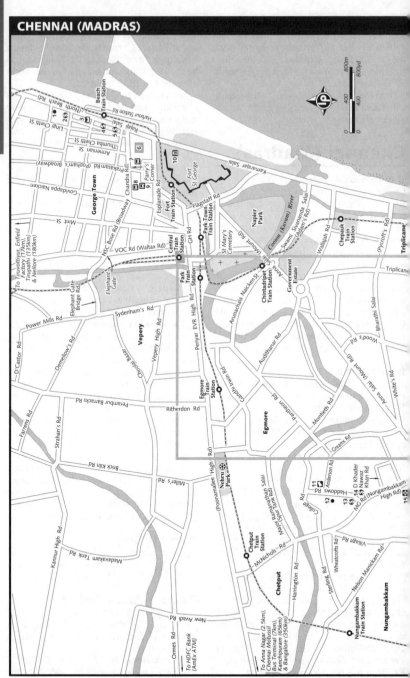

CHENNAI (MADRAS)

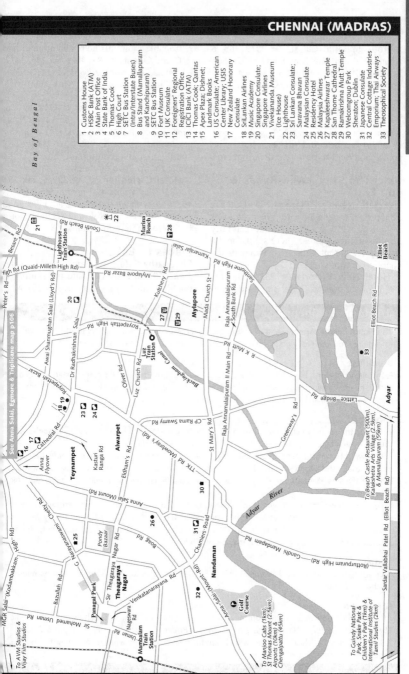

1 Customs House
2 HSBC Bank (ATM)
3 Main Post Office
4 State Bank of India
5 Thomas Cook
6 High Court
7 SETC Bus Station
    (Intra/Interstate Buses)
8 Bus Stand (Mamallapuram
    and Kanchipuram)
9 SETC Bus Station
10 Fort Museum
11 UK Consulate
12 Foreigners' Regional
    Registration Office
13 ICICI Bank (ATM)
14 Thomas Cook; Qantas
15 Apex Plaza; Distnet;
    Landmark Books
16 US Consulate; American
    Center Library; USIS
17 New Zealand Honorary
    Consulate
18 SriLankan Airlines
19 Music Academy
20 Singapore Consulate;
    Singapore Airlines
21 Vivekananda Museum
    (Ice House)
22 Lighthouse
23 Sri Lankan Consulate;
    Saravana Bhavan
24 Malaysian Consulate
25 Residency Hotel
26 Malaysia Airlines
27 Kapaleeshwarar Temple
28 San Thome Cathedral
29 Ramakrishna Mutt Temple
30 Welcomgroup Park
    Sheraton; Dublin
31 Japanese Consulate
32 Central Cottage Industries
    Emporium; Thai Airways
33 Theosophical Society

Bay of Bengal

Marina Beach

Mylapore

Elliot Beach

Adyar

Teynampet

Alwarpet

Nandaman

Theagaraya Nagar

Panagal Park

Adyar River

Golf Course

Luz Train Station

Lighthouse Train Station

Mamapuram Train Station

See Anna Salai, Egmore & Triplicane map p106

quiet, but slightly cramped, rooms with hot water in the morning.

Hotel Imperial Classic *(☎ 28191965; 6 Ghandi Irwin Rd; singles/doubles Rs 195/250)*, is set back from the road in a quiet compound. The rooms are an OK size and have geysers.

Hotel Dasaprakash *(☎ 28255111; 100 Periyar EVR High Rd; singles/doubles Rs 300/575, with air-con from Rs 480/720, deluxe rooms Rs 1020)* is a beautiful Art Deco hotel with some good (and some very ordinary) rooms.

Places to Stay – Mid-Range & Top End

The **Hotel New Park Plaza** *(☎ 28550006, fax 28550561; 29 Whannels Rd; singles/doubles from Rs 825/995)* has comfortable, centrally air-conditioned rooms. There's a bar and a rooftop restaurant with good views of the chaotic Egmore streets.

Hotel New Victoria *(☎ 28253638, fax 28250070; 3 Kennet Lane; singles/doubles Rs 975/1250)* is centrally air-conditioned and has well-appointed rooms. There's a reasonable multicuisine restaurant and bar.

Grand Orient *(☎ 28524111, fax 28523412; 693 Anna Salai; singles/doubles from Rs 1600/ 2100)* has pleasant rooms with small balconies.

Residency Hotel *(☎ 28253434, fax 28250085;* **e** *resmds@vsnl.com; 49 G Narayanaswami Chetty Rd, Theagaraya Nagar; singles/doubles from Rs 1995/2600, suites Rs 3000)* is popular, comfortable and friendly. Some rooms have city views.

Hotel Orchid Inn *(☎ 28522555, fax 284 18689; 19 Woods Rd; singles/doubles Rs 450/550, with air-con Rs 650/900)* has good rooms with TV. There's an excellent North Indian restaurant downstairs.

Places to Eat

Bhoopathy Café *(33 Gandhi Irwin Rd; meals Rs 30-50)*, directly opposite the station, is popular and does good *dosas* (Rs 20).

24 Hours in Chennai

It's colourful and enormous, and as one of India's largest cities Chennai offers plenty for travellers to explore. You can easily enjoy some of Chennai's diversities in a day's stopover.

Breakfast
Fabulous, value-for-money South Indian food is a highlight of Chennai. It's great to start a long day with a hearty meal of *idlis* (rice dumplings) and *dosas* (lentil-flour pancakes), available from the many stalls dotted all over the city.

Morning
Celebrate the revival of classical Indian music and dance while watching classes at **Kalakshetra Arts Village**, which take place between 9am and 11.15am on weekdays.

Following the artistic bent, Chennai hosts a booming film industry, and for movie buffs the good news is that **AVM Studios** *(admission free)* is open to the public. Just obtain a pass and wander through the sets at your leisure. Who knows, you could be chosen as an extra in an exciting epic Tamil tale.

For many travellers, a highlight of travelling to Goa is cruising around on a monster two-wheeled machine. See where it begins at the **Enfield motorcycle factory** *(☎ 25733310;* **w** *www.royalenfield .com; admission Rs 500)* at Tiruvottiyur, 17km north of Chennai. The half-hour tours only run on Saturday, but for the machine-mad it may be worth it.

Lunch
Give yourself a treat for lunch – dine in style at one of Chennai's top hotels, which have wonderful lunch-time buffets.

Afternoon
After the pre-noon excitement, you may wish to slow down the pace. Catch your breath in the **Theosophical Society's** 100-hectare grounds *(Adyar Bridge Rd; open 9.30am-12.30pm & 2.30pm-5.30pm Mon-Sat)*, which are filled with beautiful trees, including what is reputedly the world's largest banyan tree.

Vasanta Bhavan *(20 Gandhi Irwin Rd; dishes Rs 30)* is bustling with waiters and has an upstairs dining hall. Thalis cost Rs 25.

Udipi Home Mathsya *(cnr Halls & Police Commissioner's Rds; dishes Rs 55-90)* serves excellent veg home-style cooking from a varied menu.

Saravanaas has a branch *(48 Anna Salai)* in the forecourt of the Devi Cinema Complex. It's a great place for a quick meal. It also has an upmarket **branch** *(293 Peter's Rd)*.

Mathura Restaurant *(2nd floor, Tarapore Tower, Anna Salai)* is an excellent upmarket veg restaurant. Its Madras thali (Rs 60) comes with all the usual delicacies.

Food Plaza *(806 Anna Salai; dishes Rs 40-80)* is a good-value multicuisine restaurant set back from the road in a bamboo hut. It has air-con or open-air seating.

Gyan Vaishnav Punjabi Dhaba *(260 Anna Salai; open 11am-3pm & 7pm-11pm; dishes Rs 30-50)* offers excellent North Indian food and good-value thalis (Rs 55). You may have to wait for a seat, but it's worth it.

Only Veg *(82 Anna Salai; dishes Rs 15-20)* is spotlessly clean and does tasty snacks and juices.

The **Gallopin' Gooseberry** *(11 Greams Rd; dishes from Rs 60)* does quite a fair crack at American (hamburgers) and Italian (pasta) cuisine. It also offers an exotic range of juices.

All of the top-end hotels have lunch-time buffets ranging in price from Rs 200 to 400 plus taxes. This may seem a bit steep, but the quality (and quantity!) of the food and relaxed atmosphere make it an experience well worth trying.

Entertainment

Chennai doesn't have a bar scene as such, but most of the plush hotels have pricey bars. **Dublin**, at the Welcomgroup Park Sheraton, is the latest hot spot – a combination Irish pub/nightclub. Entry is Rs 750 per couple.

---

24 Hours in Chennai

Hit the trail to seek out Chennai's varied architectural cityscape. Worth a look are the enormous, red **High Court Building**, **San Thome Cathedral** (where the remains of St Thomas the Apostle are said to be housed) and **Sri Parthasarathy Temple** *(Thulasinga Perumal Koil St, Triplicane; open 6am-noon & 4pm-8pm daily)*. Built in the 8th century and renovated in the 16th century, the temple is one of the oldest in Chennai.

If at any stage you're travelling down Kamarajar Salai, stop at the wide expanse of Marina Beach, and take a few moments to look over the Bay of Bengal.

Traditionally considered to be an intellectual town, Chennai has its share of galleries and museums. The **Government Museum** houses a great collection of art and a strong archaeological section representing all of South India's major historical periods. The **Fort Museum's** collection of memorabilia from the British and French East India Companies and the Raj and Muslim administrations gives an insight into those eras.

If you would like to do some **shopping**, there are plenty of **government emporiums** along Anna Salai that sell goods at fixed prices. These are generally open from 10am to 6pm Monday to Friday, and 10am to 1pm on Saturday. The **stalls** around Kapaleeshwarar Temple sell lots of little knickknacks, as do the **puja shops** across the road. You might find some fun, inexpensive souvenirs here. **George Town** is interesting to explore, even if you aren't looking to buy, as the streets are often dedicated to selling just one type of item.

Dinner
Enjoy delicious vegetarian food at the **Saravanaas/Saravana Bhavan chain**, whose restaurants range from inexpensive to air-conditioned, but all serve excellent food.

Night
Classical Indian music and dance performances are often held, and are a cultural way to spend the evening. If you're interested, check the local papers or inquire at any tourist office.

Chennai has an endless turnaround of nightclubs and discos. Most of the top-end hotels have bars where you can enjoy a nightcap.

ANNA SALAI, EGMORE & TRIPLICANE

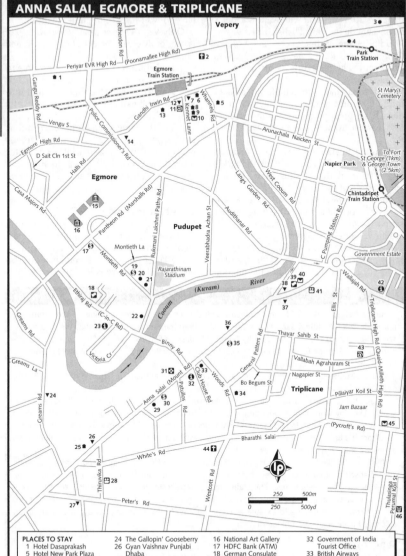

PLACES TO STAY
1 Hotel Dasaprakash
5 Hotel New Park Plaza
6 Hotel Imperial Classic;
   Hotel Imperial Supreme
8 Hotel New Victoria
9 Hotel Regent
13 Tourist Home
25 Grand Orient
34 Hotel Orchid Inn

PLACES TO EAT
7 Vasanta Bhavan
12 Bhoopathy Café
14 Udipi Home Mathsya

24 The Gallopin' Gooseberry
26 Gyan Vaishnav Punjabi
   Dhaba
27 Saravanaas
36 Food Plaza
37 Only Veg
38 Mathura Restaurant

OTHER
2 St Andrew's Church
3 Train Reservation Complex
4 TTDC Booking Office
10 Kennet Lane Post Office
11 Internet Zone
15 Government Museum

16 National Art Gallery
17 HDFC Bank (ATM)
18 German Consulate
19 Thomas Cook
20 Jet Airways; Kuwait
   Airways; Air France;
   American Airlines
21 Gulf Air
22 Indian Airlines; Air India
23 ITDC
28 Sathyam Cinema
29 Lufthansa
30 AmEx (ATM)
31 Spencer Plaza; AmEx;
   The Bookshop

32 Government of India
   Tourist Office
33 British Airways
35 State Bank of India
39 Canadian Honorary
   Consulate
40 Anna Salai Post Office
41 Devi Cinema Complex;
   Saravanaas
42 Tamil Nadu Tourist
   Complex
43 Gee Gee Net
44 Wesley Church
45 Triplicane Post Office
46 Sri Parthasarathy Temple

Music Academy (*☎ 28115619; cnr TTK Rd & Dr Radhakrishnan Salai*) is Chennai's most popular public venue for Carnatic classical music and Bharata Natyam dance. Expect to pay Rs 200 for a good seat, although there are many free performances.

Kalakshetra Arts Village (*☎ 24911169, fax 24914359; Dr Muthulakshmi Rd, Tiruvanmiyu*) is committed to the revival of classical dance and music, traditional textile design and weaving. The college hosts regular performances and visitors can watch classes from 9am to 11.15am weekdays.

There are over 100 cinemas in Chennai, most screening Tamil films. **Devi Cinema Complex** (*☎ 28555660; 48 Anna Salai*) and **Sathyam Cinema** (*☎ 28523813; 8 Thiruvika Rd*) often show English-language films.

Getting There & Away

For information on getting to/from Goa from Chennai, see the Getting There & Away chapter.

Getting Around

To/From the Airport The domestic and international terminals are 16km south of the city centre. The cheapest way to reach them is by suburban train from Egmore to Tirusulam, 500m across the road from the terminals. The trains run from 4.15am until 11.45pm (Rs 7/85 in 2nd/1st class, 40 minutes). There's also a minibus service for Rs 100 (Rs 75 during the day) between the airport and the major hotels. An autorickshaw to the airport costs about Rs 150/250 for a day/night trip and a taxi costs Rs 250.

Bus & Train The bus system in Chennai is less overburdened than in the other large Indian cities, although peak hour is still best avoided.

The suburban train is an excellent way to get between Egmore and Central Stations (Rs 5), Egmore and George Town (Rs 5), to Guindy (Rs 7) or the airport (Rs 7). To move quickly across the city, catch the more recently introduced north–south Mass Rapid Transport System (MRTS). All tickets cost Rs 5 no matter how far or long you travel.

Most government bus services for Tamil Nadu and interstate operate from the **Chennai Mofussil Bus Terminus** (*CMBT; ☎ 247 94705; Jawarhal Nehru Salai, Koyambedu*), which is 7km west of town. Bus 18B takes 40 minutes to make the trip from Anna Salai. An autorickshaw should charge about Rs 50 for the journey.

Central Goa

Central Goa is not the place for lazing on beaches – apart from Panaji's town beach, Miramar, there are none – but the region more than compensates in historical and architectural splendour (both Portuguese and Hindu), accessible villages, cycling excursions around rural islands and villages, and the natural beauty of some of Goa's best national parks and wildlife sanctuaries.

Central Goa comprises three talukas (administrative districts) – Tiswadi, Ponda and Sanguem – and the laid-back, beautifully situated state capital, Panaji (Panjim).

Panaji is Goa's most interesting town (it's a stretch of the imagination to describe the capital as a city!), with an attractive old Portuguese quarter, river cruises on the Mandovi, and some fine restaurants. About 9km to the east, Old Goa is an unmissable highlight. Half a dozen huge, whitewashed laterite churches and cathedrals, including the basilica that contains the miraculously preserved body of St Francis Xavier, are all that remain of the former Portuguese capital once said to have rivalled Lisbon in magnificence. It's now listed as a Unesco World Heritage site.

When the Portuguese arrived in Goa they set about destroying every temple and mosque they could lay their hands on. Only those that were far inland escaped. The 13th-century Mahadeva Temple at Tambdi Surla, the single surviving structure in Goa of the Kadamba dynasty, is in an isolated spot near the border with Karnataka. More accessible, and an interesting day trip from Panaji or Margao (Madgaon), the temples in the Ponda area have been rebuilt in a curious style that bears more than a passing resemblance to the churches found throughout the state.

Near Ponda, there are several working spice plantations that offer interesting tours, which include a traditional meal. In the east of the state, following the main highway out towards Londa in Karnataka, is a large wilderness and forest area comprising the two main wildlife sanctuaries in Goa – the perfect escape from Goa's developed beach life. Bondla is easily accessible and well set up for a bit of wildlife spotting, while Bhagwan Mahavir, Goa's largest national park, offers beautiful forest and Ghat scenery. Inside the park, Goa's highest waterfall,

Highlights

- Explore the rustic Portuguese quarters of Sao Tomé and Fountainhas in Panaji, stopping for lunch at Hotel Venite and staying a night in a four-poster bed at the atmospheric old Panjim Inn
- Cycle out to the magnificent churches and cathedrals of Old Goa – the astonishing remnants of the old Portuguese capital
- Glide through the waterways and mangroves of Dr Salim Ali Bird Sanctuary in a dugout canoe
- Tour one of the spice plantations near Ponda and enjoying a traditional lunch served on banana palm leaves
- Stay overnight at Bondla Wildlife Sanctuary – the best chance of seeing some of Goa's hidden fauna

Dudhsagar, is a popular 4WD excursion from Molem.

PANAJI (PANJIM)
pop 93,000
Sitting on the southern bank of the Mandovi, just out of reach of the monsoon's worst efforts, it's hard to believe that Panaji is a state capital. The low-rise, unhurried

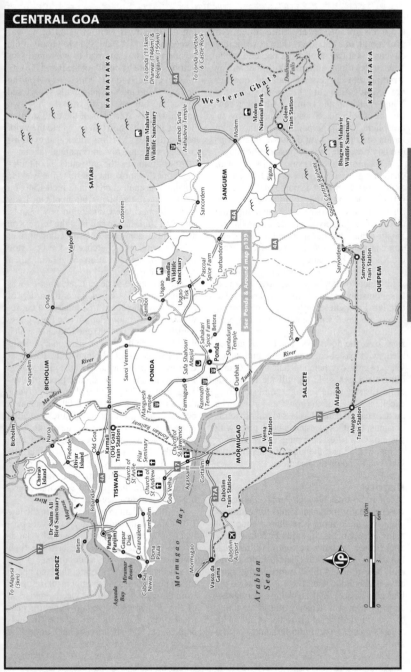

town has few noticeable public buildings, the roads and offices are more suited to a provincial market town than a principal city, and you can stroll from one end to the other in less than an hour. With the narrow winding backstreets of the old quarter, breezy location at the mouth of the Mandovi River, and compact shopping centre, the whole place has a rather sleepy atmosphere that is perpetuated by the Goan habits of taking a long daily siesta and rigorously observing every possible holiday.

While most travellers stop briefly in Panaji on their way to the beaches or to Old Goa, the town deserves at least a couple of days and is by far the best base for exploring central Goa. There are several excellent restaurants and plenty of reasonably priced accommodation. Panaji is also the transport hub of the state; you can reach almost any part of Goa from the Kadamba bus stand.

Unlike Goa's other major cities, Panaji is a great place to simply wander. The old quarters, Fontainhas and Sao Tomé, still bear a distinctive Portuguese influence. The narrow streets are lined with small shops and bars, some of which still sport original Portuguese signs over the doorways. The houses are red tiled, with pastel-coloured walls and small, vine-covered overhanging balconies. Crumbling staircases scale the hillside to the Altinho district with vantage points offering excellent views of the town and river. The modern part of Panaji has less to offer in terms of sights, but it's a pleasant enough place with some of Goa's best shopping, a bustling municipal market and the hum of daily life that you won't find on the beaches.

History

Much of the area on which Panaji now stands was originally marshland, and for centuries there was little more here than a couple of fishing settlements. In around 1500, shortly after Goa came under the control of the Muslim leader Yussuf Adil Shah, a fortress was built here to guard the entrance to the Mandovi. The building later became known as the Idalcao's Palace, 'Idalcao' being a Portuguese corruption of Adil Khan. Little, if anything, of the original structure remains, although today's Secretariat Building stands on the same site.

When the Portuguese nobleman Afonso de Albuquerque arrived in March 1510 he

quickly took the fort and set about reinforcing it. His efforts were in vain, for he was forced by Yussuf Adil Shah to abandon the position in May, and had to wait until November before he could retake it and the city of Govepuri (today's Old Goa). Having done so, Albuquerque personally supervised the rebuilding of the fortress to his own specifications. Accounts of the time say that he was in such a hurry to complete the work before the next Muslim attack that even his officers were pressed into manual labour.

Apart from this, the only other bit of building work that took place at this time was the raising of a small church, in around 1540, on the site where the huge Church of Our Lady of the Immaculate Conception now stands. Since all ships had to call in at the fortress on arrival in Goa and before proceeding upriver to the capital, the church was the first stop for the Portuguese sailors celebrating their safe arrival in India.

The first large-scale land reclamation was completed in 1634 when, under the orders of the viceroy, the count of Linhares, a causeway was built to join Panjim (the Portuguese name for the settlement) and Old Goa, which until that time had been separated by marshland. The 3km route, known as the Ribandar Causeway (from the name of the village at its eastern end), was a far-sighted piece of planning. It made Panjim a feasible alternative as the capital when, years later, Old Goa had to be abandoned because of the repeated cholera epidemics that were decimating the population. As you drive east from Panaji towards Old Goa, you can see that the ground is still marshy. The area south of the road is used for saltpans; sea water is allowed to flood the area and evaporate, leaving yellow-brown deposits of sea salt.

Limited reclamation took place in the late 17th century, though mostly as private projects undertaken by a few wealthy landowners who had chosen the area for their own estates. However, as conditions in Old Goa became more desperate, the land began to support increasing numbers of refugees from the capital. At first the viceroy and most of the noblemen moved to Panelim, near present-day Ribandar, to escape the epidemics, but when that too became unhealthy a new location was sought.

In 1759 the viceroy moved to Panjim, where he took over the fortress as his own residence. Although Mormugao had already been selected as the best location for a new capital, the fact that the viceroy himself had chosen to live in Panjim rather sealed the issue. Those who could afford it moved to Panjim, and more land was reclaimed.

By the early 19th century the city was taking shape. In 1834 Panjim became known as Nova Goa, thus signalling acceptance of its status, and in 1843 it was finally recognised by the Portuguese government as capital of Goa. A spate of building work took place to make the new capital worthy of its title. Among the public buildings erected were the army barracks (now the police headquarters and government offices) and the library. In essence though, Goa was a forgotten corner of the Portuguese empire, and lack of money and political interest meant that building work was low-key. For many years the capital remained undeveloped, leading Lieutenant Richard Burton (later to become famous as Sir Richard Burton, the 19th century traveller and diplomat) to remark that 'Panjim loses much by close inspection.'

In effect there was little change to the size and shape of the town until Goa's Independence from Portugal in 1961. After the departure of the Portuguese, the city was renamed Panaji, and a few superficial changes were made. The Secretariat Building became home to the State Assembly and a couple of statues were erected to heroes of the Goan Independence movement. In a sign of Panaji's progressiveness, a flash new Assembly Complex was built on the hill just north of Panaji and inaugurated in 2000. However, not a lot has altered in Panaji. Over the years, new building and road work has taken place, but locals and authorities are aware of retaining the city's unique atmosphere and colonial heritage.

Orientation

Despite the numerous tiny back streets, Panaji is not a difficult place to find your way around; it's interesting just to wander about and explore at leisure. The main part of the town is sandwiched between the Mandovi River to the north and the high ground of the quaint Altinho district to the south. Dayanand Bandodkar Marg is a major boulevard skirting the Mandovi all the way to the Secretariat Building before becoming Avenida Dom Joao Castro and continuing to the New Pato Bridge in the east and to Campal and Miramar in the west. The Kadamba bus stand is on the eastern side of the town, across the Ourem Creek.

Information

Tourist Offices The **Goa Tourism Development Corporation office** (*GTDC or Goa Tourism;* ☎ *2224132;* Ⓦ *www.goa-tourism .com; Dr Alvaro Costa Rd*) is just south of the Old Pato Bridge. There's not a lot of information to be gleaned here, but you can pick up maps of Goa and Panaji and book local tours. A useful first stop for information is the **tourist information counter** (☎ *2438520*) at the Kadamba bus stand.

The **Government of India tourist office** (☎ *2841653;* ⓔ *goitogoa@goatelecom.com; Church Square; open 9.30am-6pm Mon-Fri, 10am-1pm Sat*), on the 1st floor of the Communidade Building, is far more helpful, not only for information about Goa but also for onward travel. Staff here are bright and enthusiastic and qualified guides can be arranged (from Rs 280/400 per half/full day, depending on the size of the group).

Money The **State Bank of India** (*Dayanand Bandodkar Marg; open 10am-4pm Mon-Fri, 10am-1pm Sat & Sun*) is across from the Hotel Mandovi. The bank will change cash or travellers cheques.

There are plenty of efficient foreign-exchange places in Panaji. The best is **Thomas Cook** (☎ *2221312; 8 Alcon Chambers, Dayanand Bandodkar Marg; open 9.30am-6pm Mon-Sat, 10am-5pm Sun Oct-Mar only*) which changes all brands of travellers cheques commission-free and gives cash advances on Visa and MasterCard. Nearby is **American Express** (*AmEx;* ☎ *2432645; 14 Alcon Chambers Dayanand Bandodkar Marg; open 9.30am-6.30pm daily*). By comparison, visiting the local banks (even the State Bank of India) for foreign exchange is a waste of time. **Menezes Air Travel** (☎ *2432960; Ourem Rd*) is an agent for AmEx if you need replacement cheques, but there's no currency exchange here.

There are 24-hour ATMs accepting international cards (MasterCard, Cirrus, Maestro, Visa) at **HFDC** (*18th June Rd*), **ICICI** (*Dr Atmaram Borkar Rd*) and **Centurion** (*MG Rd*), and there's a **UTI Bank** ATM near the bus stand.

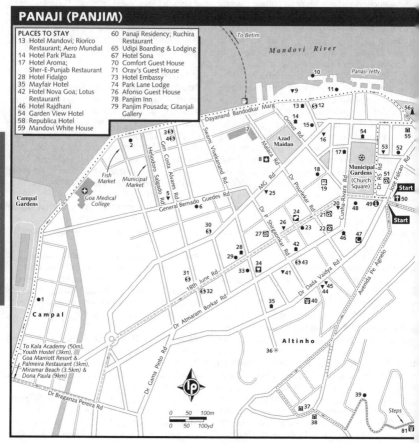

PANAJI (PANJIM)

PLACES TO STAY
13 Hotel Mandovi; Riorico Restaurant; Aero Mundial
14 Hotel Park Plaza
17 Hotel Aroma; Sher-E-Punjab Restaurant
28 Hotel Fidalgo
35 Mayfair Hotel
42 Hotel Nova Goia; Lotus Restaurant
46 Hotel Rajdhani
54 Garden View Hotel
58 Republica Hotel
59 Mandovi White House
60 Panaji Residency; Ruchira Restaurant
65 Udipi Boarding & Lodging
67 Hotel Sona
70 Comfort Guest House
71 Orav's Guest House
73 Hotel Embassy
74 Park Lane Lodge
76 Afonso Guest House
78 Panjim Inn
79 Panjim Pousada; Gitanjali Gallery

Post & Communications The **main post office** (*MG Rd; open 9.30am-5.30pm Mon-Fri, 9am-5pm Sat*) has a Speedpost parcel service and reliable post restante (*open 9.30am to 4pm Mon-Sat*). The small stationery shop on the lane next to the post office (north side) has a reasonably priced parcel-wrapping service.

You can make international telephone calls from the **central telegraph office** (*Dr Atmaram Borkar Rd; open 7am-8.30pm daily*), but there are plenty of private STD/ISD offices charging similar rates.

There are a plenty of Internet cafés in Panaji. Good places include:

Cozy Nook Travels (☎ 2425960) Cozy Nook is on 18th June Rd and access costs Rs 35 per hour.

Cyber Joint This is near the Church of Our Lady of the Immaculate Conception on Dr Dada Vaidya Rdand and access costs Rs 30 per hour.
Log Inn On the 2nd floor of Hotel Check Inn on Dr P Shirgaonkar Rd, Log Inn is open 24 hours and access costs Rs 30 per hour.
Shruti Communications Shruti is below Hotel Venite on 31st January Rd and access costs Rs 40 per hour.

Travel Agencies To confirm or book tickets on international flights, contact one of the travel agencies in Panaji.

Efficient and reliable travel agencies in Panaji include **Aero Mundial** (☎ 2424831; *Dayanand Bandodkar Marg*) at the Hotel Mandovi, **Menezes Air Travel** (☎ 2432960; *Ourem Rd*) and **Freedom Holidays** (☎ 2438320) on

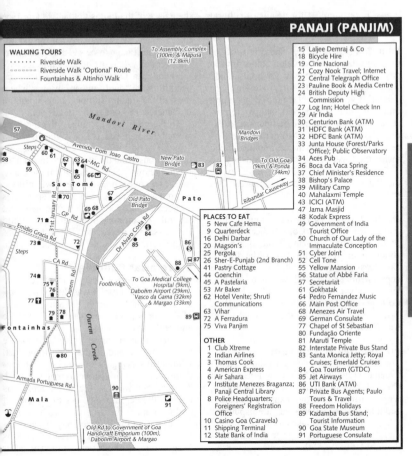

PANAJI (PANJIM)

the 3rd floor of the Patto Centre building near the Kadamba bus stand.

Bookshops & Libraries The Mandovi and Fidalgo hotels have small **bookshops** piled high with new and second-hand books and international magazines. **Pauline Book & Media Centre** (☎ 2231158; *Rani Pramila Arcade*), down a laneway off 18th June Rd, specialises in self-help, spiritual and religious titles, including lots on saints such as St Francis Xavier.

Panaji Central Library (*Malaca Rd; open 9.30am-1.15pm & 2pm-5.45pm Mon-Fri*) is on the west side of the Azad Maidan, next to the police headquarters. It's housed in the Institute Menezes Braganza. This is the oldest

public library in India. Founded in 1832 as the Publica Livraria, it is surprisingly rich in old texts, having inherited a substantial amount from the religious institutions of Old Goa as they were forced to close down.

Cultural Centres The **Alliance Française de Goa** (☎ 2223274; *ⓦ www.afindia.org; 37 Lake View Colony, Miramar; open 9.30am-1pm & 3.30pm-6.30pm Mon-Fri, 9.30am-1pm Sat*) has a small library, an art gallery and holds a range of cultural events, including film screenings and occasional exhibitions. It also offers courses in French language. Membership (January to December) costs Rs 250, and a programme of events is available on request.

See Entertainment for details of cultural shows at the Kala Academy.

Film & Photography There are lots of places in Panaji that develop colour film in anything from an hour to 24 hours (slide film is sent interstate for processing). In general if you pick a place that is operating under licence (the Kodak shops, for instance) the results should be fine. **Kodak Express** is opposite the Municipal Gardens near Kamat Hotel and there's another branch inside the foyer of the Panaji Residency.

Gokhatak (☎ 2232513; MG Rd), next to the Panaji Residency, does same-day film processing.

Medical Services The nearest medical facilities are at the old **Goa Medical College** (☎ 2224566) on Dayanand Bandodkar Marg, about 500m west of the Hotel Mandovi. It has a casualty department, but most of the departments and specialisations of the college are now based in the large **Goa Medical College Hospital** (☎ 2225727) in Bambolim, 9km south of Panaji on the National Highway (NH) 17.

Fontainhas & Sao Tomé
The old districts of Panaji are squeezed between the hillside of Altinho and the Ourem Creek. It's an attractive area to walk around, with narrow streets, overhanging balconies and a bygone Mediterranean atmosphere.

Fontainhas, which takes its name from the multitude of natural springs on the hillside, is the furthest south of the two districts. Originally this area was accessible only from the northern side and was a tangle of buildings constructed on land reclaimed from the marshes. It was not until Emidio Gracia Rd was cut through the hillside from the town centre that the district was joined more directly with the rest of Panaji. The construction of Ourem Rd, which for many years was the main thoroughfare out of Panaji to the south, also helped to open the area.

Apart from its old-world charm, Fontainhas is notable for the **Chapel of St Sebastian** (St Sebastian Rd), a small, gleamingly whitewashed church at the end of a picturesque street. Although it dates only from the 1880s, it contains a number of interesting features – in particular, at the end of the right-hand aisle, a striking **crucifix** which originally stood in the Palace of the Inquisition in Old Goa (see the boxed text 'The Goa Inquisition' later in this chapter). Worth looking out for too, although you'll have to be satisfied with peering over the wall, is the building now used by the **Fundação Oriente**. The place has been beautifully restored, and in an area where most of the traditional houses are looking a bit battered, this one really stands out.

To the north of Fontainhas, the tiny area around the main post office is known as Sao Tomé. The post office was once the tobacco trading house, and the building to the right of it was the mint. The square that these buildings face once housed the town pillory, where Panaji's justice turned into spectacles as executions took place. It was here that several conspirators involved in the Pinto Revolt (see the boxed text 'The Pinto Revolt' in the North Goa chapter) were put to death.

Secretariat Building
The first building to occupy the place of the present-day Secretariat was the fortress palace of Yussuf Adil Shah, the Muslim sultan of Bijapur who gained control of Goa at the end of the 15th century.

After the Portuguese arrived, the palace was reinforced and used as a customs post, while also serving as temporary accommodation for incoming and outgoing viceroys. The tradition was that the new viceroy was handed the ceremonial keys to the city of Old Goa under the Viceroy's Arch, and so, while waiting for the ceremony, the new appointee had to stay in Panaji or in Reis Magos across the river. Similarly, after handing over responsibility, the outgoing viceroy had to wait for his ship home outside the capital itself.

After the viceroys abandoned Old Goa, the building was adopted as the official residence from 1759 until 1918, when it was moved to the buildings on the Cabo Raj Niwas instead. From this time onwards the building was used for government offices, and until recently housed the state legislative assembly. The legislative assembly now meets in the new Assembly Complex on the hill across the river.

In a small triangle of lawn next to the Secretariat Building is an unusual **statue** of a man apparently about to strangle a woman. It's a tribute to Abbé Faria, one of Goa's most famous sons (see the boxed text later).

Walks in Old Panjim

Panaji (formerly Panjim), while growing into a modern capital, still offers flourishes of its colonial past, and its compact size and riverside location makes it perfect for exploration on foot. The following walks are marked on the Panaji (Panjim) map.

Riverside Walk (3.5km)

From the steps of the city's best landmark, the exquisite **Church of Our Lady of the Immaculate Conception**, you can survey the Church Square, the heart of Panaji and the most visible architectural reminder of Portuguese rule. Walk west to the **Municipal Gardens**, then north along Dr RS Rd to MG Rd, a busy commercial thoroughfare. On the right you'll pass the **Statue of Abbé Faria** (see the boxed text 'Abbé Faria' later).

To the right is a dilapidated **Yellow Mansion**, said to be the first house constructed in Panjim. It is the ancestral home of wealthy traders, the Mamai Kamats.

Next you come to the **Secretariat Building**, until recently the seat of the state legislative assembly, but originally the 15th-century palace of Yussuf Adil Shah. Before the Portuguese built the main road, this palace was on an island surrounded by the waters of the Mandovi. An underground tunnel led to the **Janana Khana**, the harem of the ruler.

Crossing the road to the riverfront Dayanand Bandodkar Marg, walk east towards the old steamer jetty, passing Casino Goa (the *Caravela*), Quarterdeck restaurant and the ferry across the river to Betim. A short detour south of the ferry point brings you to the **Institute Menezes Braganza**, containing a gallery and the Panaji Central Library. Further along the riverfront is the start of the bustling **Panaji Municipal Market**.

About 100m past the market is the **Campal Heritage Precinct**, a charming stretch of colonial-style bungalows, which has two of Panaji's best parks, Campal Gardens, on either side of the road. At the end of this zone is the **Kala Academy**, the centre for the performing and visual arts in Goa.

Fontainhas & Altinho (4.5km)

From the Church of Our Lady of the Immaculate Conception, walk east up the hill along Emidio Gracia Rd, then right at the four-way junction into 31st January Rd. Here you enter Fontainhas, with its winding alleys and decaying mansions. After about 150m, turn right to reach the tiny **Church of St Sebastian**. Continuing down 31st January Rd you pass the heritage hotel **Panjim Inn**. Veering right you come to the **Mala district** an area settled by Hindus after the exodus from Old Goa.

Walk up the slope, past the small **fountain** from which Fontainhas gets its name, towards **Altinho**. At the start of the hill is the **Maruti Temple**, dedicated to the monkey god Hanuman. Taking the steps to the temple you can continue walking up the hill to Altinho, which offers fabulous views over Panaji, the Mandovi and across the Ribandar Causeway. Follow the road around (past the military camp) to **Mahalaxmi Temple**, the chief minister's residence and the **Bishop's Palace**, residence of the Archbishop of Goa.

Walk down the hill from the chief minister's residence, turn right at the end and continue walking down until eventually you return to the Church Square.

CENTRAL GOA

Church of Our Lady of the Immaculate Conception

This stunning whitewashed church lords over the Municipal Gardens in the town centre. Although there has been a church on this site since about 1540, the present building dates from 1619, and it's a surprisingly large church considering the area was practically uninhabited back then.

Panaji was the first port of call for voyages from Lisbon, so Portuguese sailors would visit this church to give thanks for a safe crossing before continuing to Old Goa. By the 1850s the land in front of the church was being reclaimed and the distinctive criss-crossing staircases were added in the late 19th century. It was at about this time also that the huge bell that now hangs in the central belfry was brought to Panjim. It had previously hung in the tower of the Church of St Augustine in Old Goa, but was removed when the tower started to crumble. The bell

Abbé Faria

A pioneer in the field of hypnosis and a favourite son of Goa, Jose Custodia Faria studied under Franz Anton Mesmer – the famous hypnotist whose name led to the word 'mesmerise' – and was the first to assert that the subject's will and expectations were crucial to the success of the hypnosis.

He was born in Candolim, Goa, in 1756. His father was Portuguese and his mother Indian. When he was eight years old they were seized with religious fervour and separated, his mother to become a nun and his father a monk. He was sent from Goa to Lisbon to study for the Church, was ordained in Rome and then moved to Paris where he was involved in the French Revolution.

In Paris his interest in hypnosis developed under Mesmer. He began to practise as a hypnotic medium, but his seances, though they attracted a considerable following, were roundly condemned by the Church and he was publicly denounced. Just before he died in 1819, Faria published a seminal text on hypnosis, *On the Cause of Lucid Sleep*.

Alexander Dumas was so intrigued by the story of Abbé Faria's life and work that he based the mad monk in *The Count of Monte Cristo* on him.

is the second largest in Goa (after the Golden Bell in the Se Cathedral in Old Goa).

The church is beautifully illuminated in the lead-up to Christmas and during the Feast of Our Lady of Immaculate Conception which culminates on 8 December.

Mass is held here daily in English, Konkani and Portuguese.

City Gardens & Jama Masjid

Panaji's central square is the leafy but unkempt **Municipal Gardens**, also called Largo da Igreja (Church Square). The **Ashokan pillar** in the centre once had a statue of Vasco da Gama as its crowning glory, but is now topped by the seal of present-day India, four lions sitting back to back atop an abacus decorated with a frieze and the inscription 'truth alone triumphs'. Three relief busts once set into the walls around the garden can now be seen in the Goa State Museum.

The tiny **Jama Masjid**, barely 100m south of the Municipal Gardens, is said to have

been built about two centuries ago and has recently been comprehensively rebuilt.

The grassy **Azad Maidan** (Freedom Park) wouldn't win any prizes at a flower show. It centres on a small pavilion which now houses a modern sculpture dedicated to freedom fighter and 'Father of Goan Nationalism' Dr Tristao de Braganza Cunha (1891–1958). The domed edifice formerly held the statue of Afonso de Albuquerque that now stands in the museum in Old Goa.

Institute Menezes Braganza

At the northwest corner of the Azad Maidan, the Institute Menezes Braganza and the Central Library occupy a part of the old buildings that used to be the army headquarters. It's worth poking your head through the door, at least to see the entrance hall, which is decorated with four large blue-and-white pictures which cover the whole wall. The scenes depicted on these *azulejos* (painted tiles) are taken from the epic poem *Os Lusíadas* by Luís Vaz de Camões (see the boxed text 'Luis Vaz de Camões').

Much of the upper floor of the building is given over to the Institute Menezes Braganza, which was founded in 1871 as a scientific and literary institution. Originally called the Institute Vasco da Gama, it was renamed in 1963 in honour of the champion of the Goan Independence movement, Luís de Menezes Braganza. The Institute has a small **art gallery** that contains some rare prints and paintings.

On the lower floor of the building is the Panaji Central Library (see Bookshops & Libraries earlier).

Goa State Museum

This large, roomy museum (☎ 2458006; w www.goamuseum.nic.in; admission free; open 9.30am-5.30pm Mon-Fri), in a rather forlorn area near the Kadamba bus stand, has a dozen or so galleries featuring Christian art, Hindu and Jain sculpture and bronzes, and paintings, including miniatures, from all over India. The collection is gradually expanding and interesting exhibits include an elaborately carved 16th-century table used in the Goa Inquisition, a pair of huge rotary lottery machines containing thousands of wooden balls (the first lottery draw was in 1947), and a large wooden chariot used in Hindu fairs in the 18th century.

The first room is a sculpture gallery, containing Hindu carvings and bronzes dating from the 4th to the 8th centuries AD. The second area is a Christian art gallery with a variety of wooden sculptures of saints, devotional paintings, and some colonial wooden furniture. Also on display are some Jain busts, and three huge relief busts of Luís Vaz de Camões, Afonso de Albuquerque and Dom João de Castro, which originally stood in the Municipal Gardens. Upstairs there's a gallery containing cultural exhibits from various Goan villages, and a gallery of contemporary Goan and India art.

The Worldwide Fund for Nature was setting up a conservation display here at the time of research.

You can ask for a free guided tour; otherwise uniformed staff will silently follow you around to make sure you don't touch anything.

Mahalaxmi Temple

This modern temple off Dr Dada Vaidya Rd is not particularly imposing, or even very interesting, but if you've never visited a Hindu temple before it's worth a look inside and

Luís Vaz de Camões

Luís Vaz de Camões is regarded as Portugal's greatest poet. The young man was banished to Goa in 1553 at the age of 29 after being accused of fighting with and wounding a magistrate in Lisbon. He was obviously no soft touch, for he enlisted in the army and fought with some distinction before attracting further official disapproval by publicly criticising the administration.

His reward this time was to be exiled to the Moluccas, and he returned to Goa only in 1562. Written at this time was his most famous work, *Os Lusíadas*, an epic poem glorifying the adventures of Vasco da Gama. Classical in style and imperialist in sentiment, the poem became an icon of Portuguese nationalism.

A statue of Camões, erected in 1960, stood in the centre of Old Goa until 1983, when it was decided by many Goans that it was an unacceptable relic of colonialism. An attempt by radicals to blow it up met with only partial success, but the authorities took the hint and removed the statue. It now stands in the Archaeological Museum in Old Goa.

amply demonstrates that among the ubiquitous whitewashed churches there is a thriving Hindu community in Panaji.

Altinho

On the hillside above Panaji is the district known as Altinho. Apart from good views over the city and river, the main attraction here is the Bishop's Palace, a huge and imposing building completed in 1893. The archbishop of Goa came to reside in Panaji only early in the 20th century. He initially laid claim to the residence on Cabo Raj Niwas, the promontory that looks out over the confluence of the Mandovi and Zuari Rivers. However, it was not to be. When the Portuguese governor general realised that it was the best property in Goa, the archbishop had to change his plans and move back to Panaji.

Campal

On the way down to Miramar from Panaji the road runs through the Campal district. Just before the Kala Academy, on the seaward side of the road, is an enormous and roughly cast **cannon**, which was made in the armoury in Old Goa. It came from the fort at Banasterim where it was pointed across the Cumbarjua Canal to ward off possible attacks from the east. Opposite the cannon, on the other side of the road, is a small park in which stands a **statue** of Francis Luís Gomes, an early representative of Goa in the parliament in Lisbon, and one of the first open advocates of Independence.

Public Observatory

For anyone interested in checking out the incredibly clear night skies over Goa, the Association of Friends of Astronomy (Goa branch) has a public observatory on the roof of Junta House *(Swami Vivekanand Rd; open 7pm-9pm daily, 14 Nov-31 May)*. The local enthusiasts are only too happy to welcome visitors and explain what you're looking at. The view of Panaji by night is lovely, especially around dusk.

Organised Tours & Cruises

Goa Tourism operates hysterical hour-long cruises along the Mandovi River aboard the *Santa Monica*. You'll see this and other boats – lit up like Christmas trees – swanning around the river every evening trying to outdo each other with the volume of their

CENTRAL GOA

music. There's a sunset cruise (6pm) and a sundown cruise (7.15pm), which cost Rs 100. They include a live band performing Goan folk songs and dances. Drinks and snacks are available at an extra charge. On full-moon nights, there is a two-hour cruise at 8.30pm (Rs 150). All cruises depart from the Santa Monica jetty next to the huge Mandovi Bridge and tickets can be purchased here. A couple of private operators, **Emerald Cruises** (☎ 2431192) and **Royal Cruises** (☎ 2435599), have virtually identical trips from Santa Monica jetty each evening (Rs 100), as well as open-sea 'dolphin cruises' (Rs 500) from 10am to 1pm and backwater cruises (Rs 1000 including lunch and drinks) from 10am to 4.30pm. Their boats are bigger and rowdier (for the Indian party crowd) than the *Santa Monica*.

There's also a 'Goa By Night' bus tour at 6.30pm, which includes a river cruise and tour of illuminated sights (Rs 140).

A variety of tours of Goa are offered by Goa Tourism and private agencies. See Organised Tours in the Getting Around chapter for more information.

Places to Stay

There is a variety of accommodation available in Panaji, from old mansions to modern hotels.

Places to Stay – Budget

The **Youth Hostel** (☎ 2225433; dorm beds members/nonmembers Rs 40/60), at Miramar, 3km west of Panaji, is the cheapest place to stay in Goa but has an institutional air, is inconveniently located and there's an 8am checkout and 10pm curfew. It's popular with school groups.

Udipi Boarding & Lodging (☎ 2228047; doubles with shared bathroom Rs 100) is one of several cheap places to stay in the old part of town. It has basic and not very clean double rooms.

Comfort Guest House (☎ 5642250; 31st January Rd; doubles with shared/private bathroom Rs 232/332) is a very good value little guest house in Sao Tomé. Rooms are clean and have cable TV. There's no increase over Christmas but a 50% discount in the low season. The price includes tax.

Mandovi White House (☎ 2223928; doubles with private bathroom Rs 250, during Christmas Rs 550), behind the Panaji Residency, is a peaceful, ramshackle old villa. As it has only four rooms, some with small veranda, it's often full.

Republica Hotel (☎ 2224630; Jose Falcao Rd; singles/doubles with private bathroom Rs 200/350) is an interesting old place with good views from the balcony over to the river and the Secretariat and Panaji's tiled

Pedalling Around Panaji

If you can get past the insane traffic on the highway between the Mandovi Bridge and the Kadamba bus stand, the area around Panaji offers some enjoyable bicycle touring.

One of the best rides in the state is the 9km trip out to **Old Goa**. The pancake-flat road follows the Ribandar Causeway along the south bank of the Mandovi River, so it's a scenic ride passing through the village of Ribandar. Having a bicycle is very handy for exploring Old Goa itself, since the churches and ruins are quite scattered. Ride down to the Mandovi through the Viceroy's Arch and take the ferry across to **Divar Island** – a couple of hours spent exploring this absorbing rural outpost is perfect on a bicycle. You can ride to the southwest corner of the island where there's another ferry back across to Ribandar. Riding back towards Panaji there's yet another ferry point from where you can cross to **Chorao Island** and cycle the fringes of the Dr Salim Ali Bird Sanctuary.

Another rewarding day ride from Panaji is to head west along the Mandovi River (along Dayanand Bandodkar Marg) through the Campal district, then southwest past Miramar beach and out to **Dona Paula**, the small peninsula at the mouth of the Zuari River. There's a small hill approaching Dona Paula but generally this road is flat and wide and the traffic is light. At the roundabout at Dona Paula, turning right (coming from Panaji) takes you up to Cabo Raj Niwas, while turning left takes you across the elevated suburban area behind Panaji. You can ride all the way east to Bambolim on the main highway and then back to Panaji (a round trip of about 22km), although the highway here is busy and accident-prone. It's also possible to detour north through the suburb of **Taleigo**, at the back of Altinho, emerging on Ourem Rd in Fountainhas – ask locals for directions.

rooftops. Some of the rooms are bright with stained-glass windows, but avoid those at the back – the rooms at the front are far superior.

Hotel Embassy (☎ 2226019; *Emidio Gracia Rd; doubles/triples Rs 350/400, Christmas Rs 600/800*) is a friendly, quiet place in an old house. The rooms are certainly nothing special (some have squat toilet) but are OK value.

Afonso Guest House (☎ 2222359; *doubles Rs 350, during Christmas Rs 800*), on the same street as the Chapel of St Sebastian, is a friendly family-run place with four rooms and a pleasant rooftop terrace. Spotless doubles with hot water are worth the price.

Park Lane Lodge (☎ 2227154; e *pklaldg@ goatelecom.com; single Rs 290, doubles Rs 350-420, during Christmas Rs 550-650*) is a rambling 1930s Portuguese house with a bit of character and a variety of rooms, though they're small and more than a little overpriced. There are only six rooms and checkout is 8am. Meals are available for guests.

Orav's Guest House (☎ 2426128; *31st January Rd; doubles Rs 350*) is a reasonably clean place in Sao Tomé, though it lacks any real character compared with other guest houses in the area. The front rooms, with balconies and a bright aspect, are easily the best. There's a 9am checkout.

Places to Stay – Mid-Range

The **Panjim Inn** (☎ 2226523; w *www.panjim inn.com; 31st January Rd; singles/doubles from Rs 765/1035, large doubles Rs 1350-1575*) is by far the most charming place to stay in this (or any) range in Panaji. It's a beautiful 300-year-old mansion with a large 1st-floor veranda and leafy garden. All rooms have four-poster beds and colonial furniture. Ask to see a few rooms as they are all different.

Panjim Pousada (*31st January Rd; singles/ doubles from Rs 720/990*), across the road from Panjim Inn, is under the same management and is also a comfortable, well-furnished place. It has the Gitanjali Gallery, which has changing exhibitions of Goan and Indian artists in the bright, central entrance hall. The rooms here are perhaps even more pleasant than at the Panjim Inn. Air-con is an extra Rs 360 in the high season.

Panaji Residency (☎ 2227103; *MG Rd; doubles with/without air-con Rs 750/600, front rooms with air-con Rs 850*), run by the GTDC, is an unremarkable place on a busy road, but it's popular with travellers. There's a terrace restaurant, bar and bookshop.

Mayfair Hotel (☎ 2223317; e *mayfair@ goatelecom.com; Dr Dada Vaidya Rd; standard singles Rs 450, doubles with/without air-con Rs 700/550*) is one of Panaji's more colourful hotels, with mosaic-tile murals in the lobby. Standard rooms are small but clean, and have touches of character such as Goan oyster-shell windows. Doubles cost Rs 850 over the Christmas period.

Hotel Sona (☎ 2232281; w *www.hotelsona .com; Ourem Rd; doubles Rs 400-560, peak season Rs 600-840*) has a great location in the Sao Tomé district overlooking the Ourem River. Rooms are very simply furnished but clean with tile floors. The cheaper rooms have shared bathroom.

Hotel Aroma (☎ 2423519; w *www.sher-e -punjab.com; Cunha-Rivara Rd; doubles Rs 450-550, doubles with air-con Rs 650-850*) is a modern place that fronts onto the Municipal Gardens. The clean, airy double rooms are relatively good value but rates rise by about 20% in December. There is a noon checkout. The **Sher-E-Punjab** restaurant on the 1st floor is one of the best in Panaji (see Places to Eat).

Garden View Hotel (☎ 2227844; *Diogo de Couto Rd; singles Rs 350, doubles with/without air-con Rs 650/420*) is looking very tired but it has a good location with all rooms overlooking the Municipal Gardens. Forget it in December when rates double.

Hotel Rajdhani (☎ 2225362; *Dr Atmaram Borkar Rd; doubles with/without air-con from Rs 775/675, doubles in peak season from Rs 1250*) is a comfortable business hotel, right in the centre of town. Most rooms have air-con and all have satellite TV. There's a popular vegetarian restaurant downstairs. Checkout time is 10am.

The once-grand **Hotel Fidalgo** (☎ 2226291; *18th June Rd; singles/doubles with air-con from Rs 400/500, with fridge & TV Rs 600/700*) was being completely renovated at the time of research, which is just as well because it was becoming a bit of a ghost hotel. It will be centrally air-conditioned and rooms should cost about Rs 1000 to 1200 per double. There's a swimming pool at the back which is available for nonguests to use for around Rs 150.

Hotel Park Plaza (☎ 2422601; w *www .goaparkplaza.com; Ormuz Rd, Azad Maidan;*

CENTRAL GOA

singles/doubles Rs 595/795, with air-con Rs 795/995, peak season from Rs 995/1200) is a popular but fairly nondescript business hotel in a central location. The cheapest rooms are good value outside the peak Christmas season.

Places to Stay – Top End

Hotel Mandovi (☎ 2426270, fax 2225451; e mandovi@goatelecom.com; Dayanand Bandodkar Marg; singles/doubles from Rs 1100/1400, during peak Christmas period Rs 1600/2000, suites from Rs 2500/2950), an old, colonial hotel near the old steamer jetty, is the best of the central top-end places, though the standard rooms are nothing special. River-facing rooms are at a premium. **Riorico** is a good restaurant on the 1st floor (see Places to Eat) and there's a pleasant bar on the balcony.

Hotel Nova Goa (☎ 2226231, fax 2224958; w www.hotelnovagoa.com; Dr Atmaram Borkar Rd; singles/doubles from Rs 1100/1600, single/double suites Rs 1850/2700) is a more modern business-style hotel than Hotel Mandovi, with a garden swimming pool, the good **Lotus Restaurant** (see Places to Eat) and a business centre. Rates include a buffet breakfast. Pool-facing rooms are more expensive.

Goa Marriott Resort (☎ 2437001; w www.marriott.com; doubles US$130-165), overlooking the Mandovi at Miramar, is Panaji's top hotel. Enormous Mediterranean-style rooms face a manicured garden or overlook the estuary, there's a lovely riverside pool, well-equipped health club, tennis and squash courts and two quality restaurants. Rooms are available as package deals over the Christmas period.

Places to Eat

Panaji doesn't have the sheer number of restaurants that you'll find at beach resorts such as Calangute, but it has an excellent range, from rustic Goan cafés to upmarket hotel restaurants.

Hotel Venite (31st January Rd; Sao Tomé; mains Rs 65-110; open 8.30am-3pm & 7pm-10pm Mon-Sat) is one of the most character-laden restaurants in Goa. With four tiny balconies hanging over the street and rustic Portuguese decor, it's a fine place to enjoy a meal or just a cold beer during siesta (although it closes from 3pm to 7pm). The Goan dishes and seafood are consistently good, though not cheap by local standards. Goan

sausages, chicken cafrial (marinated in a sauce of chillies, garlic and ginger and then dry-fried) and tiger prawns are among the specialities and there are changing blackboard specials.

The 1st-floor **Udipi restaurant** at Udipi Boarding & Lodging, one street east of the Hotel Venite, has a balcony overlooking the street; it's usually crowded with Goans who come here for the inexpensive, basic but tasty food.

Vihar (MG Rd), just around the corner from the Udipi, is a spotless pure-veg place where you can get North Indian food, as well as the usual thalis for under Rs 30. It's generally busy at lunch time.

New Cafe Hema (General Bernado Guedes Rd) is a cheap, clean place near the Municipal Market serving a very good fish curry rice for Rs 20 and veg snacks for under Rs 10. Entrance is at the rear and up some stairs.

Viva Panjim (☎ 2422405; 178 Rua 31 De Janeiro; mains Rs 50-100) is a small, family-run restaurant with only six tables. There are lovingly prepared Goan fish dishes, tandoori and continental dishes, and takeaway is available.

A Ferradura (Horseshoe; ☎ 2431788; Ourem Rd, mains Rs 65-130), facing Ourem Creek, serves a wide range of Goan and Indian dishes and specialises in quality seafood. It's air-conditioned and intimate but not formal.

Magson's (18th June Rd) is just off the Municipal Gardens. It comprises a sweet shop, ice-cream parlour, Gujarati vegetarian restaurant and a deli, where you can buy Goan sausage and desserts such as bebinca (a sweet made of layers of coconut pancakes).

The **Ruchira Restaurant** (☎ 2227103; mains Rs 25-70), upstairs at the Panaji Residency, has a pleasant balcony overlooking the Mandovi River, as well as an enclosed air-con dining room. Service is a little slow (they even warn on the menu to expect a 25-minute wait!), but the food is OK and includes Goan specialities (Rs 40 to 60) as well as Indian, Chinese and Western dishes.

Pergola (MG Rd; mains Rs 35-90; open 11am-11pm daily) is a spotless place specialising in Goan and Indian dishes. The downstairs dining area is busier and slightly cheaper than the 1st-floor air-con section. Crab xacuti (cooked with a very hot sauce) costs Rs 50 and kingfish cafrial costs Rs 90.

Sher-E-Punjab (☎ 2227975; mains Rs 60-150), on the 1st floor at the Hotel Aroma, is a flash place serving arguably the best tandoori and Punjabi food in town. The butter chicken is a speciality. There's another branch on 18th June Rd.

Quarterdeck (Dayanand Bandodkar Marg; mains Rs 40-125; open 10.30am-11pm daily) is a very breezy, open-air restaurant and bar facing the Mandovi River near the Panaji jetty. The prime location means the food is overpriced but the menu covers a full range from Goan to Chinese, continental and North Indian. It's a pleasant spot for an early evening drink (large beer is Rs 60).

Riorico (☎ 2224405; Dayanand Bandodkar Marg; mains Rs 90-200), at the Hotel Mandovi, has for some time held a reputation as the city's best restaurant for Goan cuisine; while the food is good, prices are high and the service is average. There's a pleasant balcony overlooking the Mandovi River, but you can only take drinks out here.

Delhi Darbar (☎ 2222544; MG Rd; mains Rs 80-120; lunch 11am-3.30pm, dinner 7pm-11pm daily) is a Mughlai specialist and is often fully booked in the later part of the evening. Uniformed waiters and turbaned doormen usher you in a busy dining area. Half a tandoori chicken costs Rs 100.

Goenchin (☎ 2227614; mains Rs 90-200), off Dr Dada Vaidya Rd, is Panaji's top Chinese restaurant and also serves quality Thai food. The extensive menu includes chicken satay, Thai red chicken curry and chicken Manchurian. Anything on the menu marked with a red pepper will be authentically spiced and very hot. It's definitely a place for a splurge.

Lotus Restaurant (mains Rs 80-150), in the Hotel Nova Goa, is recommended for Goan and Indian cuisine and the poolside barbecue each evening is a pleasant dining experience.

Palmeira Restaurant (☎ 2437014), at the Marriott out at Miramar, is another place for a splurge meal. There's a sumptuous daily buffet (Rs 395 for breakfast, Rs 425 for lunch and Rs 495 for dinner) as well as an à la carte menu. There's also an excellent poolside brunch on Sunday (Rs 495 including a glass of wine or champagne) which includes use of the swimming pool.

There are several pastry shops in Panaji: try Pastry Cottage (Dr Atmaram Borkar Rd), near the Hotel Nova Goa, A Pastelaria (Dr Dada Vaidya Rd) or Mr Baker (Dr RS Rd) across from the Municipal Gardens.

Entertainment

Kala Academy (☎ 2223280; W www.kala academy.org; Dayanand Bandodkar Marg), on the west side of the city at Campal, is Goa's premier cultural centre. There's a cultural programme of dance, theatre, music and art exhibitions throughout the year. Many performances are in Konkani, but there are occasional English language productions.

Casino Goa (☎ 2234044; sunset gaming cruise Rs 1000 Mon-Thur, Rs 1200 Fri-Sun, dinner cruise Rs 2500-4200), aboard a small luxury ship the MV Caravela, is India's only live gaming casino and can be a fun night out. Drinks are free on all cruises and the dinner cruise includes an impressive buffet meal. On the sunset cruise you get Rs 400 in redeemable gaming chips (you have to leave the boat at 8.30pm), on the most expensive dinner cruise, all Rs 4200 are given as gaming chips. Depending on your luck, you can eat and drink all night and still come out in front. There are blackjack and poker tables, as well as roulette and slot machines. The Caravela is at the Panaji jetty.

Panaji has a few pubs, mostly frequented by young Goans rather than foreign tourists, but they make an interesting change from the beach resort bars. Aces Pub (open to 11pm daily), opposite Junta House, is a tiny two-tier place much like a little cocktail bar. Draught beer costs Rs 25, cocktails cost Rs 60 to 150. The main nightclub is Club Xtreme (☎ 2842027; open 10pm-2.30am daily) in Campal district.

Shopping

The most interesting place to browse around in Panaji is the Municipal Market, which consists of a tangled warren of alleyways, some covered and some in the open, selling everything from fresh fish to T-shirts.

Away from the market, the main shopping street in Panaji is 18th June Rd. Government of Goa Handicraft Emporium (Ourem Rd), just to the south of Fontainhas, is the place to try if you're set on rooting out some Goan handicrafts. The selection is not terribly inspiring, but it's better than you'll see anywhere else Panaji.

Another popular buy are Western brand clothes and sportswear, many of which are now being made in India. American and European designer outlets such as Levis, Nike, Lacoste and Benetton can be found on MG Rd near Delhi Darbar. Indian-made stuff costs about a third less than in the UK, but there's also some genuine imported gear.

For musical instruments, **Pedro Fernandez Music** is a small, cluttered shop with guitars, tabla (Indian drums), sitars and brass instruments, next to Vihar restaurant.

Laljee Demraj & Co (Magnum Centre, MG Rd) is a good place to pick up a fancy, decorative bottle of feni, which makes an excellent gift.

Getting There & Away

Air On the road out to Miramar, **Indian Airlines** (☎ 2237821; Dayanand Bandodkar Marg) is on the ground floor of the Dempo Building. **Jet Airways** (☎ 2438792; Shop 7-9, Sesa Ghor, Patto Plaza, Dr Alvaro Costa Rd) is near Goa Tourism. Other airlines with offices in Panaji include **Air Sahara** (☎ 2230237; General Bernado Guedes Rd) and **Air India** (☎ 2431100; 18th June Rd) next to Hotel Fidalgo.

For ticketing and flight confirmation, see Travel Agencies earlier in this section.

See the Getting There & Away chapter for information on flights from Goa.

Bus State-run bus services operate out of Panaji's **Kadamba bus stand** (☎ 2225401). Fares vary depending on the type of bus and include:

destination	one way (Rs)	hours
Bangalore	360	14
Hospet	110	9
Mangalore	125-180	11
Mumbai	276-398	15-18
Mysore	225	17
Pune	200-245	12

There are also services to Londa (Rs 35), from where you can get a daily direct train connection to Mysore and Bangalore; Hubli (Rs 65, six hours); and Belgaum (Rs 55, five hours). For Hampi, however, you're better off taking the bus rather than a bus/train combination. You can take the daily state-transport bus to Hospet (9km from Hampi) and then a local bus from here, but there are plenty of private buses, including overnight sleepers, on this route.

Many private operators have offices outside the entrance to the Kadamba bus stand, with luxury and air-con buses to Mumbai, Bangalore, Hampi and other destinations. Most private interstate buses arrive and depart from a separate interstate bus stand next to the Mandovi Bridge. **Paulo Tours & Travel** (☎ 2438531; W www.paulotravels.com), just north of the Kadamba bus stand, has nightly sleeper coaches to Hampi (Rs 450), Mumbai (Rs 375) and Bangalore (Rs 400), though these prices fluctuate – they rise from mid-December. The sleeper buses aren't the pinnacle of comfort – they can be cramped, and typically erratic Indian driving and rough roads make sleep a lottery. Ordinary nonair-con buses cost Rs 275 to Mumbai and Rs 350 to Hampi. Luxury buses can also be booked through agents in Margao, Mapusa and the beach resorts, but they still depart from Panaji.

It's possible to get buses further afield, including to Cochin and Chennai, but they are infrequent and these trips are better tackled by a combination of train and bus or by breaking the journey and changing buses.

Panaji is also a hub for local buses heading in all directions. For the southern beach resorts you'll have to change in Margao, and for points north of Calangute, you'll generally have to change in Mapusa. Some of the more popular bus routes within Goa include:

Calangute There are frequent services throughout the day and evening (Rs 7, 45 minutes).

Mapusa Frequent buses run to Mapusa and there's a separate ticket booth at the Kadamba bus stand for express services (Rs 5, 25 minutes).

Margao Direct ordinary/express buses to Margao cost Rs 10/15 (one hour). Minibuses leave from Platform 11. Change at Margao for the southern beaches.

Miramar & Dona Paula Frequent buses ply this return route (Rs 4, 20 minutes).

Old Goa Direct buses to Old Goa leave constantly (Rs 4, 25 minutes).

Ponda Regular buses run via Old Goa (Rs 8, 55 minutes).

Vasco da Gama Ordinary/express buses take one hour and cost Rs 10/15. Minibuses leave from Platform 10.

Train The train is a far more comfortable and faster option than the bus for Mumbai and Mangalore (see the Goa section in the Getting There & Away chapter). Panaji's nearest train station is Karmali (Old Goa), 12km to the east near Old Goa. You can catch a bus to Old Goa and an autorickshaw from here. Otherwise, taxis charge around Rs 80 to/from the station, and autorickshaws charge Rs 50. The busy **Konkan Railway reservation office** (open 8am-8pm Mon-Sat) is on the 1st floor of the Kadamba bus stand. Private travel agencies clustered just north of the bus stand can also make train bookings.

Boat A useful ferry service for the northern beaches is the passenger/vehicle ferry across the Mandovi River to the fishing village of Betim. It departs from the jetty on Dayanand Bandodkar Rd roughly every 15 minutes between 6am and 10pm (free for passengers, Rs 4 for motorcycles). From Betim there are buses to Calangute and Candolim via Reis Magos.

Taxi Autorickshaws, taxis and motorcycle taxis gather at several places in Panaji, including the Kadamba bus stand and around the Municipal Gardens. Typical taxi fares from Panaji include Rs 200 to Calangute, Rs 200 for a return trip to Old Goa with waiting time, and Rs 450 to Margao.

Getting Around

There's no airport bus. A taxi costs about Rs 350 and takes 40 minutes. You can share this with up to five people, but negotiate the fare before heading off.

It's possible to catch a bus from the Kadamba bus stand to Vasco da Gama, then another bus or taxi from here to Dabolim Airport.

Motorcycles and mopeds can be hired from many hotels, or directly through the touts who hang around opposite the main post office. You'll generally pay a little less than at the busy beach resorts in the high season.

Bicycles can be hired from a **shop** opposite Cine Nacional for around Rs 30 per day.

AROUND PANAJI
Miramar

Miramar, 3km southwest of the city (follow Dayanand Bandodkar Marg along the Mandovi waterfront), is Panaji's nearest beach. The couple of kilometres of exposed sand facing Aguada Bay are hardly inspiring compared to other Goan beaches, but this is a popular place to watch the sun sink into the Arabian Sea and it's an easy bicycle ride from the centre of Panaji.

CENTRAL GOA

Killer Captured at O'Coquiero

O'Coquiero, a well-known Goan restaurant in Alto Porvorim, just north of Panaji, boasts more than just a decent pomfret *recheiado* – it was the scene of one of India's most famous captures, or at least recaptures.

Charles Sobhraj was a notorious con man, jewel thief, murderer and suspected serial killer. In the mid-1970s, this charismatic Vietnamese-Indian-Frenchman was Asia's most wanted man, suspected of more than a dozen murders of travellers in Thailand, Nepal and India. After being briefly jailed in Bombay in 1973 over a bungled jewellery theft, Sobhraj managed to flit around Asia pulling off various scams, establishing a cultlike family of followers and going under enough disguises and stolen passports to elude police and the International Criminal Police Organization (Interpol). He finally came unstuck after attempting to drug a group of French tourists in Delhi in 1977. Amazingly he was charged only with that offence and one count of manslaughter and was jailed for 12 years.

With a 20-year warrant for his arrest outstanding in Thailand (and a certain death penalty), he bade his time in Delhi's gruelling Tihar Prison where he was able to lead a relatively comfortable life by befriending and manipulating prison guards and fellow prisoners. In 1986 he threw a party, drugged the prison guards and walked out.

Not long after, Sobhraj was spotted by a policeman in Goa, where authorities swooped on him in O'Coquiero Restaurant and he was sent back to Tihar Prison for another 10 years. Sobhraj later claimed he had allowed himself to be caught to escape extradition to Thailand.

In 1997 he was freed from prison and fled India a free man at the age of 52. Back in France, it's said that he makes a fortune living off his notoriety: he was reportedly paid US$15 million for a book and movie deal. A film of his life, titled *Bottom Line*, was made in 2002. For the full story, read *The Life and Crimes of Charles Sobhraj* by Australian writer Richard Neville.

The district is a wealthy one and heading inland you come across exclusive areas such as the **Lake View Colony**, where the Portuguese Consulate and the Alliance Française are based. Miramar also has a gymkhana with a (rather parched-looking) cricket ground, where you may see matches played at the weekend.

Along the seafront road, at the start of Miramar beach, is **Gaspar Dias**. Originally a fort stood here, directly opposite the fort at Reis Magos. Between them they were designed to defend the entrance to the Mandovi, although they were of limited use; in 1639 the Dutch attacked Goa and managed to destroy a number of ships before being driven off. There's no fort here now, but the most prominent position on the beachfront is taken up by a **statue** representing Hindu and Christian unity.

From Gaspar Dias, the beach runs more or less due south towards Dona Paula. Along this road, the **Goa Science Centre** (☎ 246 3426; Marine Hwy; admission Rs 10; open 10.30am-6.30pm daily) at Miramar is a hands-on learning centre, mainly for kids. Even though it's only a couple of years old, half the gadgets don't work, and it appears a bit neglected. There's a comical, animated environmental display with enormous fibreglass insects and an open-air 'science park' outside.

A reputable place for a seafood meal is **Martin's Beach Corner** (mains Rs 40-100) at Caranzalem. It's a pretty basic shack and the service is indifferent, but this unassuming place is well known to locals and the food is genuinely good. One claim to fame – which the owners seem totally unconcerned about – is that Roger Moore and Gregory Peck ate here during the filming of *The Sea Wolves*.

Dona Paula

Continuing south past Miramar, the coast road leads to Dona Paula, a small peninsula with several resort complexes that have grown up around a fishing village. Although everyone agrees that the area is named after the woman (Dona Paula de Menezes) whose tombstone can be found in the chapel in the Cabo Raj Niwas, there are numerous variations of the story about her. In one she was the viceroy's heartbroken daughter who hurled herself from the nearby cliffs. Others have it that she was the virtuous wife of a nobleman, while still others claim that she

was a lady in waiting to the viceroy's wife and also that she was the mistress of the viceroy himself. The only thing that seems certain is that she bequeathed the land, on which the village is now built, to the church.

On the westernmost point of the peninsula stands an old fortress **Cabo Raj Niwas**. Today the large estate on this headland is the residence of the Governor of Goa, known as **Raj Bhavan**. It's not accessible to the public, although you may be able to attend services at the chapel on Sunday mornings – inquire at the main gate or call (☎ 2453506). Plans to build a fort to guard the entrance to the Mandovi and Zuari Rivers were first proposed in 1540 and, although it was some years before work began, a chapel was raised on the spot almost immediately. Subsequently the fort was completed and the chapel was extended by the Portuguese viceroy to include a Franciscan friary or convent. The fort, which was equipped with several cannons, was never actually used 'in anger', and from the 1650s the buildings were requisitioned as a temporary residence for the archbishop. In 1798 it was taken over by British troops who remained in residence, apart from a brief break, until 1813.

On the southern side of the access road to the fort is the British **cemetery**, which is the last reminder of their presence. After their departure the buildings were once again taken over by the archbishop of Goa as his private residence. They didn't remain long in his possession, however, for in 1866 the viceroy took a shine to the buildings, and had them refurbished and converted into the governor's palace. You can drive up to the entrance gates (turn right at the roundabout if coming from Panaji), where there's a parking area and viewpoint with good views back across Miramar beach, the Mandovi estuary and Fort Aguada.

Continuing through the roundabout brings you to Dona Paula's small bay where there are water sports and souvenir stalls. **Dona Paula Sports Club** has a small kiosk offering jet-ski rides, water-skiing and windsurfing. At the end of the road is a pier and small outcrop of rock on which stands a **sculpture** called 'Images of India', designed by Baroness Yrsa von Leistner.

Places to Stay Across from the harbour, on the peninsula facing the sea and the mouth of ne Zuari River, are a couple of small resort otels that are quite secluded and reasonably ood value outside the high season.

O Pescador (☎ 2453876; W www.opesca or.com; singles/doubles Rs 520/920, deluxe ooms Rs 1000/1200) has a pool, small, private beach and a scattering of rooms, some f which seem to have been built among the illagers' homes. The cheaper rooms are uite plain but some have excellent views ut to sea.

Prainha (☎ 2245388; W www.prainha.com; oubles Rs 1200, cottages Rs 1400-1700), almost next door to O Pescador, has peaceful ardens, some lovely beachside cottages and swimming pool. It's a very relaxing location but a little overpriced.

Cidade de Goa (☎ 2454545; W www cidadedegoa.com; doubles Rs 5000) is an upmarket hotel a kilometre down the coast by Vaniguinim Beach (which it claims as a private beach frontage). It's mainly a package otel with little character, but it has the usual menities including a beachfront pool, health lub and a casino.

Getting There & Away Frequent buses Rs 4) to Miramar and Dona Paula leave rom the Kadamba bus stand in Panaji, and un along the riverfront road.

Dr Salim Ali Bird Sanctuary

Among the mangroves and waterways of the Mandovi River, only 4km east of Panaji, Goa's smallest wildlife reserve makes a fascinating early morning outing, even if you're ot a dedicated bird-watcher. The Dr Salim Ali Bird Sanctuary occupies a total area of only 1.8 sq km on the southwestern tip of Chorao Island, but between October and February this tiny refuge attracts an amazingly ich variety of birdlife that will keep even the most discerning twitcher happy for days.

Named after India's best-known ornithologist, the late Dr Salim Moizzudin Abdul Ali, the sanctuary was proclaimed by the 'orest Department in 1988 to protect mangroves that had grown around reclaimed marshland, and the birdlife that thrives here. Apart from the ubiquitous white egrets and purple herons, you can expect to see colourful kingfishers, eagles, cormorants, kites, woodpeckers, sandpipers, curlews, drongos nd mynahs, to name a few. Marsh crocodiles and otters have also been spotted by some visitors, along with the mudskipper fish that skim across the surface at low tide. There's a bird-watching tower in the sanctuary that can be reached by boat when the water level is not too low.

The best time to visit is either in the early morning (about 8am) or in the evening (a couple of hours before sunset), but since the Mandovi is a tidal river, boat trips depend somewhat on tide times. Quite apart from the bird-watching, a trip to the sanctuary allows you the chance to get waterborne and see Goa from a new perspective, and to that end the best way to cruise the waterways is in a dugout canoe with a local boatman. From the ferry point on Chorao Island, ask at the chai stalls and you'll soon find someone willing to take you through the dense mangrove swamps for around Rs 400 for an hour. You can do this on your own, but local Englishspeaking guides wait at the Ribandar ferry crossing and for an additional (negotiable) fee, they'll go with you and point out various bird species. The **range forest officer** at the Forest Department (☎ 2228772) at Campal, in Panaji, can also arrange local guides, and for a minimum of 10 people the Forest Department operates its own motorboat from the Ribandar ferry crossing. Contact the Forest Department for bookings and more information on the sanctuary.

Chorao Island itself can be explored by bicycle or motorcycle and you can walk around the marshlands skirting the sanctuary. Although there's not much to see on the island, the village of **Chorao** has a number of Portuguese homes and is a typical Goan backwater, which comes as a surprise being so close to the capital.

Getting There & Away To get to Chorao Island, take any bus from the Kadamba bus stand heading towards Old Goa, and ask to be let off at the Ribandar ferry crossing just beyond the east end of the Ribandar Causeway.

OLD GOA

About 9km east of Panaji, a handful of imposing churches and a couple of convents are all that remain of a city once so grand and so powerful it was said to rival Lisbon in magnificence. Known as the Rome of the East, Old Goa is without a doubt Goa's premier historical attraction and you should put aside at least a morning or afternoon to explore it.

Old Goa was not only the capital of the new Portuguese colony, but also the principal city of the Portuguese eastern empire. Its rise was meteoric – over the course of the hundred years following the Portuguese arrival in Goa, the city became famed throughout the world. One Dutch visitor compared it with Amsterdam for volume of trade and wealth. Its fall, however, was just as swift, and eventually the city was completely abandoned.

Today, although some of the churches are still in use (the tomb of St Francis Xavier is in the Basilica of Bom Jesus) many of the old buildings have become museums maintained by the Archaeological Survey of India. Old Goa can get very crowded on weekends and feast days. The best time to

visit is weekday mornings, when you can take in Mass at the Se Cathedral or Basilica Bom Jesus and explore the rest of the site before the afternoon heat sets in.

When visiting Old Goa do not come dressed in beach wear or sleeveless shirts. As a basilica, Bom Jesus is particularly sacred to Christians. Indian tourists visiting the churches show much more respect than do many Westerners – even (unnecessarily) leaving their shoes outside as they would in a Hindu temple.

History

The first large-scale settlement in the area took place in the 15th century, when a port sprang up on the banks of the Mandovi near

The Goa Inquisition

When Vasco da Gama sailed for India 'seeking spices and Christians' it was perhaps inevitable that the worst excesses of European religious zeal should reach Goa sooner or later. As it turned out, they arrived sooner.

The Inquisition was re-established in Spain and Portugal in the late 15th century against a background of rumours that many new Christians, including those who had been converted from Judaism, were secretly still observing their old faith. Many escaped the oppression in Portugal by relocating to the colonies overseas.

It wasn't long before the accusations followed them and missionaries began to be scandalised at the lax behaviour both of the new Christians and of the other Portuguese settlers. At the request of the missionaries, a deposition of the Inquisition arrived in Goa in 1560. The new tribunal was known as the Goa Inquisition, but its jurisdiction spread across the whole of the Portuguese eastern empire.

Having established itself in the sultan's old palace in Old Goa, the tribunal set about imposing its will. Hindus were forbidden to practise their faith and even the Christian population went in fear. François Pyrard, a French traveller who visited Goa from 1608 to 1610, recorded the atmosphere: 'For the least suspicion, the slightest word, whether of a child or of a slave who wishes to do his master a bad turn, is enough to hang a man…'

The tribunal sat regularly in judgment before the long carved table that today is in the Goa State Museum in Panaji, and below the crucifix that now hangs in the Chapel of St Sebastian in Panaji. The more fortunate victims were stripped of their possessions; those who were less lucky were detained indefinitely in the dungeons beneath the Palace of the Inquisition.

Those who were judged guilty underwent the notorious *auto-da-fé* (act of the faith), a public ceremony conducted in the square outside the Se Cathedral, and accompanied by the tolling of the great bell in the cathedral tower. If they failed the 'test of faith' they would usually be burned at the stake. Those who were willing to admit their heresy at the last moment were strangled before the pyre was lit. François Pyrard describes the scene:

It is upon the great feast days that they carry out their judgments. Then they cause all these poor culprits to march together in shirts steeped in sulphur and painted with flames of fire… they are led straight to the great church of A See which is hard by the prison, and are there during the mass and the sermon, wherein they receive the most strenuous remonstrances. Thereafter they are conducted to the Campo Sancto Lazaro, where the condemned are burned in the presence of the rest, who look on.

The Inquisition was suppressed in Goa in 1774.

he tiny village of Ela. While the capital of
he state was still officially to the south (what
s known today as Goa Velha), it had started
o lose importance, both because of its vul-
erability (it was sacked by Muslim invaders
rom the north in 1312 and 1470) and be-
ause the Zuari River, Goa Velha's port, had
tarted to silt up. Shortly after the arrival of
he Muslim Bahmani sultanate in 1470 the
tatus of capital and the name Govepuri were
ransferred to the new site on the north of the
nain island opposite Divar Island.

Within a short time the new capital was a
hriving city. When the Bahmani sultanate
lisintegrated, and Gove came into the hands
f the Muslim Bijapur sultanate, Gove was so
avoured by Yussuf Adil Shah that it became
is second capital. Contemporary accounts
ell of the magnificence of the city and of the
randeur of the royal palace. Over the years
ollowing his takeover, the city was enlarged,
nd strengthened with ramparts and a moat.
t became a major trading centre, a departure
oint for pilgrims to Mecca and gained
rominence for its shipbuilding.

In 1510, with the arrival of the Portuguese,
Gove (known to the Portuguese as Goa) was
he scene of not one but two takeovers.
Afonso de Albuquerque managed to gain
ontrol of the entire island briefly in March,
ut was evicted by Yussuf Adil Shah two
nonths later. Having ridden out the monsoon
n his ships, the indomitable Albuquerque
ttacked again in the autumn and on 25 No-
ember, St Catherine's Day, recaptured Gove.

With Gove now firmly under control, the
ew rulers started to build. A major impetus
vas the arrival of the religious orders. Al-
hough the first missionaries arrived with
Albuquerque as chaplains to his fleet, the
eal influx began in 1542 with the arrival of
among others) the young Francis Xavier.

In the following year the city experienced
ts first taste of the problems that were to lead
o its eventual abandonment, when a cholera
epidemic wiped out an estimated 200,000 in-
abitants. Undeterred, the missionaries built
churches, hospitals and seminaries, vying
vith each other to produce the most splendid
uildings. All were modelled on European
counterparts and consequently there are
lomes, pilasters, barrel arches and flying
uttresses by the dozen.

By the late 16th century the city had ex-
anded hugely; the city walls were removed

and the moat filled in to allow for the spread.
Goa at this time had an estimated population
of around 250,000 and was compared
favourably to the great cities of the West.

Ironically it was also at this time that
Goa's fortunes began to turn. By the end of
the 16th century, Portuguese supremacy on
the seas had been usurped by that of the
British, Dutch and French. The city's decline
was accelerated by another devastating
cholera epidemic that struck in 1635. Bouts
of disease recurred in the following years
and eventually led to plans to abandon the
city. In 1684, against considerable opposi-
tion, the viceroy ordered work to begin on a
new capital in Mormugao. His successor
abandoned the project and then restarted
work when ordered to do so by Lisbon, but
the plan never really got off the ground.

In 1695, however, the viceroy himself decided to move to Panelim (then a village outside Old Goa). Although Old Goa remained
the capital, everybody who could afford to
do so followed his example to escape the appalling health problems. In this same year the
population of the city was 20,000 – less than
a 10th of what it had been a century before.
By 1759 Panelim too had been struck by the
same problems and the viceroy again moved
his residence, this time to Panjim.

Despite Old Goa's virtual abandonment,
in 1777 the government in Lisbon ordered
the city be rebuilt, arguing that if the water
supply and drainage were thoroughly
cleaned and reconstructed the city would be
healthy. Work was abandoned five years
later when the death toll among the workers, because of cholera and malaria, became
too high to continue.

The final blow came in 1835 when the Portuguese government ordered the repression of
the religious societies and most of the missionaries were shipped home. By 1846 only
the convent of Santa Monica was in regular
use. When that was abandoned the ruins of
the great city were left all but empty.

English explorer Sir Richard Burton
recorded his impressions of the city:

...a feeling not unallied to awe creeps over one
when wandering down the deserted aisles, or
through the crowdless cloisters. In a cathedral large
enough for a first-rate city in Europe, some twenty
or thirty native Christians may be seen at their de-
votions, and in monasteries built for hundreds of
monks, a single priest is often the only inhabitant.

Finding Those Feathered Friends

The Indian subcontinent is famous for its birdlife, and Goa's equitable climate and rich vegetation support an abundance of birds. Common varieties to be seen in Goa include four different species of eagle, as well as other birds of prey such as kites, buzzards, kestrels and ospreys. There are five types of pigeon, six types of dove, five varieties of cuckoo, six of kingfisher and six of woodpecker.

A trip to one of the nearby sanctuaries or along a river early in the morning will be rewarding. Apart from the diverse bird population at the Dr Salim Ali Bird Sanctuary, a wonderful variety can be seen in Bondla and the other sanctuaries near the Western Ghats. For sea birds, Morjim beach is recommended.

Most birds live in a variety of distinct habitats according to their specialised feeding or breeding requirements. A few species eke out a living even among the city's bustle and noise. Without a doubt, **house crows** are the best example and these noisy, gregarious black birds may be seen foraging wherever people leave their scraps.

Other less obtrusive species include humble **house sparrows** that forage for crumbs around dwellings; **swallows** that dart among buildings after insects; various species of **bulbul**; and the ubiquitous **mynahs** that flash their white wing patches when they take off.

Out of Town

On the outskirts of town and in open spaces, a different range of birds can be seen. A flash of colour between ruins may turn out to be a **bee-eater**. **Indian rollers** are related to bee-eaters, but are larger and bulkier; they are attractively patterned in mauve and blue, and are common birds.

Drongos are shiny black birds with distinctively shaped tails. They typically perch on a post or even a handy cow and sally forth after insects. **Pipits** and **wagtails** strut among the stubble, sometimes in large flocks; wagtails can be recognised by their habit of pumping their tail up and down.

Common hoopoes, with their orange-brown bodies and black-and-white wings, tails and black-tipped crests, may be seen in open country, around cultivated fields and villages.

Birds of prey such as **harriers** and **buzzards** soar over open spaces looking for unwary birds and small mammals on which they feed.

Kites and **vultures** can wheel on thermals for hours on end, the kites constantly twisting their slightly forked tails. **Ospreys**, another species of large hawk, feed almost exclusively on fish that they seize with their vicious, hooked talons; ospreys patrol large tanks and other waterways.

Waterways

Waterways are rich in birdlife. Stalking on long legs at the shallow edge of tanks and ponds are various species of **egret**, graceful white birds with long necks and daggerlike bills. Their elegant poise

From the late 19th century until the mid-20th century, apart from the use of one or two buildings for military barracks, the city remained empty. When archaeological interest started to revive, work was done to clear the area and some buildings were returned to their former uses. For many of the buildings, which had been plundered for building materials or had simply fallen down, the reprieve came too late. The most stark reminder of this is the ruined tower of the Church of St Augustine, which can be seen from miles around.

Information

There's no tourist office, but **guides** are available at the main churches, or inquire at the Archaeological Museum near the Se Cathedral, which also has copies of *Old Goa* by S Rajagopalan (Rs 10), an excellent booklet about the monuments.

Se Cathedral

At over 76m long and 55m wide, this is the largest church in Asia. The cathedral was begun in 1562 on the orders of the king of Portugal (King Dom Sebastiao), to replace the older church of St Catherine, which had served as a cathedral up to this time. Progress was slow. Work on the building wasn't completed until 1619 and the altars weren't finished until 1652, some 90 years after the building's construction had first been ordered.

Little egret

Red-whiskered bulbul

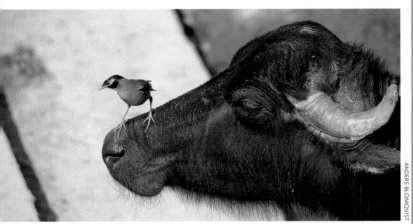
Common mynah with buffalo

Siberian black kite

Common kingfisher

Black-shouldered kite

Indian roller

Indian pond heron

Hoopoe

Pied kingfisher

Finding Those Feathered Friends

belies the deadly speed with which they spear frogs and fish. **Cattle egrets** are most commonly seen stalking among livestock looking for large insects stirred up by their namesake.

Indian **pond herons**, or **paddy birds**, are small and unobtrusive, and well camouflaged in greys and browns. Pond herons are very common, but may be almost invisible against the rubble and weeds at water's edge until they take off, showing their pure white wings.

Colourful **kingfishers** wait patiently on overhanging branches before diving down for their prey. Several species are to be seen in the area, including black-and-white **pied kingfishers**, tiny but colourful **common (or river) kingfishers** and the striking **stork-billed kingfishers**, which have massive red bills.

The water's edge is also home to smaller and drabber species, such as **plovers**, **water hens** and **coots**, which feed and nest among rank vegetation.

Forests

Although birds are easier to see around waterways, patches of forest often support a richer variety of species. Birds in forests are adapted to feeding in the different layers; some pick grubs off the forest floor, and others forage among the branches and leaves.

Among those heard more often than seen are **woodpeckers**, whose 'drumming' is caused as they chisel grubs out from under bark; colourful relatives of the woodpecker include **barbets**, which habitually sit at the topmost branches of trees and call incessantly in the early morning; and **Indian koels**, whose loud, piercing cry in spring can be maddening.

Look out for fruiting trees in the forest – they are often a magnet for birds of many species. Fruit eaters include a number of **pigeons** and **doves**, such as **green pigeons** and **imperial pigeons**; noisy flocks of colourful **parrots**; the **minivets** in their splendid red-and-black or orange-and-black plumage; and various **cuckoo-shrikes** and **mynahs**, including **hill mynahs**, an all-black bird with a distinctive yellow 'wattle' about the face. Sadly, hill mynahs are sought-after as cage birds because they can become quite tame and even learn to talk.

The jewels in the crown, for bird-watchers at least, are the huge and bizarre **hornbills** which, with their massive down-curved bills, resemble the toucans of South America. At the other end of the spectrum in both size and colour, iridescent, nectar-feeding **purple sunbirds** could be called the jewels in the canopy.

A host of smaller birds, such as **flycatchers**, **warblers**, **babblers** and little **tailorbirds** (so-called because they make a neat little 'purse' of woven grass as a nest) hawk and glean for insects in all layers of vegetation from the ground up.

CENTRAL GOA

The cathedral stands on what was the main square of the city and looking east from the main entrance it's possible to visualise something of the city's former layout. The grassy area in front of the doors was the large market square, to the left was the Senate House and to the right was the notorious Palace of the Inquisition.

The exterior of the cathedral is notable for its plain style, after the Tuscan tradition, and for the rather lopsided look that the loss of one bell tower, which collapsed in 1776, has given it. The remaining tower houses the famous Golden Bell, the largest bell in Asia, which is renowned for its rich tone.

The interior of the cathedral is also plain, and huge in its proportions. To the right as you enter is a small, locked area that contains a font made in 1532, which is said to have been used by St Francis Xavier. The two small statuettes which are inset into the main pillars are of St Francis Xavier and St Ignatius Loyola. There are four chapels on either side of the nave, two of which have screens across the entrance. Of these the **Chapel of the Blessed Sacrament** is quite outstanding, with every inch of wall and ceiling gilded and beautifully decorated – a complete contrast to the austerity of the cathedral interior.

Opposite, on the right of the nave, is the other screened chapel, the **Chapel of the Cross of Miracles**. The story goes that in 1619 a simple cross made by local shepherds

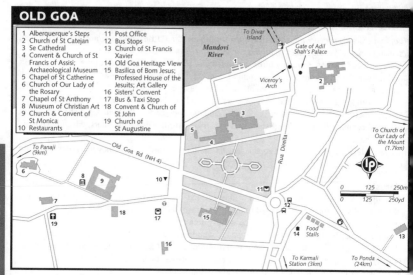

OLD GOA

1 Alberquerque's Steps
2 Church of St Catejan
3 Se Cathedral
4 Convent & Church of St
   Francis of Assisi;
   Archaeological Museum
5 Chapel of St Catherine
6 Church of Our Lady of
   the Rosary
7 Chapel of St Anthony
8 Museum of Christian Art
9 Church & Convent of
   St Monica
10 Restaurants
11 Post Office
12 Bus Stops
13 Church of St Francis
   Xavier
14 Old Goa Heritage View
15 Basilica of Bom Jesus;
   Professed House of the
   Jesuits; Art Gallery
16 Sisters' Convent
17 Bus & Taxi Stop
18 Convent & Church of
   St John
19 Church of
   St Augustine

was erected on a hillside near Old Goa. The cross grew bigger and several witnesses saw an apparition of Christ hanging on it. A church was planned on the spot where the vision had appeared and while this was being built the cross was stored nearby. When it came time to move the cross into the new church it was found that it had grown again and that the doors of the church had to be widened to accommodate it. The cross was moved to the cathedral in 1845.

Towering above the main altar is the huge gilded reredos. Its six main panels are carved with scenes from the life of St Catherine, to whom the cathedral is dedicated. She was beheaded in Alexandria and among the images here are those showing her awaiting execution and being carried to Mt Sinai by angels.

Mass takes place from Monday to Saturday at 7am and 6pm; on Sunday it's at 7.15am, 10am (High Mass) and 4pm.

Church of St Francis of Assisi

West of the Se Cathedral, the Church of St Francis of Assisi is one of the most interesting buildings in Old Goa. A small chapel was built on this site by eight Franciscan friars on their arrival in 1517. In 1521 it was replaced by a church consecrated to the Holy Ghost. This church was subsequently rebuilt in 1661, and only the doorway of the old building was left intact to be incorporated into the new structure. This original doorway, in ornate Manueline style, contrasts strongly with the rest of the facade, the plainness of which had by that time become the fashion.

The interior of the church is particularly beautiful – perhaps because the local artisans were given greater freedom with their skills here than elsewhere. The walls and ceiling are heavily gilded and covered with carved wood panels, and there are a number of large paintings on wood on the walls of the chancel. A huge arch that supports the choir, painted vividly with floral designs, and the intricately carved pulpit are worth looking out for. The reredos again dominates the scene, although with its deep recess for the tabernacle, it is different from others in Old Goa. The four statues in the lower part of the reredos are of the apostles and above the reredos is Christ on the Cross. The symbolism of this scene is unmistakable: Jesus has his right arm free to embrace St Francis, who is standing on the three vows of the Franciscan order – poverty, humility and obedience.

Like many other churches in Old Goa, this church has the tombstones of many of the Portuguese gentry laid into the floor. The font, situated just beside the door, is made up partly of a fragment of an old pillar from a Hindu temple.

Archaeological Museum

The convent at the back of the Church of St Francis of Assisi is now the Archaeological Museum *(admission Rs 5; open 10am-6.30pm daily)*. It houses fragments of sculpture from Hindu temple sites in Goa, which show Chalukyan and Hoysala influences; and stone Vetal images from the animist cult that flourished in this part of India centuries ago. Also here are two large bronze statues: that of the Portuguese poet Luís Vaz de Camões 1524–80), which once stood in the area between the Se Cathedral and the Basilica of Bom Jesus, and that of Afonso de Albuquerque, the first governor, which stood at Miramar.

Upstairs, a gallery contains portraits of the Portuguese viceroys. These paintings once hung in the official residence, and Richard Burton, who examined them while waiting for his audience with the viceroy, was unimpressed:

The collection is, or rather has been, a valuable one; unfortunately some Goth, by the order of some worse than Goth, has renewed and revived many of the best and oldest pictures, till they have assumed an almost ludicrous appearance.

Chapel of St Catherine

About 100m to the west of the Church of St Francis stands the Chapel of St Catherine. An earlier chapel was erected on this site by Afonso de Albuquerque in 1510, to commemorate his entry into the city on St Catherine's Day. In 1534 the chapel was granted cathedral status by Pope Paul III and in 1550 it was rebuilt. The inscribed stone that was added during the rebuilding states that Afonso de Albuquerque actually entered the city at this spot, and hence it is

CENTRAL GOA

The Incorrupt Body of St Francis Xavier

Goa's patron saint, Francis Xavier, was born into a wealthy and aristocratic family in Navarre, Spain, on 7 April 1506. A brilliant scholar, he studied at Paris University where he met and became friends with Ignatius Loyola and thus came to the turning point in his life. Together with five others, in August 1534, they formed the Society of Jesus and almost immediately hatched plans to travel to the Holy Land, where they hoped to convert the Muslims. Although the plans fell through, there was plenty to be done in other areas, and when missionaries were requested for the eastern empire, it seemed an ideal opportunity.

In April 1541 Xavier sailed from Portugal, arriving in Goa in May 1542. After a brief spell teaching, he commenced his travels, which took him to, among other places, Ceylon, Malacca and Japan. In February 1552 he persuaded the viceroy to allow him to plan an embassy to China, a mission which his death cut short. He died on the island of Sancian, off the Chinese coast, on 2 December 1552.

After his death his servant is said to have emptied four sacks of quicklime into his coffin to consume his flesh in case the order came to return the remains to Goa. Two months later, the body was transferred to Malacca, where it was observed to be still in perfect condition – refusing to rot despite the quicklime. The following year, Francis Xavier's body was returned to Goa, where the people were declaring its preservation a miracle.

The church was slower to acknowledge it, requiring a medical examination to establish that the body had not been embalmed. This was performed in 1556 by the viceroy's physician, who declared that all the internal organs were still intact and that no preservative agents had been used. He noticed a small wound in the chest and asked two Jesuits to put their fingers into it. He noted, 'When they withdrew them, they were covered with the blood which I smelt and found to be absolutely untainted.'

It was not until 1622 that canonisation took place. By then, holy relic hunters had started work on the 'incorrupt body'. In 1614 the right arm was removed and divided between Jesuits in Japan and Rome, and by 1636 parts of one shoulder blade and all the internal organs had been scattered through Southeast Asia. By the end of the 17th century the body was in an advanced state of desiccation and the miracle appeared to be over. The Jesuits decided to enclose the corpse in a glass coffin out of view, and it was not until the mid-19th century that the current cycle of 10-yearly expositions began (see the boxed text 'The Great St Francis Body Expo Experience').

believed that the chapel is built on what used to be the main gate of the Muslim city. The Chapel of St Catherine was rebuilt in 1952, but unfortunately it is rarely open for visitors.

Basilica of Bom Jesus

The Basilica of Bom Jesus is famous throughout the Roman Catholic world. It contains the tomb and mortal remains of St Francis Xavier, the so-called 'Apostle of the Indies' (see the boxed text 'The Incorrupt Body of St Francis Xavier'). A former pupil of St Ignatius Loyola, the founder of the Jesuit Order, St Francis Xavier's missionary voyages became legendary and, considering the state of transport at the time, they *were* nothing short of miraculous.

This is the only church in Old Goa which is not plastered on the outside, the lime plaster having been stripped off by a zealous Portuguese conservationist in 1950. Apparently the idea was that, exposed to the elements, the laterite would become more durable and thus the building would be strengthened. Despite proof to the contrary, no one has go around to putting the plaster back yet.

Construction began in 1594 and the church was completed in 1605. The facade has elements of Doric, Ionic and Corinthian design, and the pillars and detail are carved from basalt that was brought from Bassein some 300km away. Prominent in the design of the facade are the three letters 'IHS' which is the abbreviation of Jesus in Greek and were the Jesuit emblem.

The Great St Francis Body Expo Experience

The biggest event in Christian Goa happens only once every 10 years. It's the Exposition of St Francis Xavier, when the glass coffin containing the body of Goa's patron saint is brought out so that the masses can take a peak at his 450-year-old remains.

The Exposition takes place around the saint's feast day – 3 December – with the next event taking place in 2004. Lonely Planet author **Bryn Thomas** joined the crowds for the last Exposition in 1994. This is his account.

2 December

10.15pm We're squeezed into the back of the last bus of the day from Panaji to Old Goa. The bus is heavily garlanded, packed to bursting with good-natured pilgrims and the air is strongly scented with a combination of feni (Goa's favourite alcoholic drink) and cordite. More firecrackers are detonated and the bus lurches off. It's a very slow journey – many people are walking the 9km to Old Goa, some singing as they go. Horn screeching, eventually we arrive.

There are crowds of people, and a joyful, carnival atmosphere. The main churches are floodlit and there's a fair going on near the basilica. Rows of stalls sell everything from luminous green statues of St Francis to tubes of Colgate toothpaste. More attractive are the paper hats decorated with vividly coloured chicken feathers. One stall sells little wax models of human arms, legs and other pieces of anatomy. Apparently, you simply purchase the part of the body that corresponds to your malady and offer it up to St FX for an instant cure.

To the side is a little hand-operated wooden Ferris wheel, a distinctly dodgy fairground attraction. At least the people on it don't have far to fall when the whole thing collapses. The entire scene is in a time warp; attending a festival in the Middle Ages at one of the great European cathedrals must have felt something like this.

3 December

1.30am Apart from little groups of men playing cards by the light of the street lamps, most people have turned in for the night. In the main square there's row upon row of blanketed bodies; we unroll our sleeping bags on the steps of Se Cathedral. Not the best night for it as the fleas are bad and we're woken at 4am by the huge Golden Bell pealing above us. We lie there for the next hour listening to the familiar sounds of the Indian dawn (hawking, spitting and copious expectorations) while we watch the glorious sunrise.

10.15am High Mass is an impressive affair, with thousands of communicants crowded into the open-sided marquee set up outside Bom Jesus, and many more outside. No less than nine bishops

Inside the basilica the layout is simple but grand. The original vaulted ceiling has now been replaced by a simple wooden one. To the left of the door as you enter the basilica is a statue of St Francis Xavier, but yet again the huge and ornate gilded reredos that stretches from floor to ceiling behind the altar takes pride of place. The baroque detail of the ornament contrasts strongly with the classical, plain layout of the cathedral itself. As in the Church of St Francis of Assisi, the symbolism of the figures depicted is important. The reredos shows St Ignatius Loyola standing in protection over a tiny figure of the Christ child. St Ignatius' eyes are raised to a huge gilded sun above his head on which the Jesuit symbol 'IHS' is emblazoned. Above the sun is a depiction of the Trinity.

To the right of the altar, however, is the highlight for the vast majority of visitors, for it is here that the body of St Francis Xavier is kept. The body was moved into the church in 1622 and in the late 1680s the Duke of Tuscany financed the building of the marble catafalque. In exchange for his contribution he was given the pillow on which St Francis' head had been resting. He engaged the Florentine sculptor Giovanni Batista Foggini and finally, after 10 years' work, the three-tiered structure was erected in the basilica in 1698. The catafalque is constructed of jasper and marble. On each side of the second tier are bronze plaques on which are depicted, in relief, scenes from the saint's life. Atop the structure is the casket, which was designed by an Italian Jesuit

The Great St Francis Body Expo Experience

are present – this is the most important Christian festival on the subcontinent. The singing, in Konkani and English, is very good, and the choirs are accompanied by an orchestra and a band. After the service we chat to an elderly Goan who's lived in South India for the last 50 years and has just returned. 'Are you wanting to see Dead Body?' he inquires with a waggle of his head. We join the line.

1pm We've been in the queue outside Se Cathedral for half an hour and the sun beats down mercilessly. Reaching the cool shadows of the massive building is a welcome relief. At the top of the aisle lies the glass coffin and as we approach the crowd becomes more impatient. People take out their Bibles, rosaries and even postcards of the saint to touch the foot of his coffin with, drawing on his sanctity. Now we're right beside him. Four hundred and forty-two years on, there really isn't much left of poor Francis. Half his skull is showing and his face is just a mass of shrivelled, parch-

mentlike skin. Little black tufts of hair cling mosslike to the top of his head. His left ear is missing, and his right is just a small brown flap. His right arm has been sent to the Jesuits in Japan and his left hand, a decomposed ghoulish claw, rests on his chest. Just one toe remains on the right foot; three others have dropped off down the ages and the fourth was bitten off in 1554 by a mad Portuguese woman desperate for a relic. It is said that under those magnificent vestments there's little more than bare bones. The miracle of the incorrupt body is indeed over.

2.30pm We're ejected into the bright sunlight by the surging crowd. I don't feel particularly uplifted by the experience of seeing the saint's remains. A Jesuit priest comes up to talk to me. Perhaps sensing my disappointment he says, 'Remember Lazarus. He was miraculously raised from the dead but eventually he died. It's true, the miracle is over for St Francis, too, but that doesn't make it less of a miracle.' Miracle or not, simply being among the crowds of pilgrims is a tremendous experience. During the 54 days of the 1994–95 exposition more than a million people filed past the saint's body.

The body of St Fancis Xavier, Goa's patron saint, continues to draw pilgrims to the state

Marcelo Mastrili, and constructed by local silversmiths in 1637.

Passing from the chapel towards the sacristy there are a couple of items relating to St Francis' remains and, slightly further on, the stairs to a **gallery**. Even if the paintings are not to your taste, a visit to the gallery is still worthwhile, as there's a small window that looks down on the tomb of St Francis Xavier, allowing a different perspective of it.

Next door to the basilica is the **Professed House of the Jesuits**, a two-storey laterite building covered with lime plaster which actually predates the basilica, having been completed in 1585. It was from here that Jesuit missions to the east were organised. Part of the building burned down in 1633 and was partially rebuilt in 1783.

Mass is held in the basilica at 7am and 8am Monday to Saturday, and 8am and 9.15am on Sunday.

Church of St Cajetan

Modelled on the original design of St Peter's in Rome, this church was built by Italian friars of the Order of Theatines, who were sent by Pope Urban VIII to preach Christianity in the kingdom of Golconda (near Hyderabad). The friars were not permitted to work in Golconda, so they settled at Old Goa in 1640. The construction of the church began in 1655, and although it's perhaps less interesting than the other churches, it's still a beautiful building and the only truly domed church remaining in Goa. The altar is dedicated to Our Lady of Divine Providence, but the church is more popularly named after the founder of the Theatine order, St Cajetan, a contemporary of St Francis Xavier. Born in Vicenza, St Cajetan (1480–1547) spent all of his life in Italy, establishing the Order of Theatines in Rome in 1524. He was known for his work in hospitals and with 'incurables', and for his high moral stance in an increasingly corrupt Roman Catholic church. He was canonised in 1671.

The facade of the church is classical in design and the four niches on the front contain statues of apostles. Inside, clever use of internal buttresses and four huge pillars have turned the interior into a cruciform, above the centre of which is the towering dome. The inscription around the inside of the base of the dome is a verse from St Matthew's Gospel. The largest of the altars on the right side of the church is dedicated to St Cajetan himself. On the left side are paintings illustrating episodes in the life of St Cajetan. In one it appears that he is being breast-fed at some distance by an angel whose aim is remarkably accurate.

Ruins of the Church of St Augustine

All that is really left of this church is the 46m-high tower which served as a belfry and formed part of the facade of the church. The few other remnants are choked with creepers and weeds, and access is difficult. The church was constructed in 1602 by Augustinian friars who arrived at Old Goa in 1587.

It was abandoned in 1835 because of the repressive policies of the Portuguese government, which resulted in the eviction of many religious orders from Goa. The church fell into neglect and the vault collapsed in 1842. In 1931 the facade and half the tower fell down, followed by more sections in 1938. The tower's huge bell was moved in 1871 to the Church of Our Lady of the Immaculate Conception in Panjim, where it can be seen and heard today.

Church & Convent of St Monica

This huge, three-storey laterite building was commenced in 1606 and completed in 1627, only to burn down nine years later. Reconstruction started the following year and it's from this time that the buildings date. Once known as the Royal Monastery because of the royal patronage which it enjoyed, the building was the first nunnery in the east. Like the other religious institutions, it was crippled by the banning of the religious orders, but did not immediately close, although it was forbidden to recruit any further. It was finally abandoned when the last sister died in 1885. During the 1950s and 1960s the buildings housed first Portuguese and then Indian troops, before being reinstated to the church in 1968.

The building is now used by the Mater Dei Institute as a theological centre. Visitors are allowed in if they are reasonably dressed. There are fading murals on the inside of the western walls of the chapel.

Museum of Christian Art

Adjacent to the Convent of St Monica, this **museum** (admission Rs 10, children free; open

9.30am-5pm daily) contains a collection of statuary, paintings and sculptures, most of it transferred here from the Rachol Seminary. Many of the works of Goan Christian art during the Portuguese era, including much of the paintings and sculptures on display here, were produced by local Hindu artists. Among the items on show are richly embroidered priests' vestments, a number of devotional paintings and carvings, and a fair amount of silverware including crucifixes, salvers and crowns.

Church of Our Lady of the Rosary

Passing beneath the flying buttresses of the Convent of St Monica, about 250m further along the road is the Church of Our Lady of the Rosary, one of the earliest churches in Goa, which stands on the top of a high bluff. Legend has it that Albuquerque surveyed the attack on the Muslim city from this point and vowed to build a church here in thanks for his victory.

The church, which has been beautifully restored, is Manueline in style, and refreshingly simple in design. Occupying a dramatic position, there are excellent views of the Mandovi River and Divar Island, but unfortunately the church is frequently locked.

On the outside of the church the only sign of ornament are some simple rope-twist devices, which bear testimony to Portugal's reliance on seafaring. Inside, the same is true; the reredos is wonderfully plain after all the gold of those in the larger churches below, and the roof consists simply of a layer of tiles. In front of the altar, set into the floor, is the tombstone of Garcia de Sa, one of the governors, and set into the northern wall of the chancel is that of his wife, Caterina a Piro, who was the first Portuguese woman to arrive in Goa. According to legend they were married as she lay dying by St Francis Xavier himself.

Chapel of St Anthony

Opposite the ruins of the Church of St Augustine is the Chapel of St Anthony, which is now in use as part of a convent. The chapel, dedicated to the patron saint of the Portuguese army and navy, was one of the earliest to be built in Goa, again on the directions of Albuquerque, in order to celebrate the assault on the city. Like the other institutions

around it, it was abandoned in 1835, but was brought back into use at the end of the 19th century.

Viceroy's Arch

Perhaps the best way to arrive in the city of Old Goa is in the same way that visitors did in the city's heyday. Approaching along the river (and probably giving thanks for having made it at all), the first glimpse they would catch was of the busy wharf just in front of the entrance to the city. Although the city's fortifications were demolished to make way for new building, there was nonetheless an archway on the road up from the dock, to symbolise entry.

The Viceroy's Arch was erected by Vasco da Gama's grandson, who became viceroy in 1597. On the side facing the river the arch (which was restored in 1954, having collapsed) is ornamented with the deer emblem of Vasco da Gama's coat of arms. Above it in the centre of the archway is a statue of da Gama himself. On the side facing the city is a sculpture of a European woman wielding a sword over an Indian, who is lying under her feet. No prizes for guessing what the message is here. The arch originally had a third storey with a statue of St Catherine.

If you take a moment here, it's possible to imagine something of the layout of the old city. Standing on the ferry dock and looking towards the archway, the main docks at which the newly arrived ships were unloaded were to the right. The arsenal and mint were here too, although they were dismantled for building materials after the city was abandoned. To the left, the quay led into one of the busiest market areas in the city, and just to the left of the Viceroy's Arch as you face it was the Muslim ruler Yussuf Adil Shah's palace, which was eventually taken over as the viceroy's residence. All that remains of the palace now is the archway, which can be seen on the left as you approach the entrance to the Church of St Cajetan. The road running from the dock through the arch and into the city was known as the Rua Direita, and was lined with shops and businesses.

Church of Our Lady of the Mount

There is one other church in Old Goa, which often gets overlooked as it is some 2km east of the central area. Approached by a long and overgrown flight of steps, the hill on which the church stands commands an excellent **view** of the whole of Old Goa below. This is reputedly where Yussuf Adil Shah placed his artillery during the assault to recapture the city in May 1510, and again when he was defending the city in November. The church was built shortly afterwards, completed in 1519, and has been rebuilt twice since.

Special Events
The **Procession of All Saints**, on the fifth Monday in Lent, is the only procession of its sort outside Rome. Thirty statues of saints are brought out from storage and paraded around Old Goa's neighbouring villages.

The biggest festival of the year here is the **Feast of St Francis Xavier** on 3 December, preceded by a nine-day novena. There are lots of festivities and huge crowds here over this period, especially for the Exposition of St Francis Xavier's body, held once every 10 years – the next Expo is 2004. Accommodation in Panaji can be tight in the lead-up to the feast day.

Places to Stay & Eat
Most people visit Old Goa as a day trip, but there is one hotel, the GTDC **Old Goa Heritage View** (☎ 2286127; singles/doubles Rs 225/300), which has simple double rooms with private bathrooms.

Outside the basilica are two **restaurants** geared primarily to local tourists, where you can get full meals and cold drinks, including beer. They're raised up from the road and are a good spot to relax and take in the scene. You can also get cheap snacks (less than Rs 20) from the food stalls that line the road just north of the Old Goa Heritage View.

Getting There & Away
There are frequent buses to Old Goa from the Kadamba bus stand at Panaji; buses from Panaji to Ponda also pass through Old Goa. Buses to Panaji or Ponda from Old Goa leave when full (about every 10 minutes) from either the main roundabout or the bus stand in front of the Basilica Bom Jesus. The trip takes 25 minutes and costs Rs 4.

DIVAR ISLAND
The small island of Divar, which lies to the southeast of Chorao Island and directly to the north of Old Goa, is not only a useful short cut on the route from Panaji to Bicholim taluka in north Goa, but is also worth a visit in its own right. Somehow Divar Island, separated from the rest of the state by the forked waters of the Mandovi, seems even quieter and more picturesque than the villages on the mainland. The largest settlement on the island, **Piedade**, is a sleepy but picturesque Goan village – well maintained but with hints of crumbling Portuguese architecture.

Divar Island was sacred to the Hindus and it contained two particularly important temples – the Saptakoteshwara Temple (which was moved across the river to Bicholim when the Portuguese began to persecute the Hindus), and a Ganesh temple that stood on the solitary hill on Piedade. It's likely that the Ganesh temple was destroyed by Muslim troops towards the end of the 15th century, since the first church on this site was built in around 1515.

The church that occupies the hill today, the **Church of Our Lady of Compassion**, is in fine condition. It combines an impressive facade with an engagingly simple interior. The ceiling is picked out in plain white stucco designs and the windows are set well back into the walls, allowing only a dim light to penetrate into the church.

From the small park near the church there are excellent views to the north, west and south. Across the river to the south, the whitewashed towers of the churches of Old Goa are clearly visible.

Divar Island can only be reached by ferry. A boat from Old Goa (near the Viceroy's Arch) runs to the south of the island, and the east end of the island is connected by ferry to Naroa in Bicholim taluka. A less frequent ferry operates to Ribandar from the southwest of the island.

Divar makes a good outing by bicycle, especially combined with a trip to Old Goa. Most of the island is flat, but it's a tough slog getting up to the hilltop church. Although buses run between the ferry and Piedade, it would be a frustrating exercise trying to get around here by public transport – even taxis are scant.

At the north end of Divar Island, **Pleasure Island** (☎ 2280505; e islander@goatelecom.com; doubles Rs 1299, cottages Rs 1549) is a real retreat if you want to get away from anything resembling a beach or town. It's one of those typically Indian resorts set up for families and stressed businesspeople. There are overpriced cottages and rooms, a pool with waterslide, a gymnasium, activities such as tennis and a riverside location with private boat trips on offer.

GOA VELHA

Before the establishment of Old Goa as the Muslim capital, the major port and capital city under the Kadambas had been on the south side of Tiswadi Island, on the banks of the Zuari River. The Kadambas knew this city as Govepuri, but the Portuguese, distinguishing between the new capital, 'Goa', and the old site, called it 'Goa Velha'.

In its heyday, Govepuri was an international port, attracting Arab traders who began to settle in the area. In 1312 the city was almost totally destroyed by Muslim invaders from the north, and over the following years repeated invasions by the Muslims caused havoc. It wasn't until Goa was taken into the Vijayanagar empire in 1378 that trade revived, but by this time the fortunes of the old capital had begun to decline anyway, both from the crushing blow of its destruction and also from the fact that the waters on which it based its livelihood were silting up.

In 1470 the Muslim Bahmani sultanate took Goa, destroyed what was left of the old city, and moved the capital to the new site in the north, which they also called Gove but which is now known as Old Goa.

Little remains of Goa Velha, the site of which lies 3km north of the small village of Agassaim, on the northern side of the Zuari bridge. There are, however, some interesting sights to be seen nearby, and since the Panaji–Margao road runs straight through the centre of this area, the sites are easily accessible.

Church of St Andrew

Just off the main road, at the northern extent of Goa Velha, is the Church of St Andrew, which hosts an annual festival. On the Monday a fortnight before Easter, 30 statues of saints are taken from their storage place and paraded around the roads of the village. The festivities include a small fair, and the crowds that attend this festival are so big that the police have to restrict movement on the national highway that runs past the village.

The procession has its origins in the 17th century when, at the prompting of the Franciscans, a number of life-size statues were paraded as a reminder to the local people of the lives of the saints. Originally the processions started and ended at Pilar, but in 1834 the religious orders were forced to leave Goa and the statues were transferred to the Church of St Andrew. Processions lapsed and many of the original sculptures were lost or broken, until, in 1895, subscriptions were raised to obtain a new set.

Church of St Anne (Santana)

About 5km north of Goa Velha, the Church of St Anne – known to the local people simply as Santana – is one place that has really suffered from neglect over the past few years. A hand-painted sign by the side door still boasts the claim made by some observers that this is one of the greatest churches of its type (it's in baroque style with India architectural differences). However, it's hard to feel anything other than sorry for the appalling state it's in now. Even so, blackened as it is, with vegetation growing out of the facade and broken shutters hanging down, the place is still undeniably impressive. The huge front of the chapel is set off by the large cross before the building. If you peep through the doors you can see that the interior is still intact, and the whole thing has a rather ghostly air about it.

Pilar Seminary

North of Agassaim, set on a hill high above the surrounding countryside, is the Pilar Seminary, one of four built by the Portuguese (only two of which still survive, the other being Rachol Seminary, near Margao). The hill on which the seminary stands was once the site of the large Hindu temple overlooking Goa Velha. The original church on the site was built by Capuchin monks in 1613. They established a centre of learning here and named the seminary Our Lady of Pilar, after the statue they had brought with them from Spain.

Abandoned in 1835 the seminary was rescued by the Carmelites in 1858, and from 1890 became the headquarters of the Missionary Society of St Francis Xavier. The movement gradually petered out and in 1936 the buildings were handed over to the Xaverian League. Today the seminary is still in use, and is also the scene of local pilgrimages for those who come to give thanks for the life of Father Agnelo de Souza, a director of the seminary in the early 20th century who was beatified after his death.

The old Church of Our Lady of Pilar has as its centrepiece an original statue brought from Spain, and also has some attractive paintings in an alcove at the rear of the chapel. Just up the hill, in the seminary itself, there is a small museum containing some religious paintings and carvings, and some of the relics of the Hindu temples that were on or near this site.

Church of St Lawrence

About 3km south of Goa Velha, at the south end of Agassaim, is the Church of St Lawrence, a plain and battered-looking building, which houses one of the most ornate and flamboyantly decorated reredos in Goa. The heavily gilded construction behind the altar is unique not only for its wealth of detail, but for the peculiar design, which has multitudes of candlesticks projecting from the reredos itself. The panelled blue-and-white ceiling of the chancel sets the scene. Interesting too are the Jesuit 'IHS' symbols set into the tiled walls along the length of the church.

Getting There & Away

All buses running between Panaji and Margao pass through Goa Velha and Agassaim. Buses will drop you at the entrance to the Pilar Seminary. To reach the Church of St Anne you really need your own transport. However, this whole area is a good place to come for a leisurely day out on a motorcycle. The countryside is lovely and, among other things, you can see the traditional methods of salt collection, which are practised in the saltpans all around here.

PONDA & AROUND

Ponda is the major town of eastern Goa and capital of the Ponda taluka. It has grown hugely in recent years because of its location midway between south, north and east. Several large companies that distribute their goods throughout the state are based here because of the convenient access to all areas, and consequently the small town has rapidly become overcrowded. The main highway between Panaji and Londa, NH4A, now bypasses Ponda but the traffic in town is still very congested, most of it coming up on the

southern road from Margao. There's nothing of interest in the town itself.

The main reasons to visit the Ponda taluka are to explore impressive **Hindu temples** scattered among the surrounding hills, and to check out a **spice plantation**, of which there are at least four in the region that are open to the public (see the boxed text 'Spice up Your Life' later in this chapter).

For nearly 250 years after the arrival of the Portuguese, Ponda remained under the control of Muslim or Hindu rulers. When the Portuguese commenced the wholesale destruction of temples in the Old Conquests (Velhas Conquistas), many Hindus escaped across the waterway that marked the border, taking their deities with them. On the far side of the river, safe from persecution, they built new temples where the images could safely be installed. By the time Ponda itself came under Portuguese control, increased religious tolerance allowed the Hindu temples to remain.

Because all the temples around Ponda were either built from scratch or comprehensively rebuilt since the arrival of the Portuguese, they are all pretty modern in appearance. Anyone expecting the architectural wonders of, say, Madurai will be sadly disappointed.

The most interesting temples are probably the Shantadurga Temple in Quela, a short distance to the southwest of Ponda, and the Manguesh Temple at Priol, about 7km to the northwest. In between these two are several others which, because they are less prominent or simply harder to find, are less likely to be clogged with tour buses and thus more peaceful.

Manguesh Temple

This temple admirably demonstrates two features of Goan Hinduism. First, the temple is dedicated to a deity recognised only in Goa, Manguesh, and second, it exhibits a mix of architectural styles.

Manguesh was an incarnation of Shiva. Legend has it that Shiva, having lost everything to his wife Parvati in a game of dice, came to Goa in a self-imposed exile. When Parvati eventually came looking for him, he decided to frighten her and disguised himself as a tiger. In horror, Parvati cried out 'Trahi Mam Girisha' (O Lord of Mountains Save Me), whereupon Shiva promptly turned back

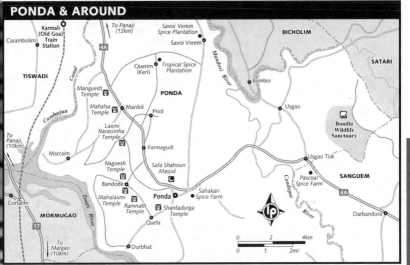

PONDA & AROUND

Karmali (Old Goa) Train Station • Carambolim
To Panaji (12km)
Savoi Verem Spice Plantation
Savoi Verem
BICHOLIM
SATARI
TISWADI
Querim (Keri) • Tropical Spice Plantation
Mandovi River
Bamboi
Manguesh Temple
PONDA
Mahalsa Temple • Mardol • Priol
Usgao
Laxmi Narasimha Temple
Bondla Wildlife Sanctuary
To Panaji (10km)
Marcaim
Farmagudi
Usgao Tisk
Naguesh Temple
Safa Shahouri Masjid
Pascoal Spice Farm
SANGUEM
Bandode
Mahalaxmi Temple • Ramnath Temple
Ponda • Sahakari Spice Farm
Candepar River
4A
Cortalim
Quela
Shantadurga Temple
Darbandora
MORMUGAO
Zuari River
To Margao (10km)
Durbhat
0   2   4km
0   1   2mi

CENTRAL GOA

into his normal form. The words 'Mam Girisha' became associated with the tale and thus the form in which he appeared at the time came to be known as Manguesh. A lingam left to mark the spot where all this had occurred was eventually discovered by a shepherd, and a temple was built to house it.

Originally the temple was based on the south side of the Zuari River, near the place where the village of Cortalim stands today. When the Portuguese took control, however, the lingam was brought to Priol and installed in a new temple. The grounds were enlarged in the mid-18th century and today there is a substantial complex, including accommodation for pilgrims and the temple administrative offices.

Architecturally, the temple is distinctly Goan; it shows the influences of both Christian and Muslim styles. Evidence of Christian influence is in the octagonal tower above the sanctum, the pillared facade of the seven-storey lamp tower, and the balustrade design around the roof. The domed roofs are evidence of the Muslim influence. The water tank in front of the temple is the oldest part of the complex. If you walk down to the right side of the temple you can also see the chariots that are used to parade the deities during the temple's festival, which takes place in the last week of January or the first week of February.

Mahalsa Temple

The Mahalsa Temple, only 1km down the road from the Manguesh Temple, is in the tiny village of Mardol. This temple's deity originally resided in an ancient shrine in the village of Verna, in Salcete taluka. The buildings were reputedly so beautiful that even the Portuguese priest whose job it was to oversee their destruction requested that they should be preserved and converted into a church. Permission was refused, but before the work began in 1543, the deity was smuggled away to safety.

Again, Mahalsa is a uniquely Goan incarnation, this time of Vishnu in a female form. Various legends suggest how Mahalsa came into being. In one, Vishnu, in a particularly tight corner during a struggle with the forces of evil, disguised himself as Mohini, the most beautiful woman ever seen, in order to distract his enemies (see the boxed text 'How the World Was Saved' later). The trick worked and Mohini, here with her name corrupted to Mahalsa, was born. To complicate matters, Mahalsa also fits into the pantheon as an incarnation of Shiva. In general, however, she is regarded by her devotees as a representative of peace; for this reason and for her multifaceted identity, she has many devotees.

Once you pass through the entrance gate and out of the busy side street, the temple is

CENTRAL GOA

How the World Was Saved

According to Hindu legend, the gods resolved to make a special potion, amrita, which would make anyone who drank it immortal. In order to make the elixir they needed to mix the ingredients on a grand scale. They used the sea as the mixing bowl and uprooted a mountain to use as the churning stick. To support the mountain Vishnu transformed himself into a tortoise, so that the rock could pivot on his shell. Finally, the serpent Vasuki was wound around the mountain and pulled backwards and forwards rapidly, so that the mountain churned the mixture and the potion was created.

As soon as the amrita was made, however, the demons who had been assisting with the process seized their chance and made off with it. All seemed lost, because with the help of the potion the demons would become immortal and invincible. Vishnu came up with the only possible solution. He transformed himself into Mohini, the most beautiful woman ever seen, who so captivated the demons that they agreed to let her distribute the elixir. Carefully she gave the bowl of amrita to the gods, while she passed a bowl of soma, or alcohol, to the demons. The ensuing battle resulted in a crushing victory for the gods and so the world was saved.

The story is a famous one in Hindu mythology, and is recalled outside the Mahalsa Temple, where the huge, brass oil lamp symbolically rests on a tortoise's shell.

Hindus celebrate this legend with what has been described as the greatest gathering of humanity on earth – the Kumbh Mela (kumbh means pitcher, the holder of the elixir, and mela means fair). It's held every three years alternately at Allahabad, Ujjain, Nasik and Haridwar – the four places where drops of the elixir fell to earth during the struggle.

pleasantly peaceful. The inner area is impressive, with its huge wooden pillars and slatted windows, and like the other temples in this area, an ornamented silver frame surrounds the doorway to the sanctum. Walk around to the back of the main building and peer through the archway to the water tank; the combination of the ancient stonework, palm trees and paddy fields beyond is quite a sight.

In front of the temple stands a large lamp tower, and a 12.5m-high brass oil lamp that is lit during festivals, and which is thought to be the largest such lamp in the world. Apart from the annual **Zatra** (festival) in February, the temple hosts two special festivals: **Zaiyanchi Puja** in August or September and **Kojagiri Purnima** after the monsoon, usually in September.

Laxmi Narasimha Temple

Almost immediately after leaving the village of Mardol on the main road, a side road to the right takes you up a hill towards the Laxmi Narasimha Temple. This is one of the most attractive of the temples around Ponda. It's dedicated to an incarnation of Vishnu, half lion and half man, that he created to defeat a formidable adversary. The deity was moved here from the area of the Old Conquests in the mid-16th century.

The best part of the temple is the incredibly ancient-looking water tank, to the left of the compound as you enter. Although the temple has a sign by the door announcing that entry is for the 'devoted and believers only' one of the priests will probably allow non-believers to have a look. Otherwise, from the gateway to the tank you get the best overall view of the place anyway, looking through the thick-pillared *mandapa* (pillared pavilion) to the inner area and the sanctum beyond.

Naguesh Temple

A short distance further south, in the village of Bandode, is the small and peaceful Naguesh Temple. The most striking part of the temple is the ancient water tank, where the overhanging palms and the weathered stone make an attractive scene. Also of note are colourful images in relief around the base of the lamp tower. Unlike its neighbours this temple was in existence well before Albuquerque ever set foot in Goa, but the buildings you see today are newish and rather uninteresting. The temple is dedicated to Shiva.

Mahalaxmi Temple

Only 4km outside Ponda, and a stone's throw from the Naguesh Temple, is the relatively uninspiring Mahalaxmi Temple. The goddess Mahalaxmi, looked upon as the mother of the world, was particularly worshipped by the Shilahara rulers and by the Kadambas, and thus has featured prominently in the Hindu pantheon in southern India. Here she wears a lingam on her head, symbolising her connection with Shiva.

Ramnath Temple

This temple is notable mainly for the impressive silver surround of the door to the sanctum. Although other temples have similar finery, the work here is exceptional, particularly the two unusual scenes depicted at the top of the lintel. The lower of the two depicts kneeling figures worshipping a lingam, while the upper one shows Vishnu lying with Lakshmi, his consort, on a couch

made up of the coils of a snake. The lingam installed in the sanctum was brought from Loutolim in Salcete taluka.

Shantadurga Temple

The Shantadurga Temple is one of the most famous shrines in Goa. Consequently, it is not only packed with those who come to worship, but also with visitors brought here by the tour-bus load.

The goddess Shantadurga is another form taken by Parvati, Shiva's consort. As the most powerful of the goddesses, Parvati could either adopt a violent form, in which case she was known as Durga, or she could help to bring peace, as Shanta. The legend goes that during a particularly savage quarrel between Shiva and Vishnu she appeared in her Durga form and helped to make peace between the

CENTRAL GOA

Spice up Your Life

One of the main reasons for the Portuguese taking Goa was to control the spice trade from the east (mostly from Indonesia), so it was a bonus to find that not only were several spices native to the territory, but also that many others could be grown here.

Spices and fruits grown in Goa's numerous plantations include cardamom, nutmeg, cinnamon, turmeric, ginger, cloves, saffron, pepper and even vanilla, alongside breadfruit, jackfruit, papaya, mango, guava and betel nut. At least four such plantations, all in Ponda taluka, are open to the public for tours where you can see spices growing, learn how they're harvested and sample and purchase various spices. The tours include a superb traditional buffet lunch, eaten off banana palm leaves and served in a shady open-air restaurant in one of the plantations. These tours are unashamedly geared towards tourists and many visitors arrive on a tour bus, but you can turn up independently and this is easily one of the best day trips you can do in Goa away from the beaches and historical sites.

Sahakari Spice Farm (☎ 2312394; W www.sahakarifarms.com; open 8am-6pm daily), on the NH4A about 1km east of Ponda, is an easily accessible 50 hectare organic plantation owned by the seventh generation of the same family. On the tour here you'll see a vanilla plantation (plants are pollinated by hand) and learn interesting trivia, such as that mixing a concoction of nutmeg and saffron with a glass of milk makes a natural Viagra! Export quantities of betel nut are grown here and you can see a demonstration (purely for tourists, of course) of the betel cutters at work. Rather than shimmy up and down the slender areca palms, they climb one tree, then swing across and grab onto another – a busy betel cutter will stay at the top of the palms for hours.

Lunch is a treat – you can sample half-a-dozen local dishes and wash them down with a fiery feni produced in the plantation's own distillery. The one-hour tour and lunch costs Rs 300.

In the tiny village of Savoi Verem, 10km to the northeast of Ponda, the **Savoi Plantation** (☎ 2340272; W www.savoiplantation.com; open 7am-6pm daily) is another long-standing tropical plantation, probably the most popular with tour groups. Again, an interesting tour and traditional lunch in the shaded restaurant area costs Rs 300. A feature here is that you can stay in farmhouse accommodation near the plantation for Rs 2000 a night, including full board. There is a small sign for the plantation on the main road through the village. Follow the loose-stone road for about 200m, and the plantation is on the left as the track starts to descend the hill.

Tropical Spice Plantation (☎ 2340329; open 8am-6pm daily), in the village of Keri, about halfway between Savoi Verem and Ponda, has similar tours; **Pascoal Farm** (☎ 2344268; open 8am-6pm daily), a little further out just off the NH4A past Usgao Tisk, also has tours for Rs 300.

two gods – thus embodying the contradiction of terms that the name Shantadurga implies. In Goa, the goddess has come to be worshipped as the goddess of peace and has traditionally had a large following.

The temple, which was built in 1738 during the reign of the ruler Shahu Raja of Satara, stands on a hillside facing the road from Ponda and makes an impressive sight.

Safa Shahouri Masjid

The oldest mosque remaining in Goa, the Safa Shahouri Masjid or Safa Masjid, is right by the NH4A on the outskirts of Ponda. Built by Ali Adil Shah in 1560, it was originally surrounded by gardens and fountains, and matched the mosques at Bijapur in size and quality. The buildings were damaged and then left to decay when the Portuguese moved into the area. Today, little remains of its former grandeur, although the Archaeological Survey of India has undertaken limited restoration.

A tiny white building set on a stone platform well back from the road, the mosque is usually kept locked. In front of it is an ancient water tank, constructed of laterite; unusually, the tank is on the south side of the building, rather than in front of the entrance, to the east. Apart from the building and the dilapidated tank, there are only a few broken pillars and random blocks of stone to mark the extent of the old buildings.

Places to Stay & Eat

It's hard to think of a good reason to stay overnight in Ponda, as the temples and spice plantations are an easy day trip from Panaji or Margao; however, it could serve as a base if you wanted to make an early start for Bondla or Dudhsagar, or if you're cycling around the region.

Hotel President (☎ 2312287; singles/doubles with private bathroom from Rs 200/300) is a central option in the Supermarket Complex, with simple but reasonably priced rooms.

The **Farmagudi Hill Retreat** (☎ 2335122; dorm beds Rs 80, doubles with/without aircon Rs 500/300-400), 4km north of Ponda on the NH4A (back towards Panaji), is a spacious GTDC resort and is more attractive than anything in Ponda. There's dormitory accommodation and all private rooms have private bathroom.

Getting There & Away

Ponda is 29km from Panaji and 18km from Margao. Although there are regular buses from Panaji (Rs 8, 55 minutes) and Margao (Rs 6, 35 minutes), the temples are scattered off the main highway, so it's best to have your own transport or charter a taxi.

BONDLA WILDLIFE SANCTUARY

Up in the lush foothills of the Western Ghats, 52km from Panaji, Bondla (admission Rs 5, car/motorcycle Rs 50/10, camera/video Rs 25/100; open 9am-5pm Fri-Wed) is the smallest of the Goa's main wildlife sanctuaries (8 sq km), but the easiest to reach from Panaji or Margao.

Sadly, although the setting is excellent and the trip provides a good opportunity to experience something of inland Goa, there's precious little to see in the wild once you get to the sanctuary. For the benefit of tourists hoping to see some animals, the Forest Department has set up a botanical garden, fenced deer park (Rs 10) and a depressing zoo with cramped enclosures housing leopards, deer and porcupines. Fauna in the wild here includes gaurs, sambars and monkeys, but unless you're prepared to spend a few days and put in the time on an observation platform, you're unlikely to see much in the wild.

Places to Stay & Eat

There's pleasant **chalet accommodation** (☎ 2229701; dorm beds Rs 50, singles/doubles Rs 200/300) at the park entrance. The circular huts each sleep two people and there's also a dormitory and a restaurant nearby. You can book in advance through the **Forest Department** (☎ 2224747) in Panaji.

Getting There & Away

Getting to Bondla is easiest with your own transport, and makes a pleasant motorcycle ride from Panaji, Margao or Ponda. By public transport there are buses from Ponda to Usgao village (Rs 5), from where you'll need to take a taxi (Rs 150) for the remaining 10km to the park. Another alternative is to catch any eastbound bus from Ponda to the turn-off known as Usgao Tisk, on the main highway (NH4A), and hope there's a taxi there to take you the 15km to the park, or at least to Usgao village. There's supposed to be a Forest Department minibus (Rs 5) that departs Usgao Tisk at 11am and 7pm, and returns from Bondla at 8.15am and 5.45pm, but it's not always running – check with the **Forest Department** (☎ 2224747) in Panaji.

MOLEM & BHAGWAN MAHAVIR WILDLIFE SANCTUARY

The village of Molem is the gateway to the Bhagwan Mahavir Wildlife Sanctuary. With an area of 240 sq km, this is the largest of Goa's four protected wildlife areas, containing within it the 107 sq km **Molem National Park**. The sanctuary is situated on the eastern border of the state, 53km from Panaji and 54km from Margao, but it is easily reached both by road and rail.

As with other Goan wildlife sanctuaries, unless you stay for at least a couple of days you're unlikely to catch a glimpse of many of the animals that inhabit the forest here, which include gaurs, sambars, leopards, spotted deer, slender loris, jungle cats, Malayan giant squirrels, pythons and cobras. There is an observation platform a few kilometres into the park; the best time to see wildlife is in the early morning or late evening.

The sanctuary's setting in the foothills of the Western Ghats is beautiful and the countryside is some of the most peaceful that you'll find in Goa, so it's a lovely place to spend a day or two. Nearby, also, are a couple of sights that are definitely worth taking in – notably the ancient temple remains at Tambdi Surla, and the cascading waterfall at Dudhsagar.

About 100m west of GTDC hotel is the **Nature Education Centre**, where you can contact the Range Forest Officer. He has the keys for vehicle access through the main park gate (admission Rs 5, motorcycles Rs 10; open 8.30am-5.30pm daily), which is about 3km east along the NH4A.

GTDC Dudhsagar Resort (☎ 2612238; doubles Rs 450, with air-con Rs 600) is just to the east of the police checkpoint in Molem. It has a rather forlorn, deserted feel to it, but the rooms are fine and there's a small restaurant.

Getting There & Away

The main entrance to the park is on the NH4A which heads eastwards out of Goa towards Belgaum and Londa. It's easy enough to get to the little truck stop that constitutes the village of Molem by public transport. Take any bus to Ponda and change to any

bus for Belgaum or Londa. Molem is 28km east of Ponda (Rs 10, 45 minutes).

However, it's far better to travel out here under your own steam on a hired motorcycle, as Molem itself is depressing, and all the sights are several kilometres away from the main road. It is extremely hard to find anyone willing to rent you a motorcycle once you get to Molem, and taxis are few and far between.

AROUND MOLEM
Tambdi Surla Mahadeva Temple

The 13th-century Mahadeva Temple found at Tambdi Surla is the only surviving structure of the glorious Kadamba dynasty in Goa. As such it is not only historically interesting, but it's also visually striking, quite unlike anything else in the state.

The temple appears to have survived the ravages of both the Muslim and Portuguese invaders purely by reason of its incredibly isolated position. No one quite knows why this spot was chosen; there was no road past here, and there's no evidence of there having been any major settlement nearby. Furthermore, the high quality black basalt of which the temple is constructed must have been brought a considerable distance – perhaps from across the ghats themselves, as such rock is nowhere to be found in Goa. All in all, the origins of the temple are something of a mystery. Although it hasn't survived completely unscathed (the headless Nandi bull in the *mandapa* is evidence of some desecration), the fact that until recently the temple was only accessible after a trek through the jungle has preserved it.

The temple itself is very small. At the eastern end, the open-sided *mandapa* is reached via doorways on three sides. The eastern of these entrances faces a set of steps down to the river, where ritual cleansing was carried out before worship. Inside the *mandapa*, the plain slab ceiling is supported by four huge **carved pillars**. The clarity of the designs on the stone is testimony not only to the skill of the artisans, but also to the quality of the rock that was imported for the construction. In particular, at about head height on each pillar there is a deeply carved groove, which is thought to have once contained small balls carved from the same piece of stone.

Above the groove, the symmetrical discus-shaped section is symbolic of the cymbals used in Hindu services. The best examples of the carvers' skills, however, are the superb **relief panel** set in the centre of the ceiling, depicting a lotus flower, and the finely carved **screen** that separates the outer hall from the inner area, or *antaralya*. On either side of the entrance to this area is a slab carving and two niches containing carvings of minor deities. Finally, beyond the inner hall is the sanctum itself, or *garbhagriha*, where the lingam resides.

The overall design of the outside of the temple is plain. On the tower itself (which appears to have lost its top section) there are three relief carvings depicting the three most important deities in the Hindu pantheon. On the north side (facing towards the access road) is Vishnu, to the west is Shiva and on the south is Brahma. On the level above these three carvings are three more, depicting each of the deities' consorts.

Getting There & Away The temple is about 13km north of Molem, and the trip out to it along quiet country lanes is wonderful. You need your own transport.

From the Molem crossroads, take the road running north towards Sancordem. After 3km or 4km there's a fork with the remains of an old, painted stone road sign. It's almost invisible, but you need to take the right-hand fork here which, according to the painted-out sign, goes to 'Bolkondo'. About 3km on there's a further fork which is signposted to Tambdi Surla. At the end of this road is a small car park area and a short path leading to the temple.

Dudhsagar Falls

On the eastern border with Karnataka, Goa's most impressive waterfalls, at 603m, are the second highest in India after Jog Falls. However, reaching them is expensive, time consuming and they are really only at their best in the monsoon, when they're inaccessible. All in all, visiting Dudhsagar (the name means 'sea of milk') will take the best part of day, and that doesn't leave a great deal of time at the falls themselves.

The best way to reach the falls independently is by local train, but with the closing of the Dudhsagar station, it's no longer as simple as getting off and walking there. You have to get off at Colem station, where locally controlled 4WD jeeps ferry groups for an extortionate Rs 1800 per jeep load (up to five people). There's a local train at 7.20am from Margao to Colem; check return train times at Margao station. The views as the line disappears up into the Western Ghats are undeniably fine.

The jeep takes you through the heart of the wildlife sanctuary, past a number of extremely scenic jungle and forest areas that would otherwise be inaccessible (there are three rivers to be forded, which would make this trip tricky by motorcycle). There is a pool suitable for swimming at the base of the falls. En route to the base of the falls it's possible to stop at the **Devil's Canyon**. Despite the dramatic name, it's an attractive spot with a deep pool formed between the steep-sided rocks. Locals say that it got its name through being a dangerous spot to swim – reputedly it's extremely deep, with strong underwater currents.

An easier alternative to taking the train is to charter a taxi (or ride a motorcycle) to Molem village (15km from the falls) or Colem station and pick up a jeep from here. Another option is to go on a full-day Goa Tourism tour from Panaji or Calangute (Rs 500, departs 9am), which also visits Old Goa, the Ponda temples and includes lunch at Molem Jungle Retreat.

North Goa

From the ramparts of Fort Aguada you can look north along the coastline for a view of almost continuous sandy beaches running right up to the border with Maharashtra, 30km away. This is by far Goa's most popular stretch of coast as far as volume of tourists is concerned. Candolim and Calangute are heavily developed and saturated with package tourists in the high season. Literally hundreds of beach shacks line the sand from Candolim to Baga, and concrete hotels dominate between the main road and the beach.

The beaches of Anjuna and Vagator are favoured by the party crowd and backpacking travellers, and at times you may get a feel for the bygone hippy days that made Goa famous (or infamous). North of the Chapora River are the quieter beaches of Morjim, Asvem and Mandrem and in the far north is Arambol (also known locally as Harmal), a developing beach scene popular with travellers escaping the crowds further south.

The famous flea market on Wednesday in Anjuna is the high point of the tourist week in north Goa, and you shouldn't miss it. There are now two smaller alternative Saturday night markets in Baga and Arpora.

North Goa is divided into four talukas (districts): Bardez, Pernem, Bicholim and Satari. Bardez is where visitors tend to spend most of their time and Mapusa is the main town here. Away from the beach are villages, farmland and a scattering of temples, but no must-see attractions, which is why few visitors explore eastwards in this part of Goa.

PANAJI TO FORT AGUADA
Along the north shore of Aguada Bay, between the bridges out of Panaji (Panjim) and the Arabian Sea, is the 'back road' to the start of the northern beaches at Candolim. From Panaji it's possible to get here by taking the regular ferry across the Mandovi River to the fishing village of **Betim** and then continuing west through **Reis Magos** and **Nerul** to the imposing Fort Aguada.

Reis Magos
A classic Portuguese **fort** and the important **Reis Magos Church**, dedicated to St Jerome, make the small village of Reis Magos worthy of a stop on the way to the beaches. It's not

Highlights

- Bargain-hunt at Anjuna beach's famous Wednesday flea market and watch the sunset from the Shore Bar
- Ride up the coast road from Chapora to Arambol and stop in at peaceful stretches of beach
- Climb the walls of Fort Aguada for superb views from this well-preserved Portuguese fort
- Enjoy the best nightlife Goa has to offer, from Tito's in Calangute or Paradiso in Anjuna to the open-air 'Goa trance' rave parties at Vagator
- Rent a room in a villager's house or cliffside chalet at Arambol and chill out on this remote beach
- Enjoy live bands, great food and hassle-free shopping at the Saturday night markets of Arpora and Baga

difficult to appreciate the importance of the site that this fort occupies, as it offers protection at the narrowest part of the Mandovi River. The fort was built in 1551 after the north bank of the river came under Portuguese control. It was rebuilt in 1703, in time to assist the desperate defence against the

NORTH GOA

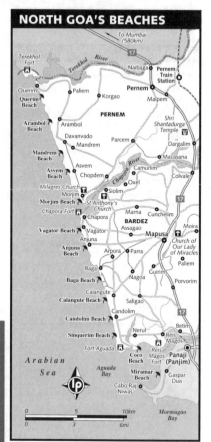

NORTH GOA'S BEACHES

shortly after the fort itself, in 1555, and was dedicated to St Jerome. A seminary was later added, and over the years it became a significant seat of learning.

Only the church remains, with its steep steps up from the road and fine views of the Mandovi River from the main doors. Outside the church, the lions portrayed in relief at the foot of the steps show signs of Hindu influence, and a crown tops off the facade. The interior of the church is impressively colourful, and contains the tombs of three viceroys. Reis Magos is the scene of a colourful festival on 6 January, when the story of the three kings is recreated, with young local boys acting the parts of the Magi.

Buses run regularly between Betim and Candolim/Calangute, so coming from either direction you can ask to be let off at the Reis Magos junction and walk the short distance to the church and fort.

Nerul & Coco Beach

About 5km further west, the village of Nerul sits on the estuary running off the Mandovi (crossed by a large, modern bridge). Signs point the way to **Coco Beach**, although you have to do a fair mount of weaving through paddy fields, coconut groves and village homes to find it. The grey sand beach, facing the Mandovi and looking across to Panaji and Miramar, is not particularly inviting, but it's quieter than Candolim or Calangute. There are a handful of beach shacks and the water is safe for swimming.

A water sports outfit set up here in 2003, but the local *ramponkars* (traditional fishermen) protested that the motorboats, waterskiers and jet skis were affecting their livelihood, so the future of water sports here is in doubt.

Albert's Odyssey (☎ 24015218; doubles Rs 400-500), an old Portuguese house among the coconut groves, faces Coco Beach. There are seven clean, spacious rooms with private bathroom and a garden restaurant at the front. The owner, Albert, also organises boat trips.

Fort Aguada

Standing on the headland overlooking the mouth of the Mandovi River, Fort Aguada occupies a magnificent position, confirmed by the fact that it was never taken by force. This is a very popular spot to watch the sunset, with uninterrupted views north and

Marathas in 1737–39, during which the whole of Bardez, with the exception of the Reis Magos and Aguada Forts, was occupied.

Although Reis Magos had the distinction of never being captured by the enemy, it was occupied by a foreign army in 1798, when the British requisitioned both it and Fort Aguada in anticipation of a possible attack by the French. After the British withdrawal in 1813 it gradually lost importance, and was eventually abandoned by the military and converted into a jail. It's not open to the public, but it's still worth coming up here for the excellent views.

The little church standing below the fortress walls is made all the more attractive by the imposing black bastions that loom above it. The first church was built here south. The motivation for building the fort came from the increasing threat of attacks by the Dutch, among others, and work was commenced in 1612.

The fort actually covers the entire headland and the river was once connected with the seashore at Candolim to form a moat, so that the headland was entirely cut off. One of the great advantages of the site was the abundance of water from natural springs on the hillside, which meant that the fort became an important watering point for ships and also led it to be named Aguada (*água* is the Portuguese word for water).

Today the main point of interest is the bastion that stands on the hilltop itself, although when compared with the overall area surrounded by defences, you realise that this is only a fraction of the fort. The buildings below the bastion on the waterfront now house the state prison, but the old bastion on the hilltop can be visited. In the main courtyard of the fort are the underground water tanks. These huge echoing chambers indicate just how seriously the architects took the threat of long sieges.

The **old lighthouse** (*admission Rs 2; open 10am-5.30pm daily*), which stands in the middle of the fort, was built in 1864 and once housed the great bell from the Church of St Augustine in Old Goa, before it was moved to the Church of Our Lady of the Immaculate Conception in Panaji.

From the top of the lighthouse (ask the caretaker to show you up) there are excellent views south across the estuary to Cabo Raj Niwas and beyond that to Mormugao and north along the whole expanse of coastline as far as the headland at Vagator. The caretaker may expect a tip for showing visitors around the old lighthouse and the underground tanks.

Nearby, the **new lighthouse** (*admission Rs 1; open 4pm-5.30pm daily*) can also be visited; no photography is allowed from it nor cameras inside it.

A short way to the east of the bastion is the pretty **Church of St Lawrence** (built in 1643), which also occupies a magnificent viewpoint.

South of the church and at the end of the road is **Aguada Jail** which houses a number of Westerners, mostly on drugs charges.

Getting There & Away To get to Fort Aguada you can ride or take a taxi along the 4km winding road that heads east from Sinquerim Beach and loops up around the headland. It's an enjoyable motorcycle ride, with good views along the top of the headland. By bicycle there's a steep initial climb, best done in the early morning. Otherwise there's a steep 2km walking trail to the fort that starts just past Marbella Guest House (see Places to Stay following).

CANDOLIM & SINQUERIM
pop 8600 • postcode 403515
Candolim beach and Sinquerim, the beach immediately below Fort Aguada, are now almost entirely the domain of the package-tour companies, although independent travellers can still find some relatively cheap rooms here, especially outside the peak season. Sinquerim Beach is a small curve of sand dominated by the five-star Taj Holiday Village and Aguada Hermitage. For the past couple of years the *River Princess*, a grounded tanker that no-one seems to want to take responsibility for, has sat forlornly about 500m offshore.

Candolim beach is a clean, straight stretch of sand running north to Calangute. It's a little quieter here, with fewer beach shacks, and it tends to attract a slightly older crowd and the few travellers who find Calangute and Baga too busy and Anjuna and Vagator too much of a scene.

Information
The main drag, roughly between Sinquerim in the south and St Anthony's Chapel in the north, is lined with souvenir shops, restaurants, hotels, travel agencies and places to make phone calls or read email.

You can change cash and travellers cheques at the **State Bank of India**. There are also numerous bureaus de change and travel agencies where you can change money and get cash advances on MasterCard and Visa reasonably efficiently. There's a **UTI Bank** ATM near Dona Alcino Resorts. The **post office** is near the north end of the village.

Davidair (☎ 2277007; Ⓦ *www.com2goa.com*) is a reputable travel agency, specialising in flights and organised tours out of Goa.

A useful landmark on the main road is the **Archana Complex**, often called the 'Elephant Shop' because of the carved elephants at the front. It changes money at good rates, provides tourist information and sells a wide range of carvings and souvenirs.

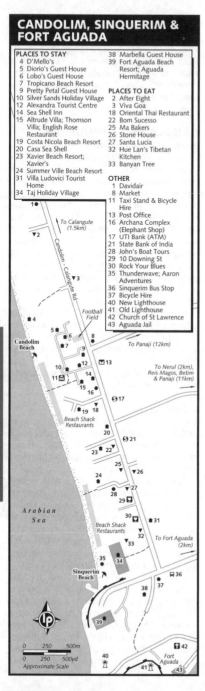

CANDOLIM, SINQUERIM & FORT AGUADA

PLACES TO STAY
4 D'Mello's
5 Diorio's Guest House
6 Lobo's Guest House
7 Tropicano Beach Resort
9 Pretty Petal Guest House
10 Silver Sands Holiday Village
12 Alexandra Tourist Centre
14 Sea Shell Inn
15 Altrude Villa; Thomson Villa; English Rose Restaurant
19 Costa Nicola Beach Resort
20 Casa Sea Shell
23 Xavier Beach Resort; Xavier's
24 Summer Ville Beach Resort
31 Villa Ludovici Tourist Home
34 Taj Holiday Village

38 Marbella Guest House
39 Fort Aguada Beach Resort; Aguada Hermitage

PLACES TO EAT
2 After Eight
3 Viva Goa
18 Oriental Thai Restaurant
22 Bom Sucesso
25 Ma Bakers
26 Stone House
27 Santa Lucia
32 Hue Lan's Tibetan Kitchen
33 Banyan Tree

OTHER
1 Davidair
8 Market
11 Taxi Stand & Bicycle Hire
13 Post Office
16 Archana Complex (Elephant Shop)
17 UTI Bank (ATM)
21 State Bank of India
28 John's Boat Tours
29 10 Downing St
30 Rock Your Blues
35 Thunderwave; Aaron Adventures
36 Sinquerim Bus Stop
37 Bicycle Hire
40 New Lighthouse
41 Old Lighthouse
42 Church of St Lawrence
43 Aguada Jail

To Calangute (1.5km)

Candolim - Calangute Rd

Football Field

Candolim Beach

To Panaji (12km)

To Nerul (2km), Reis Magos, Betim & Panaji (11km)

Beach Shack Restaurants

Arabian Sea

Beach Shack Restaurants

To Fort Aguada (2km)

Sinquerim Beach

0   250   500m
0   250   500yd
Approximate Scale

Fort Aguada

Activities

A range of **water sports** is available at the southern end of the beach at Sinquerim, so it's not the best spot for swimming. **Thunderwave** and **Aaron Adventures**, on the beach outside the Taj Holiday Village, offer adrenaline fixes such as parasailing (Rs 850 to 1300) and jet-skiing (Rs 900 for 15 minutes).

The water-sports operators and several beach shacks offer boating excursions, including dolphin-spotting for around Rs 400. The most established and best-value trips are run by **John's Boat Tours** (☎ 2479780), further up behind Candolim beach. The half-day dolphin trips (Rs 595, no-dolphin-no-pay) include lunch and drinks on the boat; and the popular full-day 'Crocodile Dundee' river trip (Rs 995) includes lunch at a spice plantation and free drinks. There's even an overnight backwater trip on a Keralan houseboat (Rs 3000).

Places to Stay

Moving south from Calangute, the hotels become progressively more expensive, with the majority in the upper-mid-range category – budget here is for rates under Rs 400. Prices listed are for the high season, but not the peak Christmas season (unless otherwise noted) when many hotels are taken over by package groups.

Places to Stay – Budget

There's a cluster of inexpensive guesthouses close to the beach at the northern end of Candolim.

D'Mello's (☎ 2275050; doubles Rs 250-500) is a very friendly family home with a garden, 15 rooms and a restaurant shack on the beach.

Further south in a series of laneways about halfway between the main road and the beach, are several good value family-run guesthouses. One of the best budget places is **Lobo's Guest House** (☎ 2279165; doubles Rs 250-400), which some good rooms upstairs and a sunny terrace.

Pretty Petal Guest House (☎ 2276184; singles/doubles from Rs 400/600, larger rooms Rs 800) is a lovely two-storey villa which has a large, well-kept garden and spacious rooms. The larger rooms have a balcony and fridge and air-con is available.

Altrude Villa (☎ 2277703; doubles Rs 400) and the **Thomson Villa** (☎ 2279297; doubles

The Pinto Revolt

In 1787 Candolim was the scene of the first serious attempt to overthrow the Portuguese. The founders of the conspiracy were mostly churchmen, angry at the racial discrimination that meant they were not allowed to occupy the highest clerical positions. Two of them, Caetano Francisco Conto and Jose Antonio Gonsalves, travelled to Portugal to plead their case in the court at Lisbon. Unsuccessful in their attempts to remove the injustice, they returned to Goa and started plotting at the home of the Pinto family in Candolim. Gradually the number of conspirators grew, as army officers and others joined the cause.

The plans were near enough to completion for a date to have been fixed, when the plot was discovered by the Portuguese authorities. A total of 47 conspirators, including 17 priests and seven army officers, were arrested. The lucky ones were sentenced to the galleys or deported, while 15 of the less fortunate were executed in Panjim.

Rs 400), side-by-side in a bare area just south of the taxi stand, are two family-run places with decent-sized rooms. There's a good open-air restaurant, the **English Rose**, which serves Goan and continental food from Rs 80.

Tropicano Beach Resort (☎ 2277732; 835B Camotim Vaddo; doubles Rs 450) is an excellent choice which has clean, pleasant doubles with private bathroom. There's a shady garden and the doors of this traditional laterite Portuguese house feature Goan glazing made from sea shells.

Diorio's Guest House (☎ 2279164; doubles Rs 500) is another attractive old home, run by a welcoming family.

Villa Ludovici Tourist Home (☎ 2479684; rooms with breakfast Rs 420) defies the up-market Candolim trend – it's a traditional family-owned Goan house with four old-fashioned, homely rooms which have private bathrooms.

Places to Stay – Mid-Range

Alexandra Tourist Centre (☎/fax 2276250; doubles with/without air-con Rs 750/660), on the lane leading to the taxi stand, is popular with British holiday-makers. It has some charm and a good restaurant.

Sea Shell Inn (☎ 2276131; e seashellgoa@hotmail.com; rooms with breakfast Rs 650, during Christmas Rs 950), on the main road, has just eight clean, comfortable rooms in an old colonial house. Its more modern sister hotel, **Casa Sea Shell**, has a pool and a good restaurant.

Moving down a small lane leading to the beach (and to John's Boat Tours) is a group of well-located mid-range package hotels. The spotlessly clean **Summer Ville Beach Resort** (☎ 2479075; w www.summerville beachresort.com; studio rooms Rs 600-950, with air-con Rs 750-1200) has a pool and comfortable rooms.

Costa Nicola Beach Resort (☎ 2276343; doubles Rs 1000-2000) is a beautiful, old Portuguese house tucked away from the main road. It has a lot more character than most mid-range places.

Xavier Beach Resort (☎ 2479489; w www .goacom.com/hotels/xavier; doubles Rs 400-800) is hidden away from the road and is a bit of a find. There are 16 comfortable rooms (Rs 200 extra for air-con), helpful management and an excellent restaurant, **Xavier's** (see Places to Eat).

Silver Sands Holiday Village (☎ 2276744; cottages Rs 700, peak season Rs 3000) has a group of cottages and rooms around a pool. Like many charter-tourist places it's good value outside the high season, but a waste of time as Christmas nears.

Places to Stay – Top End

Marbella Guest House (☎ 2479551, fax 2276509; rooms Rs 1100-2050), a beautifully restored Portuguese villa hidden down a quiet lane behind the Fort Aguada Beach Resort, is one of the finest guesthouses in the area. The house is shrouded in bougainvillea and has six airy, beautifully furnished rooms, each charmingly decorated in a different style (such as Rajasthani and Mughal). Breakfast and dinner are available on request, and the price includes tax.

Beside Sinquerim Beach, to the south of Candolim, are three five-star luxury hotels owned by the **Taj Group** (☎ 2479123, fax 2479512; e reservations.goa@tajhotels.com). There's the beachfront **Taj Holiday Village** (standard singles/doubles US$110/120, cottages US$130/140), which consists of a series of rooms and cottages in a shady, sprawling garden setting. Within the outer

NORTH GOA

walls of the old fort is the Taj Group's **Fort Aguada Beach Resort** *(singles/doubles from US$130/140, cottages US$140/150)*, which has stylish rooms, a series of cottages, and good views from the terrace patio northwards towards Calangute. The resort has a pool with a bar and five restaurants. Above it is the Taj's luxurious **Aguada Hermitage** *(1/2/3 bedroom villas US$210/280/380)*, which has northern views and sumptuous villas arranged on the hillside. There's a supplement of US$120 from 28 December to 3 January, and 18% tax on all rooms.

Places to Eat

Most hotels have restaurants, and down on the beach are dozens of shacks serving the obligatory Western breakfasts, seafood dishes and cold drinks. There's a good selection of beach shacks on Candolim beach at the end of the road opposite the post office.

Inexpensive restaurants include **Viva Goa** *(mains Rs 35-60; open 11am-midnight daily)*, a busy little place on the main road in Candolim, and **Hue Lan's Tibetan Kitchen** *(☎ 2479986; mains Rs 60-200)*, near the Taj Holiday Village, which has *momos* (dumplings) from Rs 60, along with Indian, Chinese and continental dishes.

Stone House *(☎ 2479909; mains Rs 90-150; open 11am-3pm & 6pm-midnight daily)*, on the main Calangute road, is an easily recognisable, solid laterite place. It's very mellow, with tables laid out in a garden and good grills such as steak and seafood. Mexican chicken legs cost Rs 140, and fish curry rice a pricey Rs 120. Across the road, **Ma Bakers** is good for croissants and pastries.

Oriental Thai Restaurant *(☎ 2275272; mains Rs 50-160)*, just off the main road, is an authentic Asian restaurant offering delicious spring rolls, Thai curries, a Korean barbecue and even cooking classes. The Thai chefs whip up a full range of dishes, including breakfast, continental and desserts.

Xavier's *(mains Rs 60-200)*, the restaurant at the Xavier Beach Resort, is recommended for its big range of Goan, Indian and continental food, including plenty of vegetarian dishes. There's a barbecue on Saturday evening and roast lunch on Sunday.

Bom Sucesso *(mains Rs 65-120)* has a wide range of reasonably priced snacks and meals including fish curry rice (Rs 75),

Goan sausages (Rs 95), a long list of Chinese noodles and stir fries, and the intriguing special, suckling pig. Upstairs is a sports bar catering to Brits, with darts, pool tables and live sports on TV.

Santa Lucia *(mains Rs 80-140; open from 6.30pm daily)* is an Italian place (with a Swiss chef) and one of Candolim's better restaurants for food and ambience. Pasta dishes are predominant, including a pasta buffet.

After Eight *(☎ 2279757; Rs 195-260; open 1pm-2.30pm & from 6.30pm daily)* is a fine place to splash out. The candlelit garden restaurant and cocktail bar is one of Candolim's best with a broad, innovative European and Indian menu of steaks, seafood and vegetarian dishes. There's also a quality wine list and you'll be greeted for dinner by the enthusiastic owner. Credit cards are accepted.

The superb **Banyan Tree** *(☎ 2479123, mains Rs 150-460)*, in the leafy grounds on the Taj Holiday Village, is an open-sided Thai restaurant. Green curry costs Rs 285 and seafood dishes top Rs 850. It's a great place for a special-occasion dinner and the food is genuinely spicy.

Entertainment

Candolim's more sophisticated crowd means there are a fewer boozy bars than at Calangute, but a couple of trendy places now complement the usual beach bars.

10 Downing St *(☎ 5649504; open 10.30pm-4.30am daily)* is a stylish, minimalist bar with a soundproof disco downstairs playing commercial, house and hip-hop til late. It's quite sophisticated and can get busy on weekends in the high season. There's jazz on Sundays and retro nights in the main bar. Look for the red phone box at the front.

Rock Your Blues *(RYB; open 7pm-2am Tues-Sun)*, at the southern end of the Candolim–Calangute road, is a modern club with a mixture of live music, DJs playing retro, lounge, trance and house, and a well-stocked bar – the sort of ultraslick place that's proliferating in Mumbai. A small Kingfisher costs Rs 60.

Getting There & Away

There are frequent buses between Calangute or Mapusa and Sinquerim (Rs 3). The buses stop at the T-junction at the southern end of the main road. There are also a few buses from Panaji via Betim and Nerul. The Candolim beach tourist taxi stand near Silver Sands Holiday Village has a list of 'set' prices for trips. A taxi to Dabolim Airport costs Rs 540.

You can hire bicycles near the taxi stand and there's another stall renting out bikes on the road to the Aguada Hermitage.

CALANGUTE & BAGA
pop 15,800 • postcode 403515

Welcome to Goa's package-tourist haven. The broad stretch of sand was the first beach that overlanding travellers settled on in the 1960s before moving on to Anjuna and further afield, but Calangute managed to evolve and retain the title of most popular beach in the state, becoming the epicentre of Goa's rapidly expanding charter-tourist market. This is India's answer to the Costa del Sol and, in the high season at least, central Calangute is the most overhyped, overpriced, overcrowded strip of mayhem in the state.

The village, once nestled between marshland and sand dunes among a sea of coconut palms, is now a mass of concrete hotels and guesthouses stretching almost without a break from Calangute to Baga.

Calangute beach isn't one of the best in Goa and many people will find it far too crowded – dotted with sun beds, deck chairs, meandering cows and slowly burning bodies. But for most of the charter tourists flying in from the UK, this is where the action is and there's no denying that there's plenty going on. Calangute and Baga have lots of good places to stay, some of the best restaurants in Goa, water sports, Goa's glitziest shopping and all the touts, taxis, trinket salesmen and beach bars you'll ever need. Up at the northern Baga end, the beach is a little less crowded and the landscape more interesting.

Orientation & Information

Baga and Calangute are joined by the 3km Baga Rd running parallel to and about 200m back from the beach. Many of the hotels, restaurants and shops can be found along this road.

There is no tourist office as such, but the staff in Goa Tourism's **GTDC Calangute Residency**, on the seafront, can usually help out with specific queries or with booking GTDC tours.

Money There are plenty of exchange offices in both Calangute and Baga. In Calangute, the **State Bank of India** will change cash and travellers cheques. It's more convenient to use the foreign exchange and credit card services of a reputable travel agency such as **MGM International Travels** in the market area.

Also near the market are 24-hour **UTI** and **ICICI** bank ATMs, which accept international cards, and further south on the road to Candolim is the **Centurion Bank** with an ATM.

Post & Communications The **post office** in Calangute is some way away from the main area, on a side road heading towards Panaji. There are many places in both Calangute and Baga where international phone calls can be made quickly and easily.

There are plenty of Internet cafés around the market area, on the road to Baga and along the road to Candolim. In the market area try **Edson's Cyber Café** (Rs 40/hr).

Bookshops Right on the roundabout in central Calangute, **Rama Bookshop**, operates a book exchange and carries a big range of second-hand books in many languages. There are a couple of smaller places to buy books on the road to Baga, such as **Jay Jay's Bookshop**, which buys, swaps and sells used novels.

Travel Agencies Near the roundabout in the market area, **MGM International Travels** (☎ 2276249) is the most established travel agency in Calangute. **Day Tripper Tours & Travel** (☎ 2276726; **w** www.daytrippergoa .com) on the main Calangute–Candolim road, is a good travel agency specialising in trips around Goa and interstate and dealing in flights.

Paulo Tours & Travels (☎ 2281274) has a small office near the beach in a lane called Golden Beach Rd. This is the main operator for private buses to Hampi, Mumbai and Bangalore and pick-up is available in Calangute.

Things to See & Do

The main activity in Calangute is lazing on the beach and there's no shortage of sun beds and umbrellas on this crowded strip. Most beach shacks will let you use their sun beds for free if you're eating or drinking at

NORTH GOA

CALANGUTE & BAGA

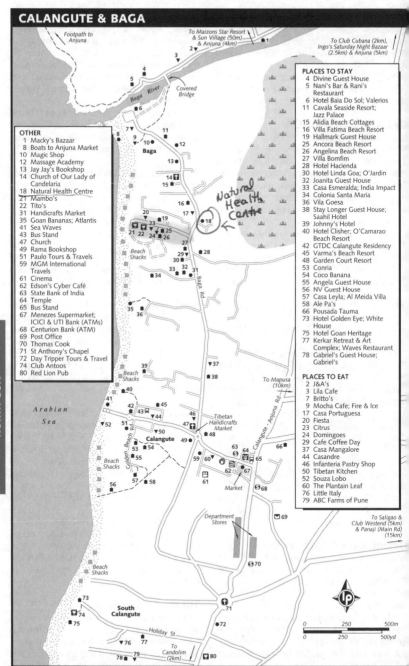

OTHER
1 Macky's Bazaar
8 Boats to Anjuna Market
10 Magic Shop
12 Massage Academy
13 Jay Jay's Bookshop
14 Church of Our Lady of Candelaria
18 Natural Health Centre
21 Mambo's
22 Tito's
31 Handicrafts Market
35 Goan Bananas; Atlantis
41 Sea Waves
43 Bus Stand
47 Church
49 Rama Bookshop
51 Paulo Tours & Travels
59 MGM International Travels
61 Cinema
62 Edson's Cyber Café
63 State Bank of India
64 Temple
65 Bus Stand
67 Menezes Supermarket; ICICI & UTI Bank (ATMs)
68 Centurion Bank (ATM)
69 Post Office
70 Thomas Cook
71 St Anthony's Chapel
72 Day Tripper Tours & Travel
74 Club Antoos
80 Red Lion Pub

PLACES TO STAY
4 Divine Guest House
5 Nani's Bar & Rani's Restaurant
6 Hotel Baia Do Sol; Valerios
11 Cavala Seaside Resort; Jazz Palace
15 Alidia Beach Cottages
16 Villa Fatima Beach Resort
19 Hallmark Guest House
25 Ancora Beach Resort
26 Angelina Beach Resort
27 Villa Bomfim
28 Hotel Hacienda
30 Hotel Linda Goa; O'Jardin
32 Joanita Guest House
33 Casa Esmeralda; India Impact
34 Colonia Santa Maria
36 Vila Goesa
38 Stay Longer Guest House; Saahil Hotel
39 Johnny's Hotel
40 Hotel Clisher; O'Camarao Beach Resort
42 GTDC Calangute Residency
47 Varma's Beach Resort
48 Garden Court Resort
53 Conria
54 Coco Banana
55 Angela Guest House
56 NV Guest House
57 Casa Leyla; Al Meida Villa
58 Ale Pa's
66 Pousada Tauma
73 Hotel Golden Eye; White House
75 Hotel Goan Heritage
77 Kerkar Retreat & Art Complex; Waves Restaurant
78 Gabriel's Guest House; Gabriel's

PLACES TO EAT
2 J&A's
3 Lila Cafe
7 Britto's
9 Mocha Cafe; Fire & Ice
17 Casa Portuguesa
20 Fiesta
23 Citrus
24 Domingoes
29 Cafe Coffee Day
37 Casa Mangalore
44 Casandre
46 Infanteria Pastry Shop
50 Tibetan Kitchen
52 Souza Lobo
60 The Plantain Leaf
76 Little Italy
79 ABC Farms of Pune

their shack, although if it's busy there's a charge of around Rs 50. Vendors are restricted from the beach and police often make a show of patrolling, but that doesn't stop people selling sunglasses, sarongs, massage and ear-cleaning services.

Goan Bananas (☎ 2276362) and **Atlantis** (W www.atlantiswatersports.com), about halfway along the beach between Calangute and Baga, both operate daily water sports and boat trips. Parasailing costs Rs 800 (Rs 1500 tandem), banana-boat rides cost Rs 300, water-skiing costs Rs 800 and jet-skiing is Rs 600. They also give lessons in windsurfing and water-skiing. **Sea Waves** offers similar water sports and parasailing near the steps on the central Calangute beach.

Boat trips to see dolphins or on the backwater to Coco Beach can be arranged through the water-sports operators, at **Day Tripper Tours & Travel** (see Travel Agencies earlier) or through **John's Boat Tours** (see Activities under Candolim & Sinquerim earlier).

If you're feeling energetic, a good **walk** is to cross the Baga River – either via the covered bridge or along the beach at low tide – and keep going for about 30 minutes around the headland to Anjuna beach. On market day (Wednesday), motorised outrigger boats regularly make the trip around the headland (Rs 50 one way) ferrying people from Baga beach to the flea market.

As with other resorts in Goa, there are many places advertising yoga courses, reiki, massage and Ayurvedic treatments. The **Massage Academy** (☎ 2279641; W www.vedamassage.com) on the main road in Baga is a very professional setup, positioned in a converted hotel, offering massage and reflexology courses from Rs 6000 (three to four days), as well as massage sessions (Rs 300 to 600).

The **Natural Health Centre** (☎ 2279036; W www.ayurvedagoaindia.com) in Baga offers a range of Ayurvedic treatments including massage (Rs 500 for one hour), reflexology, aromatherapy, acupressure and yoga. There's also a range of herbal medicines on offer and a free consultation by a Keralan doctor.

Seven- and 14-day Ayurvedic treatment courses (US$97-385) are offered at **Pousada Tauma** hotel (W www.ayurvedatauma.com).

There are two Saturday night **markets** in the Baga area that make a pleasant change

from the hype of the Anjuna Flea Market. They're much smaller, there's not as much hard sell, and they're held in the cool of the evening. The emphasis is as much on entertainment and food stalls as it is on the usual collection of handicraft, jewellery and clothing stalls. **Ingo's Saturday Night Bazaar**, on Arpora Hill, halfway between Baga and Anjuna, is spacious, well organised and has a good mix of Indian and Western-run stalls, great food stalls and local live bands. **Macky's Bazaar**, in the original market location on the Baga River (before the two organisers split and parted company), is a smaller Goan-run affair. It's walking distance from Baga. Both markets run from about 5pm to midnight from November to March.

Places to Stay

Accommodation is virtually at saturation point between central Calangute and Baga. Outside the peak season you'll have no trouble finding a room and the mid-range places that cater to charter tourists drop their rates by as much as 50%, so there are some good bargains to be found. Between 20 December and 5 January, finding a place as a 'walk-in' can be difficult.

Central Calangute The centre of Calangute is the area either side of the main road running from the market down to the beach. There are a few good budget options, particularly on the south side, but generally this is a crowded, noisy area.

There are several good places down a laneway parallel to the beach called 'Golden Beach Rd'. **Angela Guest House** (☎ 2277269; doubles Rs 150), in a pleasant area of coconut groves, offers basic, cheap doubles so it's popular with backpackers. Down a small lane just before Angela's are a couple more places, including **Conria** (☎ 2277354; doubles from Rs 300), which has large, clean rooms.

Coco Banana (☎ 2279068; W www.coco bananagoa.com; doubles Rs 450-650, mid-Dec–mid-Jan Rs 900) is a big step up in quality. Walter and Marina, a very welcoming and helpful Goan-Swiss couple, run a tight ship and keep spotless, secure rooms set around a quiet courtyard.

Down the lane in a peaceful area near the beach, **Casa Leyla** (☎ 2279068; Rs 450-600, over Christmas Rs 1500), owned by the same

NORTH GOA

family as Coco Banana, is a two-storey apartment-style place with immaculate rooms perfect for an extended stay or for a family. Behind Casa Leyla, **Al Meida Villa** (☎ 2279358; doubles Rs 150-350) is a much simpler place, but the spacious rooms are a bargain and it's run by a friendly family.

Nearby, at the end of the lane running south, **Ale Pa's** (☎ 2277479; doubles Rs 300-400, peak season Rs 1000) is a big three-story place with 10 clean, but simple, rooms. All have a balcony.

Hotel Clisher (☎ 2276873; doubles Rs 300) is a great little family-run place hidden away north of the beach road. There's an excellent seafood restaurant and 10 comfortable rooms with private bathrooms. It's just back from the beach but there's direct access to it.

O'Camarao Beach Resort (☎ 2276229; e camarao@rediffmail.com; doubles Rs 400-500), nearby, is a rambling, old Portuguese house that has the dual bonus of having character and being very close to the beach.

Near the steps to the beach, **Calangute Residency** (☎ 2276024; doubles Rs 500-650, with air-con Rs 700-800) is the GTDC hotel, an ugly bulk which dominates this part of the beach.

Varma's Beach Resort (☎ 2276077; e varmabeach@hotmail.com; doubles with/ without air-con Rs 800/600, over Christmas Rs 1650-2200) is a more pleasant family-run place with a slightly exclusive, romantic feel. Immaculate rooms are set around a private leafy courtyard garden. Some of the nicest rooms are the older ground-floor garden rooms.

Garden Court Resort (☎ 2276054; budget rooms Rs 300-350, large rooms Rs 500-800), in the thick of things at the roundabout at the start of the Calangute–Baga road, is a charming old place run by a traveller-friendly family. It has a touch of character amongst all the concrete hotels.

Pousada Tauma (☎ 2279061; w www.pou sada-tauma.com; standard/superior/deluxe suites US$185/215/295, peak season US$320/ 370/470), on the road to Panaji, describes itself as Goa's first boutique hotel and is certainly one of the most relaxing and exclusive retreats in the state. It's beautifully designed, with 12 stylish themed suites (sea theme, castle suite, garden suites) constructed in local stone around a swimming pool. There's a pool bar, fine-dining restaurant and gym. During the peak season (from 20 December to 10 January) the minimum stay is seven nights and the rates are way over the top. Ayurvedic treatment courses are available in the centre (see Things to See & Do earlier in this chapter for details).

South Calangute It's generally quieter and more rustic here than further north, and there are a few good places along the narrow lanes leading down to the beach.

NV Guest House (☎ 2279749; budget doubles Rs 150-200, 1st-floor rooms Rs 400) enjoys an excellent location close to the beach. It's run by a sociable family, and the restaurant, only a few metres from the beach, serves fresh seafood.

Further south again, at the end of a road imaginatively called Holiday St, is a group of small mid-range hotels notable mainly for their position very close to a relatively quiet stretch of the beach. **Hotel Golden Eye** (☎ 2276187; doubles Rs 650, during Christmas Rs 1000) is an efficiently run package hotel right on the beach. The Mediterranean-style **White House** (☎ 2277938; doubles Rs 600) is a spotless family-run place and great value outside the peak season. There are several other family homes with rooms to rent in this area, so it's worth having a scout around if the others are full or if you're looking for something cheaper.

Hotel Goan Heritage (☎ 2276761; w www .goanheritage.com; doubles Rs 1700, during Christmas Rs 3500), in the same beachfront area, is a large upmarket resort that has a swimming pool, gym, restaurants and rooms with satellite TV, minibar and balcony.

On Holiday St, closer to the main road, **Kerkar Retreat** (☎ 2276017; e subodhker kar@satyam.net.in; doubles Rs 1500, during Christmas Rs 3500) is a very stylish place attached to the Kerkar Art Complex. The retreat has five beautifully designed boutique rooms.

On the next road to the south (turn off opposite the Red Lion Pub), **Gabriel's Guest House** (☎ 2279486; doubles Rs 300-400), halfway down a laneway to the beach, is a pleasant family home with spotless rooms with balconies. The Goan and Italian food served at the terrace restaurant, **Gabriel's**, is superb (see Places to Eat).

Calangute to Baga The Baga Rd, running north from the roundabout in central Calangute to the Baga River, is the busiest part of the village.

Among the cheaper places, **Johnny's Hotel** (☎ 2277458; e johnnys_hotel@rediff mail.com; singles/doubles from Rs 250/300, doubles during Christmas Rs 600) is close to the beach (with easy beach access), down one of the first lanes you come to as you head north. There's a variety of plain but clean rooms in this long-running guesthouse. There's a rooftop terrace where yoga, massage and reiki sessions are held.

One of the smaller places on the main road is **Stay Longer Guest House** (☎ 227 7460; doubles from Rs 250, during Christmas Rs 600). It's an ageing place and has simple, inexpensive doubles.

Virtually next door, **Saahil Hotel** (☎ 227 6647; doubles Rs 350-500) is an attractive laterite stone building with 13 airy rooms and a pleasant open patio and dining area.

Down a lane, well shielded from the busy bustle of Calangute, **Vila Goesa** (☎ 2277535; e alobo@goatelecom.com; doubles with/without air-con Rs 1490/1380, peak season Rs 3450/2070) has a good location near the beach. Goan-style rooms are set in an attractive, shady garden resort, which has a pool, cocktail bar and restaurant. The price includes tax.

On the next lane down to the beach, well-run **Casa Esmeralda** (☎ 2277194; doubles with fan Rs 450, during Christmas Rs 1000) has seven clean rooms with private bathroom. It has an excellent terrace restaurant, **Indian Impact**.

Further down the same lane, **Colonia Santa Maria** (☎ 2276107; w www.angels resort.com; rooms Rs 1050-1550) is a fully fledged air-con package hotel with a pool, restaurant and easy beach access.

Hotel Linda Goa (☎ 2276066; w www .hotellindagoa.com; singles/doubles Rs 450/ 550, with air-con Rs 650/750) is one of a number of package-tour hotels on the main road that are reasonably priced outside the peak season. The rooms are a bit worn out but there's a pool at the back, and the recommended garden restaurant **O'Jardin**.

Next door to Hotel Linda Goa and down a small lane, **Joanita Guest House** (☎ 2277166; doubles Rs 300-350) has just four simple rooms with private bathroom alongside a Goan family home. The rooms are excellent value and face a pleasant, shady garden.

Across the road, down a small lane away from the beach, **Hotel Hacienda** (☎ 227 7348; doubles Rs 400) is a bright and breezy colonial-style house with a leafy garden.

Villa Bomfim (☎ 2276105; w www.villa bomfim.com; doubles with/without air-con Rs 1500/1300, peak season Rs 2400/2200) is not as earthy as the old colonial building housing the reception suggests, but the modern blocks surrounding a pool and landscaped garden contain large, airy rooms. There's a garden restaurant and credit cards are accepted.

Turning down the lane leading to Tito's, **Ancora Beach Resort** (☎ 2276096; doubles with/without air-con Rs 500/250-350) is 'a clean two-storey place with an Internet café and sizzler restaurant attached. The more expensive upstairs rooms face the street and have a balcony. It can get noisy around here at night, but it's great if you like to be central to the action.

Angelina Beach Resort (☎ 2279145; e an gelinabeachresort@rediffmail.com; doubles Rs 300, high season Rs 500) is one of several good family-run places set a little back from the lane where it's relatively peaceful.

Across the other side of the lane, **Hallmark Guest House** (☎ 2275030; Rs 250-300) doesn't look like much but it's reasonably priced and has immaculate tiled rooms leading onto a large balcony.

Baga These days it's hard to tell where Calangute ends and Baga begins, but it's somewhere north of the laneway leading to Tito's.

Villa Fatima Beach Resort (☎ 2277418; e fatimavi@goatelecom.com; doubles Rs 200-500), set back from the road behind a rambling Goan house, is well run and popular among backpackers. There's a restaurant and TV area in an enclosed courtyard, and easy beach access from the back.

Alidia Beach Cottages (☎ 2276835; e alidia@rediffmail.com; cottages Rs 500-800; suites with air-con Rs 1200), back behind the whitewashed Church of Our Lady of Candelaria is a very good choice; the beautifully kept rooms and cottages are well away from the road, fronting on to the beach. There are two stylish two-room suites with a modern design, large beds and balcony.

The ivy-covered brick **Cavala Seaside Resort** (☎ 2276090; W www.cavala.com; singles/doubles from Rs 450/750, doubles with aircon Rs 1300-1700) is a place that looks a bit like a miniature English manor. Rooms are comfortable and the more expensive ones are quite spacious. There are also rooms across the road where there's a bar and swimming pool. Rates double over Christmas.

Hotel Baia Do Sol (☎ 2276884; W www.ndnaik.com; rooms Rs 950-1300, cottages Rs 1500-2400), close to the Baga River at the end of the main road, tends not to take charter tourists but still keeps busy with its comfortable rooms and cottages, attractive garden and fine rooftop restaurant, **Valerios** (see Places to Eat). The more expensive rooms have air-con and river frontage. Peak season rates are about 50% higher.

North of Baga River Across the Baga River (cross through the extraordinarily ugly covered bridge and turn left) are several lovely family-run places, away from the Calangute hype.

The **Divine Guest House** (☎ 2279546; doubles Rs 300-400) has spotless rooms and a pleasant garden restaurant.

Nani's Bar & Rani's Restaurant (☎ 227 6313; rooms Rs 250-600), further around this road, is a big old Portuguese house with a variety of simple and very rustic rooms. The eight rooms are all different, there's a leafy garden and meals are served on the veranda.

At the eastern end of this road, in an area where Baga meets Arpora, is a group of resort hotels catering mainly to package tourists but also offering walk-in rates. Two of them are facing each other on the unsealed back road to Anjuna. Four-star **Sun Village** (☎ 2279409; doubles Rs 6000) is a huge place with its own shopping arcade, health club and an impressive pool. Rooms are all suites with cable TV and fridge. **Maizons Star Resort** (☎ 2279389; W www.maizons.com; singles/doubles Rs 800/1000, doubles with air-con Rs 1400) is smaller but also has all the facilities and is reasonable value.

Places to Eat

Calangute's restaurant scene now boasts some of the best dining in Goa. There are literally hundreds of small restaurants crammed into every available bit of space, and the endless string of bamboo beach shacks are a great place to watch the sun go down with a cold beer and a plate of seafood.

Calangute Near the main roundabout in central Calangute, the **Infanteria Pastry Shop** is a good stop for breakfast with an all you-can-eat buffet for Rs 125, although it's one of those places where prices have risen but standards have slipped. Fresh croissants, sandwiches, pastries and samosas sit alongside pizzas and Goan dishes.

Tibetan Kitchen (mains Rs 70-110; open 9am-3pm & 6pm-10.30pm daily), tucked away off the main beach road, offers momos and other Tibetan food, along with Indian and Chinese, in a relaxed, open-air setting.

The Plantain Leaf (mains Rs 10-40), near the market, is the best vegetarian restaurant around. It's pure veg and has thalis (from Rs 35), dosas and samosas.

The restaurant at **Hotel Clisher** (mains Rs 40-140) serves some of the best-value seafood in Calangute in a relaxed setting close to the beach. Fish curry rice costs Rs 45, Goan dishes are Rs 40 to 70 and steaks and continental dishes cost around Rs 100.

Souza Lobo (☎ 2276463; mains Rs 60-150), facing the main beach just south of the steps, has long been a favourite for quality seafood, but is becoming of victim of its own success and is not cheap compared with the beach shacks. The unassuming covered dining area is perpetually busy (especially in the evenings). Seafood prepared in Goan, Indian or continental styles is the big draw here – fish curry rice costs Rs 70, dishes such as lobster and tiger prawns can top Rs 600 to 800, depending on weight.

Casandre (☎ 2275934; mains Rs 50-180), on the road leading to the main beach, is a stylishly converted Goan house that's now a cocktail 'taverna' and restaurant. You can eat on the balcao (porch) or inside. Seafood and Goan dishes feature heavily on the menu; fish fillet with stuffed crab costs Rs 180. Cocktails range from Rs 80 to 160 and there's a pool table.

Tibetan Kitchen (mains Rs 70-140; open 9am-3pm & 6pm-10.30pm daily) is set back off the beach road in a rustic, relaxed garden setting. Along with Tibetan specialities such as momos (Rs 90) and thugpa (Tibetan noodle soup; Rs 70), there're Indian, Chinese and seafood dishes on the menu.

ABC Farms of Pune (☎ *2281182)*, just off the main Calangute–Candolim road, sells some of its wide range of cheeses produced on its Pune farm – Cheddar, Stilton, Swiss, Boursin and Parmesan among them.

Gabriel's *(mains Rs 60-200)*, the terrace restaurant at Gabriel's Guest House in south Calangute, is a fine place for home-cooked Goan and Italian food. Handmade pasta, fish pate and rich Goan sauces are the speciality and the friendly owners make guests very welcome.

Little Italy (☎ *2275368;* W *www.little italyindia.com; mains Rs 135-220; open 6pm-11pm daily)*, hidden away just off Holiday St in south Calangute, is a fine, pricey, Sicilian-run restaurant. The speciality is pizza (26 varieties), pasta and risotto, along with some interesting entrees (Sicilian antipasto costs Rs 140) and a good range of desserts and imported wine. The towering mock-classical portico is a slightly tacky eyesore. If you're dining alfresco, bring mosquito repellent!

Casa Mangalore (☎ *2277665; mains Rs 70-190; open noon-midnight daily)*, on the road to Baga, is one of the few places in Goa specialising in Mangalorean seafood. Mangalorean fish curry rice costs Rs 80 and biryanis cost Rs 70. The curry dishes are made using home-made masala. There are also some fancy desserts such as coffee-liqueur pudding and an extensive cocktail bar.

Citrus *(salads & mains Rs 50-140)*, near Tito's, is a modern European-style vegetarian restaurant with an innovative menu featuring mezes, pasta, salads, risotto and rich desserts.

Domingoes *(open from 6.30pm daily)* is a simple palm-thatch place just off the lane leading to Tito's. It specialises in excellent home-made pasta (around Rs 75 to 95) and some of the best beef steaks in Calangute (Rs 135).

Cafe Coffee Day *(coffees Rs 16-40)* is a modern, open-fronted café serving European-style coffee (espresso, cappuccino, as well as Colombian and Irish coffee), iced coffee drinks, smoothies, tea and pastries. This type of coffee shop is becoming trendy in Indian cities and it's a good place to take a break in the afternoon.

Valerios (☎ *2276884; mains Rs 65-165)*, in a relatively quiet area at Hotel Baia Do Sol in Baga, has a pleasant balcony terrace dining area as well as an enclosed restaurant

and cocktail bar. The food is mainly seafood and continental, including home-made pasta dishes, as well as a few Goan specialities.

Fiesta *(mains Rs 125-200)*, near Tito's, is one of Calangute's best restaurants for food and ambience, with a leafy alfresco dining area overlooking the beach. It specialises in Mediterranean cuisine with paella, wood-fired pizzas, ravioli and tiramisu featuring on the menu.

Waves (☎ *2276017; mains Rs 190-240; open 6.30pm-11pm Wed-Mon, 8.30pm-11pm Tues)*, at the Kerkar Art Complex in south Calangute, is a stylish garden restaurant serving gourmet steaks, seafood, Indian and vegetarian cuisine, with a Russian touch. Among the dishes on offer are chicken Kiev (Rs 210), borscht (Rs 190), prawns creole (Rs 240) and Chateaubriand (Rs 230). Like everything at Kerkar, it's beautifully done.

Baga North of the river in Baga, **Lila Cafe** (☎ *2279843; mains Rs 55-140; open 8.30am-6.30pm daily)*, is the best spot in Goa for breakfast (Rs 10 to 80), and not a bad place for lunch either. There's a German bakery, superb croissants, muesli, fresh fruit juices and home-made marmalade, all served in a relaxing garden. This is a restaurant where hippies rub shoulders with package tourists.

Mocha Cafe (☎ *2279473)*, on the beach in Baga, is a new trend for Goa – a Middle Eastern–style coffee house with cushions, low tables, aromatic hookah pipes and staff in fez hats. The specialities are exotic coffee flavours (Rs 55 to 80), rich cakes and desserts (Rs 90 to 125), but you can also get wraps, paninis and there's a well-stocked bar.

J&A's (☎ *2282364;* W *www.littleitalygoa.com; mains Rs 215-285; open from 6pm daily)*, near Lila Café, vies with Little Italy for the title of top Italian restaurant. It serves authentic Italian food in stylish alfresco surroundings, with wood-fired pizzas (from Rs 215) and some innovative pastas on the menu, along with Tuscan beef stew (Rs 245) and Mediterranean fish kababs. Imported wine costs around Rs 825 a bottle, or Rs 95 to 170 a glass, and filtered mineral water is provided free to patrons.

Britto's *(mains Rs 50-125)*, in Baga, is a long-running restaurant almost on the beach. There're good Goan and continental foods, fabulous cakes and desserts and occasional

NORTH GOA

live music. Fish curry rice costs Rs 75, prawn vindaloo is Rs 125, and Black Forest cake is Rs 40.

Casa Portuguesa (☎ 2277024; mains Rs 60-180; open from 6pm daily) is set within the walled grounds of a rambling villa. It has a unique old-world charm but the food gets mixed reviews. Goan delicacies include *sorpotel* (spicy pork stew including liver, heart and kidneys) and *bebinca* (a rich Goan dessert made from egg yolk and coconut).

Entertainment

In south Calangute, the **Kerkar Art Complex** hosts Indian classical music and dance every Tuesday from 6.45pm to 8.30pm. Performances (Rs 250) are held in the rear courtyard. Mid-range and top-end hotels occasionally stage cultural shows for tourists – look out for flyers around town.

Nightlife in Calangute revolves around bars and a few clubs. For most mainstream visitors (ie, package tourists) this is the centre of Goa's bar scene. Alcohol consumption outweighs chemical consumption here.

Tito's (ⓦ www.titosgoa.com; admission into disco Rs 200) is the number one club and bar. It has a huge terrace with two bars, a high-powered sound system, and a small, slightly seedy, enclosed disco that stays open till 3am. An overindulgence in alcohol can result in trouble in this area late at night – solo travellers should take care. Further down towards the beach, **Mambo's**, which is essentially part of Tito's, is a much earthier place with a relaxed atmosphere, wooden bar, pool tables and occasional karaoke.

Red Lion Pub in south Calangute is an English-run bar with occasional live music, karaoke, televised football matches and draught beer. It also has home-made cider and usually stays open till 1am.

The **Jazz Place**, at the Cavala Seaside Resort in Baga, has live jazz three nights a week (usually Tuesday, Friday and Sunday) during the high season.

Fire & Ice is the latest nightclub to spark up in Baga. The enclosed disco is part of the Mocha Bar on Baga Beach and is a little sister and namesake of one of Mumbai's biggest and best-known clubs.

Club Cubana (☎ 2279799; ⓦ www.club cubana.net; Xim Vaddo, Arpora; admission ladies/men/couples Rs 299/399/598; open 9pm-4am Fri-Sun) competes with Tito's for the late night drinking crowd and offers a fun night out. Once you pay the cover charge all drinks are free and there's a small enclosed dance floor with house DJs. It has a spectacular hilltop location and there's even a terrace swimming pool.

Near the beach in South Calangute, **Club Antoos** is a subterranean club with a local following.

Out at Saligao, about 5km from Calangute, **Club Westend** (☎ 2409928; open 9pm-4am daily) is another locally run club with late night parties on Tuesday and Saturday featuring Goan DJs. It's signposted just off the main road through Saligao – most taxi drivers know how to find it.

Shopping

In line with its status as the tourist capital of Goa, Calangute has also grown to be the shopping capital. Flashy Western-brand shops such as Lacoste, Levi's, Benetton, Gucci and Nike have sprouted up along the road to Candolim, just south of Calangute's market.

Also here are upmarket gold and jewellery shops, boutique fashion stores and arts and craft emporiums.

But it's probably the small-time market stalls and souvenir stands that will catch the eye of most foreign visitors – if you stay here long enough you'll be sick of the sight of them! Calangute and Baga have been swamped by Kashmiri traders eager to cash in on the tourist boom. Their incessant hassling and pressure selling can become very tedious, and the recent downturn in the tourism industry has only driven competition up. There is, however, a fantastic range of things to buy – Kashmiri carpets, embroideries and papier-mache boxes, as well as genuine and reproduction Tibetan and Rajasthani crafts, bronzes, carvings and miniature paintings. This is all the same sort of stuff you'll see at the Anjuna market, so it's worth comparing prices. If you're going to buy, bargain hard and don't be afraid to offer an amount far below the first price.

There are two permanent, but rather makeshift, **markets** along Calangute–Baga road, mostly with wares laid out on blankets. There's a Tibetan handicrafts market between the church and the roundabout in central Calangute, and another handicrafts market in Baga.

For kids (and the young at heart) there's an absorbing **magic shop** in Baga, selling all sorts of tricks, props and illusions, and the owner promises to teach you magic in three minutes.

Getting There & Away

There are frequent buses to/from Panaji (Rs 10, 45 minutes) and Mapusa (Rs 5). Most buses start or end at the market in Calangute, although a few go on to Baga.

A taxi from Panaji to Calangute or Baga costs Rs 150 to 200 and takes about 30 minutes. A motorcycle taxi to Mapusa costs Rs 50, a taxi is overpriced at Rs 100.

Getting Around

Motorcycle and moped hire is easy to arrange in Calangute and if you're here before (or after) the peak season when there are plenty of bikes around, you should be able to bargain a reasonable price – around Rs 100 a day for a Honda Kinetic if hired for a week or more – but expect to pay Rs 250 a day around Christmas. Ask around near the steps to the beach in central Calangute or around the roundabout or market area where taxis hang out. Up in Baga, ask around towards the end of the road near Britto's.

Take particular care riding on the Calangute–Baga road and near the market area where it gets very congested with buses and taxis. The sandy area leading to the covered bridge at Baga is another place where many inexperienced riders come to grief.

Bicycles can also be hired (around Rs 40 a day) in the market area – there are no shops as such, just ask around.

MAPUSA

pop 40,100 • postcode 403507

Mapusa (pronounced 'Mapsa') is the main population centre in north Goa and the main town for supplies if you are staying at Anjuna or Vagator. There's not much to see in Mapusa, though the **Friday market** *(open 8am-6.30pm)* is a raucous affair that attracts vendors and shoppers from all over Goa (and interstate). Unlike the Anjuna market it's a local event where people shop for cheap clothing and produce, but you can also find antiques, souvenirs and textiles here.

A Hindu and Christian feast day, **Feast of Our Lady of Miracles**, is held in Mapusa 16 days after Easter.

Information

There's no tourist office as such but the **Directorate of Tourism** *(☎ 2262390)*, near the Mapusa Residency, can sometimes help.

The **Goa Desc Resource Centre** *(☎ 225 2660; No 11, Liberty Apartments, Feira Alta, Mapusa, 403507)* is a local lobby group looking at issues such as human rights, women's issues and tourist development. The group holds a fortnightly discussion group, the Friday Balcao, from 4pm to 6pm, to debate issues affecting Goa and its people.

Also based in Mapusa, the **Goa Foundation** *(☎ 2256479; W www.goacom.com/goa foundation; St Britto's Apartments, Feira Alta)* is Goa's leading conservation and environment group. If you're interested in Goa's environmental issues you can call into the office here, or inquire at the Other India Bookstore.

Money Near the market, the **State Bank of India** will exchange cash and travellers cheques. A better option for currency exchange and credit card cash advances is to use one of the travel agencies such as **Pink Panther Travel** *(☎ 2263180)*, which is efficient and keeps longer hours than the bank.

There's a 24-hour ATM at the **ICICI Bank** hidden down a lane off the Mapusa–Anjuna road (opposite the police station).

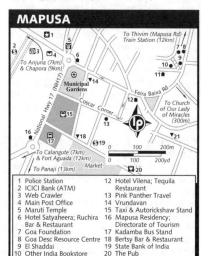

MAPUSA

1 Police Station	12 Hotel Vilena; Tequila Restaurant
2 ICICI Bank (ATM)	
3 Web Crawler	13 Pink Panther Travel
4 Main Post Office	14 Vrundavan
5 Maruti Temple	15 Taxi & Autorickshaw Stand
6 Hotel Satyaheera; Ruchira Bar & Restaurant	16 Mapusa Residency; Directorate of Tourism
7 Goa Foundation	17 Kadamba Bus Stand
8 Goa Desc Resource Centre	18 Bertsy Bar & Restaurant
9 El Shaddai	19 State Bank of India
10 Other India Bookstore	20 The Pub
11 Hotel Suhas	21 Night Food Market

El Shaddai – Homes for Kids

While you're lounging around on Goa's beaches, it's easy to forget that the state shares most of India's social problems. **El Shaddai** (☎ 2264798; **W** www.elshaddai-trust.org), based in Mapusa, is a charitable trust where travellers can get involved to help homeless or orphaned children. El Shaddai is the work of Englishwoman Anita Edgar, who was shocked by the child poverty during a trip to Goa in 1996.

With local Christian community help Anita has established four homes – three in Assagao between Vagator and Mapusa, and one in Saligao – where more than 200 local children live and receive schooling.

You can visit the homes and meet with the children between 4pm and 6pm daily. **Victory House** (☎ 2409066) in Saligao is also the nonformal school and houses boys aged eight to 15 years; **Rainbow House** (☎ 2268373) is a home for girls. **Shekinah House** (☎ 2268001) is for boys aged up to seven years; and **House of Kathleen** is the home for the youngest children.

El Shaddai also plans to establish a night shelter for homeless children in Panaji.

If you want to volunteer to help teach or play with the children, apply in advance to the trust. The head office is on the 2nd floor, St Anthony Apartments, Mapusa Clinic Rd, Mapusa. Donations of spare clothing or cash are also welcome.

Post & Communications Just to the west of Hotel Satyaheera is the **main post office**. Phone calls and faxes are handled by any of the private phone offices around the town. There are several cheap Internet places; try **Web Crawler** (Rs 20/hr), which is down a lane opposite the police station.

Bookshops If you're after books about Goa or India, or contemporary development issues, Mapusa is the place. Goa's best bookstore, the **Other India Bookstore** (☎ 226 3306; **W** www.goacom.com/books; Mapusa Clinic Rd), stocks mainly Indian titles and publishes numerous books on Goa. Specialist subjects include conservation, environment, health and self-help. You can pick up a catalogue (or check the website) and the staff are very helpful in locating hard-to-find books. It's above the Mapusa Clinic and signposted from the road.

Church of Our Lady of Miracles (St Jerome's)

Founded in 1594 and rebuilt several times since, this church is famous more for its annual festival than for its architecture. It was built by the Portuguese on the site of an old Hindu temple, which the Hindu community still holds sacred. Thus on the 16th day after Easter, the church's annual feast day is celebrated here by both Hindus and Christians – one of the best examples of the way in which Hinduism and Christianity coexist in Goa.

Places to Stay

Although there are several hotels in Mapusa's town centre, accommodation at the nearby beaches of Anjuna, Vagator and Calangute is far preferable to what's on offer here.

Hotel Suhas (☎ 2262700; dorm beds Rs 70, singles/doubles with private bathroom Rs 99/150), down a side road running off Feira Baixa Rd, is a fairly grimy, basic place but OK if you want something cheap.

Hotel Vilena (☎ 2263115; Feira Baixa Rd, doubles with shared bathroom Rs 300, with private bathroom Rs 400) is a clean place well suited to travellers. There's a bar and the rooftop **Tequila Restaurant** (see Places to Eat).

Mapusa Residency (☎ 2262794; singles/doubles Rs 325/400, doubles with air-con Rs 650), on the roundabout opposite the bus stand, is the GTDC hotel. It's pretty uninspiring but is still often full with domestic tour groups.

Hotel Satyaheera (☎ 2262849; **e** satya@goatelecom.com; doubles with/without air-con Rs 750/400), near the Maruti Temple on the northern roundabout, is the best Mapusa has to offer.

Places to Eat

For cheap street food head for the **night food market** northeast of the market, where hawkers and stalls set up around dusk.

Vrundavan (dishes Rs 10-30; open Wed-Mon), near the Municipal Gardens, is a

Fishing village, southern Goa

Fishing off Palolem beach

Fishing boats, Chapora

Municipal Market, Panaji

Fish for sale, Panaji

Disre (pipies), Panaji

Fishermen, Benaulim beach

ANJUNA

good, cheap veg thali place that also does pizzas.

The Pub *(mains Rs 20-50; open 10am-midnight Mon-Sat)* is the ideal place to escape the chaos of the Friday market for a cold beer or light meal. There's draught beer, salads and filled rolls, inexpensive pasta dishes and delicious home-made meatballs. The 1st-floor balcony gives a perfect view of the street below.

Bertsy Bar & Restaurant is another ambient little pub with a dark interior – another good spot to escape the fumes and noise on market day. There's also Internet access here.

Another traveller-friendly place is the **Tequila Restaurant** *(mains Rs 20-60)*, a breezy open-air restaurant on the rooftop of the Hotel Vilena. It's clean and the food is very reasonably priced.

Ruchira Bar & Restaurant *(☎ 2263869; mains Rs 30-100)* on the top floor of Hotel Satyaheera, is considered one of the best restaurants in Mapusa, which isn't saying much.

Getting There & Away

If you're coming by bus from Mumbai, Mapusa is the jumping-off point for the northern beaches of Goa. Private operators opposite the taxi and autorickshaw stand have buses to Mumbai (Rs 250/300 in normal/sleeper, 17 hours) and Bangalore (Rs 300/400, 15 hours). From the Kadamba bus stand, there are state-run buses to Pune (Rs 230, 15 hours) and Belgaum (Rs 47, five hours).

There are frequent local express buses to Panaji (Rs 5, 25 minutes), and every 30 minutes to Calangute (Rs 6) and Anjuna (Rs 7). Other buses go to Chapora, Candolim and Arambol (Rs 10). A motorcycle taxi to Anjuna or Calangute costs Rs 50, an autorickshaw costs Rs 70 and a taxi is around Rs 100 for the journey.

Thivim, about 12km northeast of town, is the nearest train station on the Konkan Railway. Local buses meet trains (one way to/from Mapusa Rs 5); an autorickshaw costs around Rs 80.

ANJUNA

postcode 403509

Famous throughout Goa for its Wednesday flea market, Anjuna has long held the mantle of Goa's favourite 'hippy beach'. Unlike Calangute, Anjuna has retained some of its charm.

There's a weird and wonderful collection here of defiant ex-hippies, overlanders, monks, gentle lunatics, artists, artisans, seers, searchers and itinerant expatriates who have wandered far from the organic confines of health-food emporia in San Francisco and London. They've been joined by hardcore partygoers, a mix of macho Israelis just released from military service and European ravers on charter flights, all drawn by the area's reputation for trance parties. Impromptu raves are sometimes held at legendary party spots like the Bamboo Forest, or semilegal all-night parties at the spectacular beachfront club Paradiso.

The beach itself, at the southern end at least, is one of the most alluring in north Goa and since it's not easily accessible from the village, it's rarely crowded.

Anjuna is well known as a place to procure drugs (although it doesn't have a monopoly on them). Illicit substances, though not so freely available these days, are still to be had at Anjuna, but participate at your peril – the police Anti-Narcotics Cell targets this area and regularly carries out checks on foreigners.

Take great care of your possessions in Anjuna, as theft is a big problem, especially on market day and party nights.

Orientation & Information

Anjuna is quite spread out and much of the land behind the beach is still farmland. There are three distinct areas: the main crossroads and bus stand where paths lead down to the beach; the back part of the village where you'll find the post office and convenience stores; and the flea market area a couple of kilometres to the south, which also marks the southern end of the beach.

Money On the Anjuna–Mapusa road, the **Bank of Baroda** *(open 9.30am-1.30pm Mon-Wed & Fri, 9.30am-11.30am Sat)* gives cash advances on Visa and MasterCard. There's a 'safe custody' facility here for your valuables, but you're far better off using the safe at your hotel (if you're staying in one) because you have to pay the Rs 150 monthly fee every time you retrieve your valuables. Travel agencies all change cash and travellers cheques, give cash advances on Visa and MasterCard and keep longer hours than the bank (most are open daily). There are no

NORTH GOA

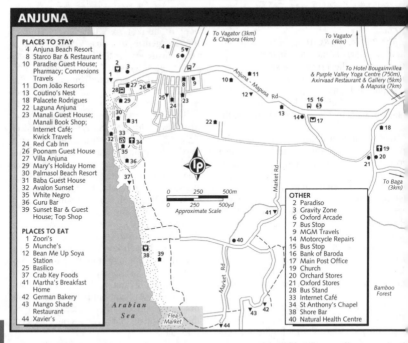

ANJUNA

PLACES TO STAY
4 Anjuna Beach Resort
8 Starco Bar & Restaurant
10 Paradise Guest House;
 Pharmacy; Connexions
 Travels
11 Dom João Resorts
13 Coutino's Nest
18 Palacete Rodrigues
22 Laguna Anjuna
23 Manali Guest House;
 Manali Book Shop;
 Internet Café;
 Kwick Travels
24 Red Cab Inn
26 Poonam Guest House
27 Villa Anjuna
29 Mary's Holiday Home
30 Palmasol Beach Resort
31 Baba Guest House
32 Avalon Sunset
35 White Negro
36 Guru Bar
39 Sunset Bar & Guest
 House; Top Shop

PLACES TO EAT
1 Zoori's
5 Munche's
12 Bean Me Up Soya
 Station
25 Basilico
37 Crab Key Foods
41 Martha's Breakfast
 Home
42 German Bakery
43 Mango Shade
 Restaurant
44 Xavier's

OTHER
2 Paradiso
3 Gravity Zone
6 Oxford Arcade
7 Bus Stop
9 MGM Travels
14 Motorcycle Repairs
15 Bus Stop
16 Bank of Baroda
17 Main Post Office
19 Church
20 Orchard Stores
21 Oxford Stores
28 Bus Stand
33 Internet Café
34 St Anthony's Chapel
38 Shore Bar
40 Natural Health Centre

To Vagator (3km) & Chapora (4km)
To Vagator (4km)
To Hotel Bougainvillea & Purple Valley Yoga Centre (750m), Axirvaad Restaurant & Gallery (5km) & Mapusa (7km)
Anjuna - Mapusa Rd
Market Rd
To Baga (3km)
Arabian Sea
Flea Market
Bamboo Forest
Market Rd
0 250 500m
0 250 500yd
Approximate Scale

ATMs in Anjuna – the nearest are in Mapusa or Calangute.

Post & Communications You can have mail sent poste restante to **Anjuna post office**. There are half-a-dozen places in the village from where you can send emails and faxes and make international phone calls.

Manali Guest House *(Rs 50/hr)* has the best Internet café in Anjuna, but there are plenty of others. There's another Internet café next to the post office and one above the beach near Avalon Sunset.

Travel Agencies There are numerous travel agencies where you can make onward travel bookings, get flights confirmed and change foreign currency. **MGM Travels** *(☎ 2274317)*, on the main road, **Kwick Travels** *(☎ 227 3477)*, at the Manali Guest House, and **Connexions Travels** *(☎ 2274439)*, next to Paradise Guest House, can all make flight and transport bookings and change money.

Bookshops There's a good range of second-hand books in the small **shop** above the Oxford Stores in the back part of the village.

Manali Book Shop, in the Manali Guest House, also has books to buy, sell or swap.

Things to See & Do

Anjuna is a place to hang out, meet people over a few drinks (or a chillum if that's your thing), watch the sunset and wait for the parties to happen. Apart from market day there's no real reason to day trip here since there's nothing to see except the 'scene' itself.

Paragliding takes place off the headland at the southern end of the beach, but usually only on market day. **Gravity Zone** is a 25m-high bungee crane on the road to the beach near Paradiso. It was out of action when we visited but was still intact and likely to resume. Jumps cost Rs 500.

The **Purple Valley Yoga Centre** *(w www .yogagoa.com; classes 7am, 9.30am, 4.30pm & 6.30pm Mon-Sat)* runs four classes a day in a private marquee in the garden of Hotel Bougainvillea. The hour-long classes cost Rs 400 (Rs 3000 for 10) and the instructors are very professional. The 9.30am and 4.30pm classes are suitable for beginners.

You can use the **swimming pool** at Villa Anjuna (see Places to Stay) for Rs 50.

ANJUNA

The Anjuna Market Experience

'Anjuna Beach in Goa is an anthropologist's dream,' said Gita Mehta in the book *Karma Cola* and that's as true today as when she wrote it back in the still-psychedelic 1970s.

The Wednesday flea market is a major attraction for people from all the Goan beaches. It's a syrupy blend of Tibetan and Kashmiri traders, colourful Gujarati tribal women, blissed-out 21st-century hippies, Indian tourists, businesspeople, Western package tourists and travellers from around the world. It's always been quite a scene, though these days it's getting a little overwhelming, with a sea of stalls numbering into the hundreds or even thousands.

The market had humble beginnings, originally started by long-term Western residents who needed to sell a few belongings from time to time so they could spend a little longer in this paradise by the sea. Many of the buyers were Indians keen to snap up a foreign bargain that could be anything from a cassette recorder to a Mars Bar, a Marks & Spencer jersey to a pair of Levi's. Until quite recently, impossibly high import duties kept these foreign goodies out of the hands of all but the richest Indians. From time to time the authorities closed the market down when the numbers of bottles of Scotch, Marlboro cigarettes or electronic devices indicated that this was becoming less of a flea market and more of a black market.

Western residents would make cakes and cookies to sell here (they still do today and chocolate chips are not the only ingredients in those cookies) and it soon became the highlight of the week, the place to catch up on the gossip, make a little money or just hang out. Although you still see Westerners trading goods and services (piercing, tattoos and haircuts), the market has developed into a souvenir bazaar, but it's none the worse for that.

Whatever you need, from a paperback to a second-hand Enfield motorcycle, you'll find it here. It is by far the best place to shop for souvenirs, and even if you're not after anything specific, it's a wonderful place to browse. You can also stock up on those essentials that you just didn't manage to get hold of before you set off from home. Day-Glo coloured rave clothing is very popular, as is beach wear. Hammocks, hand-painted T-shirts, joss stick holders, Goan trance cassettes, painting… The list goes on.

Don't expect anything to have a price tag – or if it does it'll be much more than what you should end up paying. Bargaining is most certainly the name of the game here (see the boxed text 'The Art of Haggling' under Shopping in the Facts for the Visitor chapter).

If you just want to chill out, settle yourself under the shade of a tree – or down on the beach amid a pile of like-minded folk – and enjoy a cappuccino, Goan-style. Bars, cafés, live music and the passing parade of buyers and sellers keep the show going all day. Whatever else you may have planned for your Wednesday afternoon, forget it.

The best time to visit is early morning (it starts around 8am) or late afternoon (from about 4pm); the latter is good if you plan to stay on for the sunset and party at the Shore Bar.

Places to Stay

Anjuna has several cheap guesthouses and low-key hotels scattered over a wide area. Few places front the beach since the northern end is rocky and the southern end is reserved for the flea market site and farmland. Finding a place to stay just prior to Christmas can be a problem, but either side of the peak season it should be easy to find a bargain – particularly now that travellers are moving away from Anjuna to quieter beaches. If you want to stay long term there are numerous houses available for rent (from around Rs 2000 per month). You'll need to arrive reasonably early to get the best places.

Since Anjuna mainly attracts backpackers and budget travellers, most of the accommodation is at the lower end of the scale. Mid-range here is anything over Rs 600 for a double.

Places to Stay – Budget

There are lots of no-frills budget places, especially along the Anjuna–Mapusa road leading to the bus stand and along the path above the northern end of the beach.

Manali Guest House (☎ 2273477; *rooms with shared bathroom Rs 150*) is a central place with good-value rooms (often full), a bookshop, Internet café and travel agency.

Back on the road towards Mapusa are a string of places with basic rooms, including **Starco Bar & Restaurant** *(doubles Rs 200)* which has bungalows at the back; **Paradise Guest House** *(☎ 2274439; doubles Rs 200-400)* which has a variety of clean rooms and cottages, all with private bathrooms; and **Coutino's Nest** *(☎ 2274386; doubles with shared/private bathroom Rs 200/350)*, a clean home with six rooms. It's run by a friendly family and there's a pleasant rooftop terrace.

Heading down towards the beach, turn left at the end of the road and you come to a narrow path leading across the cliff top above the beach. One of the first places along here is **Mary's Holiday Home** *(☎ 2273216; doubles with private bathroom Rs 250)*, near the bus stand, which is a clean, friendly place with rooms around a courtyard.

Further along, **Palmasol Beach Resort** *(☎ 2273258; doubles Rs 350-550)* is a good-value place with clean rooms. All have private bathrooms and hot water.

Several of the beach bars and restaurants along the path have a few rooms for rent, costing from Rs 100 to 350. Try **Guru Bar** *(☎ 2273319)*, **Crab Key Foods** *(☎ 2274554)* and **Avalon Sunset** *(☎ 2273471)*.

White Negro *(☎ 2273326; doubles Rs 500-600)* is a recommended place with some of the tidiest budget rooms in Anjuna and a very good garden restaurant. Rooms have private bathrooms, tile floors and hot water.

At the southern end of Anjuna beach (a 10-minute walk from the northern end or take the 3km loop road around the back) are a handful of places that are great if you want to be close to the best part of the beach.

Sunset Bar & Guesthouse *(☎ 2273917; Goenkar Vaddo; doubles Rs 200-300)*, down near the Shore Bar and fronting the beach, is a good choice with an interesting collection of rooms behind the restaurant. The newer rooms at the front have private bathrooms. In the same area, **Top Shop** *(☎ 2274484; doubles Rs 200-500)* also has a few rooms with private bathrooms including some bigger rooms at the front. There is a very spacious top-floor room with sea views.

Back in the village, just off the road to Vagator, are a couple more places. **Anjuna Beach Resort** *(☎ 2274499; e fabjoe@goa telecom.com; doubles Rs 350-500, apartments Rs 600)* belies the name 'resort' and is not particularly close to the beach, but it's a

family-run place with a range of rooms in a large building, plus four spotless, new ground-level apartments.

Places to Stay – Mid-Range

Villa Anjuna *(☎ 2273443; w www.anjuna villa.com; doubles Rs 500-750)*, in a prime location on the main road to the beach, is a new hotel which has comfortable rooms (with hot water) arranged around a pool.

On the back road in Anjuna village, **Palacete Rodrigues** *(☎ 2273358; rooms Rs 550-850)* is a lovely family-run colonial house built around a courtyard. Spacious, nicely furnished doubles are great value at a fixed rate and the air-con suite (Rs 850) is a bargain.

Red Cab Inn *(☎ 2274427; doubles Rs 400-600, boudoir Rs 700)*, in a warren of lanes near Manali Guest House, has an interesting selection of two- and four-bed rooms plus a split-level 'boudoir' for romantic types.

A little way back from the beach, **Poonam Guest House** *(☎ 2273247; doubles Rs 500-800, peak season Rs 1200-1400)*, has a wide range of renovated rooms from fairly average older-style doubles to spotless new suites, most of them built around a pleasant garden. Rates are way over the top in the peak Christmas season.

Dom João Resorts *(☎ 2274325; e luzco@ goatelecom.com; apartments Rs 600, peak season Rs 1200-1500)* is a large, unattractive hotel totally out of character with Anjuna (it's the only place in Anjuna built higher than two storeys). It has 42 ageing 'apartments' (with fridge, lounge area and balcony), a pool and restaurant.

Places to Stay – Top End

Laguna Anjuna *(☎ 2274305; w www.laguna anjuna.com; Soranta Vaddo; 1-/2-bedroom suites US$75/115, peak season US$125/175)* is a boutique hotel with interestingly designed circular cottages made from local laterite stone. Beds are on raised platforms and the larger suites are very spacious. It's a bit overpriced but quite stylish and there's a pool in a pleasant garden and coconut grove setting.

Hotel Bougainvillea *(Granpa's Inn; ☎ 2273271, fax 2274370; e granpas@hotmail.com; rooms Rs 1250-1900, during Christmas Rs 1950-2950)* is well back from the beach on the road to Mapusa. It's a relaxing place,

ANJUNA

with an old-fashioned resort-style feel. There's a pool in a large flower-filled garden, a bar, restaurant and pool room. The rooms vary in size and style but all are quaintly furnished.

Places to Eat

Anjuna has a few beach shacks at the southern end (near the market site), a handful of restaurants overlooking the beach along the path from the bus stand, and some refreshingly different places back in the village.

The retail needs of the expat community are served by the **Oxford Stores** and the **Orchard Stores**, opposite each other back in the village, and the **Oxford Arcade**, closer to the beach. Here you can get everything from a loaf of bread to a Christmas turkey, and such 'exotic' goodies as Vegemite, Heinz baked beans, Colgate toothpaste and imported cheese.

Martha's Breakfast Home (☎ 2273365; breakfast Rs 30-75) is a great place to start the day, serving delicious pancakes, waffles, omelettes, fresh bread and various juices in a pleasant, shady garden or on the veranda. Fruit salad with muesli and curd costs Rs 50. It also has a few rooms to rent.

German Bakery (mains Rs 25-100), further along the road to the flea market, serves herbal teas and espresso coffee as well as fresh breads and healthy soups. It's a great place to relax and read a book or meet with friends. Nearby, **Mango Shade Restaurant** (mains Rs 15-50; open 8am-5pm daily) is another good hang-out; avocado on toast is a favourite at Rs 40.

Bean Me Up Soya Station, on the Anjuna–Mapusa road, is a highly recommended vegetarian café specialising in home-made tofu and tempeh (Indonesian-style food made from soya beans), soya products and tasty soups. It's closed on Saturday.

Munche's (widely known as 'Munchies Corner') is open 24 hours so it attracts plenty of partygoers in the small hours.

There are quite a few places along the dirt path from the bus stand to the beach. **Avalon Sunset** (mains Rs 30-90) occupies a gorgeous spot overlooking the beach and is a good place to dine at sunset. The fish is good and you can get pizzas, pasta and tandoori. Further down, **Crab Key Foods** (☎ 2274554; mains Rs 40-125) also has a good beachfront perch and is great for sand-

wiches (costing less than Rs 20 to 30) and fresh seafood. You can choose a live crustacean from the pond in the middle of the dining area, which will be freshly cooked for you – stuffed crab costs Rs 125.

Zoori's (mains Rs 40-110), next to Paradiso on the cliffs near the bus stand, is a relaxing place with cushions on the floor and a great location. Breakfast is the speciality (Rs 20 to 50), as well as salads and light meals such as burgers.

Basilico (☎ 2273721; pizza & pasta Rs 75-125; open from 7pm daily) is a good Italian garden restaurant tucked in behind the Red Cab Inn. Most of the dishes are vegetarian and there's a range of salads.

Xavier's (mains Rs 80-350; open from 7pm daily), hidden away behind the flea market area, is recommended as the best place for seafood in Anjuna. Tiger prawns, lobster, red snapper, pomfret, tuna and shark are imaginatively prepared in Goan and continental styles.

Axirvaad Restaurant & Gallery (☎ 225 6949; 483 Boa Vista, Assagao; mains Rs 80-250) is 5km from Anjuna along the road to Mapusa. It's set up in a large traditional house, stylishly restored and painted in striking colours. Most of the fish dishes are steamed to preserve their flavour. This is definitely the place to go for an evening out.

Entertainment

Shore Bar is still a popular spot to sink a few beers and watch the sun go down. On market day there's usually a party here from sunset until about 10pm – on other nights it's quiet.

Paradiso is Goa's biggest club. Behind the walled entrance, an impressive series of dance floors and bars terrace down towards the beach. Some top DJs perform here in the high season (when there's usually a cover charge) and it manages to stay open very late on party nights.

Getting There & Away

There are buses every hour or so from Mapusa to Anjuna (Rs 7). They park at the end of the road to the beach and continue on to Vagator and Chapora, and some go up to Arambol. Plenty of motorcycle taxis gather at the central crossroads and you can also hire scooters and motorcycles easily from here.

VAGATOR & CHAPORA

This is one of the most rugged and interesting parts of north Goa's coastline and it's the place to be and be seen if you're seeking Goa's infamous party scene. Much of the inhabited area nestles under a canopy of dense coconut palms, and the little fishing village of Chapora is dominated by a rocky hill on top of which sits an old Portuguese fort. The fort is fairly well preserved and the views from its ramparts are superb.

Rather than the long, open stretch of sand found on most of Goa's developed coastline, secluded, sandy coves dominate around the northern side of this rocky outcrop. Although not a particularly crowded beach, Vagator is a major stop on the bus tours of north Goa, and is popular with day-trippers up from Calangute, so for a few hours each day the parts of the beach closest to the bus stop are flooded with interlopers. There are three main beaches – from north to south, Vagator (the largest), Little Vagator and Ozran Beach.

Many Westerners stay here on a long-term basis during the winter season, but it's not a tourist ghetto. The local people remain amenable and it's much more laid-back than even Anjuna – particularly at Chapora, which is little more than a narrow main street and a string of village homes between the harbour and Siolim. Vagator is where the night-time action happens, with several bars staying open late and a couple of places that are regular party venues.

Although there's little package tourism here, Vagator has a few mid-range (but low-key) resort hotels and it's likely that more development will find its way here in the future.

Zambala (see Places to Stay) has yoga and meditation classes (Rs 100) daily at 8am and just before sunset. The philosophy here is a mix of Tibetan and Western and extended retreats can be arranged.

Information

The nearest banks are in Anjuna or Mapusa, but many shops and travel agencies offer money exchange. In Vagator you can check email for around Rs 40 an hour at **Jaws**, **Bethany Inn** or closer to the beach at **Mira Cybercafe** or **Eddie's Cyberzone**.

Near the main Vagator Beach (below Sterling Vagator Beach Resort) is a small **library** (*open Mon-Tues & Thur-Sat*) run by a Swedish Christian organisation. It's a friendly place where you can borrow books (Rs 100 deposit) and chat with the volunteer workers. A free meditation session is held on Tuesday at 9pm and a Christian service on Saturday at 7pm. The **Rainbow bookshop**, opposite Primrose Cafe, stocks a small range of books.

On Chapora's narrow main street there are several STD/ISD booths as well as two small **bookstalls** and a **store** for provisions. **Soniya Travels** (☎ *2273344*) is a good agency for transport bookings, foreign exchange and Internet access. Around the corner, **Naryan Book Stall** has second-hand books to buy, swap or sell.

Chapora Fort

Though Bardez taluka was ceded to the Portuguese in 1543, the security of the territory

---

VAGATOR & CHAPORA

PLACES TO STAY
3 Shertor Villa; Sunrise Restaurant
4 Baba Restaurant
8 Helinda Restaurant
11 Sterling Vagator Beach Resort
13 Dolrina Guest House; Siddheshwar Guest House
14 Jolly Jolly Lester
16 Garden Villa Guest House
17 Jolly Jolly Roma
20 Moonlight Guest House; Sunita Guest House
24 Leoney Resort
28 Boon's Ark
29 Bethany Inn; China Town
31 Royal Resort
37 Zambala

PLACES TO EAT
1 Welcome; Paulo's Antique Bar
2 Noble Nest
7 Yak Restaurant; Scarlet Cold Drinks

19 Alcove Restaurant
21 Le Bluebird
22 Potala; Marakesh; Mira Cybercafe
27 Mango Tree
30 Pizza 'O' Live & Little Tibet Cafe
32 Robert's Place

OTHER
5 Soniya Travels; Naryan Book Stall
6 Bus Stop
9 Temple
10 Motorcycle Repairs
12 Library
15 Tin Tin Bar & Restaurant; Eddie's Cyberzone
18 Nine Bar
25 Jaws; Internet
26 Mapusa Bus Stop
33 Rainbow Bookshop
34 Primrose Cafe
35 Church
36 Bus Stop
38 Hill Top Motels

Map: Vagator & Chapora. Scale 0–250–500m / 0–250–500yd. Locations shown include Harbour, Chapora Fort, Chapora River, To Siolim (6km) & Arambol, Vagator Beach, Disco Valley, Arabian Sea, Chapora, Little Vagator Beach, Ozran Beach, Spaghetti Beach, To Mapusa (10km), To Anjuna (2km).

continued to be a major headache for many years. The lands were threatened by several enemies – the Muslims from the north, Maratha horsemen from the east and the local chieftains in the area itself.

As a result, the Portuguese set about building a series of fortifications between the mid-16th and early 17th centuries. Chapora, on the very northern edge of the new territory, was constructed in about 1617 – only five years after work began on Fort Aguada. Whereas Aguada was never taken by force, Chapora fell twice. The first time, it was reportedly taken without a shot being fired, when the captain of the fort decided to surrender to the Maratha forces of the Hindu leader Sambhaji in 1684.

The Portuguese rebuilt the fort in 1717, adding features such as tunnels that led from the bastion down to the seashore and the river bank, to enable resupply or escape in times of trouble. The fort fell again to the Marathas in 1739. Finally, when the northern taluka of Pernem came into Portuguese hands, the significance of Chapora faded, and the fort was eventually abandoned in the 1890s.

Although the ruined fort is not as interesting as Fort Aguada, it's certainly worth trekking up here for the splendid views.

Chapora Harbour

Taking the road around to the northwest of the village brings you to the small harbour, an area of pungent smells where colourful fishing boats bob idly and the day's catch is hauled in each morning and evening. At the mouth of the Chapora River, it's a good spot for photographs and you can buy fish and seafood here directly from the boats.

Places to Stay

The majority of travellers staying in Vagator or Chapora are backpackers looking for a cheap place, ravers sticking around for the party season, or long-termers who come here to hang out for the winter and become part of the Goa 'scene'. There are plenty of rooms to rent in villagers' houses, or whole houses to rent, but it helps if you get here before the real height of the season – try October or November. You can pay as little as Rs 50 a night for a basic room if you're staying a while. Houses for rent cost anything from Rs 2000 to 5000 a month, depending on their size, location and the length of the rental period.

For a short-term stay there's plenty of good, cheap accommodation, especially in Vagator.

Vagator There are many more options here than in Chapora, including several up-market places, and guesthouses are scattered around the village, mostly well back from the beach.

Dolrina Guest House (☎ 2273382; e dolrina@hotmail.com; doubles with shared bathroom Rs 150-200, doubles with private bathroom Rs 350-450) is set back from the road near the beach and has a good range of rooms. It's run by a very friendly family and there's a garden at the back.

Siddheshwar Rest House (☎ 2273963; doubles Rs 250), a little further down on the road to the beach, has four decent-sized doubles with private bathrooms beneath a restaurant. It's in a good location and the rooms are well worth this price.

Jolly Jolly Lester (☎ 2273620; singles/doubles Rs 300/400, during Christmas doubles Rs 800) has 11 clean, quiet doubles with private bathrooms behind its restaurant. The same family runs **Jolly Jolly Roma** (☎ 227 3001; singles/doubles Rs 300/400), a new place along the path leading to Little Vagator Beach, which has stylish, angular rooms.

Bethany Inn (☎ 2274520; e bethany@goatelecom.com; doubles Rs 450, 2-bedroom suites Rs 600), has a range of spacious, clean doubles and a fluid pricing policy depending on how busy the season is. In the peak season doubles can rise to Rs 700. The four-bed rooms with fridge and balcony are great value, and there's a good Internet café here.

Boon's Ark (☎ 2274045; w www.boonsark.com; rooms Rs 400-500, during Christmas Rs 800-1000), near Bethany Inn, is a recommended family-run place that has 10 clean cottage-style rooms around a garden.

Garden Villa Guest House (☎ 2273571; singles Rs 150-200, doubles Rs 300-500) is set in a barren garden but the rooms are very clean. There's also a very good restaurant here specialising in Mexican and Italian food and movies are shown here every night.

There are half-a-dozen cheap places above Little Vagator Beach, near the Nine Bar. **Moonlight Guest House** (doubles Rs 150) has four basic rooms with shared bathroom; **Sunita Guest House** (☎ 2273495; doubles with shared/private bathroom Rs 150/250), nearby, has similar rooms, but some have private bathrooms and a little veranda.

There are several places on the road leading to Little Vagator Beach. **Jackie's Daynite** (☎ 2274320; Ozran Beach Rd; rooms Rs 200-250, Rs 450 over Christmas) has some immaculate, good-value rooms set back in a small garden. There's an established bar and restaurant here.

Zambala (☎ 2273479; w www.zambala .org; doubles Rs 250) is an interesting retreat combining Indian and Western holistic philosophics with yoga and meditation. There are 15 rooms with private bathrooms.

Leoney Resort (☎ 2273634; w www .leoneyresort.com; Ozran Beach Rd; doubles Rs 1500, cottages Rs 2000) is the pick of the upmarket places in Vagator. It's a beautiful little oasis of rooms and cottages around an inviting pool and landscaped garden. The family-run place has the style of a resort, but with a personal touch. Credit cards are accepted.

The Royal Resort (☎ 2274365; e alcove 2002@yahoo.com; singles/doubles Rs 650/ 800; cottages Rs 850/1000, mid-Dec–mid-Jan rooms Rs 1000/1200, cottages Rs 1200/1500) is a tidy place and good value outside the mid-December to mid-January peak period, when you can bargain for lower than the listed prices. There's a good pool, internet café, beauty parlour, bar and a small nightclub.

Sterling Vagator Beach Resort (☎ 227 3276; e sterlinggoa@yahoo.com; doubles with/without air-con Rs 3000/2100, peak season Rs 5000/3500), in a prime location at the north end of Vagator Beach, is a sprawling hotel and time-share resort. Set in palm-shaded grounds it comprises a swimming pool, good restaurant and two types of cottages, but it's way overpriced, especially over Christmas.

Chapora This is a relatively quiet place, popular with people renting rooms or houses

Freaks, Trance & Psychedelia – Goa's Party Scene

Goa has always been a party place. When the Portuguese were here the colony became notorious as an immoral outpost where drinking and dancing lasted till dawn. The tradition continued when Goa became an important stop on the hippy trail, with 'Goa Freaks' dancing on the beaches till dawn. But the beach parties and full-moon raves of the 1970s and 80s seem like innocent affairs compared with the trance parties that replaced them in the 1990s. Today's parties are big business, drawing clubbers from the European circuit with DJs flown in from London and Europe, massive sound systems and a plethora of synthetic substances – ecstasy, acid, speed, ketamine.

The crunch came in 2000 when a central government law banned loud music in open spaces between 10pm and 6am. The law was seemingly aimed at Goa and numerous party organisers and venue owners have been charged with breaking it. Massive millennium celebrations that year were virtually shut down when organisers couldn't reach agreement with the authorities. Things aren't as free and easy any more, but the parties continue. Police claim they can't enforce the law, and money (baksheesh) still talks.

Locals see the party scene as just a bunch of self-indulgent Westerners gyrating in a drugged daze to a computer-generated, ear-splitting beat that cannot be described as music. Most Westerners consider it a chance for a good time but the hardcore element has a much more philosophical view of it all. For them it's a cosmic thing – '…to uplift people's consciousness through the trance-dance experience,' says veteran DJ Goa Gil.

Who Benefits?

Entry is free because the organisers can make their money from the drug pushers, and the police make money from the organisers. It reportedly costs organisers Rs 10,000 to stage a rave party. Locals make money by setting up stalls selling cigarettes, drinks and food. Chai ladies lay out their mats and sit in sari-clad primness dishing out cups of tea and plates of biscuits amid a sea of seminaked Westerners – shooing away those who have the gall to sit on their mat without ordering chai. A depressing sight is seeing local women with small babies wandering among the throng at 4am begging, or young boys running errands for the partygoers. A growing dependence on the long term. Get here early and you can rent a basic room for Rs 50 a night – ask around the restaurants and bars on the main street or just wander around looking for signs.

Shertor Villa (☎ 2274335; doubles with shared/private bathroom Rs 150/300) has about 20 basic rooms (there are reductions for long stays). If there's nobody here, check over the road at Noble Nest restaurant.

Baba Restaurant (☎ 2273213; doubles Rs 200) has 12 simple but clean rooms at the back, most with shared bathroom.

Helinda Restaurant (☎ 2274345; singles/doubles with shared bathroom Rs 150/200, doubles with private bathroom Rs 250-300), across the road, has some of the best rooms in Chapora. It's clean, and relaxed, but is often full.

Places to Eat

Vagator A great little place to hang out is **Potala**. It has low tables and Tibetan food, such as *momos* (Rs 50 to 75), *thugpa* (Rs 40), and herbal tea. Around the corner, **Marakesh** (mains Rs 40-90) is Goa's only Moroccan restaurant serving couscous and kofta (meatballs) while Middle Eastern music plays.

Pizza 'O' Live & Little Tibet Cafe, at the top of the hill in Vagator, cooks authentic Italian cuisine, including bruschetta, antipasto, pasta and wood-fired pizzas (Rs 80 to 120). In the afternoon you can get Tibetan food such as *momos*.

Mango Tree (mains Rs 40-80), near Pizza 'O' Live & Little Tibet Cafe, has a fair selection of dishes as well as a seafood barbecue and a nifty street-side bar with stools. Fish curry rice is only Rs 40. **Jaws** (mains Rs 35-80), nearby, is also good value for cheap snacks (burgers Rs 30), or Indian, Goan and Chinese meals.

Le Bluebird (☎ 2273695; mains Rs 100-250; open 9.30am-2pm & 7.30pm-11pm daily), a French-run place, is one of the best restaurants around. Meals are served alfresco and there are interesting continental

---

Freaks, Trance & Psychedelia – Goa's Party Scene

parties means that some villagers are forgoing their normal way of life, at least for a small part of the year.

Goa's party reputation pulls in the young travellers, which keeps the hotel and restaurant owners happy. So everyone benefits except the majority of the locals who do not happen to run hotels and restaurants. For them the parties represent endless noise pollution and an unwelcome entree for their youth into the wicked ways of the Western world.

Where to Party

Most open rave parties take place around Anjuna and Vagator, at 'party places' such as Bamboo Forest, back behind the market site in Anjuna, Disco Valley and Spaghetti Beach in Vagator, and occasionally up in Arambol. You'll sometimes see ads for parties in cafés but usually you need to just ask other travellers or taxi drivers, who are keen to ferry people around. Large groups of ravers heading off on their bikes together is a sure sign that a party is on – or that someone *thinks* they know where a party is on. Often, false alarms or last-minute cancellations will result in a lot of aimless searching. During our research trip we arrived at a party at Spaghetti Beach at around 1am. The sound system was there, the chai ladies were there and a few people were milling around – but no music. After about an hour, word got through the party was given the green light and suddenly the music fired up, continuing into the following morning.

The parties are an odd mix of ravers in psychedelic club wear, swaying to the beat and glowing like radioactive waste, tourists joining in on the Goa experience, and locals angling for business – 'taxi', 'chai', 'cigarettes'? It's a heady mix that continues on well past dawn and the beat never wanes.

Around Christmas and New Year, when police have evidently been told to turn a blind eye to the music bans, there should be a party most nights. For the rest of the November to March season there won't usually be much more than one a week, although parties are increasingly held later in the season when most of the tourists have gone home and only the hardcore ravers remain.

More permanent party venues now include Paradiso at Anjuna, a spectacular beach-front dance palace which gets going around 10pm and brings in top-name DJs.

dishes such as ratatouille (Rs 100), bouill-abaise soup (Rs 70), pullet grill (Rs 150) and aubergine Provencal. There's a good break-fast menu and a range of vegetarian dishes, plus imported wine by the bottle or glass.

China Town, next to Bethany Inn, is rec-ommended for seafood and is Vagator's best Chinese restaurant.

Robert's Place (☎ 2274392; mains Rs 25-100), on the same road as Primrose Cafe, has a massive menu (even by Goan stan-dards), but specialises in *shwarma* (sliced, grilled meat served in pita bread with salad), falafel and other Israeli dishes.

Alcove Restaurant (mains Rs 65-100) has a superb position right above Little Vagator Beach (opposite Nine Bar), a large spacious garden and a covered area with a pool table. The menu includes Indian, continental, Thai and Chinese dishes.

Zambala (see Places to Stay) has a Ti-betan café serving herbal teas, lassis and pastries, and a garden restaurant with a dif-ferent set menu each evening. Possibilities here include a vegetarian night, Goan spe-cialities and a seafood barbecue where guests are taken to the Chapora Harbour to select their own fresh fish from the boats.

Chapora There are numerous small restau-rants along the main street of Chapora vil-lage, but the best eating places are in Vagator.

In Chapora, **Baba** and **Helinda** are popu-lar, and **Sunrise Restaurant** (open from 7am daily), near Shertor Villa, opens early for breakfast. **Scarlet Cold Drinks** is the place for fresh juices, shakes (Rs 15 to 20) and muesli.

Welcome (mains Rs 30-80) is probably the best of Chapora's modest restaurants. It offers a good range of seafood, as well as the usual gamut of Goan, Indian and conti-nental dishes, served in a rustic, candlelit dining area.

Yak Restaurant, opposite Soniya Travels, also has a big menu, including Tibetan dishes, such as *momos*, and good burgers, but generally the food is nothing to write home about.

Entertainment

Vagator is the centre of north Goa's party scene – along with several established bars, impromptu rave parties are still organised here (over Christmas–New Year) at places like Disco Valley and Spaghetti Beach. Disco Valley is an open area of beach at the southern end of Vagator Beach, while Spaghetti Beach, also called Ozram Beach, is a flat area of cliff side overlooking the ocean in a deserted area south of Little Va-gator Beach. These parties are rarely adver-tised and are subject to organisers getting tacit approval from authorities. Ask around at places like Primrose Cafe, or ask motor-cycle taxi drivers.

The evening usually starts at the open-air **Nine Bar** overlooking Little Vagator Beach, where trance and house music plays to a packed floor until 10pm. Depending on re-strictions, the party then moves up to **Prim-rose Cafe**, towards the back of Vagator village, where the music usually continues till 2am or 3am under a canopy of psyche-delically painted trees.

Hill Top Motels, not far from Primrose on the back road to Anjuna, is another venue that often has outdoor parties past the 10pm music restrictions.

Alcove Restaurant, opposite Nine Bar, doesn't have a big following compared with Nine Bar, but its open cliff-top location is great at sunset. There's happy hour from 6pm to 7pm and a pool table. **Tin Tin Bar & Restaurant**, on the main road down to Va-gator Beach, occasionally has live music and you can play pool in a relaxed environ-ment here. For a quieter night, new-release movies are shown nightly at **Jaws** or **Gar-den Villa Guest House** in Vagator and **Noble Nest** in Chapora.

Chapora village doesn't have much in the way of nightlife, just a handful of restau-rants and small bars fronting the main road. **Paulo's Antique Bar** is tiny – just a few bench seats at the front – but Paulo creates a social vibe and the beer is cheap and icy cold (Rs 20 for a small King's).

Getting There & Around

Fairly frequent buses run to both Chapora and Vagator from Mapusa (Rs 10) through-out the day, some via Anjuna. The bus stop is near the road junction near Soniya Trav-els in Chapora village. Buses also continue up to Arambol via Siolim.

Vagator and Chapora villages are quite spread out and most people staying here rent a motorcycle or scooter – the Vagator hills are constantly alive with the buzz of these machines and the number of bikes outside Nine Bar or Primrose Cafe during an evening is phenomenal. You can ask about motorcycle hire down near the beach at Vagator (try the car park) or anywhere along the main street in Chapora. Bicycle hire is more difficult and the steep hills around here make cycling a relative pain.

CHAPORA TO ARAMBOL

The further you get from Panaji the quieter and less touristy the countryside becomes, although development and people are finding their way to the once-deserted beaches north of the Chapora River. Now that the huge Siolim–Chopdem Bridge crossing the river is finished (replacing the old vehicle ferry), tourist traffic along this stretch of the coast is increasing. At present there are just a few hotels between Chapora and Arambol, along with a rapidly blooming number of bamboo huts and beach shacks, but there are still some peaceful pockets of coastline here.

Heading north from Anjuna, Chapora or Mapusa, make for Siolim, the village on the south bank of the Chapora River. The main road through the village leads to the bridge which takes you across to Chopdem. From there, take the first left at the signpost to Morjim. This is the coast road, which eventually takes you the slow way up to Arambol.

Siolim

Siolim village, on the south bank of the Chapora River, is a busy little diversion if you're heading north to Arambol, but it's not a place most travellers bother to pause in, especially now that the short wait for the ferry across the river is no longer a requirement. The most interesting sight here is the unmistakable **St Anthony's Church** in the middle of the village. The cream-coloured church, with an imposing facade, was built by the Franciscans in 1568. Legend has it that a ship ran into trouble during a storm just off the coast and was saved when it found shelter in the Chapora River. The sailors believed St Anthony had rescued them and they gave the villagers of Siolim a statue of the saint, promising to build a church there. That statue now sits at the top of the magnificent reredos behind the altar.

Siolim House (☎ 2272138; ⓦ www.siolim house.com; standard/superior doubles US$100/ 126, peak season US$126/154), on the road

to Chapora, about 100m from St Anthony's Church, is a superbly restored Portuguese mansion with a central courtyard and swimming pool. The seven suites (each named after 17th-century trading ports) are all individually furnished with four-poster beds, polished floors and colonial touches – a real Goan experience that seems a world away from the touristy beach resorts.

Morjim

Crossing the bridge to Chopdem, you can head 4.5km east to Morjim, a tiny village at the mouth of the Chapora River. The beach is an exposed strip of sand heading north from the river mouth and backed as much by pine trees as by palms. At the southern car park you'll find a cluster of palm-thatch beach shacks serving food and cold drinks, along with sun beds and umbrellas catering to the small but increasing trickle of day-trippers from Calangute. As well as a clean, quiet beach, there are good views south to the headland and Chapora Fort. Rare olive ridley turtles nest at the southern end of Morjim Beach from October to March, so this is a protected area (see the boxed text 'Turtle Beaches' later).

At the northern end of Morjim Beach are more beach shacks and several places to stay. To get there you can either walk a couple of kilometres along the beach or drive back through the village, turning north on the road to Asvem and Mandrem Beach (passing Milagres Church), then left at the signposted turn-off to the beach. At the junction here, **Amigos** is a small shop offering Internet access and currency exchange.

Rooms can be rented in village homes for around Rs 150 per night, but the best places to stay are the handful of guesthouses and huts at the northern end of the beach.

Nestled in the wooded area just back from the beach are two peaceful places, about 100m apart, with rooms for rent. **Britto's Guest House** (☎ 2246245; rooms Rs 200) has six simple rooms with private bathroom and two huts on stilts. The family prepares home-cooked food and for an extra Rs 125 you can have breakfast and dinner included. A short walk south, **Goan Cafe** (☎ 2246394; rooms Rs 200) also serves good food and has five treehouses and two rooms at the back for rent.

Further north are several places lining the narrow lane running parallel to the beach.

Camp 69 *(☎ 2246458; huts or tents Rs 250)* has a group of basic palm-thatch huts and safari tents in a clearing.

Julian's Bar & Restaurant *(☎ 2246475; rooms Rs 250)* is a solid house with six rooms, all with private bathroom, on two levels. The upstairs rooms have hot water.

Olive Ridley Beach Restaurant *(☎ 224 6732; mains Rs 120-190)*, opposite Julian's, is an excellent European-run café and bar on the beach. The speciality is gourmet salads, pasta and seafood. The food is fresh and the atmosphere is congenial.

Asvem Beach

A kilometre or so north along the coast road brings you to peaceful Asvem Beach. Although virtually unheard of by travellers until a few years ago, groups of palm-thatch and bamboo huts have sprung up here, attracting visitors looking to do nothing more than relax on the beach. It's said that one of

Goa's first bamboo beach huts was built here by a British carpenter in 1996 – now they're all over the place!

The beach is small, and quite picturesque, backed by sparse stands of palm trees, but is easily accessible since the road is only about 100m back.

Gopal *(☎ 2246431; e gopal@ingoa.com; rooms & huts Rs 200-250)* is one of the original places along here. There are seven huts on stilts and a few rooms with private bathroom in a concrete block building. **Change Your Mind** *(huts Rs 150)* has also been around a while and has some of the cheapest treehouses on Asvem.

Arabian Sea *(☎ 2297432; huts Rs 300)* has slightly fancier huts and a good restaurant serving Goan, Chinese and Indian food.

Paradise Bar & Restaurant *(☎ 2297832; rooms Rs 200-300)* has rooms with private bathrooms in a concrete building. The restaurant is recommended for seafood.

Turtle Beaches

Among the litany of Goa's recent environmental problems are several notable successes. One of these, the effort to encourage rare olive ridley turtles to return to former hatching grounds on Goan beaches, continues to produce good news.

Goan beaches have provided ideal nesting places for the olive ridley turtle for many years. These giant turtles have a remarkable in-built homing device which enables them to return to nest at the beach where they first hatched – even after 15 years out at sea. One of those beaches is Morjim, but the turtle number began to dwindle dangerously because of poaching – locals were digging up the eggs and selling them in the markets for a couple of rupees each. If a turtle was found out of the water it was likely to be killed for its meat, and the shell sold. In 1972 the turtles became classified as a protected species under Indian law, but it was often difficult for the Forest Department to know where the nests were and to protect them from the egg thieves.

In 1996 the Goa Foundation, on the urging of a local resident, stepped in and enlisted the help of the Forest Department to patrol the beach and start a turtle conservation programme. A scheme offering rewards for information about new nests, and using local volunteers to monitor the nests and count the number of hatchings, has proved successful. From a reported 456 hatchings in 1997–98, 2492 hatchings were recorded from 31 nests on Morjim Beach in 2000–01, while another 2567 hatchings were recorded on Galgibaga Beach in Goa's far south. Other beaches in the programme are Querim (114 hatchings) and Agonda (715 hatchings). The influx of tourists to these once-deserted beaches (Galgibaga is an exception) is a cause for concern, but the nesting sites are protected, minimising the damage of human intervention. The practice of some locals picking up recently hatched turtles and putting them in buckets to show tourists should be discouraged, since environmentalists believe these baby turtles may not survive even if released into the sea. The Goa Foundation believes that with proper management and protection other beaches in Goa could become regular nesting grounds.

The turtle nesting season is from October to March, and the turtles usually come ashore only between the full moon and new moon nights.

TAMSIN WILSON

Mandrem

Continuing north turn left at the T-junction for Mandrem Beach, or right for Mandrem village. The beach and the majority of the accommodation is 1km or so past the village. Mandrem is another peaceful area with a broad beach and some good places to stay amongst the coconut groves. There are several groups of bamboo huts along the beach, all with semiopen-air restaurants facing the Arabian Sea. One of the best is **Dunes Holiday Village** (☎ 2297219; e dunes13@rediff mail.com; huts & cottage Rs 400), a laid-back place (in spite of the security guard at the front gate) with a choice of thatched huts, treehouses and stone cottages. Yoga and massage sessions are on offer here.

Next door, **Shankar Holiday Village** (☎ 2297948; huts with shared/private bathroom Rs 250/350) has 15 sturdy huts – some are on stilts, others have stone floors and private bathroom.

South of these huts, in a dense area of coconut groves, are some more upmarket options shielded from the road and beautifully situated near the mouth of the Mandrem River. To find them, turn at the sign saying 'Junaswada Beach'.

River Cat Villa (☎ 2297928; w www.river catvilla.com; doubles Rs 450-1200) is a very stylish Portuguese house with an unusual circular design. The more expensive rooms are spacious, beautifully furnished and decorated with mosaic tiling; the cheapest have shared bathrooms. This is one of the best guesthouses north of Calangute and with the back veranda facing the river, it oozes the tranquillity of a bohemian retreat. There's a good restaurant serving Spanish and Indian food.

Mandrem Beach Resort (☎ 2277064; doubles Rs 950, peak season Rs 1300), closer to the beach, has less character but the modern rooms are comfortable; some have river views and others have sea views.

A cheaper option near River Cat Villa is **D'Souza's Residency** (☎ 2297483; doubles Rs 150-200) which, in spite of the grandiose name, is a simple family home with a couple of rooms with private bathrooms for rent. The restaurant and juice bar at the front is a great place for fresh seafood, breakfast and cold drinks – most dishes are under Rs 50.

Fantasy Guest House (☎ 2297280; e fan tasyguesthouse@yahoo.com; doubles Rs 250) is back along the road into the village, but still an easy walk to the beach. Rooms in the slightly garish two-storey house have private bathrooms and are a bargain at this price. There's a restaurant and pub-style bar downstairs.

ARAMBOL (HARMAL)
postcode 403524

Although one of Goa's more far-flung beaches, Arambol has well and truly been discovered.

Travellers have been drifting up here for years, attracted by the remote location and prominent headland with beautiful, rocky bays. A mushrooming industry of facilities and accommodation has appeared to service them, and in the high season the beach and the road leading down to it is pretty crowded. Arambol is still a lot quieter than anything south of Vagator and generally attracts travellers looking to chill out for a while.

Orientation & Information

Buses from Mapusa stop on the main road at the back part of Arambol village, where there's a church, school and a few shops, but no bank. From here, a side road leads 1.5km down to the village, and the beach is about 500m further on. There are a few stores, travel agencies and Internet places on the road running parallel to the beach, but most services you'll need can be found on the busy, narrow path leading down to the beach.

You can buy bus and flight tickets, change cash and travellers cheques and get cash advances on MasterCard and Visa at travel agencies such as **Pedro Travels** and **Tara Travels**, both near the top end of the path to the beach. There are plenty of Internet cafés charging around Rs 40 an hour. At the north end of the beach, **Ganga Travels** has fast connections, and there are terminals at **Divya Travels** and **Cyber Zone** at Pedro Travels.

Things to See & Do

The main beach is good for **swimming**, but over the headland are several more attractive bays. At low tide, if you continue past the headland and keep walking for about 45 minutes you'll come to the near-deserted **Querim Beach**. You can also walk south along the beach to Mandrem (about one hour).

Behind the second bay is a small **freshwater pool** that's very pleasant to lie about in, although it's fast being swallowed up by

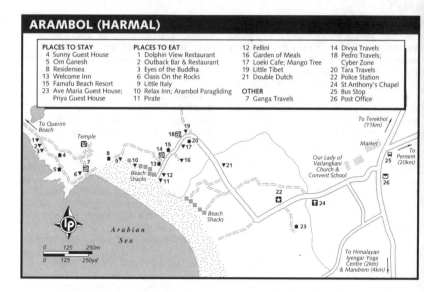

ARAMBOL (HARMAL)

PLACES TO STAY
4 Sunny Guest House
5 Om Ganesh
8 Residensea
13 Welcome Inn
15 Famafu Beach Resort
23 Ave Maria Guest House;
   Priya Guest House

PLACES TO EAT
1 Dolphin View Restaurant
2 Outback Bar & Restaurant
3 Eyes of the Buddha
6 Oasis On the Rocks
9 Little Italy
10 Relax Inn; Arambol Paragliding
11 Pirate

12 Fellini
16 Garden of Meals
17 Loeki Cafe; Mango Tree
19 Little Tibet
21 Double Dutch

OTHER
7 Ganga Travels

14 Divya Travels
18 Pedro Travels;
   Cyber Zone
20 Tara Travels
22 Police Station
24 St Anthony's Chapel
25 Bus Stop
26 Post Office

the encroaching sea and, away from the source of the spring, the water is quite brackish.

The headland at Arambol is a popular place for **paragliding**. There's an outfit called **Arambol Paragliding** (☎ 2292525; e uwe@ sify.com) based at the **Relax Inn** which charges Rs 1200 for a tandem flight and also offers certified courses (four to five days; Rs 8500).

About 2km south of Arambol, between the beach and the road to Mandrem, is the **Himalayan Iyengar Yoga Centre** (w www.hi yogacentre.com; Girkka Vaddo), which runs five-day courses in hatha yoga from December to February. This is the winter centre of the Iyengar yoga school in Dharamsala and is run by the same teacher, Sharat Arora. The five-day courses are suitable for all levels, cost Rs 1000 and start every Friday from 8.30am. Booking and registration must be done in person on Tuesday between noon and 2pm. There are also intensive two- to three-week courses for more experienced hatha-yoga devotees and special short courses combining yoga with Ayurvedic treatment and chakras (energy points).

Places to Stay

The prime accommodation is the jumble of cliff-side **chalets** (doubles Rs 200-400) on the first bay to the north of the main beach. Some

are basic rooms, but many now have private bathrooms and running water, and the sea views and sheltered location are superb. **Om Ganesh** (☎ 2297675) and **Sunny Guest House** (☎ 2297602) are two of the main places, or just ask where rooms are available at the cafés on the north side of the headland.

At the north end of the beach, **Residensea** (huts Rs 200-250) is a group of simple, lockable bamboo huts – expect to see a lot more of this type of accommodation which has already become so popular in Palolem and Mandrem.

Welcome Inn (☎ 2292510; doubles Rs 300-500), among the group of restaurants on the lane leading to the beach, has seven small, but clean, doubles with private bathrooms. A little further up, **Famafu Beach Resort** (doubles Rs 400) is out of character for Arambol – a genuine three-storey hotel with typically nondescript rooms. For the comfort of clean rooms and hot water, it's not badly priced.

There are more places and rooms in villagers' homes (from Rs 80) along the road running parallel to the beach. **Ave Maria Guest House** (☎ 2297674; e avemaria_goa@ hotmail.com; dorm beds Rs 30, doubles with shared/private bathroom Rs 150/300), in a quiet area of coconut palms back from the beach, is a solid old home run by a friendly family. There's a good rooftop restaurant, where you can also choose to sleep on a mattress at night. There's free filtered water and Internet connection. Next door, **Priya Guest House** (☎ 2292661; doubles with shared/private bathroom Rs 100/150) is popular with travellers for its cheap, clean rooms and relaxed café.

Places to Eat
There's a string of shacks lining the main beach, serving seafood, cold beer and offering similar menus and prices. Popular choices include **Pirate** and **Relax Inn**.

Along the path leading around the headland, **Oasis On the Rocks** is a simple café with a great location overlooking the beach and romantic candlelit tables perched on the cliff. Further round among the chalets, **Eyes of the Buddha** (mains Rs 30-120) also has a good seafront location and the usual extensive menu. It's a good spot for breakfast – the fruit salad with curd (Rs 40) is spectacular. Around the next bay is the popular **Outback Bar & Restaurant** and the **Dolphin View Restaurant**.

Back on the main beach, near Residensea, is Arambol's version of **Little Italy** (mains Rs 60-90), a beach shack specialising in pizza and pasta.

Most of the places to eat (and drink) are on the busy lane leading down to the beach. **Fellini** (mains Rs 60-135) is Arambol's top restaurant, specialising in Italian food. There's a good range of pizzas, calzones and pasta, as well as focaccias (Rs 40 to 75) and tiramisu (Rs 40).

Welcome Inn has a German bakery, a popular rooftop restaurant-bar and a good range of juices. Further up towards the main road it gets a bit quieter. **Mango Tree** is a pleasant garden restaurant with Indian classical music playing some nights. **Loeki Cafe** (mains Rs 25-80) has a big breakfast menu, as well as Goan, Chinese and continental dishes. It's a good place for a drink (cocktails Rs 40 to 60), and there's a jam session here on Sunday and Thursday.

Garden of Meals (open 7pm-11pm daily), about halfway down the path to the beach, serves a different set meal each night, usually with an international flavour, such as pasta, paella or couscous.

Little Tibet, at the top of the path, is an unassuming place serving momos and other Tibetan staples.

On the main road running parallel to the beach are a handful of cafés and basic restaurants. **Double Dutch** is a laid-back, bohemian-style garden café away from the crowds. It's a good spot for breakfast and there's a noticeboard advertising courses and local happenings.

Getting There & Away
There are buses from Mapusa to Arambol, via Siolim and Chopdem, every couple of hours (Rs 10, 1½ hours). Buses also head north to Terekhol and Pernem and a few buses take the back road past Mandrem and Morjim. You could get a group together and hire a taxi (around Rs 350 from Mapusa or Anjuna). From Dabolim Airport, prepaid taxis cost Rs 682 for the 65km journey.

If you're coming by bus from Mumbai you can ask to be let off at Pernem and take a local bus, taxi or autorickshaw from there. The nearest train station on the Konkan Railway is Pernem, about 2km from the town itself. Again you can get off here and catch a taxi to Arambol.

Motorcycles can be hired from touts at the main northern entrance to the beach – it costs around Rs 200 a day for a Honda Kinetic in the high season.

There are boats every Wednesday to the Anjuna Flea Market (Rs 75 each way).

NORTH OF ARAMBOL
Querim Beach
North of Arambol and south of the Terekhol River lies the almost untouched sand of Querim Beach and a couple of beach shacks. Querim is accessible from Arambol via a narrow path that leads around the headland from the second bay, or by road through exceptionally pretty countryside along the south bank of the Terekhol River. There are some very basic rooms available behind the beach shacks but visitors are better off staying in Arambol, or in Terekhol, and walking, cycling or motoring here for the day.

Terekhol Fort
At Terekhol (Tiracol), on the north bank of the river of the same name, is a small Portuguese fort with a tiny chapel within its walls. It's now an upmarket hotel, the Fort Tiracol Heritage Hotel.

Originally built by the rajas of Sawantwadi, the fort was finally captured by the viceroy, Dom Pedro de Almeida, in 1746. The fort was rebuilt and the church, which takes up almost all of the available space within the fort, was added.

The fact that the fort was on the wrong side of the natural border (the river) led it to be involved in considerable controversy. In the early 19th century the British demanded that it be handed over and later, when the first Goan-born governor, Bernado Peres da Silva, was appointed and almost immediately ousted, his supporters took over the fort. Finally, in the turbulent years before Independence, the whole of the northern border, Terekhol included, was at the centre of anti-Portuguese demonstrations, and several demonstrators were killed here.

The fort is open to visitors from 11am to 5pm daily and the trip here makes a good outing on a motorcycle. The winding 11km road from Arambol passes through villages and rice paddies and rises up to provide sensational views over the countryside and Terekhol River.

Fort Tiracol Heritage Hotel (☎ 02366-268248, 9822-589988; e nilaya@goatelecom .com; doubles with breakfast & dinner Rs 3550), within the fort itself, is an upmarket, peaceful and atmospheric place to stay. The setting is spectacular, with some of the seven rooms and the restaurant-bar facing south along the coast. The rooms in the old fort are unique, renovated and decorated in a sort of Mediterranean-meets-medieval style. The owners organise yoga, meditation and massage courses, and backwater trips on the Terekhol River.

An alternative to staying at the fort hotel – if you just want to take in the peace and solitude of far northern Goa – is the humble and optimistically named **Hygienic Restaurant** (☎ 02366-68392; doubles Rs 200) which has two simple rooms with private bathrooms. It's just below the fort and the food here is cheap (mains Rs 20 to 60) and satisfying.

There are occasional buses from Mapusa to Querim (Rs 12, two hours), on the south bank of the river, opposite Terekhol, and also between Arambol and Querim, but without your own transport you'll have to walk a couple of kilometres to reach the fort. The ferry between Querim and Terekhol runs every 30 minutes from 6am to 9.30pm, but is often suspended in the afternoon because of low tide (where the river has silted up).

INLAND BARDEZ

Away from the coast, north Goa has less to offer the tourist than the central or south parts of the state and consequently sees far fewer visitors. However, Bardez taluka has several sights east of the main highway (NH17) between Panaji and Mapusa. This is a peaceful area of rural villages, farmland, churches and temples, and makes a pleasant day trip if you have your own transport. The best way to explore this area is either by hired motorcycle or by hiring a car and driver from Panaji, Mapusa or any of the beach resorts.

The most convenient and scenic route is to follow the back roads from Panaji, along the north bank of the Mapusa River, then turn west towards Mapusa itself. Heading northeast from the Mandovi Bridge, the first village you come to is Britona. Following the road north to Aldona, visit Corjuem Fort before turning west to Mapusa and either back to Panaji or continue to the coast for Anjuna or Calangute.

Britona & Pomburpao

The parish church at Britona, **Nossa Senhora de Penha de Franca** (Our Lady of the Rock of France), occupies a fine location on the junction of the Mandovi and Mapusa Rivers, looking straight across to Chorao Island on one side, and the Ribandar Causeway on the other.

Our Lady of the Rock of France was a Spanish saint. After one particularly hair-raising voyage in which the sailors saved themselves from certain death by appealing to Our Lady, she came to be associated with seafarers, and thus was favoured by many of those who had survived the voyage to India.

The interior of the church is beautifully decorated, with a high vaulted ceiling and a simple reredos with painted scenes on it. The church is best visited in the morning and holds one service on most days – in Konkani.

About 5km north of Britona is the village of Pomburpao, where the church of **Nossa Senhora Mae de Deus** (Our Lady Mother of God) is also notable for its beautiful interior and reredos.

Aldona & Corjuem Fort

Another 4km north of Pomburpao, along the road following the banks of the Mapusa River, you reach the large village of Aldona. Catch the ferry the short distance across the

mbroidered light covers, Anjuna Flea Market

Puppet stall, Anjuna Flea Market

brics for sale, Anjuna Flea Market

Musician and fortune-teller, Anjuna beach

T-shirt stall, Anjuna Flea Market

Anjuna Flea Market

Statues for sale, Anjuna Flea Market

river to visit the abandoned Corjuem Fort on the other side of Corjuem Island.

Until the early 18th century, the Mapusa River formed the boundary of Portuguese influence, and the dark red laterite wall above the ferry point in Aldona betrays the ancient lines of the fortress that used to stand here. Around 1705, however, the Portuguese influence extended eastwards, and the small fort on Corjuem Island was built.

Squat and thick walled, standing alone on a small hillock, the fort has an ironic element of *beau geste* about it. Although there's not a whole lot to see here, it's easy to imagine this place as a solitary outpost in the jungle nearly three centuries ago, filled with homesick Portuguese soldiers, half expecting to be overrun at any moment. One of the defenders of the fort is said to have been Ursula e Lancastre, a Portuguese waif. Determined to succeed in a man's world, she disguised herself as a man and travelled the world, eventually serving as a soldier. It was not until she was captured and stripped that her secret was discovered. This did not put an end to her military career – she married the captain of the guard.

Moira

Back on the road to Mapusa there's a final stop worth making at the **Church of Our Lady of the Immaculate Conception** in the village of Moira. Built in 1636, the church has been renovated twice since then. Among the additions has been the bell from one of the seminaries in Old Goa.

BICHOLIM

To the east of Bardez, Bicholim taluka is another good place to explore, if you've hired a motorcycle, to get away from the beaches and see some Goan countryside.

With your own transport you can combine Bardez and Bicholim with a scenic loop by riding from Panaji to Old Goa, crossing by ferry to Divar Island, continuing to the north of the island and crossing by ferry again to Naroa. From here head east to Mayem Lake, then north to Bicholim.

Saptakoteshwara Temple

Among the most famous sights in the area is the Saptakoteshwara Temple, near the village of Naroa. The temple itself is tiny and beautifully complemented by its natural

NORTH GOA

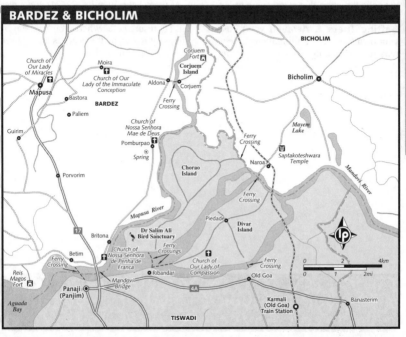

BARDEZ & BICHOLIM

surroundings. Tucked away down in a narrow emerald-green valley, the little hamlet is undisturbed by anything apart from a few mopeds and the occasional tour bus.

The deity worshipped here is an incarnation of Shiva. According to Hindu legend, the Saptarishis, or Seven Great Sages, performed penance for seven million years, a feat that pleased Shiva so much that he came to earth personally to bless them. The incarnation that he appeared in at the time was Saptakoteshwara, which was to become the favoured deity of the great Kadamba dynasty.

The lingam that now resides in this temple underwent considerable adventures before arriving here. Having been buried to avoid the ravages of the Muslims, it was recovered and placed in a great temple on Divar Island, but when the Portuguese desecrated the spot it was smuggled away and subsequently lost. Miraculously discovered again, it was placed in a simple temple on this new site. It is said that the great Hindu leader Shivaji used to come here to worship, and personally saw to it that the temple was reconstructed, leading to the small but solid structure that stands here today.

Getting There & Away If you're using your own transport, finding the temple will require some asking around. From the ferry point at Naroa (coming from Divar Island – which you reach by another ferry from Old Goa; see Divar Island in the Central Goa chapter for details), follow the road for approximately 2km before forking right down a small lane. The temple is on your left, 1.5km down this (tarmac) lane.

Mayem Lake

East of Naroa and about this 35km from Panaji, Mayem Lake is an overrated beauty spot, which has boats for hire. It's popular among India families as a picnic spot and tours run by the GTDC stop for lunch here.

You can get here from Mapusa, via Thivim and Bicholim, The road crosses some pretty desolate and sunbaked countryside, after which the small valley and the lake with its wooded shores come as a relief. Coming from Panaji, the quickest and most scenic route is to take the ferry to either Chorao or Divar Island, then another ferry across to the mainland (to Naroa if coming from Divar) then head east about 3km to the lake. This is a good outing on a motorcycle, but a bit of a long haul for little reward if you're on a bicycle.

Mayem Lake View (*☎ 2362144; doubles with/without air-con from Rs 500/300*) is the GDTC resort hotel where you can stay if you want to escape the beaches and not see another Western tourist.

South Goa

Separated from central Goa by the Zuari River, the southern part of the state has a remarkably different character to the north. If anything, the coastline of south Goa is more varied and picturesque, the beaches longer and straighter, the sand more squeaky underfoot, and the villages – even those close to the beaches – retain a very rural feeling. Overall, far fewer visitors head south, which is generally reflected in the level and type of development.

Despite this, south Goa has changed a lot over the years. The big-money resort builders favour this part of the coast and there are a dozen or so huge resort complexes punctuating the coastline, mostly at Varca, Cavelossim and Majorda. The Konkan Railway has provided better access from Mumbai (Bombay) and Mangalore, which has led to an increase in domestic tourism. One of Goa's most beautiful beaches, Palolem, has been well and truly 'discovered' in recent years, so in the high season there's a steady stream of backpackers and holidaymakers, bored with the concrete jungles of Calangute, trickling down to hang out in the beachside bamboo shacks.

There are still plenty of unspoilt patches of sand in south Goa and much to offer travellers, with lots of inexpensive guesthouses and reasonably priced hotels, particularly in Colva and Benaulim, the original south Goan resorts.

This isn't for the party crowd, though: there are no raves, and even Colva doesn't come close to the northern beaches in terms of crowds, late nights and loud music. In short, south Goa is a great place to come if you want to escape the worst of the holiday crowds, and also to avoid the hardened travellers' party scene at Anjuna and Vagator.

Away from the beaches, south Goa has a number of interesting villages and sights within easy reach of Margao (formerly Madgaon), plus the Cotigao Wildlife Sanctuary in the far south. South Goa includes the talukas (administrative districts) of Salcete, Mormugao, Quepem, Sanguem and Canacona. Margao is both the administrative centre of the region and the transport hub.

Highlights

- Chill out under the coconut palms at Palolem – the most beautiful and active of south Goa's beaches
- Explore the rural area around Chandor and visit its stunning colonial mansions
- Hire a motorcycle and ride down the coast from Cavelossim to Agonda, via the fortress of Cabo da Rama
- Spend a few relaxing days or weeks in Benaulim – a laid-back village and a beautiful beach to boot
- Cycle from Palolem to Rajbag via Patnem beach

MAHARASHTRA

Vasco da Gama p188

Colva p192
Margao (Madgaon) p182
Benaulim p195

Palolem p201

Arabian Sea

KARNATAKA

MARGAO (MADGAON)
pop 94,392 • postcode 403601

The capital of Salcete taluka, Margao is Goa's busiest city; rush hour around the Municipal Market makes central Panaji look positively comatose. For travellers, Margao is mainly of interest for its position as the service and transport centre for south Goa – this is the junction of the South Central Railway (from Vasco da Gama) and the Konkan Railway (from Mumbai or Mangalore).

While certainly not a picture of architectural elegance, Margao is worth a visit if

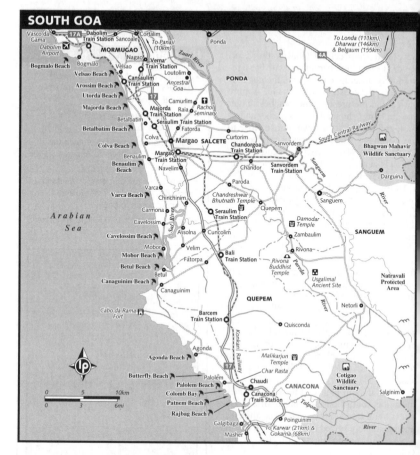

SOUTH GOA

only as a reminder that there is more to Goa than beach shacks and outrigger fishing boats. The colourful and crowded covered market provides a definitive slice of traditional India, and further away from the centre you'll see lots of traditional Portuguese houses, most looking a little worse for wear. In the shady *avenidas* (avenues) near the church there is a handful of elegant *residencias* (town houses) complete with shady *balcaos* (porches) and oyster-shell windows.

Around 8 December, Margao celebrates the **Feast of Our Lady of the Immaculate Conception** with a large fair.

Orientation

In the centre of Margao the Municipal Gardens consist of a small, shady and rather un-kempt patch of grass and trees around which half the traffic in Goa tries to pass at breakneck speed. Most of the facilities of interest to visitors are around or near this square, and the red coloured Secretariat Building at the south end of the park is a useful landmark.

Just under 1km to the north of the park is the Church of the Holy Spirit, and 1km beyond this is the main (Kadamba) bus stand and the new fish and produce market. About 1.5km southeast of the Municipal Gardens and beyond the old train station is the new train station.

Information

Tourist Offices The Goa Tourism Development Corporation (GTDC) **tourist office** (☎ 2712790; open 10am-5.30pm Mon-Sat) is in the Margao Residency, at the south end of the Municipal Gardens. The staff are friendly and reasonably helpful, and there's an interactive audiovisual information terminal which is mainly useful for amusing small children.

Money The **State Bank of India** *(Abade Faria Rd; open 10am-3.30pm Mon-Fri, 10am-1pm Sat, 10am-2pm Sun)*, on the west side of the Municipal Gardens, changes travellers cheques or cash. The **Bank of Baroda** *(Isodora Batisata Rd; open 10am-2pm Mon-Fri, 10am-noon Sat)*, to the east, gives cash advances on credit cards.

HDFC Bank has a 24-hour ATM accepting international cards on the ground floor of the Caro Centre opposite the Municipal Gardens; **Centurion Bank** has an ATM just off Luis Miranda Rd; and **UTI Bank** has an ATM near the roundabout just south of the Kadamba bus stand.

Post & Communications The **main post office** is on the north side of the Municipal Gardens. **Poste restante** *(open 8am-10.30am & 3pm-4.30pm Mon-Fri)* is held in a separate branch about 300m to the southwest, around the back of the police station.

There are plenty of places from which to make international phone calls and send faxes. Internet access is much cheaper in Margao than at the beach resorts. **Cyberlink** *(Rs 24/hr; open 8.30am-7pm Mon-Sat)* is in the Caro Centre on Abade Faria Rd; **Cyber Inn** *(Rs 20/hr; open 9am-8pm Mon-Fri)* is in the Kalika Chambers east of the Municipal Gardens on V Valaulikar Rd; and **Goa Space** *(Rs 20/hr; open 8am-11pm daily)*, directly opposite, has fast connections.

Travel Agencies Next door to Longuinhos, **Paramount Travels** *(☎ 2731150, fax 273 2572)*, is a well-established and reliable agency handling international and domestic flights. Across the road are a handful of private bus agencies that book and sell tickets to Mumbai, Bangalore, Hampi and other interstate destinations.

Bookshops & Libraries The best bookshop in south Goa is the **Golden Heart Bookshop** *(☎ 2736339)*, about 100m north of the main post office and down a small laneway off Abade Faria Rd. It has a large selection of novels and a whole section dedicated to books about Goa and India, as well as an Internet café.

The **Municipal Library** *(open 9am-1pm & 3pm-6pm Mon-Fri)* is on the west side of the Secretariat Building.

Medical Services About 500m to the northeast of the Municipal Gardens is the **main hospital** *(☎ 2223036; Padre Miranda Rd)*, which has a casualty department and a 24-hour pharmacy.

Church of the Holy Spirit
The main church in Margao is the town's most interesting attraction. The first church was built here in 1565, on the site of an important Hindu temple. Before the demolition started on the temple, local Hindus managed to rescue the statue of the god Damodara, to whom the building was dedicated. It was secretly moved to a new site in the village of Zambaulim, where there is still a large temple today.

The new church didn't last long, and was burned to the ground by Muslim raiders in the same year it was built. It was soon replaced and a seminary was established, but both were subsequently destroyed, after which the seminary was moved to Rachol.

The present church was built in 1675, and is notable not only for its size and the fine decoration inside the building, but also for the fact that it is still obviously a very active parish church. The reredos behind the altar is extremely impressive, rising from ground level to the high ceiling, but is made more distinguished by the unusual gilded and carved archway that stands in front of it. The ancient pipe organ gives the church a suitably aged feel. Access is via the side entrance.

Largo de Igreja
Largo de Igreja, the area around the Church of the Holy Spirit, features a number of traditional old Goan houses. The most famous is the **Sat Burnzam Ghor** (Seven Towered House). Originally, as its name suggests, there were seven of the distinctive high-peaked gables, of which only three remain, and the house looks imposing rather than attractive. Inside, it's reputed to be beautifully preserved and furnished, but unfortunately it is not open to visitors.

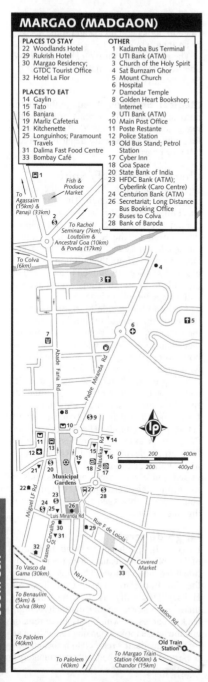

MARGAO (MADGAON)

PLACES TO STAY
22 Woodlands Hotel
29 Rukrish Hotel
30 Margao Residency;
      GTDC Tourist Office
32 Hotel La Flor

PLACES TO EAT
14 Gaylin
15 Tato
16 Banjara
19 Marliz Cafeteria
21 Kitchenette
25 Longuinhos; Paramount
      Travels
31 Dalima Fast Food Centre
33 Bombay Café

OTHER
1   Kadamba Bus Terminal
2   UTI Bank (ATM)
3   Church of the Holy Spirit
4   Sat Burnzam Ghor
5   Mount Church
6   Hospital
7   Damodar Temple
8   Golden Heart Bookshop;
      Internet
9   UTI Bank (ATM)
10 Main Post Office
11 Poste Restante
12 Police Station
13 Old Bus Stand; Petrol
      Station
17 Cyber Inn
18 Goa Space
20 State Bank of India
23 HFDC Bank (ATM);
      Cyberlink (Caro Centre)
24 Centurion Bank (ATM)
26 Secretariat; Long Distance
      Bus Booking Office
27 Buses to Colva
28 Bank of Baroda

Mount Church

About 500m east of Sat Burnzam Ghor and a fair climb up Margao's only hill is the Mount Church, a simple whitewashed building, faced by a similarly diminutive whitewashed piazza cross. A detour up here is worth it for the view: from the shade of a grove of palm trees in front of the church it's possible to see straight across the coastal plain to the beaches of Colva and Benaulim.

Markets

Margao is the market centre of south Goa. You can easily get lost in the **covered market**, also called the **New Market**, just north of Station Rd. This crowded canopy of colourful stalls is a fun place to wander around, but it's not really a place to hunt for souvenirs. Much of the merchandise here is household items, second-hand junk and cheap Indian clothing, so you'll see lots of local women poking around looking for bargains, and there are tailors' shops and material merchants where you can have clothing made.

The **fish and produce market** has been moved out of the congested town centre to a large modern covered site near the Kadamba bus stand. It's hidden from view behind the huge OSIA Commercial Arcade, which was just opening at the time of research. The main reason to visit this market is to buy fresh fish or fruit and vegetables, since it has zero local colour or flair.

Places to Stay

Although Margao has a range of hotels within most budgets, and the beaches of Colva and Benaulim are only 6km away, there's no pressing reason to stay here. Some travellers spend a night here when arriving or departing by train, and it makes a reasonable base if you're planning a tour of the attractions east of here (see Around Margao).

Most of the cheap places are strung out along Station Rd between the Municipal Gardens and the site of the old train station.

Rukrish Hotel (☎ 2715046; singles/doubles with shared bathroom Rs 95/132, doubles with private bathroom Rs 237) is central and probably the best of an unappealing range of cheapies around the bazaar area. Rooms are small and checkout time is 24 hours.

Margao Residency (☎ 2715528; singles/doubles Rs 425/500, doubles with air-con Rs 650) is the GTDC's hotel. Recent renovations have made it a more appealing choice, with clean but plain rooms.

Hotel La Flor (☎ *2731402, fax 2731382;* [e] *laflor@goatelecom.com; Erasmo Carvalho St; singles/doubles from Rs 370/470, with air-con Rs 500/570)* is Margao's best choice. It's clean, efficiently run and in a quiet but central location. Rooms come with TV and private bathroom. There is a 15% tax on all rooms.

Woodlands Hotel (☎ *2751121;* [e] *wood land@goatelecom.com; Miguel LF Rd; singles/ doubles Rs 450/540, with air-con Rs 575/660, suites Rs 725/825)* likes to think of itself as Margao's top hotel but it's looking very tired these days. There's a wide range of rooms from basic singles/doubles to air-con suites, but most are typically austere with private bathroom and TV.

Places to Eat

Bombay Café is a busy vegetarian place with cheap snacks such as samosas and *dosas* (thin, lentil-flour pancakes) – nothing over Rs 10. It's often so crowded that getting a seat is a challenge.

Tato, down a small street east of the Municipal Gardens, is another excellent vegetarian restaurant. A thali (traditional South Indian and Gujarati 'all-you-can-eat' meal) costs Rs 25, and the place is kept very clean.

Dalima Fast Food Centre (*Erasmo Carvalho St)* is tiny but you can get a decent fish curry rice for only Rs 20.

Longuinhos (☎ *2739908; Luis Miranda Rd; mains Rs 55-80),* opposite the Margao Residency, has long been Margao's classic colonial hang-out, with a languid, old-fashioned atmosphere. Unfortunately, the quality of food and service have slipped beyond recognition, but it's still a good place to sit and while away the siesta hours over a cold beer.

Marliz Cafeteria is a modern, open-fronted cafe with a wacky design. It looks out at the busy town centre and Municipal Gardens and is a great spot for coffee and cake while watching the traffic whizz by.

Banjara (☎ *2714837; D'Souza Chambers, Varde Valaulikar Rd; mains Rs 60-125; open noon-3pm & 7pm-11pm daily)* is Margao's best Indian restaurant, specialising in North Indian dishes (around Rs 95) and seafood. The subterranean air-con dining room is intimate and the service is good.

Gaylin (☎ *2733348; Varde Valaulikar Rd; mains Rs 50-95; open 11am-3pm & 6.30pm-11pm daily)* is a popular Chinese restaurant 100m north of Banjara. The dining room is intimate and the menu has a big range of soups, noodles and Cantonese dishes.

Kitchenette, near the Woodlands Hotel, is useful if you're self-catering and can't find that elusive ingredient. It's a tiny gourmet supermarket stocking everything from imported Parmesan and Gruyère cheese to pâté, strawberries and Baskin-Robbins ice cream.

Getting There & Away

Bus All local buses operate from the busy Kadamba bus stand about 1.5km north of town, but many also stop at the old bus stand in the centre of town. Catch buses to Colva and Benaulim from Kadamba or from the bus stop on the east side of the Municipal Gardens. All buses coming to Margao from Benaulim and Colva stop by the old bus station stand in the centre of town and continue to the new station stand.

There is a daily public bus to Mumbai (Rs 319, 16 hours), Bangalore (Rs 302, 14 hours) and Pune (Rs 301, 10 hours), which can be booked at the advance reservation office in the booking office inside the Secretariat building. There are also buses to Hubli (Rs 65, six hours), Belgaum (Rs 60, five hours) and Mangalore (Rs 146, 10 hours). A better option for most interstate trips is the long-distance private buses; they are more comfortable, there are more of them and they're no more expensive. Private booking offices are clustered near the Margao Residency on Luis Miranda Rd. Private buses to Mumbai and Pune (both Rs 300), Bangalore (Rs 300) and Hampi (Rs 300/450 in normal/sleeper) depart from a stand opposite the main bus stand.

Margao has good local bus connections with beaches and other towns in Goa:

Colva Beach There are hourly buses to Colva from the Kadamba bus stand and from the Municipal Gardens (east side), from 7am to 7pm (Rs 5, 20 minutes). Some services go via Benaulim (Rs 4 to Benaulim).

Palolem & Chaudi There are around eight buses a day direct to Palolem from Kadamba bus stand (Rs 12, one hour) and many others heading south to Karwar (Rs 30) that stop in nearby Chaudi, an easy autorickshaw or taxi ride to Palolem, Patnem or even Agonda beaches.

Panaji Buses depart from the Kadamba bus stand approximately every 15 minutes from 6am to 9.15pm (public bus/express Rs 10/15, about one hour). The alternative route taken by some buses is via Ponda (Rs 12, at least two hours).

Other Destinations You can find buses to most towns in Goa from the Kadamba bus stand. Timetables are approximate (the buses leave when full). There are reasonably frequent local buses to Vasco da Gama (for the airport), Ponda, Chandor and Rachol. To the smaller villages, such as Betul, Mobor and Agonda, they're much less frequent, so it's best to make inquiries at the bus stand in advance.

Train Margao's new train station, which serves both the Konkan and South Central Railways, is about 1.5km southeast of the town centre; vehicle access is via the road south of the train line. If you're walking there, however, you can cross the tracks at the footbridge past the old station. There's a **reservation hall** (✆ 2712790; open 8am-2pm & 2.15pm-8pm Mon-Sat, 8am-2pm Sun) on the 2nd floor of the main building, as well as a tourist information counter and retiring rooms. See the Getting There & Away chapter for train information.

A taxi between the train and bus stations costs about Rs 40.

The Konkan Railway provides an alternative to using the buses for travel within Goa, but since there are only a handful of services a day, and since buses to Chaudi and Palolem are easy to catch from the main bus stand, the train is only likely to be useful for getting to the far north of the state (eg, to Arambol – formerly Harmal). There are half-a-dozen trains a day north via Thivim (Mapusa Road) Station (Rs 27 for 2nd class, one hour), at least two of which stop at Pernem Station (for Arambol), and three trains south to Canacona (Rs 23, 35 minutes).

Taxi Both Colva and Benaulim are close enough to take a taxi without breaking the bank – about Rs 80 from the Municipal Market or Kadamba bus stand. If you're solo, a motorcycle taxi to either of the villages costs about Rs 40 and there are no problems taking backpacks. Autorickshaws charge around Rs 60.

If you're going further afield, prepaid taxi rates from Margao train station include Panaji Rs 480, Palolem Rs 480, Calangute Rs 600, Old Goa Rs 443, Dabolim Airport Rs 336, Anjuna Rs 696. You can bargain cheaper rates from taxis in the town centre.

AROUND MARGAO

As tempting as it is to head west to the beach, the area to the east and northeast of Margao is a rich patchwork of rice paddy fields, lush countryside, somnolent rural villages, superb colonial houses and a smattering of historical and religious sites. With a day to spare and a hired motorcycle or taxi, you can cover most of the sights listed here, assuming you don't get hopelessly lost, which is easy to do in the tangle of unsignposted back roads!

With a bicycle you could do a loop out to Chandor, up to Loutolim via Rachol Seminary and back to Margao (about 45km) in a long day. Finding a detailed map of this area is virtually impossible, and since you'll come to many multidirectional crossroads, the best advice is to keep stopping to ask directions.

Rachol Seminary & Church

Seven kilometres from Margao, near the village of Raia, is the Rachol Seminary and Church. Although there is a sign by the seminary door indicating that the seminary is not open to visitors, it's worth ringing the bell and asking if they'll show you around, or ask in advance at the Margao tourist office. After some very lean years when the religious orders were banned in Goa, the seminary is now full of life again, with more than 100 students, and is exactly as one imagines a religious college should be – ancient, peaceful and full of wonderful works of art. As you enter through the huge front door into a hall with a single central pillar, the two murals are striking – on the left wall is an image of hell, and on the right is an image of heaven.

The Portuguese first came into possession of the fortress that once stood on this site in 1520, when Krishnadevaraya, the Hindu Raja of Vijayanagar, captured it from the Muslim Sultan of Bijapur, Ismail Adil Shah, and voluntarily ceded it to the Portuguese.

The seminary, established under the sponsorship of King Sebastian of Portugal, was built by the Jesuits between 1606 and 1610 to train Goan priests. Within a short time it was a noted centre of learning, a position which was enhanced by the setting up of only the third printing press in the Portuguese eastern empire. Among the seminary's most famous members were Father Thomas Stevens, who by 1616 had translated the Bible into Konkani and Marathi, and later produced the first Konkani grammar, and Father Ribeiro, who produced the first Portuguese–Konkani dictionary in 1626.

In 1762 Rachol was raised to the status of diocesan seminary and in 1833, when other religious institutions in Goa were being forcibly closed, it was saved by its rector, Monsignor Rebello. The buildings you see today were mostly built from the early 17th century, and are contemporary with the Se Cathedral in Old Goa.

The **seminary church**, dedicated to St Ignatius Loyola, the founder of the Jesuits, is impressive mainly because it has been maintained in excellent condition. The reredos fills the whole wall above the altar with its carved and gilded yet simple design. The most striking features are the carved and painted wooden panels that cover the sides of the chancel – a mass of colour and detail. One of the side altars also displays the 'Menino Jesus', which was originally installed in the Colva church but was taken back to the seminary amid much controversy.

Loutolim

Ten kilometres from Margao and about 6km north of Rachol is the tiny, peaceful village of Loutolim. If you have your own wheels, the countryside here is a pleasure just to ride through.

Set up purely for tourists, **Ancestral Goa** (☎ 2777034; admission Rs 20; open 9am-6.30pm daily) is a mildly diverting attraction. In the terraced gardens behind the house is a series of mock-up scenarios depicting daily life in Goa under the Portuguese. There are also a number of fruit and spice plants native to Goa and, for some reason the source of great pride, the longest laterite sculpture in India.

Much more interesting, though not really tourist attractions, are a couple of grand old houses in the village. The largest of these, which visitors are occasionally permitted to view inside, is the **Miranda House**, a three-minute walk southwest from the church, down an unsurfaced access road. The two-storey whitewashed house has remained in the hands of the same family through the years; the current owner is well-known artist and illustrator Mario Miranda. This is

one of the best existing examples of Goan country-house architecture. Contact the tourist office in Margao to see if the staff can make an appointment for you.

Chandor

About 15km east of Margao, on the border between Salcete and Quepem talukas, is the small village of Chandor, once the site of the most spectacular city on the Konkan coast, Chandrapur. Capital of the ancient state of Govarashtra, Chandrapur was situated within the loop of the river which, unbelievable as it may seem today, was large enough to make the city a viable port. Although there was a town here during the time of the Mauryan empire (321–184 BC), Chandrapur's promotion to capital city came later. After several centuries of infighting following the demise of the Mauryans, the Bhojas eventually gained control of the area, and ruled almost undisturbed from Chandrapur from AD 375–525, promoting trade with other areas along the Indian coast and further afield. In AD 979, the Kadamba dynasty came to power, ruling from Chandrapur until 1052.

Ironically, Kadamba success signalled the end of Chandrapur's pre-eminence for, as the empire expanded, the Kadambas captured the port of Govepuri on the Zuari River. Within a short time more trade was flowing through Govepuri than Chandrapur, and the capital was shifted there in 1053. When Govepuri was levelled by the Muslims in 1312, the Kadambas moved the seat of power back to Chandrapur for a short time. However, it was not long before Chandrapur itself was sacked in 1327. There's now an archaeological site in the village, where the foundations of an 11th-century Hindu temple and stone Nandi (the bull, vehicle of Shiva) have been unearthed.

Chandor's premier attraction today is its beautifully preserved colonial mansions – two of the grandest, **Braganza House** and **Fernandes House** (see the boxed text 'Chandor's Colonial Mansions' later) are open to the public.

On 6 January, Chandor is one of three Goan villages that hosts the **Feast of the Three Kings** (the others are Reis Magos and Cansaulim), a colourful festival in which local boys re-enact the arrival of the three kings bearing gifts for Christ.

Chandor's Colonial Mansions

Visiting the superb colonial mansions in Chandor gives you a peek at the opulent lifestyle of the Goan landowners during the height of their fortunes in the Portuguese era. Best known is the **Braganza House** which takes up one complete side of Chandor's village square and dates back to the 17th century. It's now divided into east and west wings – two separate houses – which stretch outwards from a common front entrance.

Ongoing restoration is gradually returning the house to its former glory, but wandering through the ballrooms with their Italian marble floors, Belgian glass chandeliers and carved rosewood furniture, it's not hard to imagine the sort of parties that were thrown here. The east wing is owned by the Braganza Pereira family, and includes a small family chapel containing a carefully hidden relic of St Francis Xavier – a fingernail. The clutter of bric-a-brac collected by the family over the years gives the house an air of faded magnificence. The west wing belongs to the Menezes Braganza family, crammed with beautiful furniture and Chinese porcelain from Macau. The two large rooms behind the entrance halls contain Dr Menezes Braganza's extensive library – Luís de Menezes Braganza was a journalist and leading light in the Goan Independence movement.

The respective families give you a guided tour of their homes, and though there is no official entry fee, the owners rely on contributions for maintenance and restoration – Rs 50 to 100 is reasonable. Both houses are open daily from 10am to 5pm, but you may want to call ahead to ensure the owners will be there *(Braganza Pereira ☎ 2784227; Menezes Braganza ☎ 2784201).*

Around the corner, **Fernandes House** *(☎ 2784245)* is nowhere near as grand, but it's much older and has an interesting history. The original Hindu house here dates back more than 500 years, while the Portuguese section was built by the Fernandes family in 1821. A feature is the secret basement hideaway with an escape tunnel to the river – the Hindu occupants used it to flee attackers.

Balconied windows, Menezes Braganza House

Damodar Temple, Zambaulim

Approximately 12km southeast of Chandor and 22km from Margao on the border of Quepem and Sanguem talukas, is the small village of Zambaulim, which is home to the Damodar Temple. The deity in the sanctum was rescued in 1565 from the main temple in Margao, which was destroyed by the Portuguese to allow the Church of the Holy Spirit to be raised symbolically on the site.

The temple is fairly modern in appearance but the ancient ablutions area, built 200m back from the main buildings on the banks of the Kushavati River, is attractive and the water is said to have medicinal properties. The celebration of Shigmo here is spread over several days, and is particularly colourful (see Public Holidays & Special Events in the Facts for the Visitor chapter).

Buddhist Caves, Rivona

Continuing south from Zambaulim for about 3km, the road passes through the settlement of Rivona, which consists of little more than a few houses and drinks' stands spread out along the highway. As the road leaves the village, curling first to the left and then right, there is a small faded sign on the left, pointing to Shri Santhsa Gokarn. A short way up the dirt track (which comes to an end at a tiny temple), the Rivona caves (also called Pandava caves) are on the left. You need your own transport to get here.

It's thought that the caves were occupied by Buddhist monks who settled here some time in the 6th or 7th century AD. There's little to see, but the tiny compartments cut into the rock are an interesting reminder that religions other than Hinduism, Islam and Christianity also made it to Goa. There's a small staircase cut through the rock between the upper and lower levels of the caves; if you plan to look inside you'll need a torch (flashlight).

On the other side of the road, some way down the slope and off to the left, there is another, larger cave that is also believed to have been used by the monks.

Usgalimal Rock Carvings

Carved into laterite stone on the banks of the Kushavati River in Sanguem taluka, these prehistoric petroglyphs (rock art) show various scenes, including a dancer, wild animals, a pregnant women and a man with a harpoon. They are thought to be the work of one of Goa's earliest tribes, the Kush. The carvings are underfoot, rather than on a wall and, depending on the light, it can be difficult to make out the shapes. But if you're exploring this area with your own transport, the peaceful riverside location is worth the diversion.

To get here, continue past Rivona for about 6km and look out for the green-and-red Forest Department 'protected area' signs. An unsealed road off to the right of the main road leads 1.5km down to the river bank and carvings.

Chandreshwar Bhutnath Temple

Approximately 14km southeast of Margao near the village of Paroda, a number of hills rise out of the plain, the highest of which is Chandranath Hill (350m). At the top in a small clearing stands the Chandreshwar Bhutnath Temple, a small but attractive building in a lovely setting.

Although the present buildings date from the 17th century, there has been a temple here for more than 1500 years. The site is dedicated to the god Chandreshwar, an incarnation of Shiva who is worshipped as Lord of the Moon. Consequently it is laid out so the light of the full moon shines directly into the sanctum and illuminates the deity, which is carved from the natural rock of the hilltop. It is said that when the moonlight falls on it, the stone lingam oozes water.

Leaving through the side entrance there is another small shrine standing separately that is dedicated to the god Bhutnath, who is worshipped in the form of a simple stone pinnacle that sticks out of the ground.

To get to the temple you will need your own transport as it's a fair way off the beaten track. Head to Paroda, and ask there for the turn-off that takes you up the narrow winding hillside road. There's a small parking area near the top, from which the approach to the temple is via a steep flight of steps.

VASCO DA GAMA
pop 97,000 • postcode 403802

Vasco da Gama is a busy port and was once a major transport hub for travellers. These days it's a noisy, dirty industrial town with a seedy feel about it. It's only 4km from Dabolim Airport, so if you fly into Goa it's possible you may want to spend a night in Vasco, but there's really no need.

Situated at the base of the isthmus leading to Mormugao Harbour, Vasco sports an oil refinery and Goa's biggest red-light district at Baina, where there's also a small (filthy) beach and a steady influx of sailors and truck drivers. The city has a reputation for being the crime centre of Goa – you're safe enough in the town centre, but it is probably unwise to go wandering by yourself much further than the main part of town at night.

Information

There's **GTDC tourist information** (☎ 251 2673; open 9.30am-5.30pm Mon-Fri) in the foyer of the Vasco Residency hotel.

The **State Bank of India** (FL Gomes Rd) will exchange both travellers cheques and cash, and there are 24-hour ATMs at the **HFDC Bank** opposite the bus station, and the **Centurion Bank** on Pe José Vaz Rd near Vasco Residency.

There's Internet access at **Dajik Internet** (Rs 25/hr; Pe José Vaz Rd).

Places to Stay

Twiga Lodge (☎ 2512682; doubles with private bathroom Rs 100), near the main bus stand, is the best rock-bottom budget option in town. The dilapidated old Portuguese house has just five basic rooms with private bathrooms; it's often full so call ahead.

Vasco Residency (☎ 2513119; singles/doubles Rs 275/350, doubles with air-con Rs 600) is secure and central. Like most GTDC hotels it's a bit run-down, but it's the best cheap place in the city centre.

Hotel Karma Plaza (☎ 2518928; e karma hotel@123india.com; Rajendra Prasad Ave; standard/deluxe doubles Rs 800/1000) is the pick of the mid-range places. All the rooms have air-conditioning, it's clean and the hotel is part of a modern shopping complex with restaurants and a nightclub. Rooms attract a 10% tax.

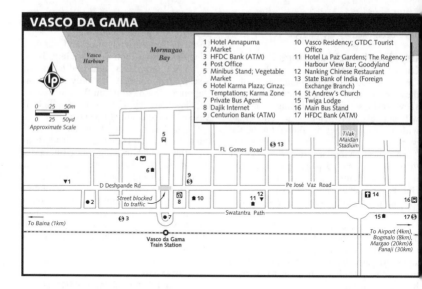

VASCO DA GAMA

1 Hotel Annapurna
2 Market
3 HFDC Bank (ATM)
4 Post Office
5 Minibus Stand; Vegetable Market
6 Hotel Karma Plaza; Ginza; Temptations; Karma Zone
7 Private Bus Agent
8 Dajik Internet
9 Centurion Bank (ATM)
10 Vasco Residency; GTDC Tourist Office
11 Hotel La Paz Gardens; The Regency; Harbour View Bar; Goodyland
12 Nanking Chinese Restaurant
13 State Bank of India (Foreign Exchange Branch)
14 St Andrew's Church
15 Twiga Lodge
16 Main Bus Stand
17 HFDC Bank (ATM)

Hotel La Paz Gardens (☎ 2512121; Swatantra Path; ⓦ www.hotellapazgardens .com; studio Rs 800, singles/doubles Rs 900/ 1200, suites from Rs 1650/2000) is the top place in town. It's a typical business hotel with air-con rooms, satellite TV, a gym and sauna, and three restaurants.

Places to Eat

There are plenty of cheap thali places around the centre. **Hotel Annapurna**, near the market, is clean and the best budget option; vegetarian thalis cost Rs 20.

Karma Plaza shopping centre has clean, modern restaurants, including **Ginza** for Chinese and Japanese and **Temptations** for burgers or ice cream, and a rooftop pub and nightclub called **Karma Zone**, which opens at 7pm.

Goodyland (mains Rs 20-50), next to Hotel La Paz Gardens, is a family-friendly fast-food place serving good pizzas, vegetarian patties, sausage rolls and refreshing ice cream.

Nanking Chinese Restaurant (mains Rs 40-80), around the corner from Goodyland, has reasonably good Cantonese food.

The Regency (mains Rs 80-150), at Hotel La Paz Gardens, is one of the better restaurants in Vasco, specialising in Goan and Indian food. Also at the La Paz is the top-floor **Harbour View Bar**.

Getting There & Away

Express minibuses run nonstop from the city bus stand north of the train station to Margao (Rs 10) and Panaji (Rs 15). Both trips take about 45 minutes. There are also regular buses from here to the airport (Rs 3) and Bogmalo (Rs 5). For long-distance state buses you have to go to Margao or Panaji, but private buses to Mumbai (Rs 250) and Bangalore (Rs 300) depart daily from outside the train station, where there are booking agents.

A taxi from the airport costs Rs 60 and an autorickshaw is Rs 50.

BOGMALO

postcode 403806

Eight kilometres southeast of Vasco, and only 4km from the airport, Bogmalo beach is a small, sandy cove dominated by the huge, five-star Bogmalo Beach Resort, which somehow evaded the restriction requiring all hotels to be built at least 500m from the high-tide line. The beach is reasonably pleasant and has an air of exclusivity, but it's really nothing special compared with the miles of white sand just a short way to the south. Most of the people staying here are charter tourists on package deals.

Bogmalo is a bit of water-sports centre – you can hire windsurfers, jet skis and boats, and **Goa Diving** (☎ 2555036) is based here at Joets Guest House (see Activities in the Facts for the Visitor chapter).

At the naval base on the road above Bogmalo beach is the **Naval Aviation Museum** (☎ 5995525; adult/child Rs 15/5, camera/video Rs 10/25; open 10am-5pm daily). It's easy to spot by the preserved military planes and helicopters sitting out the front, and by the hordes of school children waiting to go in to look around. There are displays on the history of India's navy along with uniforms, photographs, equipment and a small theatre.

Places to Stay & Eat
In keeping with its exclusivity, there are only a handful of places to stay in Bogmalo.

William's Inn (☎ 2555111; doubles with private bathroom from Rs 400) is a friendly, family-run home back from the beach. Spacious, clean rooms are good value for pricey Bogmalo. Room No 1 has a balcony and sea view.

Down on the beach, **Saritas Guest House** (☎ 2555965; e saritasguesthouse@rediffmail.com; doubles Rs 550, with air-con Rs 880) has clean but small and unremarkable rooms.

Joets Guest House (☎ 2555036; doubles Rs 700), further down the beach from Saritas, is a lively place, again with small but comfortable rooms. It's usually full from mid-December but there's a good bar and restaurant here.

Coconut Creek (☎ 2556100; e joets@goa telecom.com; 1st-floor cottages Rs 2750, cottages with air-con Rs 3250) is a very stylish resort set back from the beach in a peaceful coconut grove. There's a shady pool surrounded by 10 double-storey cottages, as well as a good restaurant serving Italian and Goan cuisine.

The ugly, high-rise of **Bogmalo Beach Resort** (☎ 2513291, fax 2512510; singles/doubles from US$51/65) presides over the southern end of Bogmalo beach. All rooms face the beach, there's a pool, restaurant and large breezy foyer. Walk-in rates triple for the three weeks over Christmas–New Year.

Apart from the hotel restaurants, there are a few beach shacks serving the usual fare of seafood, continental dishes and breakfasts but they're more expensive than you'll find elsewhere in Goa – some even quote menu prices in pounds sterling!

Getting There & Away
An irregular bus service runs between Bogmalo and Vasco da Gama (Rs 5, 25 minutes). Buses depart from the car park in front of the entrance to the Bogmalo Beach Resort. Taxis wait in the same area.

VELSAO & MAJORDA
Between Bogmalo and Colva, a 6km stretch of beach meanders south from the Mormugao headland. This is a largely undeveloped, clean beach with just a few beach shacks at the end of half-a-dozen road access points, and a handful of upmarket but slightly fading resort complexes. At the north end the beach is practically deserted – but then it's blighted by the view of the enormous agrochemical plant that stands smoking away on the headland itself.

Back from the beach are the villages of (from north to south) Velsao, Cansaulim, Majorda and Betalbatim. The beaches themselves are Velsao, Arossim, Utorda and Majorda. Occasional buses from Margao stop at Velsao and Cansaulim.

The area between Colva and Velsao makes an interesting day trip on a bicycle or motorcycle. The back lanes pass through coconut groves and working villages virtually unfettered by the tourism so prominent on other parts of the coast.

Places to Stay & Eat
There are several large resort complexes close to the beach between Velsao and Betalbatim, along with a few cheaper guesthouses set back in the villages that should suit most budgets. Development is very low-key, though, and there's no accommodation on the beach itself.

Horizon Beach Resort (☎ 2754923; w www.horizonbeachresortgoa.com; doubles with/without air-con Rs 1200/950, suites from Rs 1100) is a new resort less than 100m back from Velsao beach. It doesn't try to be too flashy – bright, modern rooms in a set of double-storey Mediterranean-style buildings around a pool and garden. There's a restaurant, bar and small gym.

Further south on the road leading to Utorda beach, **Dom Pedro's Haven** (☎ 271 3251; doubles Rs 400) has just six rooms in a lovely two-storey house. It's set among the coconut groves within walking distance of the beach.

SOUTH GOA

Shangri-la *(☎ 2881135;* **W** *www.shangrila goa.com; doubles with/without air-con Rs 535/ 425)*, on the lane leading back from Majorda beach to the coast road, is a standard hotel with plain but comfortable rooms.

Shalom *(☎ 2881016; Rs 300)*, a private house belonging to Mrs Godinho, is the best value of all with just a single self-contained flat that would suit a small family or couple. It's on the corner of the coast road and the lane down to Majorda beach.

Majorda Beach Resort *(☎ 2754871;* **W** *www.majordabeachresort.com; doubles Rs 3650)* is a beach resort at the end of the lane just back from Majorda beach. It's the fanciest hotel in this area with 120 rooms, including some villas and cottages, a pool, tennis courts and manicured garden.

There are plenty of small cafés and restaurants scattered around the villages here, and a few shacks on the beach offering the usual seafood and cold drinks. **Martin's Corner** *(☎ 2880061; mains Rs 40-80; open 11am-3pm & 6.30pm-11pm daily)* in Betalbatim, between Majorda and Colva (look for the signs from the main road), is an incredibly popular Goan restaurant and the best place around for an ambient but casual lunch or dinner. The covered dining area is usually packed. Fish curry rice costs Rs 50, *sorpotel* (pork liver and kidney cooked in thick, spicy sauce) costs Rs 60 and prawn *balchão* (seafood cooked in tangy red sauce) is Rs 80.

COLVA
pop 10,200 • postcode 403708

Colva has changed a lot since its days as a sleepy fishing village. It's now the main package-holiday resort of south Goa, but if you've been to north Goa you'll be surprised at how low-key the development is. If anything, Colva is increasingly being ignored by the package-tour companies and, except in the very busiest season, it's quite relaxed – you can easily find quiet stretches of beautiful beach to the north and south of the main village.

It's the peaceful, yet bustling, atmosphere of Colva that has made it popular with an older crowd of British and European holidaymakers (and expats) and with weekending Indian families avoiding the hype of Calangute. The market area and road leading to the main beach is busy and lined with souvenir stalls, restaurants and mid-range

The Morning Catch

Colva's days as a sleepy fishing village are long past but the activities of the local fisherman in their motorised outrigger boats are still one of the highlights of the day. Rise early (around 7am) and head down to the beach north of the main access road (in front of the Lucky Star restaurant) to see locals carrying baskets of fish – mostly small-fry mackerel caught in nets – ashore and dumping them in drying pens. It's a great photo opportunity.

hotels, but walk or cycle a kilometre or two in either direction and you'll find parched farmland, coconut groves and fish drying in the sun.

Orientation & Information

The centre of action in Colva is the roundabout area at the end of the road to the beach. This is where the taxis wait, the fruit vendors ply their trade, and a dozen or so small restaurants and shops are to be found. Colva village, where you'll find the church, post office and other facilities, is strung out a long way back along the road to Margao.

Although there is no official tourist office, the staff in the **GTDC Colva Residency** (see Places to Stay) can help with most matters, and can book GTDC tours.

Money Near the church a small **Bank of Baroda** *(open 9am-1pm Mon, Tues, Thur & Fri, 9am-11am Sat)* will change cash and travellers cheques, and give cash advances on MasterCard and Visa. Nearer to the seafront are several travel agencies that keep longer hours and can efficiently change money and give credit card cash advances. **Meeting Point Travel** has exchange facilities.

There's a 24-hour **UTI Bank** ATM on the beach road near Avloc nightclub.

Post & Communications The post office is on the lane that runs past the eastern end of the church. Poste restante can be collected daily from 9am to 1pm, and 2pm to 4pm. International phone calls can be made easily at several places, including travel agencies and Internet cafés.

There are several places offering Internet access. **Hello Mae Communication Centre** *(Rs 60/hr)*, close to the beach on the ground floor of Rodson Cottage, is not the cheapest, but has fast connections. **Ida On-ine** *(Rs 40/hr)*, above Baskin-Robbins, is a reliable air-con place.

Travel Agencies A reliable place for booking flights, buses and trains, **Meeting Point Travel** *(☎ 2788626)* is near the crossroads back from the beach.

Church of Our Lady of Mercy

Founded in 1630 and rebuilt in the 18th century, this church contains the statue of the Menino (Baby) Jesus, famous throughout Goa for its miracle-working abilities (see the boxed text 'The Miracles of Menino Jesus').

Activities & Organised Tours

Water sports have arrived at Colva, with parasailing and jet skis available in the high season. **Chris Watersports** *(☎ 2780199)* also organises dolphin trips (Rs 250 for one hour), fishing trips (Rs 500) and full-day boat trips (Rs 850). Domnick's (see Places to Eat) offers full-day boat trips to Palolem beach every Sunday, if there's sufficient demand. They cost Rs 375 including a buffet lunch and a drink. The boat trip there takes 2½ hours and there's a good chance of seeing dolphins; the return trip is by bus.

If you're not planning to stay at any of the northern beaches, it's worth making the day trip to the Wednesday **flea market** at Anjuna. Trips are advertised at the beach bars and cost about Rs 75. Tackling this trip by public bus involves three or four changes.

Places to Stay

It's still possible to rent houses long term in Colva, although there are more opportunities in Benaulim village; just ask around in the restaurants and shops. Most houses are a 20-minute walk back from the beach. Prices vary enormously, depending on location, the size of the house and the season, but in the high season you can expect to pay anything from around Rs 3000 a month up to Rs 10,000.

Places to Stay – Budget

Close to the beach, **Hotel Lucky Star** *(☎ 278 8071; e pradorbarad@hotmail.com; doubles with private bathroom from Rs 450)* has a range of comfortable though overpriced doubles. Each room has a safe and there's a very popular restaurant and bar.

Garden Cottages *(☎ 2780776; doubles Rs 150)*, in the quiet, palm-fringed 4th Ward, is a friendly place with just six rooms facing a small garden. Next door, **Joema Tourist Home** *(doubles with private bathroom Rs 200)* is another small place with four slightly better rooms, and an open-air 'candlelight café'.

Vailankanni Cottages *(☎ 2788584; rooms with private bathroom Rs 300, apartments Rs 800)*, set back from the main road to the beach, is popular with travellers for its friendly atmosphere and clean rooms.

There's a string of small guesthouses in family homes along the back road leading to Benaulim, including **Rosman Guesthouse** *(☎ 2788735; rooms with shared bathroom Rs 80-100)*; **Ma Mickey Tourist Home**

The Miracles of Menino Jesus

The original carving of the Menino Jesus was found in 1640 by a Jesuit missionary, Father Bento Ferreira, after he had been shipwrecked off the coast of Mozambique. In 1648 when Father Ferreira became the first vicar at the Church of Our Lady of Mercy in Colva, he brought the statue with him and soon noticed a strange light emanating from it. Within a short space of time it had become known for granting favours.

When the Jesuits were forced to leave Goa in 1834 they insisted that the statue should go with them, although one ring that had been on the finger of the carving was left behind in the church. This was placed on the finger of a replacement statue. Immediately the miracles started again, while the original statue, which now resides in the chapel of Rachol Seminary, is said never to have granted another request.

On the feast day, on the second Monday in October, the Menino is brought out, and there's a fair. Among those who make a special effort to appeal to the statue are young men and women in search of a partner, to whom the infant is said to be especially favourable.

(☎ 2788190; singles/doubles with shared bathroom Rs 100/150); and **Benema Guesthouse** (☎ 2788698; doubles with private bathroom Rs 150).

Navin's Inn (☎ 2788550; doubles Rs 350-400) is a very homely place in an immaculately kept family house. There are five clean rooms of varying sizes, with private bathrooms, hot water and verandas, including one small single (Rs 150). Book ahead.

Sam's Cottages (☎ 2788753; doubles Rs 300), opposite Navin's Inn, has a dozen rooms that face onto a central courtyard garden. The rooms are bright, with large windows and the whole place was being renovated at the time of research, so it should be a very good choice.

Places to Stay – Mid-Range & Top End

The **Bollywood Sea Queen Resort** (☎ 278 9040; e bollywoodseaqueen@rediffmail.com; singles/doubles Rs 1200/1800, suites Rs 3500) is a flash new (or at least renovated) hotel a couple of kilometres north of Colva's main street on the road running parallel to the beach. It's in a rather forlorn area but once you get through the lobby, the pool and garden area looks over an attractive expanse of paddy fields. The rooms are modern, spacious and all have air-con and cable TV.

GTDC Colva Residency (☎ 2788047; doubles with/without air-con Rs 700/500), facing the beach at the end of the road, is an ugly two-storey concrete construction that is saved by its excellent location. Although it looks horrible from the outside, the rooms are clean and reasonable value.

Graciano Beach Resort (☎ 2788787; e graciano@goatelecom.com; doubles Rs 900-1000, deluxe doubles Rs 1700-1800, suites Rs 2500-3000) is a possibility if the village is crammed and you want to find a space quickly. The building looks like a prison and there's a tacky fake lawn at the front, but it offers plenty of facilities. The rooms all have air-con and TV and are clean and bright, if a little small.

Colmar Beach Resort (☎ 2788043; e hotel colmar@sity.com; doubles with/without air-con Rs 700/500, cottages from Rs 1000), past the Colva Residency, has an excellent beachfront location, a swimming pool and some nice cottages, although like many of Colva's mid-range hotels it's starting to look tired. Rates double during the Christmas period.

Vincy Beach Resort (☎ 2788087; doubles with/without air-con Rs 1000/800), at the end of the road to the beach, is a long-running place – one of Colva's original hotels. The rooms are still very plain but are clean and airy, and there's a swimming pool and satellite TV.

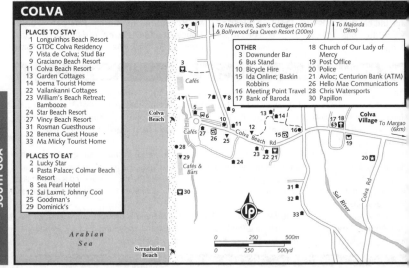

COLVA

PLACES TO STAY
1 Longuinhos Beach Resort
5 GTDC Colva Residency
7 Vista de Colva; Stud Bar
9 Graciano Beach Resort
11 Colva Beach Resort
13 Garden Cottages
14 Joema Tourist Home
22 Vailankanni Cottages
23 William's Beach Retreat; Bambooze
24 Star Beach Resort
27 Vincy Beach Resort
31 Rosman Guesthouse
32 Benema Guest House
33 Ma Micky Tourist Home

PLACES TO EAT
2 Lucky Star
4 Pasta Palace; Colmar Beach Resort
8 Sea Pearl Hotel
12 Sai Laxmi; Johnny Cool
25 Goodman's
29 Dominick's

OTHER
3 Downunder Bar
6 Bus Stand
10 Bicycle Hire
15 Ida Online; Baskin Robbins
16 Meeting Point Travel
17 Bank of Baroda
18 Church of Our Lady of Mercy
19 Post Office
20 Police
21 Avloc; Centurion Bank (ATM)
26 Hello Mae Communications
28 Chris Watersports
30 Papillon

To Navin's Inn, Sam's Cottages (100m) & Bollywood Sea Queen Resort (200m)

To Majorda (5km)

Cafés

Colva Beach

Cafés

Colva Beach Rd

Colva Village   To Margao (6km)

Arabian Sea

Sernabatim Beach

Sal River

Colva Rd

0   250   500m
0   250   500yd

Smiling girl, southern Goa

Villager, southern Goa

Waiting for a ferry, Panaji pier

Rice-sack carriers, Municipal Market, Panaji

Selling fabrics and jewellery, Mapusa market

Vista De Colva (☎ 2788144; doubles Rs 500, suites Rs 2500), opposite Sea Pearl, has some of the best rooms in Colva – it's one of the few that justifies the 'top end' tag, with prices to match. The best rooms are huge and extremely comfortable with small kitchenette and lounge, and there's a good pool and garden area. Nonguests can use the pool for Rs 50.

Star Beach Resort (☎ 2788166; W www starbeachresortgoa.com; doubles Rs 900, with air-con Rs 1200), set back from the road next to the football ground, is another mid-range place, with a pool, travel agency and massage services. Rooms are comfortable enough and have cable TV.

William's Beach Retreat (☎ 2788153; e wbretreatgoa@sify.com; doubles Rs 800, with air-con Rs 1500) is one of the best of Colva's mid-range hotels. There are comfortable ground-level rooms around a pool; rates include breakfast and tax. Nonguests can use the pool – which has a nifty pool bar – for Rs 50.

Longuinhos Beach Resort (☎ 2788068; W www.longuinhos.homestead.com; singles/ doubles Rs 800/900, with air-con Rs 1000/ 1200) is the best of the bunch in this range. It's well kept and benefits from an outstanding location right beside the beach, with direct access from the garden. The rooms are simply furnished but most have balconies and face the sea. Rates double in the peak Christmas season when the place is chock full of charter tourists.

Colva Beach Resort (☎ 2788130; e colva beachresorts2000@yahoo.com; singles/doubles Rs 700/800, doubles with air-con Rs 950), on the main road to the seafront is looking rather faded and has disconcerting hexagonal-shaped rooms.

Places to Eat

Colva has far fewer eating options than the busy northern beaches and most places turn out similar menus of seafood, continental, Indian and a few Goan dishes, along with Western breakfasts. The most popular places to eat (and drink) are the string of open-air beach shacks that line the beach either side of where the road ends. Seafood is the staple here, but don't expect fish and shellfish straight off the boat. All the shacks buy their fish daily from the market (usually at Margao) in the morning, then keep it on ice until it's required.

Domnick's (mains Rs 55-140) is one of the most established shacks on the beach and the personable owner brings a selection of the daily catch to your table, so you can choose for yourself. The other shacks – **Luke's Place**, **Rendezvous** and several others – are also very good. Most travellers staying for a while visit a few and establish their own favourite.

Goodman's (mains Rs 65-125), on the road to the beach, is the place if you're craving a cooked breakfast. The English breakfast (Rs 90) includes baked beans and sausages. It also has a lengthy menu of Goan, Indian and continental dishes and a good bar. Fish curry rice is Rs 70 and butter chicken Rs 85.

Sea Pearl Hotel (☎ 2780176; mains Rs 50-180) is recommended for seafood and Western dishes – it has a reputation as one of Colva's better seafood restaurants so it's usually very busy in the evenings. The kitchen is spotlessly clean, the service friendly and the covered dining area has a good ambience.

Lucky Star (mains Rs 50-200) has a very popular open-air restaurant with live entertainment twice a week. It has built a reputation for great steaks (Rs 110 to 200) but the menu covers the full range of seafood and Indian dishes.

Sai Laxmi (Rice Bowl; mains Rs 15-50), down a lane just off the main street, doesn't look like much from the outside, but is much more comfortable than it appears and probably serves the best South Indian vegetarian food in Colva.

Pasta Palace (mains Rs 60-150) overlooking the beach at Colmar Beach Resort, is a reliable place for Italian fare (pasta dishes Rs 60 to 90) and a pleasant spot to dine around sunset if you've tired of the beach shacks.

Bambooze (mains Rs 50-110), the restaurant at the front of William's Beach Retreat, has a good range of Goan, Indian and continental dishes served in a semi-open dining area facing the road.

Entertainment

Compared to the northern beaches, Colva and particularly Benaulim are very quiet at night, with most people content to eat out and enjoy a few drinks near the beach.

The only nightclub in the area is **Avloc** on the main road into Colva. It's a small, darkened club describing itself as the 'leisure dome' and playing anything from pop to house. It attracts a mix of curious tourists and young Indians.

Papillon is a laid-back beach bar (head south along the beach from the Colva roundabout) where you're more likely to hear Bob Marley playing than Ibiza techno.

Lucky Star and nearby beachside **Downunder Bar** are among the most popular bars in Colva, frequented by British expats and charter tourists. Downunder has an island bar right on the beach, overlooking the beach volleyball court, and pool tables.

Johnny Cool is a bit hard to find and consequently seems to have been forgotten but it has a good range of beers and an open terrace overlooking the fields of the 4th Ward. It's just off the beach road behind Sai Laxmi.

The Stud Bar, at Vista de Colva, is a bizarre cocktail bar with a Wild West theme.

Getting There & Away
Buses run from Colva to Margao about every half-hour (Rs 5, 20 minutes), departing from the roundabout in front of the GTDC Colva Residency. The first bus from Colva departs around 7.30am and the last one back from Margao leaves about 7pm.

Taxis, share taxis, autorickshaws and motorcycles can also be picked up here. A taxi from Colva to Margao costs approximately Rs 80 to 100, a motorcycle should charge about Rs 40.

Getting Around
Motorcycles and mopeds are available for hire from Rs 100 to 350 a day. The best place to ask initially is at your hotel, but also try the market area near the beach. A small stall opposite Colva Beach Resort rents bicycles for Rs 40 to 80 a day.

BENAULIM
postcode 403716
Only 2km south of Colva, Benaulim seems a world away – it's much more peaceful and rural, the beach is cleaner and less crowded and tourist facilities are few and far between. It's this rustic atmosphere that makes Benaulim a popular place for visitors staying long term. Development is beginning to make its mark round the village, but it's still a lovely place to stay.

Benaulim has a special place in Goan tradition for it is said to have been here that Parasurama's arrow landed, when he fired it into the sea and created Goa (see History in the Facts about Goa chapter).

On the main road through the village about 1.5km south of Maria Hall, **Manthan** (☎ 2271659) is a beautifully restored century old Portuguese-era home that has been converted into a heritage gallery. The furnished rooms have mosaic tile floors and contain Goan and Indian arts, crafts and antiques, most of which are for sale. Pottery, sculpture, paintings and designer clothing are on display. Even you don't want to buy pricey contemporary Goan art, Manthan is a labour of love and worth a visit to enjoy the ambience.

Yoga classes are held every Tuesday at 5pm at Pedro's Restaurant near the beach (Rs 100).

Orientation & Information
The centre of the village is the crossroad known as Maria Hall. There are limited facilities in Benaulim, and for most things it's better to go to Colva or, better still, into Margao. Travel agents, moneychangers and Internet facilities can be found on Vasvaddo Beach Rd at the crossroads west from Maria Hall.

Money The **Bank of Baroda** *(open 9am-1pm Mon, Tues, Thur & Fri, 9am-11am Sat)* has a branch by the crossroads at Maria Hall where you can change currency and get cash advances on MasterCard and Visa. There are also money-changing facilities including credit card cash advances, at the three village travel agencies. The nearest ATM is in Colva.

Post & Communications The nearest post office is in Colva. International phone calls and faxes can be made from a number of places around Benaulim, including the travel agencies. There are Internet cafes at the **GK Tourist Centre**, **New Horizons** and close to the beach, at **O Palmar Beach Cottages**. All charge around Rs 40 an hour.

Travel Agencies At the crossroads leading down to the main part of Benaulim beach **GK Tourist Centre** *(☎ 2770476; e gktourist centre@hotmail.com)* can book bus, train and flight tickets. Across the road, **New Horizons** *(☎ 2771218; e dokl@goatelecom .com)* is an efficient new travel agency handling domestic and international travels and tours within Goa.

Places to Stay

There is a wide range of budget accommodation in Benaulim, including several places right on the beach between Benaulim and Sernabatim beach.

Places to Stay – Budget

Furtado's Beach House (*☎ 2770396; doubles with private bathroom Rs 400*) has a prime beachfront location on Sernabatim, a restaurant and 10 simple double rooms.

Camilson's Beach Resort (*☎ 2788420; doubles Rs 300-600*) is a recommended place with a variety of clean rooms set in a large garden just back from the beach.

Cocohuts (*☎ 2780787; huts & rooms from Rs 200*), further south on Sernabatim beach, has a few huts, some rooms and a good beachfront restaurant. It's run by a friendly couple who offer trips on their sailing boat.

O Palmar Beach Cottages (*☎ 2771837; e opalmar@goatelecom.com; doubles Rs 350*) is near the car park on the road to Benaulim Beach. It's pretty exposed and basic but the location makes up for that.

Rosario's Inn (*☎ 2770636; doubles from Rs 150-250*), next to the football pitch, is a big place run by a friendly family. Rooms are fantastic value and come with veranda and attached bathroom. There are also some cheaper rooms with shared bathroom.

Jacinta Moraes Tourist House (*☎ 277 0187; doubles with private bathroom Rs 100-200*) has a variety of clean doubles behind the house and it's run by a hospitable family.

Tansy Cottages (*☎ 2770574; doubles Rs 150*) is another good-value family-run place. The nine rooms all have private bathroom.

D'Souza Guest House (*☎ 2770583; doubles Rs 250*), on the road to Colva, is a small family guesthouse in a Goan bungalow set in an extensive garden. Spotless rooms are a bargain so it's often full. The beauty salon here has been recommended by readers for its high level of personal pampering and D'Souza's even accepts credit cards.

Simon Cottages (*☎ 2770581; doubles from Rs 150*) is almost opposite D'Souza Guest House, although it's set back 200m into the trees – the location is about as far as it's possible to get from the tourist 'bustle' of Colva or Benaulim. Huge rooms in the two-storey house are immaculate and easily some of the best-value budget accommodation in Benaulim. To find it, follow the narrow path just off the T-junction.

Oshin Holiday Care Cottages (*☎ 277 0069; doubles Rs 300-350*) is in a very peaceful area set back from the road. Surrounded by paddy fields and catching the

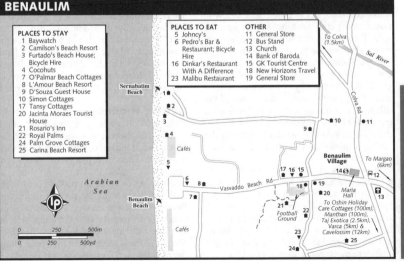

BENAULIM

PLACES TO STAY
1 Baywatch
2 Camilson's Beach Resort
3 Furtado's Beach House; Bicycle Hire
4 Cocohuts
7 O'Palmar Beach Cottages
8 L'Amour Beach Resort
9 D'Souza Guest House
10 Simon Cottages
17 Tansy Cottages
20 Jacinta Moraes Tourist House
21 Rosario's Inn
22 Royal Palms
24 Palm Grove Cottages
25 Carina Beach Resort

PLACES TO EAT
5 Johncy's
6 Pedro's Bar & Restaurant; Bicycle Hire
16 Dinkar's Restaurant With A Difference
23 Malibu Restaurant

OTHER
11 General Store
12 Bus Stand
13 Church
14 Bank of Baroda
15 GK Tourist Centre
18 New Horizons Travel
19 General Store

Sernabatim Beach

To Colva (1.5km)

Sal River

Colva Rd

Arabian Sea

Benaulim Beach

Cafés

Cafés

Vasvaddo Beach Rd

Benaulim Village

To Margao (6km)

Maria Hall

Football Ground

To Oshin Holiday Care Cottages (100m), Manthan (100m), Taj Exotica (2.5km), Varca (5km) & Cavelossim (12km)

0   250   500m
0   250   500yd

SOUTH GOA

cool sea breezes, this is a charming place. There are 12 doubles with private bathrooms and the front rooms have balconies.

Places to Stay – Mid-Range & Top End

On Sernabatim beach, **Baywatch** (☎ 277 2795; rooms Rs 600, tents Rs 700) has an interesting setup with 'Rajasthani' safari tents, complete with private bathroom (toilet and shower) and electricity. There are also spacious, clean rooms. There's a bar, restaurant and nightclub here, but it really only gets busy in the peak season.

L'Amour Beach Resort (☎ 2737960; doubles Rs 475), on the seafront just before the Benaulim beach parking area, is this mid-range standard place with cottages around a well-kept garden. Rooms are a little worn but the location is good.

Palm Grove Cottages (☎ 2770059; e palm grovecottages@yahoo.com; doubles Rs 350-450, large rooms Rs 600-800) is a very relaxing place to stay. Rooms range from basic doubles in an old house to spacious newer rooms with balcony and hot water, all set in a lush, peaceful garden. There's a glassed-in restaurant and bar. It's also unusually secure for its price range – a guard is posted on the gates.

Carina Beach Resort (☎ 2770413; doubles Rs 750, with air-con Rs 850) would be regarded as 'upmarket' and a bit fancy for Benaulim, with its security gates and uniformed staff, but it's quite low-key with a spacious garden setting and swimming pool. Rooms are comfortable enough and good value outside the peak season.

Royal Palms (☎ 2770613; e rpalms@goa telecom.com; apartments from Rs 1500, villas Rs 3500), a four-storey red-brick eyesore is easily the flashest hotel in the centre of the village. There are comfortable self-contained apartments and facilities include a pool, gym and children's park. Rates doubles during the Christmas period. Part of the hotel is a timeshare resort.

Taj Exotica (☎ 2771234; fax 2271515; e exotica.goa@tajhotels.com; doubles US$300), 3km to the south of Maria Hall, is Benaulim's top hotel. Every luxury is provided, beautifully furnished rooms have balconies facing the ocean and the landscaped lawns include a beachside golf course. In the shoulder season rates drop to US$180.

Places to Eat

The beach shacks between Benaulim and Sernabatim are all pretty good, but Benaulim has few outstanding restaurants – there's a better choice in Colva or Margao.

Johncy's (mains Rs 45-75), at the car park, has been the main beach shack in Benaulim for 15 years. It has a big menu of seafood, Indian and Chinese; fish curry rice is Rs 30. Nearby, **Pedro's Bar & Restaurant** also has good food, a covered dining area and a bar.

Further back in the village itself there are a few places but the choice isn't great.

Dinka's Restaurant With A Difference (mains Rs 70-125) is a tiny restaurant and coffee shop near GK Tourist Centre. It's unclear what the difference is, but the brief menu has some good soups and vegetarian dishes.

Malibu Restaurant, south along the road past Royal Goan Beach Club, is a pleasant outdoor place in a lush garden. It's a good spot for breakfast, Goan and Indian food.

The enclosed glass **Palm Garden Restaurant** at Palm Grove Cottages is a good choice. The kitchen is spotless and you're likely to meet a few travellers here.

For a splurge the restaurants at the **Taj Exotica** are the best in Benaulim. You can dine in style at one of three restaurants serving Goa, Mediterranean and Asian cuisine.

Getting There & Away

Buses to Margao from Benaulim (Rs 4) are frequent, and leave from the bus stand at Maria Hall. Buses heading south to Varca and Cavelossim can also be picked up at the crossroads. Minibus taxis tend to hang around opposite the Royal Goan Beach Club, while motorcycle taxis and autorickshaws are best picked up at the crossroads.

Getting Around

Benaulim village is quite spread out and a lot of accommodation is well back from the beach, so it pays to have some form of transport. There are plenty of places that rent motorcycles in Benaulim – ask at guesthouses or at the car park on the beach.

Bicycles are available for rent in front of Pedro's or outside Furtado's on Sernabatim beach for around Rs 40 to 80 a day. At low tide you can ride 15km along the beach to Mobor, at the southern end, then back along the road through Cavelossim and Varca.

Ecofriendly Pigs

You may never encounter one during your stay in Goa, but if you do there's something rather disconcerting about using a traditional Goan toilet. Basically it's no more than a normal squat-style toilet in which the pipe runs out of the building and straight into the pigsty behind the cubicle. The sound of contented snuffling is an unusual accompaniment to a normally solitary activity, and since it generally comes from somewhere pretty close beneath and behind you it can be quite alarming. However strange it may seem to Western eyes and ears, the pig loo is the perfect combination of environmental resources. By comparison, the sit-down flush loos now in use all over Goa are nothing but trouble.

The pig loo solves the problem of sewage disposal, wasted water and pig food all in one go. It does make you think twice before next ordering a plate of Goan sausages, though!

VARCA, CAVELOSSIM & MOBOR
postcodes Varca 403721 • Cavelossim 403731

The 10km strip of pristine beach south of Benaulim has become Goa's most upmarket resort frontage, hosting at least eight hotels of varying degrees of luxury facing the beaches at Varca and Cavelossim. The five-star resorts are exclusive, luxurious self-contained bubbles with pools, extensive private grounds (some have golf courses) and cavernous marble lobbies.

It's still possible to enjoy this relatively deserted stretch of coastline without spending a small fortune on accommodation. With your own transport – a bicycle, motorcycle or taxi – you can head south from Benaulim and find one of several beach access points in between the big hotels. There's generally a few beach shacks and sun beds at the end of these lanes catering to the few independent tourists who come here. Public buses run from Margao and Colva to Varca and Cavelossim villages, but you can't get right to the beach by public transport. A good spot to access the beach in Varca is just south of the Goa Renaissance Resort in a small area called Zalor. Head west at the crossroads and you'll come to a parking area and a few beach shacks. From here you can wander north or south and find a deserted bit of sand.

Cavelossim, 7km south of Varca, is more developed once you get through the village and onto the incongruous strip of shops and hotels that have sprung up here in recent years. Along the main drag are a couple of gaudy, modern shopping complexes – **Sagar** and **Luisa By the Sea** – stocking souvenirs, jewellery and designer clothing.

Both Varca and Cavelossim villages have impressive whitewashed **churches** that are worth a stop if you're exploring this region under your own steam. The ride along the back roads from Benaulim to Cavelossim takes you through coconut groves, farmland, paddy fields and small settlements.

Continuing on through Cavelossim brings you to Mobor on the tip of the peninsula where the Sal River meets the Arabian Sea. **Boat trips** on the Sal River can be organised here.

Betty's Place (☎ 2871456) runs leisurely cruises and activities such as bird-watching, dolphin-spotting (in the open sea) and fishing trips. A full-day trip, including lunch and drinks, costs Rs 650, a 1½ hour dolphin cruise is Rs 250 and a two-hour evening bird-watching trip on the river is Rs 250.

Places to Stay & Eat
Varca On the beach about 2km west of Varca village, **Radisson White Sands Resort** (☎ 2727272; ⓦ www.radisson.com; doubles US$180-320) is a new five-star resort hotel with all the trimmings.

Club Mahindra (☎ 2744555; ⓦ www.clubmahindra.com; doubles US$68), also facing Varca beach, is a reasonable choice outside the peak season for affordable luxury. It's a family-friendly place with plenty to keep kids occupied, a terraced pool, three restaurants and 135 rooms.

Goa Renaissance Resort (☎ 2745200; ⓦ www.renaissancegoa.com; standard doubles Rs 5000) is a true five-star establishment with an enormous lobby, manicured gardens stretching down to the beach, a big pool, tennis courts, golf course, nightclubs and casino. All rooms have a sea-facing balcony.

There are some relatively cheap guesthouses and hotels close to the beach between Varca and Cavelossim.

Mitchette's Bar & Restaurant (☎ 274 5732; doubles Rs 300, apartment Rs 600) is a family-run place just south of the crossroads to the beach. It has a good-value two-bedroom apartment which would be ideal for a family or group, and an inexpensive restaurant.

Further south on the same road, **Dona Sa Maria Holiday Home** (☎ 2745290; W www .donasamaria.com; doubles Rs 500) is a pleasant mid-range hotel with 18 rooms, a small pool, bar and restaurant. It's used by charter groups but you should be able to get a room outside the peak Christmas period. You can hire bikes, exchange money and use the Internet.

Cavelossim & Mobor A popular mid-range guesthouse is **Gaffino's Beach Resort** (☎ 2871441; e bradleygaffino@yahoo.com; doubles Rs 740/900, doubles with air-con Rs 700), which has an excellent restaurant.

Dona Sylvia (☎ 2871321; W www.dona sylvia.com; doubles with air-con Rs 6000) operates 'all-inclusive' package deals (includes all meals and booze) or slightly cheaper accommodation and meals packages. If all you want to do is laze around the pool, eat, drink and party, it may be for you.

Down a laneway near Gaffino's you'll find a couple more mid-range hotels and restaurants. **Sao Domingo's Holiday Home** (☎ 2871461; W www.saodomingosgoa.com; doubles Rs 800, with air-con Rs 900) is in a pleasant area of coconut palms just a few minutes walk from the River Sal. Tidy air-con rooms have balcony and hot water.

Holiday Inn Resort (☎ 2871333; W www .holidayinngoa.com; doubles US$110) is smaller than some of the resorts in this part of Goa but is still an impressive hotel with rooms arranged around a pool just back from the beach.

Besides the restaurants and bars at the flash hotels – and the handful of beach shacks – there are several good places to eat and drink in this area, although menu prices generally reflect the upscale nature of the tourism. **Goan Village** (mains Rs 60-200), opposite Sao Domingo's, is a garden restaurant with live music on weekends and a menu of Goan cuisine backed by Indian and continental staples. Fish curry rice is Rs 110, pomfret recheiado (stuffed with red masala filling) Rs 180.

Goan Fest (☎ 2871279; mains Rs 50-130) is a bit off the beaten track – along the road to the ferry crossing to Assolna – but it's a great place to sample genuine Goan cuisine in a pleasant garden setting. Dishes include pork sorpotel (Rs 90), prawn balchão (Rs 80) and chicken xacuti (hot Goan cooking sauce; Rs 90). On Monday and Thursday there's live folk dancing and you can see a demonstration of feni distilling in the minidistillery. The owners offer free transport from any hotel in the Cavelossim area. Also here is a locally owned craft gallery and shop selling an interesting collection of Goan and Indian handicrafts, jewellery, paintings, pots, woodwork and clothing.

Leela Palace (☎ 2871234, fax 2871352; W www.leelapalace.com; pavilion rooms US$250, suites US$400-1500), at the end of the road at Mobor, near the mouth of a small estuary, is one of Goa's finest resort hotels. This sprawling, imaginatively designed complex of chalets is built around an artificial lagoon. Leisure facilities include tennis and squash courts, gym, pool and health spa, golf course and casino, plus a full range of water sports. The Mobor beach is particularly good here, with palm trees providing much-needed shade. All rooms have an 18% tax.

The **Jazz Inn**, near Gaffino's on the main road to Mobor, is a popular night-time spot with live music.

BETUL TO AGONDA

To the south of Mobor is the mouth of the Sal River. To continue down the coast you either need to backtrack and head inland via Chinchinim for the National Highway (NH) 17 or take the small road leading east from Cavelossim, cross by ferry to Assolna, and then continue down the coast road.

This coast road is the most interesting way to explore southern Goa if you have your own transport – preferably a motorcycle. The area south of Betul is one of the few parts of the Goan coast where the Western Ghats project westwards far enough to form imposing headlands. The coastal road is hilly, winding and in many places poorly surfaced, but it's quiet, scenic and good for a spot of motorcycle touring. Another reason to take the coast road is that you can detour to the old fort, or what remains of it, at Cabo da Rama.

The ferry between Cavelossim and Assolna (Rs 4 for a motorcycle) runs every half-hour from around 6am to 8pm. The journey takes four minutes. To get to the ferry crossing, turn left at the sign saying 'village panchayat Cavelossim' before you get to Mobor, and continue for 2km to the river. On the other side, turn left towards Assolna then take a right in the village to head south to Betul.

Betul

Following the coast southwards from the Sal River, opposite the narrow peninsula occupied by the Leela Palace resort, is the ramshackle fishing village of Betul. Few foreign tourists stay here and, apart from getting local boatmen to take you out on the river or watching the fishermen unload their catch at the harbour, there's not much to do, but it's very peaceful and a good taste of rural Goa.

Betul Beach Resort (☎ 2730555; doubles with air-con Rs 800-1200), off the main road on the banks of the estuary, is a good choice, if a little overpriced. There are plain rooms and cottages in a garden setting, a restaurant and you can take boat trips on the river from here at high tide.

Cabo da Rama

The laterite spurs along the coastline of Goa, providing both high ground and ready-made supplies of building stone, were also natural sites for fortresses. These were used along the length of Goa's coastline – Mormugao, Aguada, Chapora and Terekhol. The headland of Cabo da Rama is no exception and there was a fortress here long before the Portuguese ever reached Goa.

The **fortress** on this site, named after Rama of the Hindu Ramayana epic who was said to have spent time in exile here with his wife Sita, was held by various rulers for many years. It was not until 1763 that it was gained by the Portuguese from the Raja of Sonda and was subsequently rebuilt; what remains today, including the rusty cannons, is entirely Portuguese.

Although the fort saw no real action after the rebuild, it was briefly occupied by British troops between 1797 and 1802 and again between 1803 and 1813, before being allowed to fall into ruin. It was used as a prison for a period until 1955.

There is little to see of the old structure beyond the front wall with its dry moat and unimposing main gate, and the small church that stands just inside the walls. The church is still used – services are held in the chapel every Sunday – and its pristine whitewash contrasts noticeably with the blackened stone of the ruined front rampart. There are excellent views from the main bastion at the top of the front wall, looking north up the coast.

Beyond the church the bare, scorched hilltop with dark laterite showing through the soil is notable mainly for its vast area. The western extent of the fortress, where the cliffs drop sharply to the sea, affords good views both to the north and south. There is practically no sign of life on the hilltop at all, apart from a few soaring fish eagles, and the occasional monkey scampering between clumps of vegetation.

To get to the fort from the coast road between Betul and Agonda, turn west at the signposted turn-off about 10km south of Betul. The road dips into a lush valley then winds steeply up to a barren plateau punctuated by farmhouses and wandering stock. The fort is at the end of this road, about 3km from the turn-off.

There are local buses direct from Margao or Betul several times daily but since there's nothing to do once you've explored the fort you should check on times for returning buses. There are a couple of simple cafés and drink stalls outside the fort entrance to while away some time while waiting for a bus, but nowhere to stay the night.

A return taxi to Cabo da Rama costs around Rs 300 from Betul and Rs 500 from Palolem, including waiting time.

Agonda

Twelve kilometres south of the turn-off to Cabo da Rama (and 8km north of Palolem), the coast road passes the small village of Agonda. Following the small road 2km to the coast you eventually come to a T-junction just behind the beach itself. The few places to stay are mainly along the road leading left from the junction. Turning right at the junction takes you through another part of the village and to the most beautiful (and unspoilt) part of Agonda beach.

Agonda beach is an almost completely untouched 2km stretch of white sand. It's a great place to chill out if you're feeling mellow and have a stack of good books, but don't come here if you like to spend your

PALOLEM

afternoons playing beach volleyball and boozing in the beach shacks – with the exception of a couple of restaurants attached to guesthouses, there are none.

Places to Stay & Eat There are several quiet guesthouses at the southern end of the beach that have been around for several years. **Dersy Beach Resort** (☎ 2647503; huts Rs 150, rooms with shared bathroom Rs 150, doubles with private bathroom Rs 200-250) has spotless doubles while across the road on the beach side they have simple palm-thatch huts.

Dunhill Resort (☎ 2647328; doubles Rs 250-300) is the most established place. The 12 clean cottage-style rooms have private bathroom. There's a bar and restaurant.

Agonda Sands, near Dunhill, is a new set of bamboo huts that was yet to open at the time of research. Expect to pay Rs 200 for a hut.

Sunset Bar (☎ 2647381), perched up on a hill at the southern end of the beach, has a great outlook and a small open-air restaurant – a great place to watch the sun sink into the Arabian Sea. There are also some rooms here.

At the north end of the beach, in an area disturbed by nothing more than villagers' homes, **Forget Me Not** (☎ 2647611; e maha hotl@goatelecom.com; cottages Rs 200, rooms with private bathroom Rs 400) is a lovely place consisting of a series of novel mud-brick cottages and a bamboo bar facing the beach. Nearby, **Karma Bar & Restaurant** is a simple bamboo bar with an upper deck, run by some friendly locals. They have a few clean rooms with private bathroom in a concrete building nearby for Rs 250.

On the road between Agonda and Palolem, near a small drink stall, look for a sign pointing to **Butterfly Beach**. A narrow path leads over a headland to this tiny secluded beach, accessible only by boat or this path. It's a stiff one-hour walk with a steep ascent then descent to the beach, so allow plenty of time to get there and back. Boat trips from Palolem also go out to Butterfly Beach so you may not be entirely alone.

Getting There & Away As with any out-of-the-way place, reaching Agonda is best with your own transport – you can cycle here from Palolem in about an hour. A taxi

from Palolem or Chaudi costs about Rs 150 and an autorickshaw Rs 90. Local buses run to Agonda from Chaudi sporadically throughout the day (Rs 5), stopping at the T-junction near the church. If you're coming from Palolem you can wait at the junction of the main highway (NH17) and the Agonda road and flag down a passing bus. Coming from Margao, there are a few direct buses, or you can go to Chaudi and get another bus from there.

PALOLEM
postcode 403702

Palolem is the most southerly of Goa's developed beaches and arguably the state's most idyllic – the argument being whether or not the addition of wall-to-wall beach shacks beneath those leaning palms has spoilt it. In the last five years it has rapidly morphed from deserted paradise into a sort of 'bamboo Calangute'.

In any case, the sweeping crescent of white sand fringed by a shady rim of coconut palms is a postcard picture. The beach is hemmed in at either end by rocky crags and there's a small island (Green Island, also known as Canacona Island) off the northern tip that you can walk across to at low tide.

Many travellers, especially backpackers, find that Palolem's mix of lazy beachside life and large numbers of fellow travellers is perfect. It's easy to meet people here, there's never a shortage of teams for beach volleyball or cricket, and there are plenty of places to stay and eat, most of them right on the beach.

Information
The lane leading from the end of the road (where buses stop) to the main beach entrance is lined with stalls selling all the usual handicrafts, souvenirs, beach clothing and sarongs.

Bliss Travels (☎ 2643456), near the main entrance to the beach, is a good travel agency, providing bus and flight bookings, currency exchange and Internet access (Rs 40 per hour). **Rainbow Travel** (☎ 2643912), on the main road in the village, is another reliable travel agency.

There are plenty of places to access the Internet in Palolem, including a 24-hour Internet café right on the beach next to Cuba.

International phone calls can be made at most Internet places.

The nearest **post office** is in Chaudi, 4km to the east.

Activities

Travellers coming to Palolem are generally looking to relax on the beach, but the growth in visitors here has resulted in plenty to do. The sea is excellent for **swimming** and you can rent boogie boards and even surfboards from stalls near the main entrance to the beach.

Boat tours to see dolphins or to visit tiny Butterfly Beach are easy to arrange – it seems just about everyone in Palolem owns an outrigger fishing boat or knows someone who does! A one-hour trip costs around Rs 150 per person and you can organise this through your accommodation or just wander along the beach and ask around. Most trips leave in the morning (around 8am) or early evening.

Yoga, massage and meditation courses are advertised at restaurants and accommodation places. Check the noticeboard outside **Brown Bread** (see Places to Eat) which has information on Ayurvedic treatments, meditation, astrology, holistic healing and tarot readings. **Bhakti Kutir**, near Colomb Bay, runs workshops in yoga, meditation and natural healing.

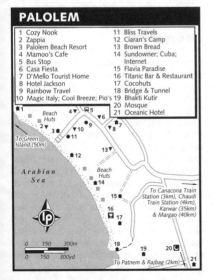

PALOLEM

1 Cozy Nook
2 Zappia
3 Palolem Beach Resort
4 Mamoo's Cafe
5 Bus Stop
6 Casa Fiesta
7 D'Mello Tourist Home
8 Hotel Jackson
9 Rainbow Travel
10 Magic Italy; Cool Breeze; Pio's
11 Bliss Travels
12 Ciaran's Camp
13 Brown Bread
14 Sundowner; Cuba; Internet
15 Flavia Paradise
16 Titanic Bar & Restaurant
17 Cocohuts
18 Bridge & Tunnel
19 Bhakti Kutir
20 Mosque
21 Oceanic Hotel

Beach Huts

To Green Island (50m)

Arabian Sea

Beach Huts

To Canacona Train Station (3km); Chaudi Train Station (4km); Karwar (35km) & Margao (40km)

0   150   300m
0   150   300yd

To Patnem & Rajbag (2km)

Places to Stay

Along the edge of the beach are around 30 groups of palm-thatch or bamboo huts grouped together in little 'villages', usually with a beach shack restaurant at the front. The most basic palm-thatch huts with sandy floor cost less than Rs 100 a double (Rs 150 in peak season). Sturdier bamboo huts with hard floor, or huts on stilts, cost from Rs 150 to 200 and from Rs 300 over the Christmas period depending on demand. There are so many places that it's just a matter of wandering along the beach until you find something that suits your budget and taste, but there are a handful of places that are a cut above the pack.

Cozy Nook (☎ 2643550; *huts & treehouses Rs 300-600*) is an excellent place in a great location at the far northern end of the beach. The owners create a very friendly atmosphere and the huts – some with private bathroom – are better than most. The owner, Aggy, also runs overnight trips out to secluded Butterfly Beach, and has another place, **Sundowner**, in the middle of the beach with cheaper huts.

Bridge & Tunnel (☎ 2642237; e *sera _goa@rediffmail.com; huts Rs 200-600*), at the far southern end of the beach, has a brilliant location, especially if you can score one of the huts perched high on the rocks. The huts are imaginatively designed with themes – one is shaped like a shark, one like a boat and another as a Hindu temple. The secluded clearing has a cushioned Arabianstyle chill-out area, a funky bar with hanging chairs and a relaxing vibe.

Ciaran's Camp (☎ 2643477; e *johnciaran@ hotmail.com; huts Rs 200-300, rooms with private bathroom Rs 600*), about halfway along the beach, is a fun place to stay with one of the best restaurants and bars in Palolem, sturdy bamboo huts, an excellent library, a private bathtub in its own hut, and rooms in a house.

Palolem Beach Resort (☎ 2643054; e *sun ila@goatelecom.com; tents Rs 300-400, rooms with private bathroom Rs 350-450*), on the right as you enter the beach, is more upmarket than most places but still low-key. There are tents with solid floor (some with private bathroom), rooms and private cottages.

There are several family-run guesthouses back in the village such as **Hotel Jackson** (*rooms Rs 100*), better known for its excellent

Cycling Around Palolem

If you tire of the beach scene there are some interesting cycling routes through the countryside around Palolem. The most obvious is down to the Talpona River mouth at Rajbag beach, stopping at Patnem beach along the way. Riding out of Palolem village (towards the highway), take the right turn at the small general store and head south, roughly parallel with the coast. The first right turn along here leads down to Colomb Bay. If you keep going straight for about 2km you come to the turn-off to Patnem beach. Back on the coast road, continue riding through paddy fields and the village of Kindlebag before reaching Rajbag and the Talpona River at the road's end. There are a couple of shacks here where you can get a drink and something to eat – and you can marvel at (or pour scorn on) the multimillion dollar resort that's just been built in this humble village.

Another possibility is to ride to Agonda beach, around 8km from Palolem. Just before you reach the highway there's a sharp left-hand turn (signposted) for the winding and hilly road to Agonda (and on to Cabo da Rama and Betul). The left-hand turn off this road to Agonda beach is not well marked but it comes before you start the steep hill climb – if your legs are getting tired you've probably gone too far. Agonda is a good antidote to Palolem and a relaxing place to spend the afternoon before riding back.

Gearless Indian bicycles can be hired in the market area at Palolem for around Rs 40 a day (Rs 80 in peak season).

If you want a guided trip on a quality bike, three-hour mountain bike tours out to Patnem and Rajbag (Rs 300) were being run on demand in 2002; ask at Ciaran's Camp in Palolem.

restaurant, with four rooms, and the long-running **D'Mello Tourist Home** (☎ 264 3057; doubles Rs 100-350), down a lane behind Hotel Jackson.

Flavia Paradise (☎ 2643673; rooms with shared bathroom Rs 150, huts Rs 150-300) is a friendly place a little back from the beach with a few cheap rooms in the house, huts and treehouses.

Cocohuts (☎ 2643296; e ppv@goatelecom .com; huts Rs 400-600), among the palms towards the southern end of the beach, was one of the original places to build huts on stilts, using the surrounding coconut palms as further supports. Its name – Cocohuts – has become synonymous with this type of accommodation at Palolem.

Oceanic Hotel (☎ 2643059; e oceanic palolem@rediff.com; singles/doubles Rs 400/ 800), English owned, is back from the beach on the road to Patnem but it's a fantastic alternative to the usual Palolem places if you want some creature comforts. There are just six bright, comfortable rooms, with private bathroom and private entrances. The restaurant here is recommended and they have the only swimming pool in Palolem.

Bhakti Kutir (☎ 2643472; e bhaktikutir@ yahoo.com; huts Rs 600-2500) is an 'eco-friendly' place ensconced in a coconut grove between Palolem and Patnem beaches. The

name means 'an abode for devotional meditation' and the Indian-German owners have set it up as a health and nature retreat, with yoga and meditation workshops an integral part of a stay here. It's very peaceful, the huts and cottages are impressive, sturdily built structures (some with private bathroom and composting toilet). It's also a family-friendly place with a 'home school' for guests' children.

Places to Eat

If you can drag yourself away from the beach shacks, all of which offer seafood, Indian, Chinese, continental and even Goan food, Palolem has a surprising range of restaurants.

Brown Bread, on the village road, is an organic wholefood café and good spot for breakfast. There's a wide range of fresh breads, cakes, cheeses and wholesome shakes and juices here, as well as a free water filter.

Hotel Jackson, back on the road behind the beach, has a good reputation for seafood and there's usually plenty of activity here.

Casa Fiesta (mains Rs 50-130), on the road running parallel to the beach, is the place for reasonably authentic Mexican food – nachos, fajitas and burritos – and decent margaritas and cocktails. There's also a range of seafood, pasta and vegetarian dishes, accompanied by Latin tunes and a cosy garden setting.

Mamoo's Café *(mains 70-90)*, near the bus stand, does a good job of Indian, continental and Italian, including highly rated lasagne (six varieties). It also has a bakery.

Magic Italy *(mains Rs 110-160)* specialises in wood-fired pizzas and pasta, mostly vegetarian and seafood. There's free filtered water and wine by the glass.

The beach-shack restaurants all turn out similar fare. The pick of the bunch is **Ciaran's Camp** *(mains Rs 50-200)* with a fish barbecue every evening and an impressive, if pricey, menu of continental and Goan cuisine. **Zappia**, a place on stilts on the beach itself, is recommended for reasonably priced seafood.

The restaurants at **Bhakti Kutir** and **Oceanic Hotel** are worth going out of your way for. The former specialises in organic and health food.

Entertainment

Palolem can be pretty quiet outside the peak season – because there are so many choices, few places are crowded. The best places for a drink (and occasional party), are **Ciaran's Camp**, **Cozy Nook**, **Bridge & Tunnel** (for a real chill-out), and **Titanic Bar & Restaurant**, all on or near the beach.

Cool Breeze, on the lane leading to the beach, is a music bar that gets pretty busy, and nearby **Pio's** has occasional live music.

Cuba, about halfway along the beach, is a hip bar with party nights and DJs.

Getting There & Away

There are around eight buses a day from Margao direct to Palolem (Rs 12, one hour), but services to Chaudi (including Karwar buses, all of which stop at Chaudi) go almost every half-hour (Rs 12). Chaudi is only 3km from Palolem, and an autorickshaw ride from there to the beach is about Rs 40. Alternatively, about 1km before Chaudi the main road passes through a small crossroads called Char Rasta (Four Roads). From this junction it's about 1.5km to Palolem, so if you get the bus driver to let you off here, it's an easy walk.

Private buses to Mumbai, Hampi, Bangalore and Mangalore can be booked at travel agents in Palolem and some will pick up in the village (check with the agent).

Between the Char Rasta crossroads and Chaudi is Canacona train station from where there are services north to Margao (Rs 10, 35 minutes) and other stations in Goa. The 5.32am *Netravati Express* goes direct to Mumbai's Lokmanya Tilak station, but it's more convenient to take a bus or train to Margao and an express train from there. Heading south the same train stops at Canacona at 11pm and goes to Kankanadi (for Mangalore) and Ernakulam (for Kochi).

SOUTH OF PALOLEM

With beach huts and shacks spreading unstoppably across the sands of Palolem beach, it's hardly surprising that travellers are drifting south in search of peace and space. Directly around the headland from Palolem is a small, rocky bay called **Colomb**, where there are a few rustic restaurants and family guesthouses sheltered in a peaceful clump of coconut trees. Given that it's only a short walk or drive (there's road access) from Palolem, it seems a world away, but there's no beach here to speak of.

Patnem

A couple of kilometres south of Palolem is beautiful Patnem beach, a small peaceful bay which runs into Kindlebag and Rajbag further south. Patnem has around a dozen laid-back beach shacks; it's much smaller and not as classically idyllic as Palolem so it's unlikely to develop as quickly as its neighbour. This is the place to escape the crowds for the time being – the sand is perfect and Patnem gets a bit of swell which is ideal for boogie boarding or windsurfing (you can rent boards in Palolem).

Most of the beach shacks have basic accommodation in palm-thatch or bamboo huts for around Rs 150 to 200 a night. Among the best places are **Kiss Restaurant & Cocohuts** *(huts Rs 200)* and **Oasis** *(☎ 2643272; huts Rs 100)* at the southern end of the beach.

Home *(☎ 2643916; e homeispatnem@ yahoo.com; doubles Rs 400-700)* is a far cry from the flimsy beach huts around it. There are eight spotless and stylish rooms of varying sizes but all with private bathroom. The Euro-style restaurant gets rave reviews and serves up superb pasta, salads and coffee (from an espresso machine).

Patnem beach is reached from the back road running south from Palolem (past Oceanic Hotel), then turning right at the

Hotel Sea View (☎ 2643110; doubles with private bathroom Rs 250-350), a guesthouse with clean doubles about 200m back from the beach. Alternatively, walk about 20 minutes along the path from Palolem via Colomb Bay.

Rajbag

Beyond Patnem is **Rajbag beach**, an exposed but isolated stretch of sand, which ends at the mouth of the Talpona River. It's an easy walk along the beach between Patnem and Rajbag, but this once deserted beach is now dominated by the massive new five-star **Goa Grand Intercontinental Resort** (W www.intercontinental.com/goa), which was yet to open at the time of research. Unsurprisingly, the hotel was a source of controversy as it was partly built on ground held sacred by local people. A small Hindu temple stood at the proposed entrance to the resort (and its nine-hole golf course). Finding they were unable to demolish the temple, the developers built a fence – and the entire resort – around it and now market it as part of the attraction!

A narrow road runs behind the beach from Patnem, via the tiny village of Kindlebag, to the Talpona River and there's a sandy path from there to the beach. Local boatmen can ferry you across the river if you want to explore further south to **Galgibaga**, a small beach and protected area visited by rare olive ridley turtles. There are a couple of rustic restaurant-shacks on the banks of the Talpona where the road ends.

At Kindlebag, **Molyma Resorts** (☎ 264 3028; e molyma2001@yahoo.com.in; singles/doubles with private bathroom Rs 200/300), a fair way back from the beach, is the only cheap place to stay in this area but it has a rather deserted, forlorn feel. You really need your own transport to stay here.

Although there are other beaches to the south of Rajbag, they are inaccessible by road, apart from **Polem beach**, which is at the very southern tip of Goa, only a couple of kilometres from the state border. There have been attempts to provide some limited accommodation here in the past, but these seem to have foundered, and as the land is part of a designated green belt, it seems unlikely that there will be any guesthouses here in the future.

COTIGAO WILDLIFE SANCTUARY

Proclaimed as a conservation area in 1962, Cotigao (admission Rs 5, camera/video Rs 25/100, motorcycle/car Rs 10/50; open 7am-5.30pm daily) is the second-largest sanctuary in Goa with an area of 86 sq km. Unfortunately, as with any nature reserve, most of the animals prefer to remain hidden, so to have a chance of seeing much fauna you will have to stay here for at least one night, spending either the late evening or early morning in the tree-top watchtower or the observation post.

For those who have the time and patience there is the chance to see, among other species, Indian bison or gaur, barking deer, sambar and jackals. If you come here on a day trip, there are pleasant walks through the forest and the area contains some unspoilt ghat scenery.

There's a small Nature Interpretation Centre and reception about 1.5km in from the main road. Also here is a single **cottage** for rent at Rs 200 a double, along with a small canteen. Facilities are minimal so it pays to bring your own food. The only other accommodation is the **Forest Rest House**, 3km further south along the main road at Poinguinim, which can be booked through the **Forest Department** (in Chaudi ☎ 2644263).

The park boundary is a further 1.5km in from the reception centre, and the two observation towers are 6km and 9km from the park entrance, so it makes sense to have your own transport or be prepared to put in a lot of walking. The ideal situation is to stay in Palolem, rent a motorcycle and make an early start from there.

The entrance to the park is 7km southeast of Chaudi. As you head south from Chaudi, the first entrance you come to (signposted 'Govt of Goa Forest Check Post') allows access to the area generally. The second, some 2km further on, is the entrance to the wildlife sanctuary. Any bus heading south to Karwar can drop you on the main road, but it's then 2km down the side road before you come to the park entrance itself.

Excursions

If you have time during your stay in Goa, it would a shame not to experience some other aspects of India. There are several interesting excursions that are no more than a day's journey over the border in Karnataka.

About 60km south of the southern border of Goa is **Gokarna**. The village itself is one of the most holy Hindu sites in South India, but it's the beautiful, near-deserted beaches that have drawn travellers over the years – many of them ex-Goa hippies escaping the hype! About 50km southeast of Gokarna are **Jog Falls**, the highest in India. The ultimate excursion from Goa, however, is to **Hampi**, the magnificent ruined city of the Vijayanagar Empire and a renowned travellers centre. Hampi is easy to reach by bus from Goa.

KARWAR
☎ 08382

Dull, sleepy Karwar, near the mouth of the Kali Nadi River, has very little of interest to tempt the traveller. But, being just 13km south of Goa, it is an important transport hub linking Goa with some excursions into Karnataka.

Getting There & Away

Karwar is a main station on the Konkan Railway, so most express trains stop here. The bus stand, on the southern edge of the town centre, is well connected for buses to and from Gokarna and Jog Falls.

GOKARNA
☎ 08386

Gokarna (Cow's Ear), 50km south of Karwar, attracts a potpourri of Hindu pilgrims, Sanskrit scholars and hippies, as well as travellers seeking a mellow beach.

For Hindus, Gokarna is one of the most sacred sites in South India. It's a sleepy, charming town with wooden houses on the main street and some attractive traditional houses in nearby alleys.

Information

There are no banks with foreign exchange here, but the **Pai STD shop** (Main St) exchanges money. A **sub-post office** (1st floor, cnr Car & Main Sts) and several STD/ISD places are in town. Internet nooks are read-

ily available on Main and Car Sts, most charging Rs 40 per hour.

Temples

Foreigners are not allowed inside Gokarna's temples, but you'll certainly bear witness to religious rituals around town. At the western end of Car St is the **Mahabaleshwara Temple**, home to a revered Shiva lingam. Nearby is the **Ganapati Temple**, which honours the role Ganesh played in rescuing the lingam. Near the temple are two gargantuan chariots, which barrel down the main street on 'Shiva power' (as thousands of bananas are tossed at them for luck!) during the mind-blowing Shivaratri Festival in February/March.

South of the **Venkataraman Temple** is **Koorti Teertha**, the large temple tank, where locals, pilgrims and immaculately dressed Brahmins perform their ablutions next to dhobi-wallahs (people who wash clothes) on the ghats.

Beaches

Travellers have been drifting into Gokarna for years now, lured by stories of beaches that rival anything Goa has to offer. The closest decent stretch of sand, and the first of four near-perfect beaches, is **Kudle Beach** (pronounced **kood**-lee), a 20-minute walk to the south of the village. To reach it, follow the footpath that begins on the southern side of the Ganapati Temple and heads southward.

At the southern end of Kudle a track climbs over the next headland and a further 20-minute walk brings you to **Om Beach**, which has a handful of chai shops and shacks. The other beaches – **Half-Moon** and **Paradise** – are a series of 30-minute walks to the south, each one more isolated.

Don't walk between the beaches and Gokarna after dark – it's easy to get lost and muggings have occurred. For a small fee, you can safely leave valuables and baggage at Vaibhav Nivas and Nimmu House in Gokarna (see Places to Stay).

Places to Stay

The choice in Gokarna is between a rudimentary shack on the beach on the beach – where you can chill out with little to disturb

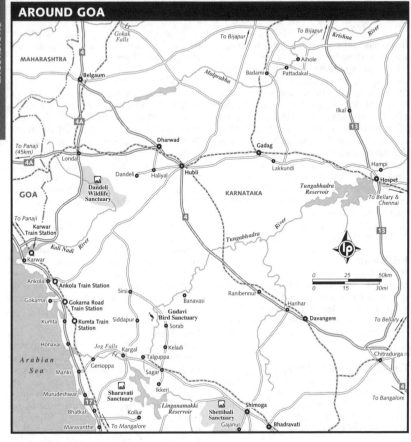

AROUND GOA

your peace – or a basic, but more comfortable, room in town.

Most beach places provide a bedroll, but bring your own sleep sheet or sleeping bag. Padlocks are provided. There are simple communal washing and toilet facilities.

The **Spanish Place** (*huts with shared bathroom Rs 70, doubles Rs 200*), a very chill spot in the middle stretch of Kudle Beach, has palm-thatch huts, as well as two garden rooms with private bathing facilities but shared toilet.

Namaste (*basic huts/rooms with shared bathroom Rs 50/100*), on Om Beach, is where the action's at during the high season. It has Internet connections (*Rs 60/hr*), and a spacious restaurant/hang-out that some travellers can muster no reason to leave.

There is more choice in the village. **Nimmu House** (☎ *56730; Manibhadra Rd; doubles with shared bathroom Rs 70, with private bathroom Rs 120-150*), set in relaxed, green grounds, has simple rooms, but it's the best place in town for ambience. It's on a side street near the Mahabaleshwara Temple and the town beach.

Vaibhav Nivas (☎ *56714; rooms with shared bathroom from Rs 50/80, doubles with private bathroom Rs 120*), off Main St on the way into town, has snug rooms and a restaurant serving Western snacks and meals.

Hotel Gokarna International (☎ *56622; Main St; singles/doubles Rs 150/200, deluxe doubles with TV Rs 400, with air-con Rs 600*), is a clean, modern place about 500m up the main road from the bus stand. It has two

EXCURSIONS

restaurants, a bar with cold beer and an ice-cream parlour.

Places to Eat

Prema Restaurant *(dishes Rs 20-50)*, upstairs in the alley next to the Mahabaleshwara Temple, serves good *masala dosas* (curried vegetables inside a lentil-flour pancake) (Rs 10) and coffee milkshakes, plus a range of travellers' fare.

Pai Restaurant *(thalis Rs 16)*, halfway along Main St, is a friendly place with fresh vegetarian meals and snacks.

Namaste Cafe *(meals Rs 40-100)*, on Om Beach, serves Western stand-bys, but its sizzler dishes (Rs 55 to 95) are a true hit.

Getting There & Away

Gokarna's bus stand is just off Main St as you enter town. Buses head north to Karwar (Rs 23, 1½ hours, four daily), which is the place to pick up a bus for Goa. Deluxe buses go to Mysore (Rs 225, 11 hours) at 6.45am, to Hospet (for Hampi; Rs 110, eight hours) at 7am and to Bangalore (Rs 268, 10 hours) at 7pm. Coming from Goa, take any bus to Karwar and change there.

The Konkan Railway is the best way to reach Goa and Mangalore, even though only a couple of slow passenger trains currently stop at Gokarna Road station (☎ 70487), 9km from town. An 11.30am train rolls north to Margao (Madgaon; Rs 24, 1½ hours); another leaves at 6.15pm. Autorickshaws want about Rs 75 to take you out to the station, but buses head there from the bus stand hourly (Rs 5). Many of the hotels, as well as small travel agencies on Main St, can book tickets.

Express trains stop at Ankola and Kumta stations, both about 25km from Gokarna and accessible by local bus. The last bus to Kumta leaves Gokarna at 7pm.

JOG FALLS
☎ 08183 • pop 12,570

Jog Falls are the highest in India, but unfortunately they don't live up to their former glory: the Linganamakki Dam further up the Sharavati River limits the water flow. The tallest of the four falls is the Raja, which drops 293m.

The spectacular countryside here is perfect for gentle hiking. The bottom of the falls is accessible via the 1200-plus steps that start close to the bus stand; beware of leeches during the wet season.

There's a tourist office (☎ 44747; open 10am-5pm Mon-Sat) close to the bus stand.

Places to Stay & Eat

The **Inspection Bungalow** *(rooms per person Rs 60)* sits at the top of the falls about 3km from the bus stand and offers stellar views. You must book in advance with the **Public Works Department** *(☎ 0838-322164)* in Siddapur. The starting point for Raja Falls is reached on a short trail from here.

The Karnataka State Tourism Development Corporation (KSTDC) **Hotel Mayura Gerusoppa** *(☎ 44747; singles/doubles Rs 220/ 300)* is splendidly situated on the other side of the gorge, overlooking the falls; it's about 150m from the car park. The rooms are almost big enough to get lost in, but they're a bit musty. Its run-of-the-mill restaurant *(meals from Rs 20)* is next to the tourist office.

Getting There & Away

Jog Falls has good bus connections, though the roads to/from the coast are fairly tortuous. There are two buses a day to Karwar (Rs 120, five hours) via Kumta (Rs 35, 2½ hours), where you can change to get to Gokarna or Goa.

HAMPI
☎ 08394

The ruins of Vijayanagar, near the village of Hampi, are some of the most fascinating in India. They're set in a strange and sublime boulder-strewn landscape that resonates with a magical air. Once the capital of one of the largest Hindu empires in Indian history, Vijayanagar was founded by the Telugu princes in 1336 and hit the peak of its power in the 16th century. With a population of about 500,000, the empire controlled the regional spice trade and cotton industry, and its busy bazaars were centres of international commerce. The empire came to a sudden end in 1565 when the city was ransacked by a confederacy of Deccan sultanates.

Hampi is a thriving travellers centre, and many visitors end up staying here a while. It's possible to see the main sites in a day or two – by bicycle, moped or, if you start early, on foot – but this goes against the laid-back grain of Hampi.

Orientation & Information

Hampi Bazaar, the main travellers centre, and the small village of Kamalapuram to the south are the two main points of entry. The ruins themselves can be divided into two main areas: the Sacred Centre, around Hampi Bazaar, and the Royal Centre, to the south around Kamalapuram.

The **tourist office** (☎ 41339; Hampi Bazaar; open 10am-5.30pm Sat-Thur), on the main street, can arrange guides for Rs 500 per day or Rs 350 for half a day. Books and maps of Hampi are available from **Aspiration Stores** (☎ 41254; Hampi Bazaar), near the entrance to the Virupaksha Temple.

Canara Bank (☎ 41236; Hampi Bazaar; open 11am-2pm Mon-Tues & Thur-Fri, 11am-12.30pm Sat) changes travellers cheques and gives cash advances on credit cards, but there are numerous authorised moneychangers. Internet cafés – all with erratic connections – are easy to come by; they charge Rs 60 per hour.

Hampi is generally a safe and alluring place, but don't wander around the ruins alone at dawn or dusk, particularly on the climb up Matanga Hill, as there have been problems with muggings in the past. Foreigners are asked to register at the **police station** inside the Virupaksha Temple upon arrival.

Hampi Bazaar (Sacred Centre)

The **Virupaksha Temple** (☎ 441241; admission Rs 2; open 6.30am-8pm daily), at the western end of the bazaar, is one of the earliest structures in the city. The main *gopuram* (gateway tower), almost 50m high, was built in 1442, with a smaller one added in 1510. The main shrine is dedicated to Virupaksha, a form of Shiva. Overlooking Virupaksha Temple to the south, **Hemakuta Hill** has a scattering of early ruins including Jain temples and a monolithic **sculpture** of Narasimha (Vishnu in his man-lion incarnation). It's worth the short walk up for the view over the bazaar.

Vittala Temple

From the eastern end of Hampi Bazaar a 2km track, navigable only on foot, leads northeast to the undisputed highlight of the ruins, the 16th-century World Heritage–listed Vittala Temple (foreigner US$5; open 8am-6pm daily). Work most likely started on the temple during the reign of Krishnadevaraya (1509–29) and, despite the fact it was never finished or consecrated, the temple's incredible sculptural work is the pinnacle of Vijayanagar art. The outer 'musical' pillars reverberate when tapped, although this is discouraged to avoid further damage. There's an ornate stone chariot in the temple courtyard containing an image of Garuda. Its wheels were once capable of turning.

You should keep your entry ticket, as it is good for same-day admission into the Zenana Enclosure and Elephant Stables in the Royal Centre.

Sule Bazaar & Achyutaraya Temple

Halfway along the path from Hampi Bazaar to the Vittala Temple, a track to the right leads to deserted Sule Bazaar, which gives you some idea of what Hampi Bazaar might have looked like if it hadn't been repopulated (locals once again occupy the ancient buildings lining the main street of Hampi Bazaar). At the southern end of this area is the Achyutaraya Temple. Its isolated location at the foot of Matanga Hill makes it utterly atmospheric.

Royal Centre

This area of Hampi is quite different from the northern section, since most of the rounded boulders that once littered the site have been used to create a mind-boggling proliferation of beautiful stone walls. It's a 2km walk on a track from the Achyutaraya Temple, but most people get to it from the Hampi Bazaar–Kamalapuram road. This area is easily explored by bicycle since a decent dirt road runs through its heart.

Within various enclosures here are the rest of Hampi's major attractions, including the **Lotus Mahal** and the **Elephant Stables** (foreigner US$5; open 8am-6pm daily). The former is a delicately designed pavilion in a walled compound known as the **Zenana Enclosure**. It's an amazing synthesis of Hindu and Islamic styles and it gets its name from the lotus bud carved in the centre of the domed and vaulted ceiling. The Elephant Stables is a grand building with domed chambers, where the state elephants once resided.

Further south is the Royal Centre area, with its various temples and elaborate waterworks, plus the **Underground Virupaksha Temple** and the impressive **Queen's Bath**.

Traditional sweets

Uned (local bread)

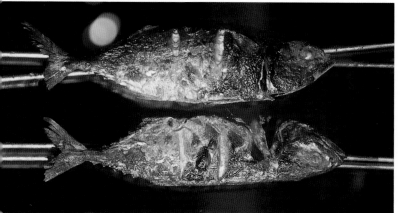
Barbecued mackerel

Feni

Bebinca (traditional Goan dessert)

Volleyball at sunset, Arambol beach

Palolem beach

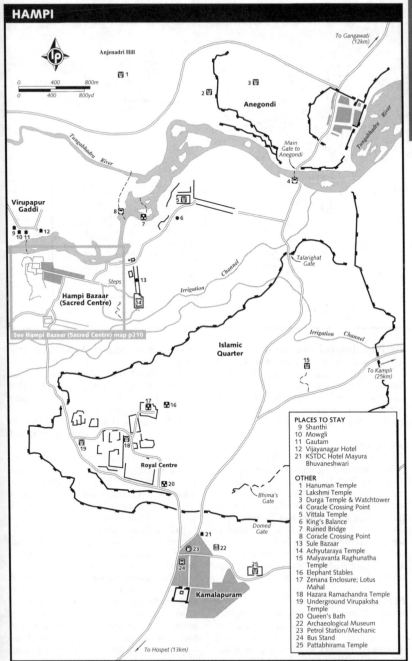

HAMPI

Anjenadri Hill

Anegondi

Tungabhadra River

Tungabhadra River

Main Gate to Anegondi

Virupapur Gaddi

Talarighat Gate

Irrigation Channel

Steps

Hampi Bazaar (Sacred Centre)

See Hampi Bazaar (Sacred Centre) map p210

Islamic Quarter

Irrigation Channel

To Kampli (25km)

Royal Centre

Bhima's Gate

Domed Gate

Kamalapuram

To Hospet (13km)

To Gangawati (12km)

PLACES TO STAY
9 Shanthi
10 Mowgli
11 Gautam
12 Vijayanagar Hotel
21 KSTDC Hotel Mayura
      Bhuvaneshwari

OTHER
1 Hanuman Temple
2 Lakshmi Temple
3 Durga Temple & Watchtower
4 Coracle Crossing Point
5 Vittala Temple
6 King's Balance
7 Ruined Bridge
8 Coracle Crossing Point
13 Sule Bazaar
14 Achyutaraya Temple
15 Malyavanta Raghunatha
      Temple
16 Elephant Stables
17 Zenana Enclosure; Lotus
      Mahal
18 Hazara Ramachandra Temple
19 Underground Virupaksha
      Temple
20 Queen's Bath
22 Archaeological Museum
23 Petrol Station/Mechanic
24 Bus Stand
25 Pattabhirama Temple

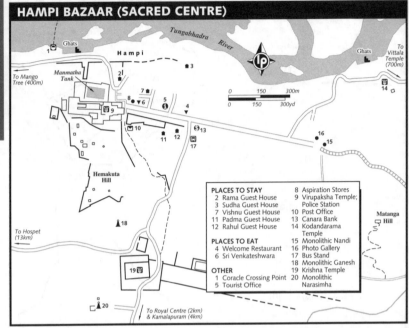

HAMPI BAZAAR (SACRED CENTRE)

PLACES TO STAY
2 Rama Guest House
3 Sudha Guest House
7 Vishnu Guest House
11 Padma Guest House
12 Rahul Guest House

PLACES TO EAT
4 Welcome Restaurant
6 Sri Venkateshwara

OTHER
1 Coracle Crossing Point
5 Tourist Office

8 Aspiration Stores
9 Virupaksha Temple;
   Police Station
10 Post Office
13 Canara Bank
14 Kodandarama
   Temple
15 Monolithic Nandi
16 Photo Gallery
17 Bus Stand
18 Monolithic Ganesh
19 Krishna Temple
20 Monolithic
   Narasimha

Archaeological Museum

The archaeological museum (☎ 41561; admission Rs 5; Kamalapuram; open 10am-5pm Sat-Thur) has well-displayed collections of sculptures from local ruins, Neolithic tools, 16th-century weaponry and a large floor model of the Vijayanagar ruins.

Anegondi

To the north of the Tungabhadra River is the ruined fortified stronghold of Anegondi. The unruffled area, amid paddy fields, makes for a good afternoon's ambling. Among the numerous small temples is the tiny whitewashed **Hanuman Temple** (open 6.30am-7.30pm daily), which is perched on top of a prominent, rocky hill.

To get to Anegondi to have a look around, take a coracle across the river then follow the dusty road north.

Places to Stay

Hampi Bazaar Dozens of basic lodges dot the alleys leading off the main road. Accommodation is simple (squat toilets and running cold water), so if you require something more comfortable, you'll have to

shack up in Hospet (see Hospet, later in this chapter).

Rama Guest House (doubles with private bathroom Rs 150) has three ultra-clean doubles equipped with mosquito nets. Its restaurant serves excellent food.

Vishnu Guest House (☎ 41415; doubles Rs 150) is a family home that exudes friendliness.

Rahul Guest House (☎ 41648; basic singles Rs 70, singles/doubles Rs 150/200, doubles with air-con Rs 350-500), across from the bus stand, is a reliable place with a range of choices, the cheapest being spartan singles with shared bathroom and no fan.

Padma Guest House (☎ 41331; doubles with air-cooler & shared bathroom Rs 250) has some of the cosiest rooms around, plus a rooftop restaurant.

Sudha Guest House (☎ 41451; singles with shared bathroom Rs 80-100, doubles with private bathroom Rs 200-350), situated apart from the others, is a gem. Its singles are basic, but the polished downstairs doubles have both squat and sit-down flush toilets. Its rooftop restaurant offers gorgeous views.

Virupapur Gaddi Hampi's most laid-back scene is just north of the river in Virupapur Gaddi, where guesthouses cater to those who find even Hampi Bazaar too hectic. During the high season, this is the place to be for parties after hours. To reach it, take a coracle (Rs 5) from the ghats north of the Virupaksha Temple.

Vijayanagar Hotel (☎ 367640; huts Rs 80, doubles with shared/private bathroom Rs 100/175), just above the coracle stop, is a spacious compound with little thatched huts and basic rooms in a concrete building.

Gautam (☎ 367754; single/double huts with shared bathroom Rs 100/125, single/double huts with private bathroom Rs 150/250) is run by a local farming family. It has palm-thatched huts, clean and cosy rooms, and a small café.

Mowgli (☎ 387033; single/double huts with shared bathroom Rs 100/150, huts with private bathroom Rs 300) is a very amiable place with a range of accommodations in shaded grounds.

Shanthi (☎ 387038; rooms with shared bathroom Rs 100-120, huts with private bathroom Rs 250), the next place along from Mowgli, is a friendly and relaxed hang-out with a variety of choice in rooms. The huts have awesome paddy-field and river views. The kitchen does exceptional thalis (Rs 30) and pizzas (Rs 70 to 85).

Kamalapuram On very still grounds in the northern outskirts of Kamalapuram, KSTDC **Hotel Mayura Bhuvaneshwari** (☎ 41574; singles/doubles Rs 250/300, with air-con Rs 400/450) is modern and well maintained. Decent rooms, some with mosquito nets, have private bathrooms.

Places to Eat
Hampi isn't renowned for its cuisine, but simple restaurants line the main street of Hampi Bazaar and more are interspersed among the guesthouses in the dusty streets behind the tourist office.

Sri Venkateshwara (Main Rd; meals Rs 25-50), on the right as you near the Virupaksha Temple, is the most established restaurant and offers a wide range of dishes, including Western breakfasts.

Welcome Restaurant (Main Rd; dishes Rs 20-45), as well as offering the usual suspects, makes a worthy attempt at Korean food.

The **Mango Tree** (dishes Rs 25-40) is away from the crowds, about 400m west of the ghats down a path through a banana plantation. Its thalis (Rs 30) are a treat, and the straw mats atop the terrace are ideal spots to stretch out with a book.

Due to Hampi's religious significance, alcohol is not permitted – but that doesn't mean you won't find a discreet beer or two. If you want a legal drink, there's a bar at Hotel Mayura Bhuvaneshwari in Kamalapuram.

Getting There & Away
While private buses from Goa and Bangalore (325km) will drop you in Hampi, you have to go to Hospet to catch a bus out. Local buses run roughly every hour from Hampi Bazaar to Hospet (Rs 6, 30 minutes). The first bus from Hospet is at 6.30am, the last one back leaves Hampi at 8.30pm. An auto-rickshaw costs Rs 80.

If you're going to or coming from Goa, the overnight sleeper bus (Rs 400), which runs during the high season, is a popular option. Numerous travel agents in Hampi Bazaar can book onward bus, train and plane tickets or arrange a car and driver.

Getting Around
Once you've seen the Vittala and Achyutaraya Temples and Sule Bazaar, hiring a cycle to explore the rest of the ruins is a rational thing to do. The road between Hampi Bazaar and Kamalapuram has key monuments haphazardly signposted along its length. Bicycles cost around Rs 30 per day in Hampi Bazaar. Mopeds are also for hire for around Rs 200 plus petrol. You can take your bicycle (extra Rs 5) or motorcycle (extra Rs 10), across the river with you on the coracles.

Autorickshaws and taxis are available for sightseeing, and will drop you as close to each of the major ruins as they can. A five-hour autorickshaw tour costs at least Rs 250.

HOSPET
☎ 0839 • pop 163,284
Hospet is an active regional centre with none of Hampi's atmosphere, but you'll need to pass through here to make transport connections. It has some good accommodation and restaurants, but otherwise there's zero reason to linger long.

The **tourist office** (☎ 428537; Old Bus Stand Rd; open 7.30am-7.30pm daily) has maps and information on Hampi. **State Bank of India** *(☎ 428470; Station Rd)* changes currency and **Andhra Bank** *(☎ 428249)*, next to Hanuman Temple, gives cash advances on Visa and MasterCard.

Organised Tours
The daily KSTDC tour to the three main sites at Hampi and to Tungabhadra Dam departs at 9.30am and returns at 5.30pm (Rs 80). Bookings can be made at the hotels or the tourist office, which is where the tours depart from.

Places to Stay & Eat
Hotel Priyadarshini *(☎ 427313, fax 424709; e priyainnhampi@india.com; Station Rd; singles/doubles from Rs 140/250, with air-con Rs 500-650)*, between the bus and train stations, is a well-run place with very acceptable rooms and an open-air restaurant.

Hotel Malligi *(☎ 428101, fax 427038; e malligihome@hotmail.com; 6/143 Jabunatha Rd; old wing rooms Rs 200-330, newer wing rooms with air-con Rs 550-2250)* is near the southern canal running through Hospet. It has a range of rooms, an inviting swimming pool (Rs 25 for nonguests) and **Waves Restaurant**.

Getting There & Away
Buses to Hampi depart from bay No 10 of the busy **bus stand** *(☎ 428802)* every 30 minutes (Rs 6).

Express buses run to Bangalore (Rs 120/150 in ordinary/deluxe, nine hours, more than 10 daily). An overnight bus leaves for Margao (Madgaon; Rs 145 in semideluxe, 10 hours) at 6.30pm.

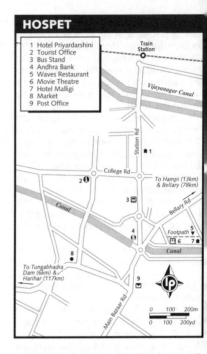

HOSPET

1 Hotel Priyadarshini
2 Tourist Office
3 Bus Stand
4 Andhra Bank
5 Waves Restaurant
6 Movie Theatre
7 Hotel Malligi
8 Market
9 Post Office

Hospet train station is a 20-minute walk or Rs 10 autorickshaw ride from the centre of town. The daily *Hampi Express* heads to Bangalore at 8.10pm (Rs 210/945 in sleeper/2-tier air-con, 10½ hours), or go to Guntakal (Rs 42, three hours) and catch a Bangalore-bound express there. Every Tuesday and Friday, an 8.50am express heads to Vasco da Gama in Goa (Rs 145/652 in sleeper/2-tier air-con, 9½ hours).

Language

As a legacy of its unusual colonial history, Goa has inherited a mixture of languages. Portuguese is still spoken as a second language by a few Goans, although it is gradually dying out. The official language of India is Hindi, which children in Goa are obliged to learn in school. Konkani (which has five different scripts) is now accepted as the official language of the state, and Marathi is also taught as a standard subject.

Ironically the primary language used in many schools is actually English. Arguments about continuing or abandoning this policy of placing such importance on English rage on. How can Indians get away from their colonial past, many ask, if they are still forced to use the language of the colonisers? Others feel that continuing use of English is a distinct advantage to their children, who will need it if they are to find good jobs in the future. Meanwhile, children in Goa are taught three or four languages as a standard part of the school syllabus.

You'll find that English is widely spoken in Goa's tourist areas. For a comprehensive guide to Hindi, get a copy of Lonely Planet's *Hindi & Urdu phrasebook*.

HINDI & KONKANI
Useful Words & Phrases

English	Hindi	Konkani
Hello.	namaste	paypadta
Excuse me.	maaf kijiyeh	upkar korxi
Please.	meharbani seh	upkar kor
Yes/No.	haan/nahin	oi/naah
Thank you.	dhanyabad	dev borem korum
big	bhada	hodlo
small	chhota	dhakto
today	aaj	aaj
day	din	dees
night	raat	racho
week	haftah	athovda
month	mahina	mohino
year	saal	voros
medicine	dava-ee	vokot
egg	aanda	tatee
butter	makkhan	masko
fruit	phal	phala

rice	chaaval	sheet
sugar	chini	sakor
vegetables	sabzi	bhaji
water	paani	udok
ice	baraf	jell
tea	chai	chao
coffee	kaafi	kofi
milk	dudh	dudh

Do you speak English?
kya aap angrezi samajhte hain? (H)
to English hulonk jhana? (K)
I don't understand.
meri samajh men nahin aaya (H)
mhaka kay samzona (K)
Where is a hotel?
hotal kahan hai? (H)
hotel khoy aasa? (K)
How far is ...?
... kitni duur hai? (H)
anig kitya phoode ...? (K)
How do I get to ...?
... kaiseh jaateh hai? (H)
maka kashe ... meltole? (K)
How much?
kitneh paiseh? kitneh hai? (H)
kitke poishe laqthele? (K)
This is expensive.
yeh bahut mehnga hai (H)
chod marog (K)
Show me the menu.
mujheh minu dikhaiyeh (H)
tumcho aaije meno kithe aasa (K)
The bill, please.
bill de dijiyeh (H)
bill aad (K)
What's your name?
aapka shubh naam kya hai? (H)
tuje naav kide? (K)
What is the time?
kitneh bajeh hain? (H)
vurra kitki jali? (K)
How are you?
aap kaiseh hain? (H)
kosso assa? (m) *koxem assa?* (f) (K)
Very well, thank you.
bahut acha, shukriya (H)
bhore jaung (K)

Beware of *acha*, an all-purpose word for 'OK'. It can also mean 'OK, I understand what you're saying, but it isn't OK'.

213

LANGUAGE

Numbers

Where we count in tens, hundreds, thousands, millions and billions, the Indian numbering system goes tens, hundreds, thousands, hundred thousands, ten millions. A hundred thousand is a lakh, and 10 million is a crore. These two words are almost always used in place of their English equivalent. Thus you'll see 10 lakh rather than one million and one crore rather than 10 million. Furthermore, the numerals are generally written that way too – thus three hundred thousand appears as 3,00,000 not 300,000, and ten million, five hundred thousand would appear numerically as 1,05,00,000 (one crore, five lakh) not 10,500,000. If you say something costs five crore or is worth 10 lakh, it always means 'of rupees'.

When counting from 10 to 100 in Hindi, there's no standard formula for compiling numbers – they are all different. Here we've just given you enough to go on with!

Given the many different ways of writing Konkani, the Konkani words included in this chapter are only approximate transliterations. To complicate matters further, there are two different counting systems in Konkani. Hindu Goans use the system shown in the list below, but for Catholic Goans there are differences: – *vis-ani-ek* rather than *ekvis* for 21, for example.

	Hindi	Konkani
1	ek	ek
2	do	don
3	tin	tin
4	char	char
5	panch	panch
6	chhe	sou
7	saat	sat
8	aath	att
9	nau	nov
10	das	dha
11	gyaranh	ikra
12	baranh	bara
13	teranh	tera
14	chodanh	chouda
15	pandranh	pondra
16	solanh	sollah
17	staranh	sottra
18	aatharanh	ottra
19	unnis	ekonis
20	bis	vis

21	ikkis	ekvis
22	bais	bavis
23	teis	tevis
24	chobis	chouvis
25	pachis	ponchis
26	chhabis	sovis
27	sattais	satavis
28	athais	attavis
29	unnattis	ekontis
30	tis	tis
35	paintis	posstis
40	chalis	chalis
45	paintalis	ponchechali
50	panchas	ponnas
55	pachpan	ponchavan
60	saath	saatt
65	painsath	pansatt
70	sattar	sottor
75	pachhattar	ponchator
80	assi	oixim
85	pachasi	ponchalsh
90	nabbe	novodh
95	pachanabbe	ponchanov
100	so	xembor
200	do so	donshe
1000	ek hazaar	ek hazaar
2000	do hazaar	don hazaar
100,000	lakh	lakh
10 million	crore	crore

GOAN FOOD & DRINK

Goan cuisine is distinct from Indian cuisine, having been influenced by Portuguese rule. The following is a glossary of some food and drink terms you might spot on a Goan menu. For general Indian food and drink items that you're likely to come across in Goa, see the Indian Food & Drink glossary.

ambot tik – sour curry dish made with meat or fish and flavoured with tamarind

balchão – fish or prawns cooked in a rich spicy tomato sauce; balchão de peixe is made with fish, balchão de porco is made with pork
bebinca – richly layered, pancake-like Goan dessert made from egg yolk and coconut

cabidela – a rich pork dish
cafrial – method of preparation in which the meat, usually chicken, is marinated in

sauce of chillies, garlic and ginger and then dry-fried

caldeirada – a mild curry of fish or prawns layered in a vegetable stew

caldinha – meat or vegetable dish cooked in spices and coconut milk

chourico – spicy pork sausages, dried and smoked then cooked in hot sauce

doce – sweet made with chickpeas and coconut

dodol – traditional Christmas sweet made with rice flour, coconut milk, *jaggery* and cashew nuts

feni – Goa's most famous drink, feni is a liquor distilled from coconut *toddy* or the juice of cashew apples

fish curry rice – Goa's staple dish, a simple concoction of fish or prawns in a mild to hot curry and served with steamed rice

fofos – fish rolls, spiced and fried in bread crumbs

kokum – dried fruit used as a spice

mergolho – vegetable dish made with pumpkin and papaya

neureos – deep-fried sweet made with coconut, cashews and raisins

sanna – steamed rolls or cakes made with rice flour, ground coconut and *toddy*

sorpotel – pork liver, heart or kidney cooked in a thick, slightly sour, spicy sauce and flavoured with *feni*

uned – small, round, crusty rolls

uttapam – similar to a *dosa*

vindaloo – very hot curry, usually using pork, spiced with chillies, vinegar and garlic

xacuti – method of cooking where a very hot sauce of spices and coconut milk is used to marinate meat (usually chicken) until quite dry

INDIAN FOOD & DRINK

chai – tea; in India it's usually sugary, milky and lightly spiced

chapati – unleavened Indian bread

chota – small spirit drink measure (as in 'chota peg')

curd – milk with acid or rennet added to solidify it

dhal – stew of lentils; India's staple meal

dosa – paper-thin pancake made from lentil flour (curried vegetables wrapped inside a dosa make it a masala dosa)

gram – legumes

idli – South Indian rice dumpling

IMFL – Indian Made Foreign Liquor; beer or spirits produced in India

jaggery – hard, brown, sugarlike sweetener made from kitul palm sap

kachori – Indian-style breakfast of *puri* and vegetables

kulfi – frozen pistachio-flavoured sweet, similar to ice cream

lassi – refreshing yogurt and iced-water drink

pakoras – small pieces of vegetable dipped in chickpea-flour batter and deep-fried

puri – flat pieces of dough that puff up when deep-fried

ragi – cereal grain

sabzi – curried vegetables

thali – traditional South Indian and Gujarati 'all-you-can-eat' meal

toddy – sap collected from palm trees, it is fermented and distilled – once to produce *uraq*, and again to produce *feni*

uraq – liquor produced at the first distillation of coconut *toddy* or cashew juice

Glossary

The glossary that follows is a sample of the words and terms you may come across during your Goan travels. For definitions of Goan and Indian food and drink, see the listings in the Language chapter.

Adivasi – tribal person
amrita – immortality
Arjuna – *Mahabharata* hero and military commander who married *Krishna's* sister (Subhadra), took up arms against and overcame all manner of demons
autorickshaw – small, noisy, three-wheeled, motorised contraption for transporting passengers short distances; cheaper than taxis
avatar – incarnation of a deity, usually *Vishnu*
Ayurveda – ancient study of the healing arts and herbal medicine
azulejos – decorative ceramic tiles

babu – lower-level clerical worker (derogatory term)
baksheesh – tip, bribe or donation
balcao – shady porch, usually with benches built into the walls, which stands at the front of a traditional Goan house
bandh – general strike
betel – nut of the areca palm; the nut is mildly intoxicating and is chewed with *paan* as a stimulant and digestive
Bhagavad Gita – Hindu song of the Divine One; *Krishna's* lessons to *Arjuna,* emphasising the philosophy of bhakti (faith); part of the *Mahabharata*
Bhairava – the Terrible; refers to the eight incarnations of *Shiva* in his demonic form
bhang – dried leaves and flowering shoots of the cannabis plant
bhojanayalas – basic restaurant or snack bar serving vegetarian food
Brahma – source of all existence and also worshipped as the creator in the Hindu *Trimurti* (triad); depicted as having four heads (a fifth was burnt by *Shiva's* 'central eye' when Brahma spoke disrespectfully)
Brahmanism – early form of Hinduism that evolved from Vedism (see *Vedas*); named after the *Brahmin* priests and the god *Brahma*
Brahmin – member of the priest caste, the highest Hindu caste
bund – embankment or dike, used in Goa to protect *khazans* (low-lying areas)

caste – one of the four classes into which Hindu society is divided; one's hereditary station in life
Chandra – the moon, or the moon as a god, worshipped particularly in Goa at the Chandreshwar Bhutnath Temple, on Chandranath Hill
charas – resin of the cannabis plant; also referred to as hashish
chillum – pipe of a hookah; used to describe the small clay pipes for smoking *ganja*
communidades – traditional system of land management in Goa
coracle – small boat made of waterproofed hides stretched over a frame
crore – 10 million

Dalit – preferred term for India's casteless class; see *Untouchable*
darshan – offering or audience with someone; viewing of a deity
deaknni – traditional Goan dance
deepastambha – lamp tower, a prominent and distinctive feature of many temples
devadasi – temple dancer
Devi – *Shiva's* wife
dhaba – basic restaurant or snack bar
Dhangars – tribe of Goa's indigenous people
dharma – Hindu and Buddhist moral code of behaviour; natural law
dhirio – Goan version of bullfighting, which was finally banned in 1997
dhobi ghat – place where clothes are washed
Dravidian – member of one of the aboriginal races of India pushed south by the Indo-Europeans and now mixed with them; the Dravidian languages include Tamil, Malayalam, Telugu and Kannada
dulpod – traditional Goan dance
durbar – royal court; also used to describe a government
Durga – the Inaccessible; a form of *Shiva's* wife *Devi,* a beautiful but fierce woman riding a tiger; major goddess of the Sakti cult

fado – type of song popular in the Portuguese colonial time, delivered in an operatic style

Ganesh – the Hindu god of good fortune, elephant-headed son of *Shiva* and *Parvati* and probably the most popular god in the Hindu pantheon; also known as Ganpati

Ganga – Ganges River; also the Hindu goddess representing the sacred Ganges River

ganj – market

ganja – dried flowering tips of cannabis plant; highly potent form of marijuana

gaon – village

garbhagriha – inner sanctum of a Hindu temple; where the deity resides

ghat – steps or landing on a river; range of hills, or road up hills; the Western Ghats are the range of mountains that run along India's west coast – effectively forming the eastern border of Goa

GTDC – Goa Tourism Development Corporation; Goa Tourism

Hanuman – Hindu monkey god, prominent in the *Ramayana*, follower of *Rama*

Harijan – name given by Gandhi to India's *Untouchables*; the term is, however, no longer considered acceptable (see *Dalit* and *Untouchable*)

Indra – the most important and prestigious of the Vedic (see *Vedas*) gods of India; god of rain, thunder, lightning and war

ji – honorific that can be added to the end of almost anything; thus babaji, Gandhiji

Kali – the Black; a terrible form of *Shiva's* wife *Devi;* depicted with black skin, dripping with blood, surrounded by snakes and wearing a necklace of skulls

Kama – Hindu god of love

karma – principle of retributive justice for past deeds

kell tiatr – form of *tiatr*

khadi – homespun cloth

khazans – low-lying areas alongside Goa's rivers, reclaimed by building *bunds;* the flow of salt and fresh water is regulated to allow the land to be used for a variety of purposes

Krishna – *Vishnu's* eighth incarnation, often coloured blue; a popular Hindu deity, he revealed the *Bhagavad Gita* to *Arjuna*

Kshatriya – Hindu caste of warriors and administrators

KTC – Kadamba Transport Corporation; Goa's state bus company

kumeri – slash and burn agriculture

Kunbis – sometimes called Goa's aborigines, Kunbis are descendants of Goa's first inhabitants, and are among the state's poorest groups, living mainly from agriculture

kusada – sea snake

lakh – 100,000 units

Lakshmana – half-brother and aide of *Rama* in the *Ramayana*

Lakshmi – *Vishnu's* consort, Hindu goddess of wealth; sprang forth from the ocean holding a lotus; also referred to as Padma (lotus)

lathi – bamboo stick often used by police

lingam – phallic symbol; symbol of *Shiva*

Mahabharata – Great Vedic (see *Vedas*) epic of the Bharata dynasty; an epic poem, containing about 10,000 verses, describing the battle between the Pandavas and the Kauravas

Mahadeva – Great God; *Shiva*

Mahadevi – Great Goddess; *Devi*

mahatma – literally 'great soul'

Maheshwara – Great Lord; *Shiva*

maidan – open grassed area in a city

mandala – circle; symbol used in Hindu and Buddhist art to symbolise the universe

mandapa – pillared pavilion of a temple

mando – famous song/dance style, introduced originally by the Goan Catholic community

Manguesh – an incarnation of *Shiva,* worshipped particularly in Goa

mantra – sacred word or syllable used by Buddhists and Hindus to aid concentration; metrical psalms of praise found in the *Vedas*

Manueline – style of architecture typical of that built by the Portuguese during the reign of Manuel I, 1495–1521

Maratha – warlike central Indian people who controlled much of India at various times; fought the *Mughals*

marg – major road

masjid – mosque

Moghul – see *Mughal*

moksha – liberation from the cycle of rebirth

monsoon – rainy season between June and October

Mughal – Muslim dynasty of Indian emperors from Babur to Aurangzeb

Nanda – cowherd who raised *Krishna*

Nandi – bull, vehicle of *Shiva;* his images are usually found at *Shiva* temples

Narasimha – man-lion incarnation of *Vishnu*

Nataraja – *Shiva* in his incarnation as the cosmic dancer

niwas – house, building

paan – mixture of betel nut and various spices, chewed for its mildly intoxicating effect, and as a digestive after meals

panchayat – local government; a panchayat area typically consists of two to three villages, from which a number of volunteers are elected to represent the interests of the local people (the elected representative is called the panch; the elected leader is the sarpanch)

Parasurama – sixth incarnation of *Vishnu*, and the 'founder' of Goa

Parvati – the Mountaineer; a form of *Devi*

pousada – Portuguese for hostel

prasad – food offering

puja – literally 'respect'; an offering or prayers

Puranas – set of 18 encyclopaedic Sanskrit stories, written in verse, relating to the *Trimurti* dating from the period of the Guptas (5th century AD)

raj – rule or sovereignty

raja, rana – king

Rama – seventh incarnation of *Vishnu*

Ramayana – story of *Rama* and *Sita* and their conflict with *Ravana*; one of India's most well-known legends, retold in various forms throughout almost all Southeast Asia

ramponkar – traditional Goan fisherman, fishing the coastal waters from a wooden boat, using a hand-hauled net, or rampon

ratha – temple chariot or car used in religious festivals

Ravana – demon king of Lanka who abducted *Sita*

reredos – ornamented screen that stands behind the altar in Goan churches

sagar – lake, reservoir

saquão – central courtyard in traditional Goan houses

Sati – wife of *Shiva;* became a sati (honourable woman) by immolating herself (although banned more than a century ago, the act of sati is occasionally performed, though not in Goa)

satyagraha – literally 'insistence on truth'; nonviolent protest involving a fast, popularised by Gandhi; protesters are satyagrahis

Scheduled Castes – official term for *Dalits* or *Untouchables*

Shaivite – follower of *Shiva*

Shaivism – the worship of *Shiva*

Shiva – also spelt as *Siva;* the Destroyer; also the Creator, in which form he is worshipped as a *lingam*

shri – also spelt as sri, sree, shree; honorific; these days the Indian equivalent of Mr or Mrs

Sita – in the *Vedas* the goddess of agriculture; more commonly associated with the *Ramayana,* in which she is abducted by Ravana and carted off to Lanka

Sudra – caste of labourers

Surya – the sun; a major deity in the *Vedas*

susegad – uniquely Goan expression meaning relaxed or laid-back

sutra – string; a list of rules expressed in verse, the most famous being the Kamasutra

swami – title given to initiated Hindu monks meaning 'lord of the self'; a title of respect

tabla – pair of drums

taluka – administrative district or region

tank – reservoir

tiatr – locally written and produced drama in the Konkani language

tikka – mark devout Hindus put on their foreheads with tikka powder

toddy tapper – one who draws the toddy from palm trees

torana – architrave over a temple entrance

Trimurti – Triple Form; the Hindu triad – *Brahma, Shiva* and *Vishnu*

Uma – light; *Shiva's* consort

Untouchable – lowest caste or 'casteless' for whom the most menial tasks are reserved; the name derives from the belief that higher castes risk defilement if they touch one (formerly known as *Harijan*, now *Dalit*)

Upanishads – esoteric doctrine; ancient texts forming part of the *Vedas* (although of a later date), they delve into weighty matters such as the nature of the universe and the soul

vaddo – also spelt as waddo; section or ward of a village

Vaishnavaites – followers of *Vishnu*

Vamana – the fifth incarnation of *Vishnu*, as the dwarf

varna – concept of caste

Varuna – supreme Vedic god

Vedas – Hindu sacred books; a collection of hymns composed in preclassical Sanskrit during the second millennium BC and divided into four books: Rig-Veda, Yajur-Veda, Sama-Veda and Atharva-Veda

Velips – traditional, forest-dwelling people

vimana – principal part of a Hindu temple

Vishnu – part of the *Trimurti* with *Brahma* and *Shiva;* the Preserver and Restorer

wallah – man or person; can be added onto almost anything, thus dhobi-wallah, taxi-wallah, Delhi-wallah

See also the glossary, 'Eating out'

Although Goan food has similarities with that in the rest of India – rice, vegetable curries and *daal*, for example – there are many Goan specialities, which are usually served with local bread. Common ingredients in Goan cooking include coconut and cashew (*kaju*) nuts, pork and a wide variety of seafood. Not surprisingly, the food in this region is hot, making full use of the small bird's-eye chillies that are grown locally. Chilli was only introduced to Goa by the Portuguese, adding just one more ingredient to an already richly flavoured, and highly spiced diet. One recipe for the popular *sorpotel* suggests that in addition to other spices you should use 20 dry chillies for 1 kg pork plus liver and heart, with four green chillies thrown in for good measure! Goa's Christians have no qualms about using pork (not eaten by Muslims and most Hindus). A state dominated by its coastline, Goa freely uses the harvest from its seas. The standard 'fish curry and rice', the common Goan meal, has become a catchphrase. Most beach shacks offer a good choice (depending on the day's catch), and will usually include preparations of kingfish, tuna, mackerel, pomfret, tiger prawns and shark. You will find fried mussels, squid, lobsters, baked oysters, boiled clams and stuffed crabs as specialities.

South Indian Vegetarians are well provided for in Goa. South Indian Brahmin food, for example, is wholly distinctive, with tamarind and coconut being typical ingredients. Three of its snacks – *dosai*, *idli* and *wada* (*vadai*) – are good vegetarian options.

North Indian North Indian cooking is often called *Mughlai*, hinting at the Muslim influence on North Indian diet over the last six centuries. Cream and *ghee* are favourite cooking mediums, and spices, herbs, nuts and fruit are all ingredients added to dishes, which usually have meat as the main focus of the meal. Several different kinds of *kebab*, meatballs and minced meat preparations are served alongside *biriyani* or *pulao*. *Tandoori* dishes, marinated meat cooked in a special earthenware oven, come from the far northwest, but are widely popular.

Thali A *thali* is a complete meal served on a plate or stainless steel tray. Several preparations, placed in small bowls, surround the central serving of wholewheat *puris* and rice. A vegetarian *thali* basically includes chapati, rice, *daal*, two vegetable curries and poppadum, although there are regional variations. Fish, mutton or chicken curries are popular non-vegetarian dishes, which can be quite hot and spicy. A variety of sweet and hot pickles are offered – mango and lime are two of the most popular. These can be exceptionally hot, and are designed to be taken in minute quantities alongside the main dishes. Plain *dahi* (yoghurt) is usually included, which acts as a bland cooling dish to accompany highly spiced food. You may wish to order a sweet to end the meal.

European Many hotel restaurants and beach cafés offer European options, eg toasted sandwiches, stuffed pancakes, apple pies, crumbles and cheese cakes. Italian favourites, eg pizzas and pastas with sundried tomatoes, mozarella cheese, olives, are well established. Western confectionery, in general, is disappointing. Ice creams (eg *Cadbury's*, *Dollops*, *Kwality's*, *Walls*), on the other hand, can be exceptionally good .

Fruit & nuts Home of one of India's most famous mangoes, the *alfonso*, Goa has a wide range of fruit. Some are highly seasonal – mangoes in the hot season, for example – while others (eg bananas) are available throughout the year. The extremely rich jackfruit is common, as are papaya and watermelons. Cashew nuts and pineapples (brought from South America) and papaya (brought from the Philippines) were introduced to Goa by the Portuguese.

Index

Text

Boxed Text

MAP LEGEND

CITY ROUTES

Freeway .... Freeway		⊐ ⊐ ⊐ ⊐ ...... Unsealed Road
Highway .... Primary Road		.... One-Way Street
Road .... Secondary Road		.... Pedestrian Street
Street .... Street		.... Stepped Street
Lane .... Lane		⇥ ═ ═ .... Tunnel
┼──────┼ .... Roadblocks		════════ .... Footbridge

REGIONAL ROUTES

════════ .... Tollway, Freeway
════════ .... Primary Road
════════ .... Secondary Road
════════ .... Minor Road

BOUNDARIES

━·━·━·━ .... International
━·━·━·· .... State
─ ─ ─ .... Disputed
▆▂▃▆▂ .... Fortified Wall

HYDROGRAPHY

~~ .... River, Creek		⬬ ⬬ ..Dry Lake, Salt Lake
·━·━·━ .... Canal		⊙ ⟶· .... Spring, Rapids
⬭ .... Lake, Tank		⊙ ⊣⊦ ⋐ .... Waterfalls

TRANSPORT ROUTES & STATIONS

━━●━ .... Train	⊢─┼──⊟┼·· Cable Car, Chairlift
Ⓜ .... Metro	─ ─ ─ ⊟ .... Ferry
━━⊡━ .... Tramway	▨▨▨ .... Path in Park
------------------- Bus Route	─ ─ ─ ─ ─ .... Walking Trail
═══════ .... Monorail	· · · · · · · · .... Walking Tour

AREA FEATURES

▬▬ .... Building		⛺ .... National Park		🏖 .... Beach	+ + + ... Cemetery
▨ ⚙ .... Park, Garden		▨▨ .... Market		Rocks	▬▬ .... Urban

MAP SYMBOLS

✪ **CAPITAL** .... National Capital	⊟ ⊟ ... Bus Terminal, Stop	▣ .... Jain Temple	▣ .... Pub, Bar
◉ **CAPITAL** .... State Capital	▰ ⊟ ... Cathedral, Church	⚏ .... Lighthouse	▣ .... Ruins
◉ **City** ...... City, Large Town	⌂ .... Cave	☀ .... Lookout	◉ ..... Shopping Centre
◉ **Town** .... Town	⊞ .... Cinema	⚱ .... Monument	◉ .... Spring
◉ Village .... Village	▣ ..Embassy, Consulate	Ⓒ .... Mosque	⛫ .... Stately Home
■ .... Place to Stay	⊡ .... Fort	▲ .... Mountain, Hill	⊟ .... Taxi
▼ .... Place to Eat	⛲ .... Fountain	⌒⌒ .... Mountain Range	⊟ .... Telephone
● .... Point of Interest	▙ .... Ghat	🏛 .... Museum, Gallery	⊟ .... Theatre
✕ .... Airport	◕ .... Golf Course	▣ .... Parking Area	⊙ .... Toilet
⊖ .... Bank	⯄ .... Hindu Temple	◉ .. Petrol/Gas Station	❶ ..... Tourist Information
⌇ .... Bird Sanctuary	✚ .... Hospital	✚ .... Police Station	⊟ .... Transport (General)
▣ ...... Buddhist Temple	▣ .... Internet Cafe	✉ .... Post Office	🐾 Wildlife Sanctuary, Zoo

Note: not all symbols displayed above appear in this book

LONELY PLANET OFFICES

Australia

Locked Bag 1, Footscray, Victoria 3011
☎ 03 8379 8000 fax 03 8379 8111
email: talk2us@lonelyplanet.com.au

USA

150 Linden St, Oakland, CA 94607
☎ 510 893 8555 TOLL FREE: 800 275 8555
fax 510 893 8572
email: info@lonelyplanet.com

UK

72-82 Rosebery Ave, London, EC1R 4RW
☎ 020 7841 9000 fax 020 7841 9001
email: go@lonelyplanet.co.uk

France

1 rue du Dahomey, 75011 Paris
☎ 01 55 25 33 00 fax 01 55 25 33 01
email: bip@lonelyplanet.fr
www.lonelyplanet.fr

World Wide Web: www.lonelyplanet.com *or* AOL keyword: lp
Lonely Planet Images: www.lonelyplanetimages.com